Imagining Harmony

Imagining Harmony

POETRY, EMPATHY, AND COMMUNITY
IN MID-TOKUGAWA CONFUCIANISM
AND NATIVISM

Peter Flueckiger

STANFORD UNIVERSITY PRESS
STANFORD, CALIFORNIA

Stanford University Press
Stanford, California

Printed in the United States of America on acid-free, archival-quality paper

Library of Congress Cataloging-in-Publication Data

Flueckiger, Peter, 1970–
  Imagining harmony : poetry, empathy, and community in mid-Tokugawa Confucianism and nativism / Peter Flueckiger.
      p. cm.
  Includes bibliographical references and index.
  ISBN 978-0-8047-6157-4 (cloth : alk. paper)
      1. Japanese poetry—18th century—History and criticism—Theory, etc. 2. Literature and society—Japan—History—18th century. 3. Nativism in literature. 4. Culture in literature. 5. Philosophy, Confucian. I. Title.
  PL733.4.F58 2011
  895.6'13209355—dc22

                          2010013338

Typeset by Bruce Lundquist in 11/14 Adobe Garamond

In memory of my father

Contents

Acknowledgments   ix

    Introduction   1

1   Nature, Culture, and Society in Confucian Literary
    Thought: Chinese Traditions and Their Early
    Tokugawa Reception   33

2   The Confucian Way as Cultural Transformation:
    Ogyū Sorai   61

3   Poetry and the Cultivation of the Confucian Gentleman:
    The Literary Thought of Ogyū Sorai   90

4   The Fragmentation of the Sorai School and the Crisis
    of Authenticity: Hattori Nankaku and Dazai Shundai   116

5   Kamo no Mabuchi and the Emergence of
    a Nativist Poetics   145

6   Motoori Norinaga and the Cultural Construction
    of Japan   173

    Epilogue   210

Character List   215
Notes   233
Bibliography   263
Index   279

Acknowledgments

I would like to thank first of all Haruo Shirane at Columbia, who encouraged me to pursue premodern Japanese literary studies, and guided this project at every stage. I also received invaluable guidance from Kurozumi Makoto at the University of Tokyo, who shared his broad knowledge of Ogyū Sorai and Tokugawa intellectual history through his seminars and countless personal conversations. My understanding of Sorai is deeply indebted as well to Hiraishi Naoaki's rigorous seminars on *Bendō* and *Benmei* at the University of Tokyo. Seminars with Nagashima Hiroaki, at the University of Tokyo, and Suzuki Jun, at the National Institute for Japanese Literature, contributed to my knowledge of eighteenth-century waka and literati culture. I have learned much about Dazai Shundai from my discussions with Kojima Yasunori of International Christian University.

The perspectives on modern Japan that I have gained from Paul Anderer, Karatani Kōjin, and Tomi Suzuki have informed my interpretations of how Tokugawa literature and thought relate to various modern Japanese political ideologies and conceptions of cultural identity. I owe much as well to Martin Kern, Paul Rouzer, and Wei Shang, who provided the training in Classical Chinese language and literature that made it possible for me to pursue research on Chinese literary thought and Tokugawa Confucianism.

Since I came to Pomona College in 2003, my colleagues in the Department of Asian Languages and Literatures and the Asian Studies Program have provided a supportive environment for my development as a teacher and scholar. I am particularly indebted to Sam Yamashita for not only being a valuable mentor and colleague, but also sharing his expertise on Ogyū Sorai and Tokugawa intellectual history, and painstakingly reviewing my entire manuscript.

The comments from the readers for Stanford University Press were very helpful to me in revising my manuscript. I would also like to thank Carolyn Brown, Stacy Wagner, Jessica Walsh, and the other staff at Stanford who steered me through the publication process. Eileen Cheng, Ari Levine, Kiri Paramore, and Morgan Pitelka all reviewed portions of the manuscript at various stages, and I am grateful to them for their candid feedback and suggestions for improvement.

Portions of Chapters 1 and 3 appeared in "The *Shijing* in Tokugawa Ancient Learning," in *Monumenta Serica* 55 (2007). Portions of Chapter 5 appeared in "Reflections on the Meaning of Our Country: Kamo no Mabuchi's *Kokuikō*, in *Monumenta Nipponica* 63, no. 2 (Autumn 2008). I am grateful to the editors for their permission to use this material.

Research on this project in Japan from 2000 to 2002 was funded by a Fulbright IIE Fellowship. In the summer of 2004 I was able to conduct further research in Japan thanks to a grant I received through Pomona College funded by the Freeman Foundation. A Japan Foundation Short-Term Research Fellowship made it possible for me to return to Japan again to work on this project in the summer of 2006.

Imagining Harmony

Introduction

A distinctive feature of much eighteenth-century Japanese philosophical and political discourse is the prominent place it gave to poetry in imagining the ideal society. Theories about poetry had long been used in Japan to talk about issues beyond the composition of poetry itself, but this tendency became especially pronounced in the eighteenth century. Many writers of this time viewed emotionality as the essential truth of human nature, and claimed that poetry had a unique capacity to express and communicate authentic emotions. They also valued poetry as a vehicle for accessing the languages and cultures of the past. They looked to idealized visions of ancient China or Japan as the source of a "Way" (*michi*) that could be used to give order to society, and investigated these historical cultures through the philological analysis of ancient texts. They saw poetry, specifically classical genres in either Chinese or Japanese, as the purest form of ancient language, making the study and composition of such poetry a crucial component of philological training. They valued such language not only as a scholarly tool, but also for how it embodied aesthetic qualities and cultural forms that could put people of the present in touch with normatively correct cultures from the past. Their emphasis on poetry as a way to become immersed in ancient languages and cultures gave rise to what could be called a neoclassical approach to composition, in which they composed poetry by imitating canonical models from the past.

This study investigates how eighteenth-century Japanese writers, by describing poetry as both a vehicle for emotional expression and a source of linguistic and cultural knowledge, integrated poetry into their visions of political community. It was above all in the philosophy of the Confucian scholar Ogyū Sorai (1666–1728) that an interest in historical cultures was combined with an emphasis on emotionality in this way. Sorai, the subject of Chapters 2 and 3, argued that Confucianism should be understood as a philosophy of rulership, rather than a means for personal moral cultivation, and he not only generated novel and influential interpretations of the Confucian classics, but also formulated detailed proposals for political reform. He saw the study and composition of classical Chinese poetry by the governing elite as key to the practice of the Confucian Way, and his views were inherited and modified by his disciples, whom I discuss in Chapter 4, such as Dazai Shundai (1680–1747), who further developed his ideas on Confucian government, and Hattori Nankaku (1683–1759), who was most famous as a poet. The Sorai school saw China as the source of culture and civilization, and they were criticized in the eighteenth century by scholars, often referred to in English-language scholarship as "nativists," who argued for the superiority of ancient Japanese culture and saw China as having corrupted Japan's original virtues.[1] The two most prominent eighteenth-century nativists were Kamo no Mabuchi (1697–1769), whom I write about in Chapter 5, and Motoori Norinaga (1730–1801), the subject of Chapter 6, both of whom shared with Sorai a belief in the importance of poetry in achieving a harmonious society, but argued that only Japanese poetry could play such a role.

When examining these figures' literary thought, it is not only the great importance they place on poetry that stands out, but also the diversity of roles that they assign to it, even within the theories of a single writer. These roles can at times even seem to represent conflicting visions of poetry, especially when it comes to how the emotional expressiveness of poetry relates to its other roles. The same writers who extolled authentic emotions often demanded that these emotions conform to a narrow set of classical poetic models, and while they rejected the application of moral judgments to the emotions expressed in poetry, they still tied poetry to a normative Way meant to give order to society. Many modern scholars, as I discuss below, have viewed these juxtapositions of ideals as contradictions that arose from the incipient but incomplete modernity of eighteenth-century literary thought. Such interpretations identify the centrality of emotions as a characteristically modern aspect of the Sorai school and nativism, while taking their neoclassical literary ideals and their political applications of poetry as detractions from this emphasis on emotions, and signs of their failure to entirely cast off premodern restrictions on emotional expression.

I take a different approach in that I see the combination of these diverse elements in theories of poetry from this time not as a contradiction or a sign of these theories' incomplete development, but instead as a product of a specific type of discourse in eighteenth-century Japan on the role of culture as a unifying force. When Japanese intellectuals of this time looked to ancient cultures as the source of a normative Way, they typically defined the value of such a Way in terms of its ability to structure society as a whole that exceeds the sum of its parts, so that individuals and their relationships take on meaning through their incorporation into a totality that transcends them. This vision of society was motivated by an unease these figures expressed with living in a world they perceived as fragmented. Such a perception had much to do with the transformations brought about by urban and commercial growth in the seventeenth and eighteenth centuries, which made it increasingly difficult to govern effectively with the political structures of the Tokugawa regime, premised as they were on a feudal agrarian economy presided over by the samurai class. Urban commoners (*chōnin*), despite their economic prosperity, lacked political power, while samurai, who had themselves become urbanized, found their fixed rice stipends no guarantee of financial stability in a complex commercial economy, as the purchasing power of these stipends fluctuated greatly depending on market conditions. Both commoners and samurai searched for new ways of defining the basis of a harmonious and well-governed society, and they often framed their efforts in terms of the restoration of a lost wholeness that they imagined had existed in ancient China or Japan, when human relationships were assumed to be more stable and meaningful than in the degraded present.

This notion of a cultural unity was an alternative to the metaphysical unity offered by the Confucianism of the Song dynasty (960–1279) scholar Zhu Xi (1130–1200), a common target of criticism among the eighteenth-century writers I discuss.[2] According to Zhu Xi's philosophy, all things in the cosmos are united in a single moral order (the Way) through their possession of a universal "principle" (Ch. *li*, Jp. *ri*). Principle is equated with Heaven (Ch. *tian*, Jp. *ten*), the highest source of authority, while at the same time being inherent in the "original nature" (Ch. *benran zhi xing*, Jp. *honzen no sei*) of each individual human. This original nature is the essential core of what it means to be human, and is characterized by perfect virtue. Zhu Xi's notion of universal principle thus links the human nature of each individual to the norms that govern the various totalities—familial, political, and cosmic—within which the individual is situated. Many of his Tokugawa critics, though, argued that social and political unity could only come about through the mediation of cultural norms external to and transcending human nature. Zhu Xi's idea of a universal principle inherent in human nature, they charged, merely encouraged people to assert their own subjective prejudices as universally valid, leading to the fragmentation and strife that plagued their world.

This replacement of a metaphysical Way with a cultural one was accompanied by a shift from Zhu Xi's view of a morally defined human nature to a notion of human nature as being at core emotional. In Zhu Xi's system, morality and emotionality are interpreted through the notions of principle and material force (Ch. *qi*, Jp. *ki*). In this schema, universal principle is the source of all things' participation in the Way, but only exists on the level of abstract value; what allows things to come into being in their physical concreteness is the material force with which they are endowed, which is different for all things. Principle cannot exist without material force, but at the same time principle maintains a philosophical priority over material force, as principle is the source of normative correctness, while material force is only good to the extent that it facilitates the expression of principle. In humans, principle is represented by such virtues as humaneness (Ch. *ren*, Jp. *jin*) and rightness (Ch. *yi*, Jp. *gi*), while material force is represented by the emotions (Ch. *qing*, Jp. *jō*). Emotions are a necessary vehicle for the manifestation of virtues, but they are at the same time potentially dangerous, as unregulated emotions can obscure people's inner virtue and prevent it from being put into practice. While it is possible for emotions to be morally good, this goodness is always defined through the conformity of emotions to an underlying moral principle that finds expression in them.

Proponents of a cultural conception of the Way in eighteenth-century Japan denied the existence of the morally perfect original nature posited by Zhu Xi, instead defining human nature in emotional terms, and taking Zhu Xi to task for suppressing this nature.[3] At the same time, these critics of Zhu Xi themselves saw emotions as in need of regulation and socialization, and their lack of faith in an inner moral perfection, which had played such a regulatory role for Zhu Xi, made them turn instead to cultural norms external to human nature. This shift to a culturally defined Way and a view of human nature as emotional, however, complicated the relationship between the Way and human nature for eighteenth-century writers. It was important for them that the ancient cultures they identified with the Way be linked to human nature, as without such a link these cultures would be artificial constructs that would run the risk of alienating people from their authentic being. For Zhu Xi there had been a direct connection between the Way and human nature, as the universal principle that defined the Way for him was itself the innermost essence of this nature. For his eighteenth-century critics, though, the integration of human nature with the Way involved bringing together dissimilar things. Or, to the extent that cultural norms were identified with human nature, as they were with many nativists, this was seen as a nature from which people had become alienated, meaning that they could never regain it through their own natural emotions, but rather needed to subject these emotions to training through external cultural forms. The ways in which eighteenth-century writers negotiated the gap between an emotionally defined human nature and a culturally based Way then represented, I will argue, different methods of theorizing the incorporation of individuals into a social whole, entailing certain visions of the basis of community and the possibilities for political subjectivity within such a community.

One type of connection that eighteenth-century writers drew between the Way and human emotions was to depict the norms of the Way as having been created by taking into consideration the natural emotions of those who are meant to follow it. In this view, the Way is not identical to or directly derived from the emotional nature of humans, but neither can it contradict this nature. In other words, while the Way is cultural, this culture must work within certain limitations imposed by a human nature that exists outside of it. Another, more complex dimension to the relationship between the Way and human emotions emerged out of the idea that the Way not only takes account of preexisting natural emotions, but also transforms and socializes the emotions of those who are immersed in the Way, turning their emotions themselves into something culturally constructed. The cultural construction of emotions, moreover, works through a virtuous feedback loop, in which the emotions nurtured by a cultural Way are in turn a source of this culture's cohesiveness. Sorai, for example, believed that living within the feudal social arrangements established by the sage kings causes people to develop feelings of affection for each other, which then provide such a society with an organic unity lacking in impersonal, law-based societies. Even when eighteenth-century writers saw emotions as culturally formed, though, they still typically connected these in some way to natural emotions, such as with Sorai's argument that humans have an innate tendency toward mutual affection and cooperation, a tendency that the Way of the sages harnesses and develops in order to achieve forms of society that people, despite their generally virtuous instincts, would not be able to arrive at of their own spontaneous accord.

I see the prominence of poetry in eighteenth-century discourse as owing much to how it was viewed as capable of simultaneously embodying an emotional human nature and culturally defined social norms. By straddling the divide between human nature and culture, poetry came to serve as a site of contestation for questions of how people are meant to be cultivated by cultural norms, where the source of these norms' legitimacy lies, and what kind of agency people can exercise in relation to them. This negotiation of the relationship between human nature and culture took place most notably in the frequent debates over how natural emotions in poetry relate to both poetic standards from the past and political applications for poetry. While these debates often show a concern for how authentic emotionality can come into conflict with other elements and functions of poetry, I argue that it is misleading to view such concerns simply in terms of a quest for emotional liberation, as this interpretation overlooks how a strong interest in both emotionality and the norms that regulate and socialize it were outgrowths of a common discourse, and thus inextricably linked. To put it another way, valuing emotions did not necessarily amount to liberating them.

These philosophical discussions of poetry are my primary focus, although they were not the only reason for the strong interest in classical forms of Chinese and Japanese poetry in the eighteenth century. For many of its practitioners, such poetry served primarily as a form of cultural capital that allowed them to imagine themselves as belonging to a world of elegance, as well as to form communities based on this shared world of elevated literary taste, such as through the composition of poetry in various social settings. The sociological context of poetic composition in the eighteenth century is a complex topic involving such phenomena as literati networks and private academies, a full treatment of which merits a study of its own.[4] I do, however, touch on the general outlines of how philosophical ideas about poetry intersected with the role that it played as cultural capital for different figures and their followers, such as with Sorai's idea of poetry as a means of educating an elite class of gentleman scholars and making them fit to govern.

Because of my specific focus on the eighteenth-century discourse represented by the Sorai school and nativism, I do not attempt to give a comprehensive account of Tokugawa theoretical writings on waka or kanshi, or stylistic developments in these genres during this period. A recent work, Roger Thomas' *The Way of Shikishima*, surveys waka poetry and poetics over the entire Tokugawa period. This study overlaps to some degree with my own, but I write about a narrower group of figures in greater depth, particularly in my exploration of the relationship of discourse on poetry in eighteenth-century Japan to both contemporary and earlier Confucian philosophical and literary discourses. A study that provides a broad coverage of Tokugawa kanshi is *Écriture, lecture et poésie*, by Marguerite-Marie Parvulesco, who, while touching on some of the philosophical issues that I discuss, analyzes this poetry mainly from a literary standpoint.[5]

My approach puts my work in a somewhat ambiguous position between literary studies and intellectual history, but I would argue that these disciplinary divisions of the modern academy are a barrier to grasping the full import of Tokugawa discourse on poetry. A central contention of this book is that we need to take seriously the ways in which writers of this time combined poetry with cultural and intellectual pursuits that to the modern reader lie outside the rubric of "literature," rather than dismissing such efforts as evidence of these figures' failure to grasp some purported essence of what poetry or literature should be. These writers saw poetry as embodying qualities that contributed to the ideal society, and it was only natural to them to integrate poetry with other means for achieving such a society, such as historical study, the exegesis of the Confucian classics, music, or devotion to the Shinto gods, and to use discourse on poetry to engage in philosophical explorations of the basis of good governance and social harmony.

Ogyū Sorai and his Tokugawa Antecedents

Ogyū Sorai is famous for declaring that the Confucian Way "was created by the ancient kings, and is not the Way existing spontaneously in Heaven-and-Earth," and that it was created for the purpose of "bringing peace to the realm."[6] His idea of a humanly created Way whose essence lies in the practice of effective governance was directed against the ideas, present in many interpretations of Confucianism in Japan at the time, that the Way is the manifestation of a cosmic or natural order, or of a metaphysical principle, and that the purpose of the Way is to promote the moral perfection of the individual.[7] Sorai saw the quest for moral purity as constraining human nature, rather than bringing it to completion, and argued that the authentic Confucian Way did not try to deny the imperfections and diversity of human nature.

While Sorai's interpretation of Confucianism represented a significant new intellectual paradigm in eighteenth-century Japan, many aspects of his philosophy were prefigured by earlier developments in Tokugawa philosophy and literature. Sorai and other eighteenth-century figures, for example, were critical of the application of moral judgments to the emotions expressed in poetry, as they believed such judgments make it impossible to encounter people in the full reality of their humanity, instead reducing them to rigid categories of good and bad. In discussing human emotions in this way, they were participating in a widespread discourse on emotions in the Tokugawa period, one that sought more authentic forms of human experience, interpersonal relationships, and communal identity by appealing to emotionality as the basic reality that was suppressed by existing social conventions and political structures.[8] In popular literature, for example, the domestic-life plays (*sewamono*) of Chikamatsu Monzaemon (1653–1724) depict urban commoner characters who find true love in socially prohibited relationships, bringing human emotions (*ninjō*) into conflict with the demands of duty (*giri*). Chikamatsu's plays present such conflicts as irresolvable in this world, leaving the characters with no choice but to seek escape in love suicide, with the promise that the lovers can at least be together in the next world. A later genre that stresses human sentiment is the *ninjōbon* ("books of human emotions") of the early nineteenth century, the most famous writer of which was Tamenaga Shunsui (1790–1843). Unlike the tragic figures of love suicide plays, though, the lovers in *ninjōbon* are able to resolve the conflicts that keep them apart, providing a fantasy world in which emotions do not necessarily have to be suppressed in favor of social compliance.

In Tokugawa philosophical discourse, positive views of human emotions were often presented as critiques of the philosophy of Zhu Xi. A number of early Tokugawa Confucians criticized him for putting too much emphasis on principle at the expense of material force, and as a result failing to recognize the importance of activity and vitality, including the emotional lives of humans. In his *Taigiroku* (1713), for example, Kaibara Ekiken (1630–1714) writes, "Principle and material force are necessarily a single thing. The reason I cannot follow Zhu Xi is because of how he makes principle and material force out to be two separate things."[9] He argues that Song Confucians "make nothingness the basis of existence" (p. 13), and in this regard their theories "are not based on Confucius and Mencius, but rather come from Buddhism and Daoism" (p. 14). Itō Jinsai (1627–1705) attacks Zhu Xi's idea of principle along similar lines, writing, "The term 'the Way' is a living word, as it describes the wonder of constant generation and transformation. Terms like 'principle' are dead words. . . . The sages take Heaven-and-Earth to be a living thing. . . . Laozi takes emptiness to be the Way, and views Heaven-and-Earth as a dead thing."[10] Jinsai takes issue with Zhu Xi's view of human emotionality, arguing that it is in fact not an authentic Confucian teaching at all, but rather comes from the Daoist belief that "all things come into being from nothingness," and that to return to this nothingness it is necessary to "extinguish desires and return to the inborn nature."[11] Both Jinsai and Ekiken claimed that Zhu Xi's theorizing distorted the Confucian Way by making it abstruse and lofty, when in fact, they argued, it was something that anyone could easily practice. Jinsai was from a merchant class background, and Ekiken, while of samurai origins himself, produced many works geared toward a popular audience. Their interest in human emotions and everyday life can be seen, then, much like Chikamatsu's plays, as an attempt to validate the lives of commoners and to challenge, even if not the actual legitimacy of the Tokugawa regime, at least its claim to authority over all aspects of its subjects' lives.

Sorai shared the belief of figures like Ekiken and Jinsai that the Confucian Way, properly conceived, treats humans as active, emotional beings, and like them criticized Zhu Xi for defining the Way in terms of a static purity. He expressed dissatisfaction with Jinsai, though, for thinking that the Way could be achieved through the outward extension of qualities inherent in the self. Jinsai had sought to remedy the perceived solipsism and subjectivism of Zhu Xi's philosophy by replacing its inward orientation, which located the Way in the purification of the individual self, with an external orientation, in which the Way could only exist within actual interpersonal relationships.[12] Sorai praised Jinsai for his criticisms of Zhu Xi, but thought that Jinsai did not go far enough, and still fell within the same subjectivist trap as Zhu Xi. To truly escape subjectivism, Sorai believed, it was necessary not only to cultivate the Way through active social relationships, but also to structure these relationships through the objective standards provided by the historical examples of the ancient Chinese sage kings. In this way, Sorai frames his own views in relation to those of Zhu Xi and Jinsai, each of whom more-over represents for him broader tendencies in Song and Ming (1368–1644) dynasty Confucianism, one emphasizing quietude and principle, and the other activity and emotionality.

Sorai's presentation of the problem of subjectivism reflects a different at-titude from Jinsai's toward the emergence of an urban commercial culture in the Tokugawa period. While Jinsai's critique of Zhu Xi's subjectivism was part of an attempt to define this dynamic urban society as a locus of ethical cultivation, Sorai's appeal to the norms of the sage kings reflects his profound unease with this same urban society, as he saw the Way of the sages as a corrective to the infiltration of merchant values. Sorai was one of a number of Tokugawa intellectuals who tried to solidify the position of the samurai as a governing elite, and provide a more pragmatic vision of ruler-ship than that offered by the moral idealism of Zhu Xi. Kumazawa Banzan (1619–1691), in his *Daigaku wakumon*, proposes an extensive series of po-litical and economic reforms that he saw as necessary to rescue Tokugawa society, and emphasizes the need for rulers to go beyond just moral purity: "Even though a ruler may have a humane heart, if he does not practice humane government, this is empty virtue."[13] He also points out the need to rely on norms passed down from the ancient sages, commenting that just as even a highly skilled carpenter must make use of a compass and square, great rulers too must grasp the "methods of the ancient kings" (*sen'ō no hō*) if they are to govern the realm effectively (p. 416). At the same time, these methods need to be applied with an eye to the specific circumstances in which they are to be practiced, which Banzan expresses as "time, place, and rank," and "historical changes and human emotions" (p. 416). For this reason, even though "the methods of the ancient kings are recorded in the classics and commentaries," they are ultimately "difficult to express on paper" (p. 416). Although Banzan's concern for policymaking is quite differ-ent from the philosophies of Ekiken and Jinsai, then, he is like them in his concern for engaging with the dynamic reality of society.[14]

Yamaga Sokō (1622–1685), another figure concerned with proper ruler-ship, adapted Confucianism to define the role of the samurai as a military elite. He wrote at a time when the samurai class was being transformed into a civil bureaucracy, but saw it as important for samurai to uphold martial values in order to maintain their distinctive role as moral leaders in soci-ety. Sokō, like the figures discussed above, made a point of affirming the emotional nature of humans, noting that "theories of being without desires for the most part come from Buddhism and Daoism."[15] He is also similar to these other figures in rejecting the idea of Confucianism as a form of esoteric metaphysics, arguing that "the teachings of the sages consist simply of the everyday."[16] He faults Zhu Xi for presenting a distorted view of Confucianism, and writes that in the Song "the learning of the sages changed greatly, and while scholars were Confucian on the surface, in reality they deviated from Confucianism."[17] Sokō sees this loss of true Confucian teachings as the culmination of a process that had been going on since the Han dynasty (206 B.C.–A.D. 220), and his desire to return to pre-Han interpretations of Confucianism is a point he had in common with both Jinsai and Sorai, which has led to the three of them being labeled as advocates of "Ancient Learning" (*kogaku*).[18]

I have provided only a very rough sketch of early Tokugawa Confucians whose ideas overlap with those of Sorai, but we can see that his concern for proper government as the content of Confucianism, his emphasis on the active and emotional character of humans, and his philological orientation were far from unprecedented in the Tokugawa period. Much of his originality lay in how he elaborated the philosophical concepts described above in new directions, such as in his views on the relationship between human nature and social norms, a relationship in which poetry, as a vehicle for educating rulers in the emotions of those they govern, played an important role. He was also distinctive in Tokugawa Japan for the strong literary consciousness that informed his philology. His earliest renown as a scholar came through his studies of the Chinese language and the problem of translation, and his views on ancient Chinese developed further through his encounter with the writings of the Ming literary movement known as Ancient Phraseology (Ch. *guwenci*, Jp. *kobunji*), the leaders of which were Li Panlong (1514–1570) and Wang Shizhen (1526–1590). These Ming writers strove to enter into the language of the past by closely imitating a narrow literary canon, an approach that Sorai followed in his own poetry, which was based heavily on the High Tang poetry extolled by the Ancient Phraseology poets.[19] Ming Ancient Phraseology had been a primarily literary movement, but Sorai extended these writers' views on language to the study of the Confucian Way, portraying the linguistic consciousness gained through poetic composition as a means to accessing the historical culture, recorded in the Confucian classics, that he saw as the source of the Way. Sorai's scholarly paradigm was then developed in new directions by eighteenth-century nativists such as Mabuchi and Norinaga. While nativists were critical of Sorai's adulation of Chinese culture, arguing that it was ancient Japan, not China, that should be turned to for models of government and literary expression, they shared with Sorai a belief in the need to access ancient cultures by inhabiting their linguistic and literary worlds, and an emphasis on the study and composition of ancient poetry as a means to such a communion with the past.

Maruyama Masao on Sorai's Modernity

Sorai was brought to prominence in postwar scholarship primarily through Maruyama Masao's seminal *Nihon seiji shisōshi kenkyū* (Studies in the History of Japanese Political Thought), and virtually all postwar interpretations of Sorai engage in some way with Maruyama's work.[20] Maruyama argues that by seeing social norms as humanly constructed rather than natural, and shifting the content of the Confucian Way from morality to politics, Sorai created the beginnings of a modern political consciousness in Japan. He does not go so far as to claim that Sorai created a fully modern political philosophy, and in fact stresses how Sorai idealized feudal social relationships and strove to buttress the Tokugawa regime. His point, though, is that Sorai, in his effort to uphold an increasingly fragile feudal social order, unwittingly introduced a political logic that was foreign to this order, and would ultimately work to undermine it. Although he mainly treats Sorai as a political philosopher, he also discusses how Sorai's political philosophy gives rise to what Maruyama portrays as a characteristically modern vision of literature, one in which literature is conceived of as the free expression of the emotional interiority of the individual.

Maruyama approaches Sorai's political modernity from two main directions. First, he argues that the notion of the political order as "invention" (*sakui*) rather than "nature" (*shizen*) is the decisive break that Sorai made with Zhu Xi, for whom the political order, the cosmic or natural order, and the inner moral virtue of humans are all regulated by a single universal "principle." Maruyama argues that Zhu Xi's system adheres to a logic in which social hierarchies and other norms governing human society are manifestations of a static natural order, and thus are not subject to change by human agents. By depicting social norms as human constructs, Maruyama maintains, Sorai introduces a political logic in which social bonds are seen as contingent rather than necessary. Maruyama uses the sociological notions of Gemeinschaft and Gesellschaft to interpret this contrast between Zhu Xi and Sorai, arguing that Sorai's political philosophy represents a movement away from a consciousness of society as Gemeinschaft, in other words as an organic community of immutable social arrangements that are experienced by the individual as a necessary given, toward a consciousness of society as Gesellschaft, in other words as made up of contractual bonds entered into freely by autonomous individuals for the pursuit of particular interests, a view that Maruyama sees as characteristic of modern bourgeois society.[21]

In his second argument for Sorai's modernity, Maruyama emphasizes his politicization of Confucianism, by which he means not just that Sorai sees Confucianism as a tool for government, but more specifically that he takes up politics as an autonomous sphere of activity, rather than as an extension of morality.[22] Part and parcel of this is what Maruyama calls Sorai's externalization of the Confucian Way. In one sense this refers to how for Sorai the Way is embodied in institutions that have their origins outside of human nature, but more importantly, Maruyama argues that Sorai sees the Way as only concerned with the external behavior of people, and not with their inner private lives, such as their emotions or their personal moral values. He maintains that this is an important criterion in the development of a modern political consciousness, writing that "nonmodern, or more properly speaking premodern thought does not generally recognize the opposition between the public and the private," and that "the independence of the public sphere in all areas of cultural activity, which at the same time entails the liberation of the private sphere, is surely an important distinguishing characteristic of the 'modern.'"[23]

Maruyama connects this depiction of modernization to literature by asserting that after Sorai shifted the Confucian Way away from Zhu Xi's idea of moral norms rooted in human nature, and toward political norms that lie outside human nature, "the only thing that could rush in to fill this interior, private sphere that had been emptied out by the externalization of the Way was the natural human emotionality that had been suppressed by the moral rationalism of Zhu Xi" (pp. 109–10). This affirmation of emotions is manifested, he argues, in the Sorai school's strong interest in literary composition: "As one would expect, the natural emotions that were liberated from moral rigorism in the philosophy of Sorai went in the direction of a 'carefree elegance and literary talent.' It is not without reason that Sorai's academy had a reputation for giving primacy to the literary arts" (p. 111).

Maruyama argues that while Sorai himself incorporated both the public and the private in his scholarship, these two aspects of his philosophy became detached in the work of his followers. He sees Dazai Shundai as having inherited the public, political side of Sorai's philosophy, while Hattori Nankaku carried on its private, literary side. Maruyama depicts this division in the Sorai school as a process of fragmentation and degeneration, writing that even though Shundai and Nankaku each grasped only a part of Sorai's learning, and lacked their teacher's capacity for integrating diverse fields of study, "in the typical manner of epigones, they either consciously or unconsciously took the particular aspect that they inherited and absolutized it as the essence of Sorai's learning itself" (p. 143).

Maruyama finds a more dynamic development of Sorai's thought in nativism, especially the philosophy of Motoori Norinaga. First of all he argues that, like Nankaku, "Nativism inherited the private, apolitical side of Sorai's philosophy, while completely rejecting its public side" (p. 178). He sees Norinaga as going further than the Sorai school, though, in that Norinaga's literary ideal of *mono no aware* ("the pathos of things") actively affirmed emotions, rather than merely granting them a negative freedom as what is left unregulated when the Confucian Way confines itself to the public sphere (p. 169). While Maruyama depicts Norinaga as exercising a nonpolitical option within the structure created by Sorai's philosophy, he sees certain differences between Norinaga's early work, which focused almost entirely on classical Japanese literary studies, and his later scholarship, which attempted to elucidate Japan's "Ancient Way" (*kodō*) or "Way of the Gods" as an alternative to Confucianism. In his early literary thought, Maruyama maintains, Norinaga did allow that the expression of emotions through literature could have certain social benefits, a position Sorai had taken as well, but Maruyama characterizes such ideas as peripheral to the basic import of Norinaga's (and Sorai's) literary thought, which was to free literature from ethics and politics (p. 172). He claims that in Norinaga's later thought, though, the pure, unregulated emotions expressed in poetry became themselves equated with the Shinto Way, so that "literature, which had been liberated from being used for self-cultivation or government, once again appears to have taken on a social and political character" (p. 173). Maruyama sees this view of literature as ultimately damaging to politics, though, as "the fact that literature, while remaining literature, was politicized meant, to look at it from the other side, that politics was made literary; to put it somewhat paradoxically, this is nothing other than the depoliticization of politics" (p. 174). In the context of Maruyama's modernization narrative, then, Norinaga's abandonment of politics as an active pursuit represents a step backwards from the incipient modernity of Sorai.

One problem with Maruyama's reading of Sorai is that the idea of the

Confucian Way as something created by humans for the purpose of governance has a long tradition in Confucianism, going back to such philosophers as Xunzi, making it difficult to use this idea as an index of modernity. While such human invention of the Way by sages was seen in earlier Confucianism as backed up by and answerable to Heaven, meaning that the sages are not completely autonomous actors, Sorai is no different in this regard.[24] The role of Heaven in Sorai's philosophy will be an important aspect of my analysis, and I stress how Sorai uses Heaven not just as an authority on high to be obeyed, but also as a source for critical reflection on humanly created governments and social norms.

The primary focus of my critique of Maruyama, however, is a questioning of his picture of Sorai as having opened up a private interiority in which emotions were freed from normative demands. Even if we accept that a separation of the public and private, and of politics and morality, is characteristically modern, it is questionable whether Sorai really proposed this in the way Maruyama claims he did. While Maruyama maintains that Sorai's externalization and politicization of the Way entails a retreat of the Way from making any claims on people's inner emotions or moral values, Sorai defines the music of the sages as "the Way of governing the inborn nature and the emotions,"[25] and argues that the promotion of the everyday morality that he defines as the content of the "Mean" (Ch. *zhongyong*, Jp. *chūyō*)—virtues such as filial piety, brotherly obedience, loyalty, and faithfulness—is an important part of government.[26] With Norinaga, too, there is reason to question the existence of an unregulated sphere of private emotionality. Maruyama argues that Norinaga freed emotions from all norms, but eventually politicized this emotionality by equating it with the Shinto Way. What such an interpretation overlooks, though, is how even in his earliest literary writings Norinaga depicted emotions as in need of regulation and socialization, presenting classical Japanese literature as a tool for instilling correct emotional responses.

Certain problems with Maruyama's claims about the liberation of emotionality in Sorai's philosophy are alluded to in the later interpretations of Sorai discussed below, but the full implications of a reconsideration of this point for our understanding of eighteenth-century literary thought have not been fully explored. This book attempts to fill this gap by presenting an alternative framework for understanding eighteenth-century writers' views on emotionality and poetry, one that recognizes the importance they placed not only on emotions themselves, but also on the incorporation of emotions into systems of social norms.

Sorai as Philosopher of Culture

Some scholars have countered Maruyama's positive portrayal of Sorai by arguing that the authoritarian aspects of Sorai's philosophy, such as his demand that people have total faith in the sages, are not merely a product of his political logic not being carried through to its proper conclusion, but are an integral part of this logic itself. Wm. Theodore de Bary, for example, in "Sagehood as Secular and Spiritual Ideal in Tokugawa Neo-Confucianism," reverses Maruyama's judgment of the relative modernity of Song Confucianism and Sorai, writing of Sorai's "fearful reaction to the liberal humanism of the Song and Ming," a humanism that de Bary defines in terms of "Neo-Confucian idealism and egalitarianism,"[27] a reference to the idea that all humans innately possess the Way within their inborn nature. John Tucker, in the introduction to *Ogyū Sorai's Philosophical Masterworks*, likewise contrasts Sorai unfavorably with the egalitarianism of the Neo-Confucian tradition, and writes that "Sorai's thought was not a modernizing force, but rather [was] one appealing anachronistically to the fundamentals of an archaic political tradition for the sake of fashioning an ideology of shogunal absolutism."[28] Maruyama depicts Zhu Xi as negating political agency by making the Way inherent in nature, and argues that Sorai takes the first step in escaping this kind of static, a priori vision of the Way by imagining a limited number of sages as active creators of social norms, an intermediate stage that he sees as analogous to the period of absolute monarchy in European history. According to de Bary and Tucker, though, political subjectivity was there all along in the Neo-Confucian tradition, and Sorai's conception of the sages is in fact a constriction of Neo-Confucianism's assertion of the universal potential for sagehood, as represented by humans' innate capacity for the moral cultivation of the self and the rational investigation of the external world.

I also portray the authoritarian aspects of Sorai as integral to his philosophical logic, but do so from a different direction by interpreting his humanly created Way as a kind of symbolic or ideological system that functions on a transcendental level to structure and limit the consciousness of those who inhabit it, and mediate their perception of and engagement with the social world. Naoki Sakai reads Sorai along these lines in *Voices of the Past*, where he argues that Sorai envisions the ideal community as a cultural and linguistic interior that is radically incommensurable with what lies outside it, while making those who inhabit it completely transparent to each other.

He compares Sorai's formulation of community with the kind of ideology that constructs languages as closed systems of meaning that are separated from other languages, while allowing immediate comprehension to obtain among their native speakers. The kind of cultural interiority proposed by Sorai, Sakai argues, admits no internal difference or conflict, creating a society in which "there is absolutely no room for the otherness of the Other."[29] He connects this notion of interiority to Sorai's vision of social control, in which institutions are "completely internalized and consequently rendered invisible and transparent" (p. 280), so that "the motivation for social action appears to originate in the spontaneous participation of each subject" (p. 281). In contrast, then, to Maruyama's description of Sorai as liberating the interior life of individuals by limiting the Way to external compliance, Sakai maintains that for Sorai the Way is meant to permeate individuals on the deepest level, so that individual interiority is from the start completely determined by and identical with a communal interiority.

While I share this view that Sorai envisions the Confucian Way as a framework of cultural value that shapes people from within, I differ from Sakai in that I see Sorai as in fact quite concerned with the dangers of attempting to eradicate all forms of difference within society, and of defining the culture of the sages as a totally closed system. Sorai's belief in the importance of valuing human differences is a point emphasized by Tetsuo Najita, who portrays Sorai as seeking social unity through the political integration of diverse capacities. In *Tokugawa Political Writings*, Najita calls attention to how Sorai insisted on the maintenance of the specific qualities that people were endowed with by Heaven, rather than trying to force people into a single mold. He characterizes Sorai as an essentially optimistic philosopher: "Rather than an oppressive bureaucratic polity, it would appear that Sorai held to a romantic and dynamic vision of people living and working together in a 'human community' (*ningenkai*). Sharing a common living place, people would bring together many different talents (*unyō ei'i no sai*) and build a flourishing society."[30] Najita sees this vision of the Confucian Way as a profoundly ethical one, and rejects Maruyama's claim that Sorai proposed a separation of ethics from politics (pp. xvi, xxiv–xxv). One manifestation of Sorai's idea of diverse human capacities is his insistence on the necessity of social hierarchy, and Najita readily acknowledges this elitism as a negative aspect of his philosophy, mentioning that it was recognized and criticized even in the eighteenth century (p. liii). Still, Najita ultimately finds positive value in Sorai's idea of an ethical community built upon the respect for and nurturing of the diverse capacities of its members.

Olivier Ansart, in *L'empire du rite*, similarly writes about the importance of diverse human capacities in Sorai's political philosophy. At the same time, he overlaps with Sakai in portraying Sorai's Way as a system of symbolic value that people inhabit and are structured by, one that Ansart describes as defined by the rites as "an exhaustive, totalizing system of meaning."[31] Ansart uses the term "Nature" (with a capital "N") to refer to this system, a choice of terminology that distinguishes this world of humanly created value from the natural world (which he simply calls "nature"), while at the same time calling attention to how people are meant to internalize the rites to the point that they are *as if* natural. In contrast to Maruyama's view of Sorai's private sphere as an inviolable personal interiority, Ansart argues that for Sorai the "private" simply consists of the raw material of "nature" that has not yet been integrated into "Nature." He comments, "In this sense, with Sorai there is not the slightest 'discontinuity' between the public and private domains. Private capacities and sentiments do not exist except as material that must be *forcibly* organized and introduced into the public domain" (p. 149). Ansart notes the similarity of Sorai's conception of learning the Way to the hermeneutic circle, in that Sorai portrays the Way as something that people must be placed within and accept as an entirety before they can grasp specific elements of it, a process that necessarily involves an act of faith, as the Way as a whole cannot be comprehended from an outside perspective through rational analysis (p. 85). Ansart does not see such forced internalization as eradicating the differences between individuals, though, as he argues that Sorai demands that such differences be maintained even when people have internalized the Way. He notes that in contrast to Song Confucianism, where the possession of a universal principle by all individual things and people means that the part can stand in for the whole, for Sorai, "a political capacity, humaneness, must assure the coherence and guarantee the sense of a system made of profoundly heterogeneous components" (p. 81). More specifically, people's specific talents predispose them toward developing different virtues, which then allow them to serve society in different ways.

My reading of Sorai is similar to Ansart's in that I see Sorai as conceiving of the Confucian Way as a vehicle for assimilating people into a common framework of symbolic value, while at the same time promoting the individual differences that allow people to contribute to society in the manner most suited to their particular inborn qualities. I put greater importance than Ansart does, though, on Sorai's treatment of the relationship between nature and the Way. Ansart claims that for Sorai the rites are created by humans "without owing anything to nature or to Heaven" (p. 23), and "the Way is nothing other than the artificial and autonomous order of politics, devoid of the least anchoring in nature" (p. 65). I agree with Ansart's assertion that Sorai posits a qualitative gap between nature and the Way, but I contend that Sorai nevertheless does see the Way as needing to respond to a nature that lies outside it, such as with how, as I noted earlier, he makes the Way answerable to Heaven. A number of interpreters of Sorai have pointed out the relationship between his Way and a broadly conceived notion of nature, such as when Samuel Yamashita argues that "Sorai's thought was distinguished . . . by its affirmation of both nature and artifice," and notes that this "nature" includes "heaven, spirits, and natural phenomena," as well as, on a human level, "the physical nature, emotions, and desires."[32] I would agree, and in this study I focus particularly on how Sorai uses poetry as a method of relating the Way to the natural qualities of humans.

In the case of Heaven this nature is a source of authority that comes from above, but by demanding that the Way take account of empirical reality, particularly the reality of human nature and human emotionality, Sorai also requires that the Way reach down to respond to the most ordinary aspects of people's being. Ultimately these different notions of nature are connected, though, in that Sorai sees human nature as bestowed by Heaven, so that to ignore or violate it is in fact an offense against Heaven itself. Such external reference points to the Way are significant, I argue, because they prevent Sorai's Way from becoming a completely self-validating and totalizing system of value, instead placing constraints on what the Way can do and how it can shape people, and allowing for a degree of critical reflection on existing political structures, something that readings such as de Bary's and Sakai's do not find in Sorai. My interpretation therefore recognizes a certain element of the political agency that Maruyama had found in Sorai, but it does so from a different perspective.

One way to define the term "culture" is in terms of the kind of world of symbolic value I have described, and in discussing Sorai and other eighteenth-century figures I use the notions of culture and nature as an alternative to Maruyama's schema of invention versus nature.[33] Maruyama's contrast between nature and invention, and the shift from the former to the latter, indicates a process of liberation through which the norms governing human society go from being seen as given and immutable to being something that individuals can actively shape to serve their own interests. "Culture," though, understood as something that structures people on a transcendental level, necessarily involves an element that eludes the control of individuals. A second definition of the term relevant to this study is "culture" in the sense of refined forms of literary expression, music, and ritual traditionally associated with social elites. These two kinds of culture are connected in Sorai's philosophy, in that he sees elegant forms of language, literature, ritual, and music as necessary for internalizing the norms through which society can be regulated. Although I am not using "culture" as a translation for any one single term in Sorai's writings, it does overlap with the range of meanings of the Chinese term *wen* (Jp. *bun*), which can refer to both senses of "culture" mentioned above, indicating literary or artistic refinement, as well as the "patterning" through which social relationships are given order and integrated into a system of symbolic value.[34]

In Maruyama's modernization narrative, invention is a more liberated, advanced stage of political consciousness than nature. In drawing a contrast between nature and culture, however, I simply see these as different philosophical discourses for legitimating social structures, and do not see one as inherently more liberating than the other. A point that some scholars have made with regard to Zhu Xi's system is that it embodies a tension between optimism and rigorism; it is optimistic in that it portrays the Way as inherent in human nature, but it is rigorist in that the positing of such a morally pure vision of human nature, and the linking of this purity to an objective natural order that must be conformed to, creates a strict demand for human perfection.[35] One way to judge the possibility for the positive exercise of subjectivity among followers of Zhu Xi, then, is by the extent to which they develop the liberating, optimistic side or the authoritarian, rigorist side of his philosophy. With a cultural paradigm of Confucianism, though, the question is not so much one of optimism versus rigorism as it is one of the extent to which cultural frameworks are seen as engaging with some exterior point of reference, as I argued above that they are with Sorai, as opposed to views that see culture as a closed system that determines all aspects of people's being, thus precluding the development of any independent subjectivity. I see eighteenth-century discourse on poetry as an important arena in which writers of the time defined the boundaries between culture and what lies outside it, and therefore as crucial to their articulations of how culture is meant to function as a means of regulating society.

Emotions and Linguistic Form in Sorai's Poetics

Modern scholars have often praised Sorai's literary thought for its positive view of human emotions, but they have typically been critical of his imitative poetry, faulting it for not living up to an ideal of literature as the free expression of the individual self through the transparent medium of colloquial language. An early example of this kind of criticism of Sorai is the assessment of him by Inoue Tetsujirō, who, writing in 1902, attacks his poetry by comparing it unfavorably with the Meiji ideal of *genbun itchi* (the "unification of the spoken and written languages"): "It would have been better if Sorai had used *genbun itchi*, rather than ancient phraseology. His method of lining up difficult characters and phrases in an effort to display ancient elegance is nothing more than a ridiculous vanity on his part."[36]

More complex is the analysis of Hino Tatsuo, who offers an explanation of why Sorai would simultaneously promote emotionality in poetry and an imitative approach to composition: "We need to understand that the imitativeness and classicism of [Sorai's] Ancient Phraseology school was a detour that necessarily had to be taken as poetry in Chinese broke free of the moralism of Zhu Xi's philosophy and moved toward becoming something in which one composes freely on one's own feelings."[37] Hino argues that Sorai clings to classical models of expression due to a philosophical emphasis on regulation through external forms: "Sorai defines the Way of the sages as ritual and music, which are forms external to human nature. If the forms of social life make up the institutions of the sages, which are the core of Sorai's political thought, then he must have, consciously or unconsciously, made use of literature as a form for the heart within the private sphere."[38]

Hino's comparison of Sorai's use of classical literary models to his views on the ritual and music of the sages has some validity, but is not without its limitations. He is right to focus on how Sorai turns to cultural norms for emotionality as a replacement for the moral norms of Zhu Xi, and literary models do have a basic similarity with ritual and music in that for Sorai these are all cultural forms created at a certain point in history, rather than something inherent in human nature, and must be mastered through imitation until they come to seem natural. Hino's characterization of ritual and music as functioning for Sorai in the political or public sphere, though, and poetry in the private sphere, is more problematic. As I discuss in Chapter 3, poetry is for Sorai integrated into a matrix of complementary and interdependent cultural practices that do not allow for clear distinctions between the public and private, or the political and the literary. He depicts the music of the sages, for example, as functioning to regulate people's inner emotions, and describes poetry as giving the ruling class a familiarity with human emotions, which allows it to govern effectively, as well as more specifically valuing classical poetic models for the training they provide in the language in which the creations of the sages have been recorded.

Another aspect of Hino's analysis I find problematic is his reliance on a modern notion of free self-expression as the authentic essence of literature. In his emphasis on the different kinds of constraints imposed on literature, such as his description of Sorai's literary formalism as a middle point between moral didacticism and free expression, I see Hino as participating in a narrative in which the achievement of modernity is depicted in terms of the removal of artificial distortions and impediments, so that things are free to be what they naturally are. He writes, for example, that "the anchoring of the self in expression is a fundamental desire of humans," and describes how with the Sorai school, "the essential meaning that literature has for humans gradually came to be discovered."[39] In this way, he describes the need for self-expression in literature not as the product of an ideologically and historically specific construction of modernity, but simply as something that asserts itself spontaneously when barriers to expression are removed. A similar narrative is present in Maruyama, as he portrays the private sphere of emotionality as having been suppressed in Tokugawa Japan by Zhu Xi's moral view of literature, the removal of which allowed pent-up private emotions to burst forth in their natural state.

A picture of Sorai's neoclassical poetics as a more purposefully chosen approach to language and literature appears in Yoshikawa Kōjirō's "Soraigaku an."[40] In contrast to Hino's argument that a desire for emotional expression is the primary impetus behind Sorai's interest in poetry, Yoshikawa focuses on the role of poetry in Sorai's philological project. Hino does not ignore this aspect of Sorai's literary thought, but he downplays its significance when he comments, "It is difficult to completely explain [Sorai's] strong interest in literature simply through reference to such utilitarian motives. One must think that he had a deep-rooted desire to anchor the self in expression."[41] Yoshikawa, though, gives a more central place to the role of poetry in Sorai's philology by stressing the linguistic aspects of his view of the Confucian Way: "The language of ancient phraseology in the Six Classics is [for Sorai] in itself an expression of the Way. Therefore, to apprehend the language of ancient phraseology in the Six Classics is at the same time to apprehend the Way of the ancient kings."[42] Yoshikawa writes of this ancient phraseology that Sorai "regarded it as the perfected form of language, and as something that can be grasped through poetry and prose, that is to say through literary language" (p. 653). He notes that for Sorai it was crucial for scholars of the present to become one with the language of the Six Classics, a process that requires "not just to read ancient phraseology, but also to write it oneself" (p. 632). He also comments on how Sorai values the language of his favored poetic canon for its capacity to convey emotionality, writing that for Sorai, "[Emotions] cannot be exhausted by logic. The only thing that can express emotions is 'language with grace, rhythm, luster, and mystery'" (p. 693).[43] For Yoshikawa, then, Sorai's neoclassical approach to composition is not merely an unfortunate appendage to a more essential role of poetry as emotional self-expression, but is central to why Sorai was interested in poetry in the first place.

My approach is closer to Yoshikawa's than to Hino's, but I explore in more detail than Yoshikawa the role of emotionality in Sorai's philosophy, and the issues that arise not only in Sorai, but also in eighteenth-century discourse more generally, from the juxtaposition of emotionality and classical literary models. I argued earlier that eighteenth century writers' interests in cultural forms and natural emotionality are interdependent, in that they both emerged out of a common discourse on a culturally defined Way that must at the same time connect with human nature. The relationship between these two aspects of poetry, as I noted, then became an axis along which broader philosophical issues were contested. Sorai's idealization of the language of a canon of Chinese poetry as uniquely capable of manifesting human emotions is indicative, I argue, of a certain political stance, one that takes the culture of the Chinese sages as interacting with and building upon an emotionally defined human nature, without contradicting it or violating its natural qualities. This is an essentially optimistic view of the Confucian Way as humane rulership, but one that was subjected to various critiques by Sorai's opponents as well as many of his followers. These figures presented different visions of the relationship between human nature and culture, which are manifested in their views of poetry by a problematization of the relationship between spontaneous emotions and neoclassical norms of expression.

Japanese Culture as Emotional Closure: Norinaga's Poetics

Norinaga, like Sorai, rejected the Song Confucian idea of a Way rooted in natural principle, and turned instead to a notion of the Way as a creation.

He posited the Japanese gods, however, rather than Sorai's human sages, as the creators of the Way, and promoted unquestioning obedience to the gods as well as their human descendants, the Japanese emperors. Before developing his theory of the Way of the Gods, though, Norinaga focused his scholarship on classical Japanese literary texts, and the relationship of his early literary studies to his more overtly political later work has been the subject of considerable debate. While most scholars have recognized some political component to Norinaga's literary thought, assessments of the nature and extent of his politicization of literature have been varied. This relationship between his early and late thought has been particularly significant to assessments of Norinaga in the postwar period, as his emperor-centered nationalism was discredited after the war, but many scholars have turned to his literary thought, which they depict as humanistic and modern, in order to rehabilitate aspects of his legacy. Others, though, have seen his early literary thought as itself incorporating politically problematic elements. I take this latter view, and develop it by exploring in more depth Norinaga's relationship to the broader eighteenth-century discourse on human nature and culture that I see him as participating in.

The most positive assessment of Norinaga's literary thought has come from those who see it as essentially unconnected to his later thought. A pioneering English-language study of nativism, for example, Peter Nosco's *Remembering Paradise*, characterizes Norinaga as a champion of human sentiment, and as essentially unconcerned with making literature serve political ends. Nosco notes that Norinaga sees the communication of emotions in poetry as aiding in government, but stresses how Norinaga defines this political role as an indirect one, and not as part of the essence of poetry. He comments that "the basic tone of Norinaga's poetics is consistent with what others have called the 'emotionalism' of National Learning, that is, the unrestrained affirmation of the affective dimensions of human experience."[44] Nosco distances the ideals expressed in Norinaga's poetics from his Ancient Way thought, arguing that "there is no wholly satisfactory manner in which to reconcile these apparently contradictory preferences other than to recognize them as complementary and opposing facets of his remarkable intellect and erudition" (p. 161).

Maruyama, as discussed earlier, sees Norinaga's literary thought as bringing to completion the liberation of emotionality that he sees as characteristic of the private side of Sorai's literary thought. He acknowledges that Norinaga found political uses for poetry, but maintains that these were not the primary import of his literary thought. At the same time, he does draw a connection between Norinaga's poetics and his Ancient Way thought, arguing that Norinaga's vision of the Ancient Way involves the absolutization of free emotions in his literary thought. Maruyama writes that with Norinaga, "*mono no aware*, which is the essence of poetry, is elevated just as it is to being the essence of Shinto itself," and maintains that "nativism gave interior emotions, purified of all normativity, a positive role by equating these emotions, just as they are, with the Way."[45] He sees Norinaga's literary thought as praiseworthy for its liberation of emotions, but is critical of Norinaga's eventual raising of this emotionality to a political principle, as he sees this as compromising politics as an arena for the active exercise of subjectivity.

Many other scholars have argued for a connection between Norinaga's praise for pure emotionality on the one hand, and his political passivity and acceptance of the existing Tokugawa regime on the other. Matsumoto Sannosuke, in *Kokugaku seiji shisō no kenkyū*, writes, "The fact that [nativism] opposed the normativism of Confucianism, and promoted a valorization of emotions, is certainly something worth being proud of for its freshness in the context of that time."[46] He goes on, however, to note that "valuing the emotions of the common people by no means amounted to valuing the common people themselves" (p. 147). Saigō Nobutsuna makes a similar point, writing in *Kokugaku no hihan* that in contrast to Sorai's two-part criticism of Zhu Xi, which involves both an affirmation of human emotions and a political critique of Zhu Xi's philosophy, "the position from which nativism criticized Zhu Xi learning was entirely permeated by the single element of affirming private desires."[47] He claims that because of how nativism "distanced the self from everything social, and set it loose, humanity ended up being expressed as an irrationality devoid of intellect" (p. 96). Like Matsumoto, then, he sees the emotionalism of nativism as leading to an atrophying of political consciousness.

H. D. Harootunian, in *Things Seen and Unseen*, criticizes this kind of negative assessment of the political potential of nativism, and also finds a much greater political component within Norinaga's early literary thought itself, rather than just in its later transformation into the philosophy of the Ancient Way. He stresses the communal dimension to emotionality in Norinaga's poetics, a reading that can be contrasted with how Maruyama defines Norinaga's literary thought in terms of private interiority. Harootunian argues that the immediacy of expression that Norinaga imagines in his poetics, where there is no disjunction between language and lived experience, is connected to a vision of a community united by empathy, one "unbound by the constraints of history or social forms."[48] While he acknowledges that at this stage nativism did not have an active political program, he maintains that the notion of community that Norinaga constructed in his poetics "created a space for a subject that could be mobilized for ideological contestation against the received authority and its form of representation."[49] He sees Norinaga's focus on emotionality as a challenge to existing hierarchies, in that in his poetics, "a demonstration of spontaneous and natural feeling, rather than studied rationality, distinguished the high and the low" (p. 98). For this reason, he argues, "it would be wrong to conclude that Motoori was simply exacting passive submissiveness from contemporary townspeople by turning their attention to aesthetics and sensibility rather than political power" (p. 114).

I make a more critical assessment of Norinaga's affective model of community, though, by calling attention to how it demands conformity to specific emotional responses, and in doing so suppresses true engagement with others as others. As opposed to the views of Maruyama and others I discussed earlier, I do not see the politically problematic aspects of Norinaga's literary thought as deriving simply from an absolutization of emotionality, or from a passivity engendered by privileging sentiment over reason. Instead, I emphasize how Norinaga does not accept all natural emotions as valid, but posits a set of emotional norms based on the sentiments expressed in a canon of classical Japanese waka and monogatari. Kojima Yasunori makes reference to this emotional normativity to call into question the view of *mono no aware* as emotional passivity, writing, "'Knowing *mono no aware*' was not something that could be achieved simply through passive feeling. It was necessary to encounter things, discern their respective essences, and feel in an appropriate form in response to things that ought to inspire feeling. 'Knowing *mono no aware*' is something that entails effort and training."[50] Momokawa Takahito writes along similar lines: "Norinaga does not do anything like affirm a 'liberation' of human emotions. . . . Upholding feelings of '*mono no aware*' requires considerable effort."[51] I would agree with these assessments, and add that the loss of political subjectivity that comes with Norinaga's poetics has less to do with passivity than with a demand to actively adhere to emotional norms, and to internalize those norms to the point that they are identified as one's own authentic feelings.

Norinaga values waka as a way to communicate emotions and thus establish bonds of empathy, but I argue that one consequence of his normative model of emotions is that he sees such communication as only possible between those who have already internalized the correct emotional responses through immersion in a specific literary canon. The implications of Norinaga's norms of feeling for his model of sociality are emphasized by Tomiko Yoda in "Fractured Dialogues: *Mono no aware* and Poetic Communication in the *Tale of Genji*," where she describes how Norinaga downplays the tension and dissonance within poetic exchanges in the *Genji*. She notes that for Norinaga, "the particularity of individual instances of communication . . . is neutralized by the uniformity of experience (*mono no aware*) rooted in the nature of all human beings."[52] She writes that because of this idea that poetry only conveys universal emotions, as well as Norinaga's demand that poetry be totally transparent, "the 'communication' that Norinaga evokes is patently non-dialogic or non-interactive" (p. 541). She depicts Norinaga's literary ideal as a kind of empathy without otherness, writing, "*Mono no aware* in its purest form may be best described as the empathy of a spectator who identifies with the other without engaging in a relation of exchange or negotiation" (p. 541).

I agree with this picture of how Norinaga conceives of poetry as functioning in interpersonal relationships, and argue that the lack of genuine dialogue in his model of communication is connected to a view of culture that, unlike Sorai's, does not recognize any reference point outside of culture itself. Harootunian contends that by privileging emotions, rather than rationality and morality, as the basis for knowledge, Norinaga "avoided precisely the kind of closure demanded by Neo-Confucianism" (p. 105). I would say, on the contrary, that Norinaga replaces the rational and moral closure of Zhu Xi with an emotional closure, one that eliminates any real otherness by demanding conformity to norms of feeling, and excluding from legitimate social intercourse those who fail to conform to such norms. Norinaga claims that the emotional norms he promotes represent a universal human nature, but he uses this appeal to human nature to create a kind of theory of emotional false consciousness, in which the spontaneity of people's emotions does not exempt these emotions from being condemned as inauthentic. He maintains that a process of historical decline has introduced a gap between people's natural emotions and the emotions that they ought to feel, and he sees the study of classical Japanese poetry as a means to closing this gap.

Koyasu Nobukuni has described Norinaga's discourses on language and the Japanese gods as being constructed through a tautological logic that offers no source of validation other than the superiority of Japan itself.[53] I see a similarly self-enclosed and self-validating logic at work in Norinaga's poetics, as the homogenization of experience that he advocates can be understood in terms of a collapse in the distinction between culture and human nature, or between culture and its outside. For Norinaga Japanese culture is itself the essence of human nature, making the emotional and aesthetic responses embodied in classical Japanese literature into universal imperatives, but without any justification other than the assertion that they are correct. It is through their parallel constructions of Japanese culture as a closed system, then, that I connect Norinaga's literary thought to his philosophy of the Ancient Way. By presenting the politicality of Norinaga's literary thought in this way, I am trying to move away from the idea of the literary Norinaga as a "good Norinaga" who was then transformed into a "bad Norinaga" with his formulation of the Ancient Way. Such a view is implicit even in many interpretations of Norinaga that are critical of his literary thought, as they depict the political consequences of his literary ideas as the result of a good thing, namely free emotionality, being taken too far. I see Norinaga's writings on waka and monogatari, though, as from the start incorporating a notion of community based on the regulation and homogenization of emotions, and find it problematic to turn to his literary ideas as an example of a more liberated vision of Japanese cultural identity.

Confucianism and the Discourse of Emotions in Eighteenth-Century Literary Thought

In questioning the view of eighteenth-century literary thought as the discovery of free emotionality, I am also reconsidering the relationship of the Sorai school and nativism to earlier Confucian views of poetry. A contrast between instrumental and emotional views of literature plays a central role in many interpretations of Tokugawa literary thought, with a modern liberation of emotionality depicted in terms of a casting off of Confucian tradition, which is seen as suppressing emotionality by subordinating it to political and didactic ends. Maruyama, for example, notes that Sorai saw emotional expression in poetry as contributing to the Way of the sages, as Sorai described the Way as being originally constructed based on human emotions, which poetry allows us to become conversant in. Maruyama ultimately sees emotionality and politics as contradictory elements of Sorai's theory, though, and downplays the significance of the connection Sorai draws between poetry and the Confucian Way, arguing that his views on poetry "could be said to stand on the outer limit of Confucian views of the arts."[54] He presents Sorai as a victim of the Confucian tradition's last tenuous grasp on literature, commenting that his view of poetry "of course could not escape from the ultimate restriction represented by the Way of the sages," and that "the removal of this final restriction was only carried out with the arrival of nativism."[55]

Other scholars overlap with Maruyama in viewing the focus on emotionality among Sorai and others as fundamentally at odds with the application of poetry to social and political ends. Wakamizu Suguru, for example, after describing a number of different aspects of Sorai's view of the *Book of Odes*, and noting how he values it for the insight its poems provide into human emotions, concludes by writing, "However, in all three of these views of the *Book of Odes* politics shows its face, and Sorai was not able to completely sweep away the old Confucian thought. This was perhaps inevitable given the perspective of Sorai as a Confucian. As Sorai was unable to separate the *Odes* from the 'Classics,' and see it purely as a text of human emotionality, it was ultimately not possible for him to break free of the fetters of the past, in other words to separate literature from Confucian thought."[56] This interpretation is premised on the idea that Confucianism is unnatural and oppressive in how it fails to make literature autonomous of political concerns, a failure that keeps literature from playing its proper role as uninhibited emotional expression. In this view, Sorai shows some signs of moving away from Confucianism by taking a positive view of human emotions, but is still trapped within political views of literature that stubbornly persist from the past.

I depart from these kinds of interpretations by questioning the notion of a simple opposition between emotionality and social utility in Confucianism. Instead, I find it more appropriate to characterize Confucian views of literature in terms of how they depict humans as emotional beings whose emotionality must be socialized through some kind of norms, and how they theorize poetry as contributing to this process of socialization through its capacity to convey emotions. From this perspective, I argue, we can see the Sorai school and nativism as working within a basic paradigm shared with the earlier Chinese views of literature that they criticize, even while they conceive of emotionality and its regulation in new ways, and reject outright certain prominent features of earlier views, most notably the direct application of moral judgments to poetry.

One point I make with regard to the eighteenth-century figures who are the focus of this book is that when they bring up the importance of emotional expression in poetry, they do so in the context of interpersonal relationships, such as by stressing the need to know the emotions of others, and communicate our own emotions to others. Kurozumi Makoto, for example, notes that for Sorai, "while the literary arts pertain to the interior of individuals, they at the same time reach out into society," and writes that Sorai "from the beginning speaks of literature as a way of learning to empathize with and relive the experiences of others and other worlds."[57] Norinaga describes a similar interpersonal dimension to poetry by insisting that emotional expression is only meaningful to the poet if this expression is communicated to and understood by another. Eighteenth-century writers defined the problems of their society in terms of subjectivism and self-absorption, and devoted much of both their philosophical writings and their commentaries on Tokugawa society to the problem of how to connect to other people. In order to form meaningful interpersonal bonds, they argued, we need to understand others on an emotional level, an understanding made possible by the communication of emotions in poetry. Contrary, then, to the common assumption that a valorization of emotionality is inherently a demand for individual self-expression, I approach the emphasis on human emotions among the Tokugawa figures I discuss as fundamentally a social and political concern. This social aspect to their interest in emotionality meant that they did not simply value emotions as experiences of individuals, but saw it as important that the particularity of individuals' emotions be mediated in some way with universal social structures that transcend the individual. For these thinkers, poetry was valuable for how it brought emotions out of the sphere of an isolated subjectivity, and into an interpersonal space where the communication of these emotions could inspire empathy in others, thus providing rulers, for example, with the knowledge of their subjects needed to enact effective policies, or giving ordinary people the sensitivity to others' feelings that would make them behave ethically in their everyday social interactions.

While I see this interest in the social aspects of emotionality as a common thread uniting eighteenth-century Japanese theories with earlier Confucian views, my point is not to define a single authentically Confucian view of poetry, a task that is inherently problematic. There are many possible Confucian views of poetry, depending on which elements of Confucian literary thought we choose to emphasize, as well as how we define Confucianism itself as a tradition (such as through reference to the Six Classics, the *Analects*, Warring States philosophy, or any number of later commentarial approaches, metaphysical doctrines, or bodies of social practice). When I speak of a concern with emotionality and its regulation as typically Confucian, then, this is meant as a descriptive account of the theories I examine of writers who identify as Confucian, and not an essentialist statement about what defines Confucianism as Confucianism. Along the same lines, when I argue that nativists participated in a discourse shared by the Confucians they criticized, I am not claiming that these nativists were somehow "really Confucian." Moreover, I am not simply trying to identify Confucian "influences," such as through the frequent citing of the *Analects* and other canonical Confucian texts by eighteenth-century authors.[58]

My reason for bringing up the "Confucian" label has less to do with attempting to define it than with examining how it has been used to generate a certain narrative of the history of Tokugawa literary thought, one that I contend obscures important aspects of its ideological character. This narrative depicts Confucian literary thought as a monolithic tradition unchanging over time, characterized by such traits as moral didacticism, utilitarianism, and the politicization of literature, and then credits Tokugawa figures like Sorai and Norinaga with breaking away from this tradition by valuing literature as the expression of authentic human emotions.[59] Interpretations that follow such a narrative do not ignore the political aspects of eighteenth-century literary thought, but they dissociate this politicization of literature from the new ideas about emotionality emerging in this period. They do so by assigning politics and emotionality different roles in a teleological narrative of the achievement of modernity through the overcoming of premodern, and specifically Confucian, modes of thinking about literature. The juxtaposition of the "premodern" politicization of literature with the "modern" valorization of emotionality is then seen as indicative of an intermediate stage in the modernization of literature, in which the seeds of modernity are sown, but are unable to come to fruition. Key to such a view is the idea that the so-called modern elements are the essential core of a theory and the source of its originality, while the so-called premodern elements are to be dismissed as vestigial habits of thought that persist beyond their presumed obsolescence. This distinction makes it possible to acknowledge the existence of "premodern" or "Confucian" elements in eighteenth-century figures' literary theories, while downplaying the importance of these elements, and to create a narrative of the modern struggling to break free from the premodern. Maruyama, for example, presents an image of an internal division within Sorai's literary thought when he writes that Sorai "put primary importance on liberating the literary arts from ethics and politics, only touching as a secondary matter upon the political and social benefits of literature."[60] A similar division between the "modern" elements as the essence of a theory, and the "premodern" elements as obstacles to be overcome, can be seen in discussions of eighteenth-century neoclassical poetry, such as the statement by Hino cited earlier in which he describes the Sorai school's imitative approach to composition as a "detour" on the road to truly free expression.

I question the supposed opposition between a unified Confucian tradition and an eighteenth-century repudiation of this tradition from two directions. First, by examining the two major paradigms for interpreting the *Book of Odes*, the Mao tradition dating from the Han and Zhu Xi's views from the Song, both of which I discuss in Chapter 1, I show how Confucians prior to the Tokugawa period are far from uniform in how they conceive of poetry as functioning to cultivate people in the Confucian Way.[61] Second, in my readings of Tokugawa figures, I argue that they were not merely affirming emotions in the face of a vaguely conceived Confucian didacticism or politicization of literature, but were engaging with very specific philosophical points in earlier Confucian theories, challenging the models of socializing emotions that these theories entail, while at the same time presenting their own alternative theories for how emotions should be managed through poetry.

In this way, I see views of emotionality and its social applications as interdependent and developing in tandem in the eighteenth century, rather than as opposing forces in the process of breaking loose from each other. Instead of speaking of the political applications that eighteenth-century writers find for poetry simply as accidental appendages, inherited from earlier traditions, to their new emotion-based theories of literature, I argue that these figures actively created new political uses for poetry, and I focus on how new ways of valuing emotionality in the eighteenth century were accompanied by new demands for how emotions were to be regulated and socialized. In contrast to the kind of modernization narrative described above, then, I see the "modern" emphasis on emotionality in eighteenth-century Japan as inseparable from the "premodern" use of literature for political ends, a judgment that calls into question the appropriateness of the "modern" and "premodern" labels to begin with, and the narrative of emotional liberation that these labels imply. In this way, I present the history of eighteenth-century literary thought not as a gradual removal of constraints on emotionality, but rather as a series of reconfigurations of the relationship between emotions and normative conceptions of the social order.

ONE

Nature, Culture, and Society in Confucian Literary Thought
Chinese Traditions and Their Early Tokugawa Reception

As Japanese intellectuals in the seventeenth century turned to Confucianism as a philosophy to define norms for the new society taking shape under Tokugawa rule, they drew on a range of Chinese and Korean interpretations of Confucianism, particularly those of the Song and Ming dynasties in China, and of sixteenth-century Korea. Confucianism had long been used in Japan as a source of ideas about poetry, with the prefaces to the *Kokinshū* (905), for example, borrowing from the "Daxu" (Great Preface) to the *Shi jing* (Book of Odes), the anthology of poetry that was one of the canonical texts of Confucianism. In the Tokugawa period, though, Confucianism came to play a much more expanded role as a philosophy for defining human nature, self-cultivation, and social norms, a development that was accompanied by an increased engagement with Confucian writings on poetry in order to discuss what role poetry should play in promoting morality, social harmony, and good government, or whether it should play any such role at all.

It was Song Confucianism, especially the philosophy of Zhu Xi, that most often became the basis for Confucian interpretations of poetry and other literary writings in the early Tokugawa period. Nakamura Yukihiko has described three views of literature prevalent among early Tokugawa followers of Song Confucianism.[1] The first of these is the view that literature "transmits the Way" (*saidō*). As an example of this he cites the statement of Hayashi Razan (1583–1657) on the relationship between the Way (Jp. *dō/michi*, Ch. *dao*) and *bun* (Ch. *wen*), a term that, as discussed in the Introduction, can refer to culture in general, or more narrowly to writing or literary writing: "When there is the Way, then there is culture/literary writing. When there is no Way, there is no culture/literary writing. . . . The Way is the root of culture/literary writing, and culture/literary writing is a branch of the Way."[2] Culture and literary writing, then, only have value to the extent that they express the Way that lies at their root. The second theory that Nakamura cites is that literature is useless and harmful because it represents "toying with things and losing the will" (*ganbutsu sōshi*), such as when Yamazaki Ansai (1618–1682) writes, "The fact that people of the world go forth in wantonness, knowing no path of return, is because of the *Genji monogatari* (Tale of Genji) and *Ise monogatari* (Tales of Ise)."[3] The third view is that literature serves for "approving virtue and chastising vice" (*kanzen chōaku*), that is, that it teaches morality by providing examples of good behavior for people to model themselves on, and bad behavior to teach them the consequences of vice. An example of this view is the account of Andō Tameakira (1659–1716) of the function of the *Tale of Genji*: "This tale speaks entirely of human emotions and social conditions, shows the manners and customs of those of the high, middle, and low ranks of the aristocracy through their amorous affairs, and without explicitly praising or censuring, causes the reader to make judgments of virtue and vice."[4]

These views, as discussed in detail later, each emphasize different facets of Zhu Xi's philosophy, but they share the idea that literature should be judged according to its capacity to effectively convey the moral values that Zhu Xi sees as the content of the Confucian Way. One way to interpret his ideas, then, would be to see them as manifestations of a typically Confucian didactic approach toward literature. It is important to keep in mind, though, that his views on literature do not merely represent a static and timeless Confucian tradition, but are the product of a specific set of assumptions about human nature and its relationship to the Confucian Way, assumptions tied to a major reconceptualization of Confucianism in the Song. In other words, Zhu Xi formulates one variety of Confucian literary thought, rooted in one interpretation of Confucianism. More specifically, his reading of the *Odes* involves a rethinking of over a millennium of Confucian commentarial tradition, as represented by the Mao school of *Odes* commentary dating from the Western Han dynasty (206 B.C.–A.D. 8). In order to highlight the distinctive characteristics of Zhu Xi's approach to the *Odes*, and to literature more generally, we will first look at the Mao tradition that it displaced. This will then allow us to see, in our discussion of Tokugawa critics of Zhu Xi, how new views of literature, with an equal claim to being Confucian, could be generated out of critiques of Zhu Xi.

The Mao Tradition of Odes Interpretation and the Culture of King Wen

The Mao school was one of four schools of *Odes* interpretation that arose in the Western Han, and is the source of the text of the *Odes* used today.[5] In the Mao school of interpretation, a specific moral content was attributed to each of the Odes, creating what Steven Van Zoeren describes as "a hermeneutic that saw the moral significance of the Odes to lie in their inscription and preservation of the paradigmatically normative aims, or *zhi*, of their authors."[6] Van Zoeren notes that the music accompanying the Odes had long been seen as having a normative function, specifically through its capacity to regulate the emotions, and characterizes the Mao school as introducing a new approach to the Odes with its idea that their actual words can play such a normative role as well.[7] This view that the words of the Odes have moral significance in and of themselves necessitated a stabilization of the meaning of the Odes, in contrast to the older practice, prevalent particularly in formalized speech situations such as diplomatic encounters, in which the words of the Odes were quoted as a kind of rhetorical embellishment to speech, without regard for adhering to any notion of a fixed original meaning. This concern for stabilizing the meaning of the words of the Odes, as well as establishing their moral significance, is reflected in the interpretive apparatus produced by the Mao school, which includes interlinear commentaries that clarify the meaning of particular words and phrases, as well as a note known as a "Minor Preface" (*xiaoxu*) that is appended to each poem to explain its moral import.[8]

The Mao tradition was then carried on and expanded upon by the *Maoshi jian* (Annotations on the *Mao Odes*), by the Eastern Han dynasty (25–220) scholar Zheng Xuan (127–200), and the *Maoshi zhengyi* (Correct Significance of the *Mao Odes*), edited by the early Tang dynasty (618–907) scholar Kong Yingda (574–648). Kong Yingda's work was one of a set of commentaries produced by Tang court scholars between 631 and 653 that are together known as the *Wujing zhengyi* (Correct Significance of the Five Classics).[9] These commentaries represented an attempt by the newly ascendant Tang dynasty to match its political unification of China with a unification and systematization of the Confucian textual tradition, a process that Peter Bol describes as follows: "For each Classic the compilers chose a definitive commentary from the range of possible Han and post-Han commentaries and appended subcommentaries to elucidate the Classic, elaborate on the main commentary, note alternative views, and generally survey the exegetical tradition that had grown up around each Classic."[10] In this sense, the *Correct Significance* project was a fundamentally preservationist one, concerned with synthesizing and unifying what was already there, rather than with generating self-consciously new interpretations. Despite this stated intention of upholding tradition, the *Correct Significance of the "Mao Odes"* was more than just a neutral conduit for the transmission of earlier ideas, as its interpretations played a role in actively constructing the Mao tradition as a philosophically coherent approach to the *Odes*.

In addition to the Minor Prefaces, which explain the meaning of individual poems, the Mao text of the *Odes* includes a "Great Preface," which provides more general theoretical statements about poetry.[11] The "Great Preface" presents a variety of perspectives on the nature and function of poetry, describing it as a manifestation of emotionality, a tool for political critique, a means for instructing people in morality, and a way of connecting with the world of spirits, as well as providing classifications of rhetorical techniques and genres. Van Zoeren describes an important difference between the *Correct Significance* commentary and the "Great Preface" itself when he writes:

> The "Preface" was a bricolage, a compilation patched together from earlier texts and logia that was anything but systematic. It aimed to be comprehensive only in the sense that it attempted to bring together what its compilers thought the most important, authoritative traditions concerning the Odes. The *Correct Significance*, on the other hand, undertook to present a unified and comprehensive, even systematic, account of the Odes. It was therefore constantly forced to explain that the relatively narrow and particular claims made in the "Preface" in fact presupposed or implied a more general, unified vision.[12]

I will examine two specific areas in which the *Correct Significance* commentary elaborates on the "Great Preface" to provide a more systematic philosophical framework for thinking about the Odes, the first of these being the division between "orthodox" (*zheng*) and "mutated" (*bian*) Odes, and the second the relationship between the words and the music of the Odes.

The *Odes* is divided into four main sections: the "Airs of the States" ("Guofeng"), which contains poems that are thought to have folk origins; the "Lesser Elegantiae" ("Xiaoya") and "Greater Elegantiae" ("Daya"), which appear to be products of court culture and include, among other things, accounts of Zhou dynasty (c. 1027–256 B.C.) history and celebratory songs for events such as banquets; and the "Hymns" ("Song"), which consists mainly of pieces to be performed at ancestral rites of the royal house. In the Mao tradition, the Airs of the States and the Elegantiae are classified as either "orthodox" or "mutated," depending on whether they derive from the idealized time in which the moral transformation effected by King Wen held sway or from degenerate later ages.

The "Great Preface" begins with an explanation of the didactic role of the first poem of the *Odes*, "Guanju":

> "Guanju" depicts the virtue of the Queen Consort. It is the beginning of the Airs/moral instruction (*feng*).[13] It is that by which the realm is influenced (*feng*) and the relations between husbands and wives are made correct. Therefore it is used among the people of the villages, and it is used by the feudal states. "Airs" (*feng*) means "influence" (*feng*) and "teaching." Influence moves people, and teaching transforms them.

In its explication of this passage, the *Correct Significance* emphasizes the connection of the subject of this poem (the virtuous character of the Queen Consort, who by this time was identified specifically as the Queen Consort of King Wen) to the larger process of moral instruction that the *Odes* promotes: "If the relations between husband and wife are correct, then the relations between parent and child will be affectionate. If relations between parent and child are affectionate, then relations between ruler and minister will be respectful."[14] "Guanju" is included in "Zhounan," the first section of the "Airs of the States," which together with "Shaonan," the second section, constitutes the orthodox Airs. A later passage of the "Great Preface" comments more generally about these sections of the *Odes*, "The 'Zhounan' and 'Shaonan' are the Way of correct beginning, and the foundation of kingly transformation." The *Correct Significance* explains, much as it had with regard to "Guanju," that while the poems of the "Zhounan" and "Shaonan" may deal with everyday matters, these examples of exemplary moral behavior are the basis upon which the transformation of the realm is built.

The mutated Odes are discussed in the "Great Preface" as a form of protest against the degraded times that their creators lived in:

> When the kingly Way decayed, ritual and rightness were abandoned, the ability of government to teach was lost, the states came to follow different methods of governance, and families each followed different customs, then the mutated Airs and mutated Elegantiae were produced. The historians of the states clearly understood the signs of success and failure, were pained by the abandonment of proper human relations, and lamented the harshness of punishments and government. They sang their emotions in order to influence (*feng*) their superiors. They were aware of how things had changed, and longed for the old customs. Therefore the mutated Airs arise out of emotions, but remain within ritual and rightness. That they arise out of emotions is the inborn nature (*xing*) of the people; that they remain within ritual and rightness is because of the beneficence of the ancient kings.

In its commentary on this passage, the *Correct Significance* describes how the mutated Odes are characterized by critical reflection, in the form of praise and blame, on the government of the time, and explains how this practice of praise and blame is dependent on a certain set of historical circumstances framed within a historical metanarrative of moral decline.

The first condition for the emergence of the mutated Odes is the "decay of the kingly Way." This is not just for the rather straightforward reason that this decline gives people something to criticize, but also because it brings about a shift in people's consciousness, a shift that is particularly important in explaining why poems of praise, as well as blame, only come into being with the mutated Odes: "The mutated Airs and mutated Elegantiae are necessarily created only after the decay of the kingly Way. When the Way is present in the realm, then the common people do not critique the government. Peace goes on for generation after generation, so praise and blame do not arise. The reason for this is that when one is not familiar with the bad, then one does not know that the good is good" (p. 46). The perfection of the kingly Way in the past thus becomes associated with a kind of blissful ignorance of political matters; no power of reflection is needed on the part of the people, because they already live in a perfect society.

The second condition necessary for the emergence of the mutated Odes is that there be consciousness of some positive norm against which to judge contemporary reality. The continuation of the passage quoted above argues that, just as knowledge of the bad is necessary in order to judge the good, knowledge of the good is necessary to judge the bad: "When one has never known anything but the bad, then one does not know that the bad is bad" (p. 46). The specific source of this knowledge of the good is the lingering memory of the kingly Way. The mutated Odes are then presented as emerging out of the disjunction between this ideal Way and the less than ideal contemporary reality that the creators of these Odes faced: "The mutated Airs and the mutated Elegantiae were composed at a time when the kingly Way had begun to decay and proper government had begun to be lost, but when it was still possible to correct and reform these, and pursue and recover them. Therefore the poets took the old exemplars and used them as the basis for remonstration" (p. 47). The mutated Odes are the product, then, of a kind of intermediate stage in moral history, when people have begun to reflect upon right and wrong in the face of an imperfect world, but things have not declined so far as to make them completely lose sight of the proper norms (which existed at a determinate point in the past).

In explaining the relationship between the descriptions of the mutated Odes as "arising out of emotions" and "remaining within ritual and rightness," the *Correct Significance* elaborates further on the idea that the mutated Odes come about from the poet's awareness of the disjuncture between the current state of affairs and an ideal past. It comments that "arising out of emotions" refers to how these poems depict the emotions of the common people of the present, while "remaining within ritual and rightness" refers to how the customs of the past serve as a fixed norm against which the present is measured. The *Correct Significance* also notes that the passage says that these poems "remain within ritual and rightness," instead of that they "are in keeping with ritual and rightness." It explains that the mutated Odes describe actions not in keeping with ritual and rightness, but that the goal of these descriptions is to criticize immorality and reestablish ritual and rightness, so the poems are ultimately expressions of moral intentions. Ritual and rightness serve as the guiding norms, then, even if the things being described violate them, such as in poems that describe illicit sexual liaisons.

To return to its commentary on the first line of the "Great Preface," the *Correct Significance* makes the initially somewhat puzzling point that "Guanju," which is one of the orthodox Airs, describes the virtue of the Queen Consort, but does not explicitly *praise* her. To understand what this distinction is supposed to mean, we need to look at the role that the *Correct Significance* sees praise and blame as playing in the mutated Odes. It is easy enough to understand how the poets who created the mutated Odes would find fault with the degenerate society around them, but the commentary argues that the same historical environment gives rise to poems of praise as well: "The mutated Odes come from a time when proper government and teachings had been lost and there were many people who did bad things, so when there was someone who nonetheless was able to do something good, they were praised" (p. 36).

"Guanju," on the other hand, while *describing* the virtue of the Queen Consort, "does not praise her for being able to act as she does" (p. 36). The difference is that while the praiseworthy people of the mutated Odes go against the grain of their fallen societies, orthodox Odes (such as "Guanju") depict a society in which, due to the influence of King Wen, moral action comes to people automatically. In light of the specific way that "praising" is talked about with respect to the mutated Odes, we can see that when the *Correct Significance* emphasizes that the Queen Consort is not praised, the point is not that she is not praiseworthy, but that her actions are not based on any distinctive capacity of hers to act morally. In other words, "Guanju" is meant to extol not the Queen Consort as an individual so much as the underlying ethos (that of the idealized culture of King Wen) of which her virtue is a manifestation. With the mutated Odes, in contrast, the point is to single out those individuals who responded properly even within a degenerate world (although the ultimate source of norms, as with the orthodox Odes, is the culture of King Wen).

WORDS AND MUSIC IN THE MAO TRADITION

Another issue systematized more clearly in the *Correct Significance* commentary is the relationship between the words of the Odes and their music. As mentioned earlier, the Mao tradition was based on the extension to poetry of a capacity for moral transformation that had previously been the province of music. We can see this merging of poetic and musical discourses in the following three statements, presented one after the other in the "Great Preface," of how people express themselves in poetry:

> Poetry is that to which the intention (*zhi*) goes. In the heart it is the intention; released in words it is a poem.

Emotions (*qing*) move on the inside, and take form in words. When words are insufficient, then we sigh our emotions. When sighing is insufficient, then we draw them out in song. When drawing them out in song is insufficient, then unconsciously our hands dance them and our feet tap them.

Emotions are released in sounds (*sheng*). Sounds form patterning (*wen*), and this is called tones (*yin*).

The first of these is based on earlier accounts of poetry as the expression of intentions in words, the third draws on musical discourse when it speaks of the expression of emotions in tones, and the second bridges these by describing how emotions are manifested first in words, and then in song and dance.[15] In the "Great Preface" these three formulae of expression are simply lined up together, but the *Correct Significance* spells out how the reader is meant to form equivalences between them, such as by equating "intentions" with "emotions," and thus positioning the second formula as a restatement of the first: "'Emotions move on the inside' corresponds to 'in the heart it is the intention,' and 'take form in words' corresponds to 'when released in words it is the poem.'"[16] The *Correct Significance* further solidifies the relationship between poetry, song, and music when it describes them as elements of a single continuous process: "In the *Han shu* (History of the Han) it says, 'When words are recited it is called poetry. When the voice is intoned it is called song.' That is, when in the heart it is the intention. What come out of the mouth are words. When words are recited it is a poem. When this is intoned it is song. When this is put to the eight types of instruments it is called music. These are all only names for different stages of the same thing" (p. 38).

The second of the statements cited above is organized as a series of increasingly expressive stages, but the *Correct Significance* commentary on the third statement introduces a new element by describing the progression from words to tones not just as a quantitative increase in expressiveness, but as a shift to a qualitatively distinct mode of expression, one that is free of the possibility for falsehood that plagues language: "Sounds can depict emotions, and then emotions become completely visible. By hearing tones, one can know of good and bad government. . . . When people's words are different from their intentions, this is called dissembling. But when emotions are seen through sounds, then this dissembling can also be recognized" (p. 39). The danger of failing to make such distinctions is that it will be impossible for poetry to carry out its role as a vehicle of moral transformation, as incorrect intentions could present themselves as correct ones, or correct intentions could mistakenly be seen as incorrect. Despite the promise of transparency offered by tones, though, it still requires a certain skill to discern intentions through tones, as "it is only one who is expert in music who can distinguish whether the words are proper but the intention is not, or whether the words are warped but the intention is straight" (p. 39).

Although many of the Odes, specifically the Airs of the States, are described as having origins in the common people, the need to accurately identify intentions means that poetry cannot serve as a teaching simply by having ordinary people listen to each other's compositions. Instead, a music official listens to the songs that people have created, chooses those with proper intentions, and sets them to music created by the ruler. It is only then that these compositions are suitable for use in the moral instruction of the people. The *Correct Significance* notes that this process of collecting songs from the people, and then in turn teaching the people with them, involves two different types of relationship between emotions and tones. In the first, "Sadness and pleasure emerge from the emotions of the people. Musical tones follow along with the people and change accordingly" (p. 41). In the second, though, "Music is created by the king, and the people change in accordance with musical tones" (p. 41). In the first case, then, tones emerge spontaneously from people's natural emotions, while the second is a conscious process of creation by rulers that is designed to regulate people's emotions. The *Correct Significance* explains how these two forms of relationship between music and emotionality coexist: "Music originally emerged from the people, and then it turns back and teaches the people. This is like how clouds emerge from mountains, and then rain back down upon these same mountains" (p. 41). The people are taught with poetry that was created by the people to begin with, then, but this process is only possible through the mediating role played by rulers and officials, who have expertise that the people lack.

While the *Correct Significance* sees the music of the Odes as crucial to their role as a form of moral instruction, the problem it faced in its own time was how to deal with the fact that this music had been lost. The solution it offers is to present the prefaces to the poems, which give explanations of their moral significance, as substitutes for their lost music, allowing contemporary readers to gain perfect understanding of the intentions of the Odes.[17] In this way, the commentary justifies its own importance by presenting itself as the solution to the problem of textual opacity (partly semantic, but more importantly moral) that it had raised earlier.

Describing the culture of the early Tang court, in which the *Correct Significance* commentaries were produced, Peter Bol writes, "The characteristic assumption of this . . . worldview . . . was to think of values as cultural forms. 'Xue,' learning as a moral activity, meant mastering the appropriate cultural forms so well that one could reproduce them and vary them to fit the situation."[18] He then describes how in the early Tang view these cultural forms were seen as inheritances from an ideal past, which was accessible through the textual canon of the Classics. In contrast to the view (deriving from Zhu Xi) that we saw Hayashi Razan express, in which the cultural and literary forms represented by the term *wen* are seen as something appended externally to a Way that exists autonomously of these forms, for early Tang Confucians *wen* is constitutive of the Way from the very start. We can see the idea of values as cultural forms in the *Correct Significance* commentary on the "Great Preface," which portrays the correctness of the intentions expressed in the Odes as deriving from the civilizing project of King Wen. The didactic possibilities of poetry then become tied to its capacity to serve as a vehicle for communicating these cultural forms. This is achieved by communicating to the reader "intentions" that are influenced by these cultural forms, whether directly (in the case of the orthodox Odes) or as a kind of lingering cultural memory (in the case of the mutated Odes). The prefaces to the Odes, which explain their moral function, then serve as replacements for the lost music of the Odes, guaranteeing the transparent communicability of the intentions inscribed in the Odes.

Zhu Xi's Reading of the Odes *and the Way as Natural Principle*

The Mao tradition came under attack from various quarters during the Tang and Song, and in the late Song Zhu Xi produced a definitive new paradigm for reading the *Odes*.[19] Zhu Xi's most complete theoretical statement on poetry is the preface to *Shi jizhuan* (Collected Transmissions on the Odes), his commentary on the *Odes*. This preface opens with a description of the emotional process that gives rise to poetry:

> Somebody asked, "Why is it that poetry is produced?" I responded, "Humans are born at rest; this is the Heavenly inborn nature (*tian zhi xing*). They feel in response to things, and their inborn nature is put into motion; these are the desires of the inborn nature (*xing zhi yu*). When people have desires,

then they cannot help but have thoughts. When they have thoughts, they cannot help but put these into words. When people put thoughts into words, but these cannot be exhausted by words alone, then they will be released in a resonance of sighs and exclamations, which will come out in spontaneous tones and rhythms and be unstoppable. This is why poetry is produced."[20]

Much like the "Great Preface," Zhu Xi sees poetry as a product of the spontaneous release of pent-up emotions through a series of increasingly expressive stages. The description of this in terms of the "Heavenly inborn nature" and the "desires of the inborn nature," though, brings in Zhu Xi's own conceptual framework for understanding the emotions, in which emotions are something that threatens to draw people away from their morally perfect human nature.

The sentences that speak of the "Heavenly inborn nature" and the "desires of the inborn nature" are a direct quotation from the "Yue ji" (Record of Music) chapter of the *Li ji* (Record of Ritual), a collection of texts related to ritual that date back to the Zhou, and were assembled in their current form in the Han. The "Record of Music" discusses not just music itself, but the significance of music as a tool for regulating human emotions, and we can better understand Zhu Xi's use of terminology from this text by looking at his essay entitled *Yue ji dongjing shuo* (An Explanation of Rest and Motion in the "Record of Music"), in which he discusses the same passage that he quotes in the preface to his commentary on the *Odes*:

> In the "Record of Music" it says, "Humans are born at rest; this is the Heavenly inborn nature. They feel in response to things, and their inborn nature is put into motion; these are the desires of the inborn nature." This speaks of the mystery of the inborn nature and emotions. It describes that which humans possess innately at birth. At birth people innately receive the centrality of Heaven-and-Earth (*tiandi zhi zhong*). When they have not yet felt anything, they are purely good, and are endowed with the totality of principle (*li*). This is what is called the "inborn nature" (*xing*). But when people have such an inborn nature, it will necessarily take on form. When the inborn nature takes on form, then there will be a heart (*xin*), and this heart will be unable to help but feel in response to things. When the heart feels in response to things and moves, then the desires of the inborn nature emerge. With these there is a division between the good and the bad. The desires of the inborn nature are namely the emotions (*qing*).[21]

In Zhu Xi's philosophy, the Way is rooted in a universal "principle" that inheres in all things. Because this principle represents the normative standard for the cosmos, it is also referred to above as the "centrality of Heaven-and-Earth." Zhu Xi's comment that people receive this innately comes from his idea that humans possess principle in their "inborn nature," also referred to as the "Heavenly inborn nature" or the "original inborn nature" (*benran zhi xing*), which consists of such virtues as humaneness, wisdom, ritual propriety, and rightness. The inborn nature is "at rest" in that principle exists on an unchanging, abstract level. This autonomous existence of principle is really just theoretical, though, as principle is always manifested in conjunction with "material force" (*qi*), which is what allows things to exist in their concrete materiality, taking them away from a state of "rest" and putting them in "motion." Zhu Xi does not specifically use the term "material force" in the above passage, but it is this combination of principle and material force that he is alluding to when he writes that the inborn nature "necessarily takes on form." For humans, material force is represented by the "emotions" (or "desires"), and the "heart" is then what encompasses both the emotions and the inborn nature.[22] While the inborn nature, being identical to principle, is purely good, emotions can be either good or bad, depending on whether they are in keeping with or violate principle.

Applying this philosophical framework to the passage from Zhu Xi's preface, we can see that the emotional basis of poetry means that poetry results from a movement away from the unambiguous moral virtue of the original inborn nature. Since the emotions expressed in poetry are extrinsic to the Way, and threaten to distract us from it, we could conclude that poetry is something we are better off avoiding, leading to the kind of negative view of poetry that we saw earlier expressed as "toying with things and losing the will." Zhu Xi does allow for the possibility of a positive role for poetry in promoting the Way, though, such as expressed in the other two views of poetry promoted by followers of Song Confucianism in seventeenth-century Japan, which I examine below in terms of how these relate to Zhu Xi's theory of the inborn nature and the emotions.

EMOTIONAL CORRECTNESS
AND "TRANSMITTING THE WAY"

Though Zhu Xi sees the inborn nature, and the Way that inheres in it, as abstracted from human emotionality, and sees the particularity of emotions as making them liable to selfishness and partiality, he does not see the emotions as something that can or should be actually eliminated. As his follower Chen Chun (1159–1223) explains in *Beixi ziyi*, a lexicon of key terms of Zhu Xi's philosophy, "Emotions are the activity of the heart. They are something that humans cannot do without, and are not something bad. However, when it comes to the causes of emotions, they each have their proper norms."[23] What is important is that emotions be morally correct, so that they express rather than obstruct the inborn nature, and it is poetry that arises from such emotions that is considered to "transmit the Way." Even if such poetry and the emotions expressed in it are not themselves constitutive of the Way, the fact that the Way always needs some concrete form in which to be manifested lends value to poetry as one possible vehicle for this.

The above quotation from Chen Chun comes from a discussion of a passage in the *Doctrine of the Mean* that is one of the key passages used by Song Confucians to discuss emotional cultivation. The passage is given here together with Zhu Xi's commentary:

> [*Doctrine of the Mean* text:] When joy, anger, sadness, and pleasure are not yet manifested, this is called centrality (*zhong*). When they are manifested and attain their proper measure, this is called harmony (*he*). Centrality is the great root of the realm. Harmony is the achievement of the Way in the realm.[24]
>
> [Zhu Xi commentary:] . . . Joy, anger, sadness, and pleasure are emotions. The inborn nature indicates the state in which these are not yet manifested. In this state there is no bias in any one direction, so this is called "centrality." When these emotions are manifested and all attain their proper measure, this represents the correctness of the emotions (*qing zhi zheng*). In this case the emotions do not contradict the inborn nature, so this is called "harmony." The great root is the inborn nature bestowed by Heaven (*tianming zhi xing*). The principle of the realm entirely emerges from this inborn nature, and it is the essence (*ti*) of the Way. The "achievement of the Way" indicates following the inborn nature. It is that which the realm relies on in both past and present, and is the application (*yong*) of the Way.[25]

In Zhu Xi's interpretation of this passage we can see the basic dichotomy between the inborn nature and the emotions, here expressed in terms of the emotions being "not yet manifested" versus being "manifested."

"Centrality" and "harmony" represent two different forms of moral perfection, one on the level of the inborn nature and the other on the level of the emotions. The perfection represented by centrality is guaranteed simply by the fact that centrality exists within the inborn nature, which is completely autonomous of any emotions that would threaten to draw it away from its original goodness. The perfection of harmony is more complex, in that it is achieved within the emotions, which have the potential to be either good or bad. Harmony, Zhu Xi argues, is achieved when the emotions "attain their proper measure," a phrase that Chen Chun explains as follows in the continuation of the passage from *Beixi ziyi* that was quoted earlier:

> For example, to feel joyful when one should feel joyful, to feel angry when one should feel angry, to feel sad when one should feel sad, to feel happy when one should feel happy, to feel compassion when one should feel compassion, to feel shame and disapproval when one should feel shame and disapproval, to feel deference when one should feel deference, and to feel right and wrong when one should feel right and wrong—this is in accord with proper norms, and is what is meant by emotions "being manifested and attaining their proper measure."[26]

When we feel the right emotions at the right time, the emotions are in "harmony" with the inborn nature, in the sense that these emotions do not contradict the inborn nature.

The relationship between centrality and harmony for Zhu Xi can therefore be seen as one between a norm and the realization or practice of that norm. Another way this relationship is expressed in Zhu Xi's commentary on the *Doctrine of the Mean* passage is through the paired terms "essence" (*ti*) and "application" (*yong*). The essence of something is what gives it value through its participation in the universal principle that governs the cosmos, while the application of something is the concrete manifestation of that essence within the realm of material force. As Zhu Xi points out in his commentary, the Way is achieved by following principle, or the essence, but this achievement itself takes place on the level of application. Zhu Xi has a reputation as an opponent of emotionality, as he does not value emotions in themselves, but only sees them as valid to the extent that they conform to a (morally defined) inborn nature. It is also important to keep in mind, though, that he sees emotions as the medium through which the Way goes from being an abstract potentiality to being practiced in society, with the consequence that poetry, which arises from emotions, can play a role in expressing and communicating the Way.

APPROVING VIRTUE AND CHASTISING VICE

One of the most radical departures that Zhu Xi makes from the Mao tradition is his rejection of the idea that all the Odes are expressions of moral intentions. In the Mao tradition, it was the moral correctness of the intentions expressed in the Odes that made them appropriate as teachings, but Zhu Xi's theory of "approving virtue and chastising vice" provides a way for expressions of both morally correct and incorrect emotions to guide the reader toward morality.

Zhu Xi's introduction of the possibility for immoral Odes can be seen in his redefinition of the distinction between orthodox and mutated Odes, concepts that Zhu Xi, like the Mao tradition, applies to two categories of poems, the Airs of the States and the Elegantiae. Zhu Xi defines the mutated Elegantiae in much the same terms as the Mao tradition, writing in the preface to *Shi jizhuan* that the mutated Elegantiae "were produced by wise men and gentlemen of the time who were concerned about their age and lamented its customs."[27] Describing the Airs, on the other hand, he writes that "only in the 'Zhounan' and 'Shaonan' was virtue achieved under the gentle transformation of King Wen, making it possible for all people to achieve correctness in their inborn nature and emotions." He distinguishes these from the rest of the Airs, in which "there were differences in correctness and incorrectness, and right and wrong" (p. 2).

Despite the inclusion of poems that are expressions of morally incorrect emotions, Zhu Xi still believes that all of the Odes can aid in the moral cultivation of the reader, as he indicates in his account of the process through which Confucius edited the *Odes*: "[Confucius] eliminated those whose virtue did not suffice to serve as a model or whose vice did not suffice to serve as an admonition. . . . They have thus allowed those who study them to reflect on right and wrong, so that the virtuous use them as models and the wicked use them to reform themselves" (p. 2). He also takes up this issue in his commentary on the *Analects* passage that states that the Odes contain "no crooked thoughts (*si wu xie*),"[28] explaining, "As for the words of the Odes, those that are morally good are sufficient to evoke approval from people's good heart, and those that are morally bad are sufficient to inspire a strong desire to punish such badness. Therefore the function of the Odes all amounts to causing people to achieve correctness in their emotions and inborn nature."[29] The Odes all have a moral capacity, then, but this capacity lies in the responses they inspire in the reader, and is not intrinsic to the poems themselves, or the cultural world that gave rise to them.

A central assumption here is that the reader already possesses, in the form of the purely good inborn nature, an inner moral compass that is able to distinguish virtue from vice. This moral faculty may be obscured, but it is always there as a latent capacity, and the point of presenting various examples of virtue and vice is to allow for the exercise and cultivation of this innate moral faculty. The goal, then, is to unlock what the reader in a deeper sense already knows, and not, strictly speaking, to impart any new information. To this end, the examples of virtue and vice given in the *Odes* are chosen with an eye toward their effectiveness in awakening the reader's faculty of moral judgment, which can subsequently be applied to an unlimited range of possible experiences, which may or may not resemble the specific examples given in the *Odes*.

This view of the education provided by the *Odes*, which sees it as a process of uncovering the original inborn nature of the reader, also has consequences for how we interpret the relationship between the instructor in the Way (the sage) and the student (the non-sage reader). We have already seen how one function of the sage is to serve as a source of paradigmatic emotions, but in the theory of "approving virtue and chastising vice," the role of the sage is to choose poems that are effective in arousing feelings of moral approval and disapproval. This role is based on the idea that both teacher and student share the same inborn nature, but have realized this nature to different degrees, so that the task of the teacher is to guide the student in a process of uncovering, within the student's own innermost nature, that which both student and teacher have always already possessed. While there is an asymmetrical aspect to this relationship to the extent that the sage has greater access to this nature, access that allows the sage to take on the role of teacher, the relationship has a symmetrical aspect as well, in that it is based on the existence of a common nature.

"INVESTIGATING THINGS" THROUGH THE ODES

Zhu Xi's theory of how the Odes can be used for "approving virtue and chastising vice" can be seen as part of a more general model of cultivating the Way that he refers to as "investigating things" (*gewu*), in which people come to understand principle by closely examining how it is manifested in various external things, such as objects in the natural world. The term "investigating things" has its origin in the *Great Learning*, where it is described as the first step in self-cultivation:

> When things are investigated, knowledge becomes complete. When knowledge is complete, intentions become sincere. When intentions are sincere, the heart becomes correct. When the heart is correct, the self is cultivated.

When the self is cultivated, one's house becomes ordered. When one's house is ordered, the state is well governed. When the state is well governed, the realm is made peaceful.[30]

In Zhu Xi's commentary on this passage, he glosses "things are investigated" as "completely extending to the limits of the principle of things."[31] For Zhu Xi, the same principle that is discovered in external things is the basis for the inborn nature of humans, so the process described in the *Great Learning* passage is one in which people uncover their inborn nature through the investigation of things, and then extend their perfectly cultivated nature outward in an expanding sphere of influence to properly order the self, the household, and eventually the realm as a whole.

The same idea is extended to textual studies in the section on "Methods of Reading" (*dushu fa*) in *Zhuzi yulei* (Master Zhu's Classified Conversations):

> Reading is an example of "investigating things." At first one pursues one section, savors its content in detail, and repeats this many times. One may spend a day or two on only one section. Then, once one can use this section as a foundation, one stands firmly on it and moves on to the next section. In this way, after advancing by reading things over and over in the proper sequence, and pursuing what one reads in depth, and thoroughly inquiring into it, only then will one come to entirely understand its principles.[32]

Studying texts then becomes a matter of the reader's own inner principle getting in touch with the principle embodied in the text: "It is only when the principle of things accords with one's own heart that one truly understands. In reading, it is necessary that the principle within oneself extend everywhere, so that things become clear" (p. 162). Here we can see how the reader's inner principle is not only revealed through reading as a practice of "investigating things," but also represents the condition of possibility of proper textual interpretation.

One implication of this view of reading is that the purpose of textual study is less to impart new knowledge than to remind people of what they in a sense already know:

> When people are born, they already possess within themselves the totality of principle. The reason to read books is that there are many things that one has not experienced. Sages have experienced many things and understood them. Therefore they put these down in writing in order to show them to others. The important thing when reading is to understand many principles. When

we understand these, they are all something that was within us originally, and not something brought in from outside and added on. (p. 161)

The role of the sage as textual editor, as we saw with Zhu Xi's description of how Confucius edited the *Odes*, is to present readers with things that best serve to guide them toward an understanding of the principle that in fact already lies latent in their inborn nature.

The application of the methodology of "investigating things" to the study of poetry is described in the closing section of the preface to Zhu Xi's *Shi jizhuan*, which is part of a section responding to the question, "How should one study poetry?"

> One should look at the general framework of the phrases of poems, and also go into detailed exegesis of individual words. One should chant them in order to bring them to life, and completely immerse oneself in them in order to embody them. One should observe in them the hidden nuances of the emotions and inborn nature they express, and find the driving force behind them. If one does this, then without needing to seek elsewhere, it will be sufficient to achieve the Way of cultivating the self and the household, and regulating the realm.[33]

Although this passage contains no direct mention of the term "investigating things," the description of the proper method of reading poetry echoes the passage from *Zhuzi yulei* that discusses how reading is a form of "investigating things," and the final sentence is an allusion to the *Great Learning* passage that is the locus classicus of the term. Approaching poetry as something to be investigated for its inner principle is ultimately the same as viewing it through the lens of "approving virtue and chastising vice," as virtue and vice derive from being in accord or conflict with principle. Expressing this process as "investigating things," however, calls attention to how Zhu Xi does not just approach poetry morally, but also ties these moral judgments to a specific definition of the dynamic between the external and the internal, in which the external world serves as a stimulus for the cultivation of the self, which is then applied outward again to benefit the world.

Itō Jinsai: Empathy, Ethics, and the Odes

Itō Jinsai was one of the most prominent critics of Song Confucianism in seventeenth-century Japan, and had a large impact on later Tokugawa scholars, especially Ogyū Sorai. Jinsai came from a Kyoto merchant family of modest means, and in his youth studied the philosophy of Zhu Xi. In 1662 he opened a private academy in Kyoto called the Kogidō (Hall of Ancient Meanings), which eventually attracted more than three thousand students, and through his teaching and lecturing he began to develop his own interpretations of Confucian texts. These were collected in his commentaries *Rongo kogi* (Ancient Meanings of the *Analects*), *Mōshi kogi* (Ancient Meanings of the *Mencius*), *Chūyō hakki* (An Exposition of the *Doctrine of the Mean*), and *Daigaku teihon* (The Authentic Text of the *Great Learning*). Other of his major texts include *Gomō jigi* (The Meaning of Terms in the *Analects* and *Mencius*), a digest of his commentaries on the *Analects* and *Mencius*, and *Dōjimon* (Questions from Children), a collection of essays on various topics.

As discussed in the Introduction, Jinsai was critical of what he saw as the abstract theorizing of Song Confucianism, which he rejected in favor of an emphasis on emotionality and on practical ethics cultivated by ordinary people in their everyday lives. In *Gomō jigi*, he singles out the preface to *Shi jizhuan* as an example of Zhu Xi's denial of the active, emotional character of humans, arguing that such an attitude is not truly Confucian:

> The "Record of Music" says, "Humans are born at rest; this is the Heavenly inborn nature. They feel in response to things, and their inborn nature is put into motion; these are the desires of the inborn nature." Zhu Xi took this and put it at the head of the preface to his *Shi jizhuan*, and believed it to be truly in keeping with the principles of the sages. He did not realize that this originally came from Laozi, and that it is really far removed from the Way of the sages. . . . The meaning of Laozi's theory is that all things come into being from nothingness. Thus, the inborn nature of humans is in the beginning authentic and at rest, but once it takes form, desires spring into motion and emotions take over, and people are assailed by immorality. Therefore, his Way is based on entirely extinguishing desires and returning to the inborn nature. . . . The learning of Confucians is not like this.[34]

This view of emotionality is reflected in Jinsai's comments on poetry, where he refuses to subordinate the emotions expressed in poetry to any underlying moral principle. As we will see, though, he still does see poetry as contributing to moral cultivation, specifically through its capacity to make people reach outside themselves and empathetically grasp the experiences of others.

THE INTERPERSONAL SPACE OF MORAL CULTIVATION

Both Zhu Xi and Jinsai equate the Confucian Way with moral virtue, but they posit different relationships between this virtue and human nature. This difference comes through in their interpretations of the *Mencius* passage on the "Four Beginnings" (Ch. *siduan*, Jp. *shitan*), which begins by stating, "Humans all have a heart that cannot bear the suffering of others."[35] This is demonstrated, the passage continues, by the fact that upon seeing a small child about to fall into a well, no person would fail to feel compassion, a sentiment that moreover arises completely spontaneously, and not out of any calculated motive, such as a desire to be praised or to please others. Therefore, it says, "we can see that whoever does not have the heart of compassion is not human, whoever does not have the heart of shame and disapproval is not human, whoever does not have the heart of deference is not human, and whoever does not have the heart of right and wrong is not human."

This passage provides an argument for the essential goodness of human nature, and is one of the classic statements on this issue in the Confucian textual tradition. It has given rise to various interpretations, though, particularly with regard to how the spontaneous feelings listed above, the capacity for which is depicted as an essential part of what it means to be human, relate to Confucian moral virtues. The continuation of the passage cited above describes this relationship by saying, "The heart of compassion is the beginning (Ch. *duan*, Jp. *tan*) of humaneness (Ch. *ren*, Jp. *jin*). The heart of shame and disapproval is the beginning of rightness (Ch. *yi*, Jp. *gi*). The heart of deference is the beginning of ritual propriety (Ch. *li*, Jp. *rei*). The heart of right and wrong is the beginning of wisdom (Ch. *zhi*, Jp. *chi*)."

Zhu Xi's commentary maps the passage onto his schema of the division between principle and material force, here represented by the inborn nature (Ch. *xing*, Jp. *sei*) versus the emotions (Ch. *qing*, Jp. *jō*):

> Compassion, shame and disapproval, deference, and right and wrong are emotions. Humaneness, rightness, ritual propriety, and wisdom are the inborn nature. The heart is that which encompasses the emotions and the inborn nature. A "beginning" is like the tip of a thread. So when emotions are released, one can see the original state of the inborn nature, in the way that something inside can be known through the part of it that is visible on the outside.[36]

In this view, humans possess the totality of virtue by birth, and this innate virtue is then manifested in certain emotions. In *Gomō jigi*, Jinsai criticizes Zhu Xi by arguing that the term "beginning" refers not to an outer manifestation of something hidden inside, but rather to the fundamental origin of a thing. The implication is that it is not that people have, for example, an innate virtue of humaneness, which is manifested outwardly in the emotion of compassion, but rather that they begin with the innate feeling of compassion, which is the starting point for the cultivation of humaneness.[37] Jinsai's critique of Zhu Xi reflects his rejection of Zhu Xi's idea that people can find the Way by reaching inside themselves to a set of virtues that are abstracted from their actual practice. When we locate virtues in a static inborn nature, Jinsai argues, then "humaneness, rightness, ritual propriety, and wisdom become empty vessels."[38] For Jinsai, the Way can only be achieved by means of an outward movement in which, through people's everyday social interactions with others, they develop and expand the qualities with which they are born. Another way to put this is that for Jinsai virtue is not a principle that underlies what we might call moral sentiments, but is an extension and development of these sentiments themselves.

Jinsai also emphasizes that in order to cultivate virtue properly through social interactions, these interactions cannot simply be based on outward extensions of the self, but must take into account the feelings and perspectives of others. This idea is expressed in his discussion of the term "considerateness" (Ch. *shu*, Jp. *jo*)[39] in *Gomō jigi*, where he stresses how considerateness involves truly encountering others as others, and not simply reaching out to them based on a point of view that is ultimately only a product of our own prejudices. He writes, "People are very clear about their own likes and dislikes, but when it comes to the likes and dislikes of others, these are indistinct and we do not know how to perceive them. Therefore people often grow distant from each other."[40] This can be overcome, though, if we make a genuine effort to understand others and empathize with them: "If when dealing with others we have consideration for what their likes and dislikes are, as well as what situation they are in and what they do, then it will be as if their hearts are our own hearts, and their selves are our own selves" (p. 65). This will then lead, he argues, to a tolerance for the weaknesses of others, as we will realize that "people's misdeeds come from things that are unavoidable, or from situations that are difficult to bear" (pp. 65–66).

EMPATHY, COMMUNICATION,
AND THE CREATION OF POETIC MEANING

Jinsai sees the *Book of Odes* as one way to learn about the emotions of others, writing in *Dōjimon*, "Poetry speaks the emotions and inborn nature. Although the people of the realm are many, and the lives of past and present are innumerable, when we look into the source of their emotions, they do not depart from the three hundred Odes. When these are followed then the world will be well governed, and when they are violated it will go into chaos."[41] His son and intellectual heir Itō Tōgai (1670–1736) makes a similar point in his *Dokushi yōryō* (Essentials of Reading the Odes) when he writes, "Poetry reflects human emotions. If you are not conversant in human emotions, then when you go out into the world you will be incapable of interacting with others."[42]

Jinsai's emphasis on poetry as an expression of natural emotions comes through in his commentary on *Analects* II.2, where he departs from Zhu Xi by interpreting the statement that the Odes contain "no crooked thoughts" not as a comment on moral virtue, but simply as a declaration that the Odes are "direct" (Ch. *zhi*, Jp. *choku*).[43] At the same time, he does not deny that the Odes can function for "approving virtue and chastising vice." In *Gomō jigi*, he opens his section on the *Odes* by citing Zhu Xi's commentary on the "no crooked thoughts" passage: "As for the method of reading the Odes, it is true that those that are virtuous inspire approval from people's good heart, and those that express vice inspire a desire to condemn such vice."[44] Statements to the same effect appear in *Rongo kogi*, such as that the Odes "are sufficient to arouse a heart that likes virtue and dislikes vice."[45]

Despite his willingness to see moral cultivation as at least one of the functions of the Odes, Jinsai differs from both Zhu Xi and the Mao tradition by refusing to attribute a fixed moral value to each of the Odes, or even a fixed meaning in the first place. In *Gomō jigi* he writes, "The use of poetry lies not in the original intention of the author, but in what the reader feels."[46] Because of this, he charges, "Things like Zheng Xuan's *Maoshi jian* and Zhu Xi's *Shi jizhuan* pointlessly state the circumstances that led to a poem being composed, and do not know how ancient people read the Odes" (p. 87). He notes, for example, "In the lines, 'My troubled heart grieves, I am resented by the herd of petty men,' Zhuang Jiang of Wei laments being neglected by her husband. Mencius quotes this, though, and uses it to speak of Confucius" (p. 87).[47] He points out that the moral value of a poem can even be reversed through this kind of quotation, writing, "The poem on the plum tree is licentious, but Confucius quotes this to clarify that the Way is very near at hand" (p. 87).[48] Jinsai extends this idea of the readerly construction of meaning to the "Six Principles" of poetry, which the "Great Preface" describes as follows: "There are six principles (*yi*) in the Odes. The first is the Airs (*feng*). The second is exposition (*fu*). The third is comparison (*bi*). The fourth is evocation (*xing*). The fifth is the Elegantiae (*ya*). The sixth is the Hymns (*song*)."[49] Jinsai writes, "In my view, the Six Principles of poetry lie not in the intentions of the poems' creators, but rather in how readers use them" (p. 87). Because of this, he maintains, there is no fixed method of defining poems as belonging to these six categories: "Each individual poem encompasses the Six Principles, and the Six Principles permeate the three hundred Odes" (p. 88).

Jinsai does not provide an explicit theoretical account of the process through which the Odes can cultivate a sense of moral judgment in the reader, and the ability of readers to assign moral values at odds with those of the poems' creators may seem to undermine the ability of poetry to serve as any kind of moral teaching. His reading of the Four Beginnings passage in *Mencius*, though, suggests how his valorization of poetry as direct emotional expression, and his denial of fixed meaning in poetry, can coexist with his belief in the role of poetry in moral cultivation. In Zhu Xi's reading of the Four Beginnings, he sees the emotions represented by the Four Beginnings as valuable to the extent that they make people aware of the moral virtues that underlie these emotions. In the same way, he conceives of the process of reading the Odes as one of uncovering the fixed moral values, either virtuous or wicked, that underlie the emotions expressed in each poem. For Jinsai, however, the Four Beginnings are not expressions of fully formed moral virtues, but are instead the raw material out of which virtues can eventually be fashioned. We can see a parallel to this in his view of the Odes, in that he finds value in the process of actively giving meaning to the Odes, instead of simply trying to decode them for their preexisting moral significance.

These contrasting models of self-cultivation also help explain why Jinsai, despite his emphasis on the Odes as direct emotional expression, is actually less willing than Zhu Xi to read them as expressions of immorality. Jinsai's idea of the readerly construction of meaning in the Odes is not without boundaries, as he grants that the Minor Prefaces do have some value, and criticizes Zhu Xi for discarding them entirely. Jinsai specifically notes how without the Minor Prefaces, there are Odes that would appear to be expressions of extreme lewdness. Zhu Xi had accepted such readings under the rubric of "chastising vice," but Jinsai, while not insisting that the Odes are expressions of perfect virtue, finds it implausible that people would give voice to the kinds of sentiments that Zhu Xi at times attributes to them. He explains his objection to Zhu Xi with reference to one of the Four Beginnings, arguing that the "heart of shame and disapproval" would make people refrain from openly expressing certain emotions (p. 89).[50] Zhu Xi's tolerance of lewdness is rooted in his view of the reader of the Odes as a judge of virtue and vice, empowered by the possession of an innate moral purity. Jinsai's model of reading, in contrast, puts the reader and the creators of the Odes on a more equal plane in terms of their level of moral cultivation, in that they are both assumed to possess a basically good but imperfectly developed inborn nature. Rather than judging and categorizing the Odes, the reader is meant to actively engage with the Odes and the sentiments they express, with these interactions, much like relationships with other human beings, then serving to further develop the seeds of goodness present in the reader.[51]

The creation of meaning by readers of the Odes creates a potential problem, though, in light of Jinsai's declaration of the need for people to reach out and grasp the experiences of others who are different from themselves. If people can make poems mean what they want them to mean, then it would seem that their study of poetry would simply reinforce their existing prejudices, leading them into the kind of solipsism for which Jinsai faults Zhu Xi. This problem is mitigated, however, by the fact that Jinsai sees poetry not just as an object of study for isolated individuals, but as something to be used in the context of interpersonal encounters. He gives great attention, for example, to passages in the *Analects* where quotations from the Odes are used as a means of communication. One of these passages is *Analects* I.15:

> Zigong said, "Poor yet not obsequious, rich yet not proud—what do you think of this?" The Master replied, "That is fine, but it does not match being poor and joyful, and being rich and liking ritual." Zigong replied, "In the *Odes* it says, 'like being cut, like being filed, like being carved, like being polished.' This has the same meaning as what you say." The Master replied, "With one like Zigong I can begin to discuss the Odes. I tell him one thing and he knows what remains unsaid."

Here Zigong begins by describing a goal for self-cultivation, and Confucius responds by putting forth an even higher ideal. Zigong then quotes from the Ode "Qiyu" (Mao #55), in which the quoted lines are in the voice of a subject praising his lord's refinement, to echo Confucius' statement on the importance of constant improvement. A similar passage is *Analects* III.8:

> Zixia asked, "'The dimples of her charming smile / The clearly defined black and white of her beautiful eyes / The plain ground for the patterns'— What does this mean?" The Master said, "The colors go on after the plain ground." "Do the rites then come afterwards?" The Master said "You, Shang, are the one who brings out my meaning. Now I can begin to discuss the Odes with you."

The lines quoted are from the Ode "Shuoren" (Mao #57), where they describe the beauty of a bride, but they are used in the *Analects* passage to make a point about the nature of ritual.[52]

In his interpretations of these passages, Jinsai emphasizes that the lack of fixed meaning in the Odes makes it particularly difficult to grasp the intention of one who uses the Odes in conversation. In his commentary on *Analects* I.15 he writes, "Poetry is a living thing (Ch. *huowu*, Jp. *katsubutsu*). Its words from the start have no fixed meaning. Its meaning has no fixed standard. It is fluid and changing."[53] His description of poetry as a "living thing" is significant in that he often uses the contrast of life versus death to describe how the true Confucian Way differs from Daoism, Buddhism, and Zhu Xi's Confucianism, all of which he sees as valuing emptiness and nothingness. We can see this in his discussion of the term "principle," which he sees as simply the regularities of inert objects, and not as the metaphysical source of value posited by philosophers like Zhu Xi. Jinsai writes, "The term 'the Way' is a living word, as it describes the wonder of constant generation and transformation. Terms like 'principle' are dead words. . . . The sages take Heaven-and-Earth to be a living thing. . . . Laozi takes emptiness to be the Way, and views Heaven-and-Earth as a dead thing."[54]

Jinsai's characterization of the Confucian Way as something "living" refers to how it involves the active social relationships of humans, and with poetry as well he uses the notion of a "living thing" to point to how poetry takes on meaning only within the context of its active use. In his commentary on *Analects* III.8 he writes:

> Poetry has no form. It changes depending on the things it encounters. It can be made round, or made square. Depending on what people see, sometimes it is sad and sometimes it is joyful. Depending on what people encounter,

a single affair can extend to a thousand principles, and a single word can achieve a thousand meanings. Therefore if you are not one who can hear one thing and understand two, then you will not be able to exhaust the emotions in poetry.[55]

Because a poem can have many meanings, and because these meanings differ depending on the person who encounters the poem, the meaning to be grasped in conversation is not something that can be arrived at through scholarly inquiry, or through memorizing the Odes. In order to be qualified to discuss the Odes, it is necessary not only to have a knowledge of the content of the Odes themselves, but also to be the kind of person who is capable of empathetically grasping the experiences of others, and understanding what a specific person means in a specific situation. The interpretation of the Odes, then, is practiced within an interpersonal space, and not just between a solitary reader and a text.

Jinsai does not provide a single unified theory of the Odes, but his discussions of the role of the Odes are brought together by a concern for reaching out to others. Zhu Xi also discusses the value of reaching outside the self, such as in his idea of "investigating things," but the ultimate goal of this process is to uncover the moral principle that already exists fully formed within the self. For Jinsai, in contrast, moral virtues only come to completion as a product of social interactions, rather than being a principle underlying these interactions. Ethical cultivation therefore requires that people encounter others explicitly as others, introducing an element of uncertainty that is absent in Zhu Xi's model of interpersonal relations. This indeterminacy that Jinsai sees as inherent in social relations is then mirrored in the indeterminacy he finds in the meaning of the Odes.[56] For both the Mao school and Zhu Xi, the ethical function of the Odes requires that a fixed moral value be assigned to each of the Odes, but for Jinsai it is precisely because the Odes can mean many things that they force people to actively give them meaning, and empathetically grasp the meanings given to them by others, processes that provide the foundation for the cultivation of ethical social relations.

Conclusion

It would certainly be possible to read the theories discussed in this chapter as the story of the gradually lessening grip of morality on poetry, starting with the Mao tradition's attempt to read all the Odes as morally correct, progressing to Zhu Xi's idea that each Ode is morally good or morally bad, but in either case serves to cultivate moral goodness in the reader, and finally arriving at Jinsai's view that the Odes may cultivate the reader morally, but do not have a fixed moral content in and of themselves. What such an analysis leaves out, though, is how Zhu Xi and Jinsai, while providing less literally moral readings of the *Odes*, at the same time integrate it into new conceptions of the Confucian Way. If we compare the differences between how the theories in this chapter envision the education provided by the *Odes*, we can see a parallel to the differences in their views on the basis of the Confucian Way as a means to ensuring ethical social relationships. For the Mao tradition the *Odes* is a vehicle for internalizing the culture of the ancient sage kings, for Zhu Xi it puts people in touch with the principle latent in their inborn nature, and for Jinsai it helps spur on the active interpersonal engagements that he sees as crucial to Confucian moral cultivation.

It is this concern for active social relationships that is at the core of many Tokugawa writers' attacks on earlier Confucian ideas on poetry, especially their criticisms of Zhu Xi. While on one level their criticisms are directed at his didacticism, the broader issue is how this didacticism results in a failure to connect with others. Given the centrality of social relationships in Confucian traditions of ethical and political philosophy, we could even say that Tokugawa writers like Jinsai rejected Zhu Xi's view of poetry not because it was too Confucian, but because it was not Confucian enough. In the chapters that follow, we will see how other Tokugawa writers pursued a similar critique of Zhu Xi, in which they argued for the need to recognize and overcome the gaps separating people socially, and saw poetry as a vehicle through which people could be bound together to form a well-ordered society.

The Confucian Way as Cultural Transformation

Ogyū Sorai

Ogyū Sorai sought to make Confucianism relevant to managing Tokugawa society, leading him to refuse to equate the Confucian Way with individual moral purity, instead depicting it as a tool for governance. Moreover, he saw the Way as a human creation, rather than an extension of the natural order of the cosmos. While he was strongly critical of those who believed that the Way could be achieved through individual cultivation, his vision of the Way still did, as discussed in the Introduction, involve a certain idea of transforming people from within. In this chapter I examine why he thought such a transformation was necessary in early eighteenth-century Japan, and how he envisioned the cultivation of the Way by individuals as a process of socialization. I give particular attention to his depiction of the relationship between the Way as a cultural system and the raw material of human nature that it works upon, and how his conception of this relationship is tied to a vision of government as the coordination of distinct human abilities toward a common goal.

Sorai's Life and Writings

Sorai was born in Edo in 1666 into a family of samurai lineage. His father served as personal physician to Tokugawa Tsunayoshi (1646–1709), who would later reign as the fifth Tokugawa shogun from 1680 until 1709. In 1679 Sorai moved to Kazusa (present-day Chiba Prefecture) when his father was sent into exile there for an offense committed against Tsunayoshi. He stayed there until 1690, when his father was pardoned by Tsunayoshi and the family returned to live in Edo. Before his family went into exile, Sorai was enrolled in the Confucian academy run by Hayashi Gahō (1618–1680), the son of Hayashi Razan. The relative remoteness of Kazusa meant that Sorai had few opportunities for formal study there, but he would later credit his status as a self-taught outsider with giving him a freshness of perspective that allowed him to see the errors of the conventional scholarly methodologies of the time.

Upon his return to Edo, Sorai opened a private academy and set himself up as a teacher of the Chinese classics. His interpretations of the classics were conventional, based on the commentaries of Zhu Xi, but he already at this early stage began to distinguish himself as an innovative teacher of the Chinese language. His lectures on language from this time would later form the basis for *Yakubun sentei* (A Guide to Translation), a Chinese-Japanese dictionary that focuses on the problem of how different Chinese words can share the same Japanese translation, so that the translation taken by itself can obscure important nuances in the original text. His growing reputation as a scholar eventually led to him being brought to the attention of Yanagisawa Yoshiyasu (1658–1714), Tsunayoshi's chamberlain (*sobayōnin*). *I*n interview was arranged, and Yoshiyasu, impressed with Sorai's abilities, ʾired him as a house Confucian scholar.

Sorai served Yoshiyasu from 1696 until 1709, when Tsunayoshi died and Yoshiyasu, having lost his patron, retired from the political scene. Tsunayoshi was an active supporter of Confucian scholarship, giving the Hayashi school a new home in an official bakufu center for Confucian study and ritual, and even lecturing on the Confucian classics himself on a regular basis. This taste for Confucianism extended to his public policies as well, such as the posting of signboards exhorting the people to follow Confucian virtues. Yoshiyasu shared his patron's enthusiasm for Confucianism and for scholarship in general, and he created a salon atmosphere in his house by gathering together many of the most talented scholars of the day, including some who would later become disciples of Sorai, such as Hattori Nankaku and Andō Tōya (1683–1719).

Sorai's official duties while employed with Yoshiyasu involved a large amount of relatively uninspiring editing work, but he gained much from the debates and other interactions he was able to have with the scholars in Yoshiyasu's salon, and encountered many scholarly trends that made an important impact on his formulation of an original philosophy later in his career. His interests during his time with Yoshiyasu were mainly linguistic and literary, and he extended his study of Chinese by learning to speak colloquial Chinese from teachers who served as interpreters in Nagasaki, where trade with China was carried out. Most important perhaps was Sorai's discovery, toward the end of his service with Yoshiyasu, of the Ming writers Li Panlong and Wang Shizhen, leaders of the so-called Ancient Phraseology (Ch. *guwenci*, Jp. *kobunji*) movement of the Ming.[1] The neoclassical style of poetry championed by these writers, based particularly on poetic models from the High Tang, had an enormous effect on Sorai's own poetic taste. Beyond the matter of literary style, their sensibility for ancient language led Sorai to doubt his own understanding of ancient Chinese and seek to grasp it more directly. Eventually he would come to the conclusion that later commentators such as Zhu Xi had fundamentally misunderstood the *Analects* and other Confucian classics because they failed to grasp ancient language as ancient language, instead distorting it by reading it from the perspective of modern language. In this sense, philosophy was always for Sorai intimately linked to literary and linguistic studies.[2]

One of the most famous episodes in Sorai's life was his unsuccessful attempt to establish a dialogue with Itō Jinsai. In 1703 Sorai wrote Jinsai a letter praising his scholarship, a letter that remained unanswered when Jinsai died in 1705. It is unclear why Jinsai never responded—perhaps he was already too ill at the time, or perhaps he simply did not give much attention to unsolicited mail—but in any case Sorai took great offence, which was compounded when his letter was included in a collection of letters to Jinsai published after his death. Sorai's response to this perceived affront was to pen a scathing critique of Jinsai's philosophy entitled *Ken'en zuihitsu* (Jottings from the Miscanthus Garden), written in 1709 and published in 1714. Sorai would later repudiate this work, which attacked Jinsai essentially from a Song Confucian standpoint, but together with *Yakubun sentei*, the first part of which was published in 1711, it was responsible for cementing Sorai's reputation in the years immediately following his departure from service with Yoshiyasu.

After leaving Yoshiyasu's service Sorai once again set up a private academy, and over the next decade produced his most important original philosophical works. Some of the students in his new academy were carryovers from his time with Yoshiyasu, but he also gained important new disciples such as Dazai Shundai, who joined his school in 1711. One of the first works Sorai produced after *Ken'en zuihitsu* was *Gakusoku* (Regulations for Learning), a brief methodological primer. His two most famous philosophical works, drafts of which he completed by 1717, are *Benmei* (On Distinguishing Names) and *Bendō* (On Distinguishing the Way). *Benmei* is a philosophical lexicon, in which a series of terms such as "virtue" (Ch. *de*, Jp. *toku*), "humaneness" (Ch. *ren*, Jp. *jin*), and "ritual" (Ch. *li*, Jp. *rei*) are explained through citations from passages where they appear in the Confucian classics.[3] *Bendō* is a kind of digest of *Benmei*, made up of a series of brief sections that each make a particular point about the Confucian Way. After *Bendō* and *Benmei*, Sorai produced commentaries on the *Analects* (*Rongo chō*, or *Clarification of the "Analects"*), the *Doctrine of the Mean* (*Chūyō kai*, or *Interpretation of the "Doctrine of the Mean"*), and the *Great Learning* (*Daigaku kai*, or *Interpretation of the "Great Learning"*).

Sorai's writings in the 1720s, up until his death in 1727, were more oriented toward political policy, and show how he envisioned the practical application of the Way of the ancient Chinese sage kings in the context of contemporary Japan. This emphasis on policy coincided with a reestablishment of links between Sorai and the bakufu, beginning in 1721 when he received a request from a representative of the shogun to punctuate a Qing dynasty (1644–1911) legal text, the *Liuyu yanyi*. Over the following years he continued to be charged with various scholarly assignments, and also presented two works on politics to the bakufu, *Taiheisaku* (A Proposal for Great Peace), which consists largely of philosophical reflections on politics, and *Seidan* (A Discourse on Government), which outlines in much more detailed and concrete terms a comprehensive program of reform for the Tokugawa government.[4] While neither of these works was published until modern times, Sorai also dealt with many issues of governance in *Sorai sensei tōmonsho* (Master Sorai's Responsals), a wide-ranging work published in 1727 that provides an accessible introduction to his philosophy, and is said to be made up of his letters to two domain officials with whom he was corresponding.[5] Sorai's respected role as an advisor to the bakufu is evidenced by a formal audience he was granted with Yoshimune in 1727, and certain bakufu policies may have come about as the result of Sorai's suggestions.[6] There are also sources that suggest that Sorai had been offered an official position with Yoshimune and declined, and was on the verge of being asked again when he died.[7] Sorai's activities with the bakufu and his efforts to have an effect on contemporary policy are significant in that they come at the end of a period in which prominent Japanese Confucians strove to fulfill the role of the Confucian scholar-official. The loss of this role among Sorai's disciples would have a profound effect on how they carried on his teachings, leading them to search for new kinds of meaning in Confucianism and Chinese literary studies.[8]

Crisis and Reform in Early Eighteenth-Century Politics

Sorai's early career in Edo, first as a private teacher and then as a member of the salon of Yanagisawa Yoshiyasu, took place during the Genroku period (1688–1704), a time marked by the emergence of the urban merchant class as a powerful force both financially and culturally. The peace brought about by the consolidation of Tokugawa rule at the beginning of the seventeenth century had generated conditions conducive to commercial growth, such as by allowing for the development of a reliable transportation and communication infrastructure. Apart from the general role of stability in facilitating economic growth, the Tokugawa policies of having the samurai live in castle towns (rather than scattered throughout the countryside), and of forcing daimyo to maintain lavish residences in Edo, to which they commuted from their home domains under the system of alternate attendance (*sankin kōtai*), led to the growth of urban centers with large concentrations of samurai. The samurai were relieved by the advent of peace from the need to engage in the actual business of fighting, and they came to occupy themselves more and more with civil administration, while being supported financially by stipends paid in rice. It was considered unseemly for samurai to engage in commercial activity, so the increasingly complex financial business of the country was left to the merchant class, which as a consequence grew in wealth and influence throughout the seventeenth century.

While the merchant class showed great economic and cultural dynamism, from the point of view of the samurai this was not necessarily a welcome development; the merchant class played an important function (one which the samurai had no intention of taking over themselves), but the wealth of the merchants threatened to disturb the official social hierarchy in which samurai were at the top, followed by peasants, artisans, and finally merchants at the bottom. Despite the stable incomes provided to samurai by their stipends, the fact that these stipends were paid in rice meant that fluctuations in the rice market could make the real value of stipends vary greatly from year to year, and many samurai ended up becoming severely indebted to merchant class financiers. The ostentatious display of wealth on the part of merchants was another source of concern, and during Tsunayoshi's reign there was a sharp increase in the number of sumptuary edicts dictating exactly what clothes, houses, and other items were permissible to people of different statuses. These edicts, which were aimed not only at merchants, but also at samurai, were an attempt to maintain a rigid social hierarchy, if only on the level of appearance, as well as to curb excessive consumption in general. A more extreme solution than sumptuary edicts was simply to confiscate the wealth of merchants, such as when in 1705 the bakufu seized the entire assets of the Yodoya merchant house of Osaka.

Another issue the bakufu faced during the Genroku period (and the reign of Tsunayoshi in general) was a fiscal crisis precipitated by the gradual depletion of the bullion reserves that had originally been built up by Tokugawa Ieyasu (1542–1616) at the founding of the Tokugawa regime. The bakufu's response was to debase the currency in 1695, melting down gold and silver coins and issuing new coins with lower percentages of precious metal content. This netted the bakufu a considerable sum, but was only a short-term solution, as it did not take long for people to discount the value of the new coinage while hoarding the older coins.

Tsunayoshi was succeeded as shogun by Tokugawa Ienobu (1663–1712, r. 1709–1712), and then by the child Tokugawa Ietsugu (1709–1716, r. 1713–1716). Tsunayoshi had attempted to reform society by commanding through exhortation and legislation that people obey Confucian moral precepts, but Ienobu eased up on these policies, particularly such unpopular measures as Tsunayoshi's laws that called for severe punishment of those who failed to display benevolence toward animals. During the reigns of Ienobu and Ietsugu, the most influential Confucian scholar within the bakufu was Arai Hakuseki (1657–1725), whose contributions to policymaking during this period included convincing the bakufu to reverse Tsunayoshi's policy of currency debasement.[9]

The brief reigns of Ienobu and Ietsugu were followed by the much longer reign of Tokugawa Yoshimune (1684–1751), who was shogun from 1716 until his retirement in 1745. Yoshimune's reign was notable for a series of reforms known as the Kyōhō Reforms (a name taken from the Kyōhō period, which lasted from 1716 to 1736). This reform program addressed the same basic issues that the bakufu had been concerned with since the time of Tsunayoshi, namely the fiscal difficulties of the bakufu and the excessive influence of the merchant class. Specific policies enacted as part of this reform project included sumptuary laws, a temporary reduction of alternate attendance duty for daimyo, tightened control over the activities of merchants (including price controls and restrictions on moneylending), and reforms in the system for assessing land taxes that were designed to provide more revenue to the bakufu. In the area of currency, Yoshimune began by following the revaluation policy of Hakuseki (even though Hakuseki had lost his position in the bakufu with the death of Ietsugu), although in 1736 the bakufu reverted to a policy of debasement after a series of fiscal crises precipitated by wild fluctuations in the rice market.

It was in the context of the early stages of the Kyōhō Reforms that Sorai produced his treatises on government, and his hope was that these proposals would have some influence on the direction of Yoshimune's policies. Sorai was a keen observer of the changes going on in the society around him, and for him the economic transformations, expansion in popular culture, and upending of social hierarchies that he witnessed were not signs of a vibrant and dynamic society, but were rather indications of a breakdown in the proper order of things. In order to reverse this trend, Sorai thought it was necessary to put into practice the teachings of the sage kings of ancient China, an approach to reform that was guided by his belief that human society was originally given order through the civilizing process enacted by these sage kings, whose creations continued to provide the best guide for governing society in the present.

Objectivity as Cultural Framework

One theme that shows up repeatedly in Sorai's writings is the danger of relying on one's own personal opinions and inclinations, such as when he writes:

> Different people see things differently. This is what happens when they each use their own heart to determine that this is the Mean, or that is the naturally proper course. When people look from the north, they see the south. What serves as a standard? . . . This is, for example, like when two peasants have a dispute over a property boundary. If there is no official to hear their cases, then what can serve as a standard?[10]

A concern for avoiding the subjective and private, in favor of the objective and public, is common throughout Confucian thought, but Sorai defines this issue in distinct opposition to both Zhu Xi and Jinsai. For Zhu Xi, subjectivism is only a problem to the extent that material force (Ch. *qi*, Jp. *ki*), which he equates with the emotions (Ch. *qing*, Jp. *jō*), has not been properly brought under control. Once people have regained access to the principle (Ch. *li*, Jp. *ri*) that resides in their original inborn nature (Ch. *benran zhi xing*, Jp. *honzen no sei*), which is the innermost core of their being, there is a perfect unity of the subjective and the objective. One reason Sorai is skeptical about this kind of inner-directed definition of self-cultivation is that he denies the dualistic structure of human nature posited by Zhu Xi, arguing for a monism of material force, in which material force is not described as an outer covering laid over the inborn nature (Ch. *xing*, Jp. *sei*), but is instead seen as the only inborn nature that people have: "The inborn nature refers to the qualities with which people are born. It is what Song Confucians call 'material force.'"[11] Zhu Xi sees the individual differences embodied in material force as an outer layer of the self, and defines self-cultivation and the achievement of the Way in terms of the ability to regain access to the original inborn nature, which is identical for all humans and provides them with a perfectly objective standpoint. For Sorai, though, this original inborn nature simply does not exist, and each individual is irreducibly different. When people look inward, then, instead of encountering a deep layer of the self in which subjectivity and objectivity are perfectly united, they simply find more of the same particular material force of which they are constituted. To put it another way, all they find is their self, not some greater and more primal universal "Self" that transcends the individual.

As described in Chapter 1, Jinsai also argued for a monism of material force, and criticized Zhu Xi for seeking the Way by looking inward to the original inborn nature. In his critique of Zhu Xi's reading of the Four Beginnings passage in *Mencius*, for example, Jinsai denies that the Four Beginnings are outward manifestations of inner virtues latent in the inborn nature, a nature that exists prior to any actual application of these virtues, and instead argues that virtues are the product of the active exercise of the innate capacities represented by the Four Beginnings. While Sorai agrees with Jinsai on the need to avoid the abstraction and navel-gazing that both of them see as characteristic of Zhu Xi, he finds fault with Jinsai for failing to properly regulate the sphere of social relations within which the Way is realized. The *Mencius* passage describes the Four Beginnings as something that all people possess, just as all people possess four limbs, and Jinsai sees the development of these into the four corresponding virtues of humaneness, rightness, ritual propriety, and wisdom as being like extending the four limbs outward.[12] The problem Sorai finds with this interpretation is that he sees it as ignoring the fact that the Four Beginnings can only be cultivated through the mediation of external norms. He explains, "Those who do not realize this see a problem with how ritual and music are something external, and are not in the self. Such people do not have faith in the teachings of the sages, and try to achieve humaneness through their own personal intelligence."[13] While Sorai sees Jinsai as having corrected certain errors of Zhu Xi, then, he sees him as ultimately just as prone to subjectivism.

One way Sorai describes the objectivity provided by the Way of the sages is as a set of behavioral norms external to human nature. Because the Way exists outside human nature, he is adamant about the need to look to the specific historical creations of the sages, criticizing those who would try to bypass these with their own private speculations on the Way, commenting, "If one were to look inside oneself in order to find the principle of how things should be, and call this the Way of the sages, it would be an extreme delusion."[14] In one metaphor, he compares the creations of the sages to the tools of a carpenter:

> To follow the Way of the sages is called "correctness" (Ch. *zheng*, Jp. *sei*). To fail to follow the Way of the sages is called "deviance" (Ch. *xie*, Jp. *ja*). . . . This can be compared to the compass, square, and level. These are tools for making things correct. When a compass is followed then a circle will be correct, when a square is followed then an angle will be correct, and when a level is followed then things will be correctly level.[15]

Just as it is impossible to draw a circle freehand, or determine whether something is level simply by eyeballing it, people cannot find the standards to govern society by relying on what seems to them personally to be right.

A more complex formulation of the role of external norms comes through in Sorai's idea that people can understand things only by assimilating themselves to the cultural frame of reference within which these things are generated.[16] This idea that things become comprehensible through the frame or symbolic system in which they are situated can be contrasted with how in Zhu Xi's philosophy things take on meaning and value by being rooted in a universal principle, and people's ability to understand things outside of themselves is premised on the a priori possession of this principle in human nature. Sorai's view should also be distinguished from the view that finds norms in culture rather than in nature, but defines these norms simply as a set of rules for people to follow. For Sorai such rules can only be understood by one who has internalized the sphere of cultural value within which they are situated, a sphere that can itself never be reduced to a set of rules.

One version of this idea of cultural frames of reference appears in Sorai's early writings on language and the problem of translation, such as the methodological introduction to *Yakubun sentei*, in which he lays down a series of guidelines for the study of the Chinese language. Central to his approach is his rejection of the practice of reading Chinese through *wakun*, the system in which Japanese pronunciations are assigned to Chinese characters, which are then rearranged to fit the order of Japanese syntax, and supplemented with the particles and verb endings needed to produce a grammatically Japanese sentence. He argues that people overlook the shortcomings of *wakun* because they remain convinced that it is a direct rendering of the Chinese text, and fail to grasp that it is in reality a form of translation (*yaku*). By defining *wakun* as translation, Sorai is insisting that people see the original text and the *wakun* text as belonging to two distinct linguistic worlds, those of Chinese and of Japanese. As an alternative to *wakun*, he promotes translation into vernacular Japanese, a method that makes no effort to conceal its true nature as translation.

Another problem he finds with *wakun* is that it is an artificial form of language that provides neither access to the original Chinese nor an adequate translation into Japanese. The use of ordinary Japanese to translate has the benefit that "the common is easy and close to human emotions, so that when we use this to translate Chinese, we avoid giving people the impression of [the original Chinese] being anything out of the ordinary."[17] In other words, vernacular translation calls attention to how ancient Chinese is in fact nothing more than the ordinary language of its time, and is not any kind of lofty philosophical code to be deciphered, as the stilted language of *wakun* would lead people to believe. At the same time, he notes that there is a fundamental asymmetry between Chinese and Japanese, so that translation into vernacular Japanese should not be taken as a substitute for the original.[18] The result is that such translation is "neither identical to nor separated from (*fusokufuri*)" the Chinese original.[19] He connects this kind of relationship between translation and original to the metaphor of the "fishtrap and rabbit snare (*sentei*)" used in the title of *Yakubun sentei*, which can be rendered literally as "a fishtrap and rabbit snare of translation." The idea behind this metaphor, borrowed from a passage in *Zhuangzi*, is that a translation, like a fishtrap or rabbit snare, is a means to an end, and should be discarded once it has served its purpose.[20] Just as people put away fishtraps and rabbit snares after using them to catch fish and rabbits, vernacular Japanese is a tool that can be used to gain a hold on the Chinese original, but should eventually be set aside in favor of the original text, to which it will never be completely equal.

Tied to Sorai's presentation of separate languages as distinct spheres of meaning is the idea that to know a language means to inhabit its world, rather than to grasp it as an external object of knowledge. Sorai calls attention to what it means to be outside versus inside a language when he gives the following description of the process of learning Chinese:

> The most important task for scholars is that they come to know the essential character of the language of the Chinese. Moreover, this essential character is something that the Chinese themselves are not aware of. Why would this be any different from how people who live on Mount Lu cannot see what it is like?[21] It is because we seek out [the features of Chinese] from the perspective of the Japanese language that we are then able to see how [Chinese] is different. This is, for example, like how a southerner who always stays in the south is unaware of the characteristics of his region, whereas when a northerner comes to the south, he realizes how hot it is there.[22]

In one sense Sorai sees Japanese as having a better knowledge of Chinese than the Chinese themselves, in that only a Japanese has the outside perspective that would be necessary to produce something like a textbook of Chinese grammar. In his view, though, the kind of theoretical knowledge of Chinese that is available to an outsider such as a Japanese is not really a better form of knowledge. What he ultimately values is the knowledge of the native speaker who, although not able to describe the rules of his language, is not in need of such descriptions either. The goal of studying Chinese, then, is to achieve a leap of understanding, irreducible to any set of grammatical rules or mastery of items of vocabulary, that allows the student to enter into the linguistic world of ancient Chinese.

The notion of inhabiting worlds of meaning is also central to Sorai's policy writings, most notably in his emphasis on custom (*fūzoku*), which he defines as a kind of general framework within which people operate epistemologically, determining the limits of what is intelligible for them. In *Taiheisaku* he writes:

> If we were to try to explain the city to a country person, no matter how intelligent he was . . . how could he understand? It is only when we bring

him to the city and leave him there for two or three years that at some point he is changed, and without knowing it becomes a city person. Then when he looks back at his hometown it becomes comical to him. . . . To be changed in such a way, down to one's very heart, is simply a matter of the difference between being imbued or not imbued [by custom], and has nothing to do with the meticulousness of one's training or one's ingenuity. To explain to someone who does not study the Way of the sages, and to try to get him to understand it, is like speaking of the city to a country person. . . . This is because such a person is imbued with the customs of his own province and time, and neither the state of his heart nor the workings of his intelligence go outside their enclosure (*kuruwa*).[23]

Custom is not merely an aggregation of discrete items of knowledge, but is rather the condition of possibility of that knowledge, and thus always exceeds the sum of its content. This is why no matter how exhaustive a description of the city we may give to a person from the country, we can never get him to understand the city. Although Sorai's contention that people can never see beyond the limits of their own sphere of custom may seem to imply a pessimistic outlook on reforming society, he makes it clear in the passage above that even though custom determines what is intelligible to us at a given point in time, custom can nevertheless be changed. The transformation of custom is a central goal of his program for political reform, and we will turn next to how this is manifested in certain of his policy proposals.

The Establishment of Institutions

In *Seidan*, Sorai claims that it is only possible to reform society by turning back to the sages of ancient China: "When it comes to the Way of governing the realm and the provinces, there is nothing better than the Way of the ancient sages. The ancient sages Yao, Shun, Yu, Tang, Wen, Wu, and the Duke of Zhou governed the realm well, and bequeathed this Way to later ages. Without relying on this Way, it is not possible to know how to provide relief for the people."[24] This is not meant to imply, though, that it is necessary or even desirable to literally copy ancient Chinese civilization. Instead, he believed that the founder of each dynasty needed to create institutions (*seido*) based on the creations of the ancient sage kings, while still taking into account contemporary circumstances.

Institutions are designed to shape customs, and as such they are directed toward defining the basic modes of social organization, rather than just dictating specific behaviors. Sorai was critical of attempts to carry out reforms simply by passing laws, without striving to change people's mindset and habits. An example of this stance is his attitude toward the sumptuary regulations issued by the bakufu, which were meant to stem the spread of luxury goods to merchants and low-ranking samurai. Sorai was sympathetic to the goals of these regulations, as he considered the growth in the consumption of luxuries to be a major drain on the economy, as well as a disruption of the proper social hierarchy. He saw the bakufu's legal remedies to this problem, though, as ultimately futile:

> When we look at the situation of recent times, there are often decrees ordering frugality, but even though extravagance is prohibited, it does not go away. Even though theft is punished, theft does not come to a stop, and even though the punishment for bribery is severe, bribery does not cease. The military arts are promoted, but the warriors become weaker by the day; the practices of the samurai and the customs of the common people become worse every day. Prices skyrocket, throwing both high and low into penury, and the fact that there are no methods for dealing with this is because they try to control it simply by issuing orders and passing laws. This is, for example, like ordering people from the mountains to learn to swim, or ordering people from the coast to burn charcoal. To do so would be to set aside that which custom permits people to do, and to try to govern through laws. When one does this one is trying to force what cannot be done, so in the end this is impossible.[25]

The only way to create lasting reforms, according to Sorai, is to change customs. Instead of the piecemeal measure of issuing sumptuary restrictions, he argues that excessive consumption can be brought under control only by altering the fundamental structures within which people live. This idea was the basis for his most radical proposal, which was to have the samurai move out of the cities and back to the land, where he thought they would naturally develop simpler tastes and of their own accord stop desiring luxury goods. He applies a similar logic to the question of how to provide relief for the poor, arguing that it is useless simply to hand out money without making more fundamental changes to society: "Even if we were to try to help people by distributing every last coin in the treasury, things would soon return to their former state."[26]

Sorai follows Chinese historiographical convention in taking the dynasty as the basic unit of history, and he argues that it is the responsibility of the founders of a dynasty to establish appropriate institutions. Although all dynasties must come to an end at some point, as "faults will emerge even in the creations of sages, and these faults lead to the world being sent into chaos,"[27] this decline can be forestalled if the founders of a dynasty create institutions that anticipate potential problems: "Through the ritual, music, and institutions of the founding ruler, the conditions of the age and the sources of troubles can be known several hundred years in advance. 'Sages' refers to those founding rulers who consider the future well, and establish ritual, music, and institutions in such a manner that there will be few faults."[28] Although history, in Sorai's view, is a constant cycle in which dynasties are created, descend into chaos, and then are replaced by new dynasties, this does not mean that all dynasties are created equal, and he emphasizes how properly established dynasties last longer: "The Xia lasted six hundred years, the Yin seven hundred years, and the Zhou eight hundred years, and the fact they held up for so long is a sign of their being founded by sages. From the Han and Tang onward, though, there was no ritual and music. The reason that none of these later dynasties lasted more than three hundred years is that they did not have good institutions, and therefore the world quickly declined and descended into chaos."[29]

Sorai applies this same model of history and dynastic change to explain how Japan had arrived at its contemporary state of disorder, and to situate his own historical moment within a broader narrative of the importation of the culture of the sages to Japan. In *Seidan* he writes,

> In Japan, as well, Fujiwara no Fuhito [659–720] created the *ritsuryō* system based on the methods of the Tang court, and this was used to govern the country. After three hundred years, though, the realm passed into the hands of warriors. After that, the Kamakura government disappeared in a hundred years, and the Muromachi government collapsed into great chaos within a hundred years. These were both lacking in learning, and did not know to follow the government of the ancient kings of the Three Dynasties, and so their duration was extremely ancient.[30]

In this way, even the diluted version of the Way of the sages that had been borrowed from the Tang disappeared, and the country was left bereft of any guiding principles for government.

The establishment of the Tokugawa regime successfully put a stop to the warfare that had been raging since the collapse of the Muromachi, but Sorai criticizes how the Tokugawa government failed to carry out its task of establishing institutions. Describing the establishment of the Tokugawa bakufu in *Seidan*, he writes, "It came after a period of great chaos, and yet it did not reform the customs of this world that had entirely lost institutions in everything, and instead simply left things as they were. Because of this, today there are no institutions, and it has become a world in which both the high and the low simply do as they please."[31] He is not so much critical of the founder Ieyasu's skills at rulership, though, as of his failure to prepare for the future by setting up institutions that would guarantee good government even in the hands of lesser rulers than himself. In one metaphor, Sorai writes of the founding of the Tokugawa regime: "It is like raising the sails of a boat in a strong wind and launching it, but not having an anchor."[32]

Sorai's descriptions of the consequences of this lack of institutions focus on how society has become fragmented, with people lacking any objective norms. This concern for subjectivism, which is also evident in his critique of Song Confucianism, is paralleled by an argument that people have come to interact with each other as isolated individuals, connected only through monetary exchange and contractual arrangements, rather than through feelings of mutual obligation or a sense of membership in a family or other communal body. For example, he deplores the replacement of hereditary servants with contract labor, and argues that if servants are going to be hired for wages, then the employer should be able to obtain solid background information on servants directly from their native place, rather than the current practice of having servants backed up by guarantors who simply provide their services for a fee, and do not have any actual connection to the person being hired.[33]

These problems are caused above all, he argues, by the Tokugawa policies of removing the samurai from the countryside and concentrating them in castle towns, and of subjecting daimyo to the alternate attendance requirement, making it necessary for them to spend vast amounts of money and maintain large retinues in Edo. Living apart from the people they govern, he maintains, samurai come to see themselves as individuals, and fail to connect to the governed other than as a source of tax revenue. In cities they "live as if in an inn," paying for everything in cash, and driving themselves into poverty.[34] He also complains about the encroachment of urban commercial values into the countryside and the peasantry: "When there is no border between the city and the country, the farmers gradually turn to commerce and the realm grows impoverished."[35] While he sees cities and commerce as necessary evils, he views the countryside as the source of true wealth, as well as an environment that encourages frugality, and argues that to preserve economic health it is necessary to prevent the countryside from being infected by urban values.

It was in response to this diagnosis of his society's ills that Sorai came up with his proposal to resettle the samurai in the countryside, where he believed they would naturally develop feelings of empathy for the common people, as well as lead more frugal lives, saving them from financial hardship on an individual level, and on a broader class level from subordination to the merchant class. This proposal is related to his idealization of feudal (Ch. *fengjian*, Jp. *hōken*) social relationships, where "feudalism" refers specifically to the decentralized government characteristic of the Three Dynasties of ancient China, in which local rulers have power over their own fiefs and live in direct contact with the people they govern. This arrangement is in contrast to the centralized bureaucracies of later Chinese history, in which territories are administered by officials appointed from the capital. He sees these different forms of rule as leading to different forms of human relationships, commenting, "In the Way of feudalism, the relationship to the people is like that of a father and son within a house. In a [centralized] system of prefectures and counties (Ch. *junxian*, Jp. *gunken*), though, they rely only on laws; everything is explicit and impartial, but there is no kindness and affection."[36]

Sorai's fear of urbanization, and nostalgia for an imagined feudal past of humane and empathetic rulership, indicates a reactionary streak in his political philosophy. This impression is strengthened by his concern for fixing people in place socially, which he believes will ultimately result in a moral transformation of the people: "When none fail to devote themselves to their families' occupations, then people's hearts will all return to sincerity, and all the various bad things of today will disappear."[37] He extends this desire to control movement to the sphere of literal physical movement as well. When people are permitted to move around, he writes, they "have no long-lasting feelings; they do not care about their neighbors, and their neighbors do not care about them."[38] On the other hand, "If people were forbidden to move freely to other provinces, people all throughout Japan would be fixed in their places, and would be attached to the land there. Therefore people would always be under control, there would be none who abandoned their native places, and so there would be none with no defined status."[39] Sorai's proposals, which are designed to counteract the social changes that were occurring in Japan at the time, end up relying on a draconian control of society in an ultimately futile attempt to stem the tide of history. He does, however, recognize certain limits on the ability of rulers to mold people into a vision of an ideal society, as I explore next in my discussion of his idea of the need for the Way to respond to human nature.

The Way and Human Nature

Sorai's emphasis on the frames of reference through which people's consciousness is structured is also manifested in his privileging of relationships between insiders to a culture or worldview over relationships between insiders and outsiders. In *Bendō*, for example, he argues that it is only really possible to talk about the Way to those who in a sense already understand it. The job of the teacher is not to explain the Way through logic, but to instill it in students by remaking them from within. Through such a teaching method, he writes, "After a long period of time, we transform people's eyes and ears, as well as their hearts and thoughts. Therefore without even awaiting our words, they spontaneously understand."[40] He contrasts this with the argumentative style of Zisi (the author of the *Doctrine of the Mean*) and Mencius, whom he charges with practicing what he calls the "Way of the litigant," instead of the "Way of teaching people."[41] What drove them to such a practice, he explains, is that they were "disputing with outsiders,"[42] by which he is referring to how they were trying to refute the attacks made on the Confucian Way by the likes of the Daoists. Unlike Sorai's vision of the teacher, who instructs by transforming the outsider into an insider, and only then explaining, the litigant deals with the outsider as outsider, meaning that he cannot presume the kind of spontaneous understanding that is the privilege of the insider, and must lay things out logically and discursively in an attempt to win over his audience, an attempt that Sorai considers ultimately counterproductive.

There is undoubtedly an element of authoritarianism in Sorai's philosophy of pedagogy, or at least a tendency to be closed off to other perspectives. Although he argues that the norms governing human social interactions are cultural constructs, this does not mean that he takes all such constructs as equal, or that he sees anything productive about the dialogic encounter of spheres of consciousness generated by different frameworks of cultural assumptions. Far from seeing dialogue with outsiders (such as the debates of Zisi and Mencius with Daoists) as a stimulus to gaining new perspectives on the Confucian Way, Sorai is deeply suspicious of such debates, which he believes cause people to compromise and distort their own views in an attempt to make them convincing to outsiders.

In his discussion of the differences between the "teacher" and the "litigant," for example, he criticizes the litigant for pandering excessively to the listener: "The fault of Zisi, Mencius, and those who came later is that they explain things in great detail in an effort to make them easily comprehensible to the listener. This is the Way of the litigant. It hastily tries to sell its arguments, and thus places authority in the other. The Way of teaching people is not like this; it puts authority in oneself."[43] He expresses a similar attitude when he stresses that faith in one's teacher is the precondition for all learning:

> Those who try to use words to make others submit have never succeeded in doing so. Those who teach concern themselves with those who have faith in them. The subjects of the ancient kings had faith in the ancient kings, and the disciples of Confucius had faith in Confucius; this is why their teachings could sink in. Mencius, however, took those who did not have faith in him, and tried to get them to have faith in him through his words.[44]

This idea can be seen in certain aspects of Sorai's views on the practice of governance, such as his advice not to remonstrate with rulers unless you have their trust; he explains that "it is pointless to try to reason with people who do not have faith in you," and that such attempts will always degenerate into an endless conflict where neither side will give way.[45] These examples show a logic similar to that at work in Sorai's distinction between customs and laws. Just as laws can only be effective with people whose customs have already been transformed, we can only really communicate with those who have already been made into insiders to our worldview.

It may seem, then, that Sorai is replacing the alleged solipsism of Zhu Xi with what could be called a cultural solipsism, that is to say, an attitude that refuses to see outside the confines of its own sphere of cultural assumptions, or address itself to anyone who does not already share them. While there is certainly room for such charges, these aspects of Sorai's philosophy are mitigated by his insistence that the culturally constructed norms of the sages must respond to a preexisting human nature. The highest source of authority for Sorai is Heaven, and the duty to respect human nature ultimately derives from the fact that the inborn qualities of humans are bestowed by Heaven: "The material [nature] is the inborn nature (*sei*) from Heaven. If we tried to go against this by using human power to prevail over Heaven, this would be impossible."[46] By explicitly identifying the material nature as that which is given by Heaven, Sorai is targeting Zhu Xi's idea that there is an original nature, distinct from the material nature, that connects humans to Heaven, and that self-cultivation involves transforming the material nature so that it conforms to the original nature. For Sorai such a notion of the original nature is in fact an affront to Heaven, as it is based in a denial of what Heaven has granted us as humans.

The relationship between the raw state of human nature and its cultivation by the Way is the focus of Sorai's interpretation of the passage from the opening of the *Doctrine of the Mean* that states, "That which Heaven mandates is the inborn nature; that which follows the inborn nature is the Way."[47] Zhu Xi's reading of this passage takes the inborn nature to be equivalent to principle, and says that the Way "follows" the inborn nature in that "if people follow the spontaneous state of their inborn nature, then in matters of everyday life they will never fail to find the proper path."[48] That is, because humans are endowed from birth with the normative principle that governs all things, all they need to do in order to do the right thing is follow this inner principle. This is the view that in the previous section we saw Sorai criticize for its unstable subjectivism, but this criticism does not lead him to reject the *Doctrine of the Mean* passage. Instead, he argues that the problem lies not with the *Doctrine of the Mean* itself, but with Zhu Xi's misinterpretation of it, particularly his misunderstanding of what it means for the Way to "follow" the inborn nature.

The source of Zhu Xi's error, Sorai argues, lies in his failure to take into account the fact that the *Doctrine of the Mean* is not an autonomous text that can be read as an expression of abstract philosophical truths, but is embedded in a specific historical and discursive context within which its statements take on meanings different from those they would take on were they to be read in complete isolation. In *Bendō* he explains, "When in the *Doctrine of the Mean* it says such things as 'that which follows the inborn nature is the Way,' this is because at that time the theory of Laozi had arisen, which condemned the Way of the sages as something false. Therefore Zisi wrote this text [the *Doctrine of the Mean*] in order to promote our Confucian Way."[49] He goes on to argue that what Zisi was trying to say was not that the inborn nature and the Way are equivalent, or that the Way is a direct extension of the inborn nature, but simply that the Confucian Way does not violate human nature in the manner charged by Daoists:

> [The *Doctrine of the Mean*] says that the ancient kings created the Way by following the inborn nature of humans. It does not say that the Way exists naturally (*shizen*) in Heaven-and-Earth, nor does it say that the Way simply follows human nature just as it is, without adding any artifice (*sakui*). This is, for example, like cutting down trees to build a palace. You build it

by following the innate qualities (*sei*) of the wood. However, how could a palace be considered the natural state (*shizen*) of wood?[50]

In response to the Daoist charge that the Confucian Way is a construct, then, Zisi responds by conceding that it is a construct, while denying that it is an arbitrary construct.

Even though Sorai stresses both the constructed character of the Way and its connection to human nature, he does not describe this in terms of a tension between nature and artifice. Instead, he sees the function of the Way in terms of how it nourishes and develops the innate qualities of things, and integrates them into a broader order in which they are put to use for specific ends:

> The teachings of the ancient kings, which are ritual, music, the *Odes*, and the *Documents*, are like the gentle breezes and irrigating rains that make the myriad things grow. Although the qualities of the myriad things are different, they are all the same in how they grow through receiving nourishment. Bamboo receives it and becomes complete as bamboo, trees receive it and become complete as trees, grass receives it and becomes complete as grass, and grain receives it and becomes complete as grain. When these have become complete, then they provide plentifully for the uses of buildings, clothing, and food.[51]

As I explore next in my discussion of Sorai's conception of "virtue," this idea of the Way as something that responds to the natural state of things, while at the same time developing them into something that goes beyond nature, carries over into his views on how the Way should be cultivated by different individuals, and how individuals should be organized under the guidance of rulers.

"Attaining the Way" through Virtues

On the level of individuals, Sorai argues that the Way interacts with the inborn nature to give rise to virtues. He begins his discussion of the term "virtue" (Ch. *de*, Jp. *toku*) in *Benmei* with the definition, "'Virtue' means 'to attain.' It refers to that which each person attains in the Way."[52] In the previous section we saw how Sorai describes the Way as being built upon the innate qualities of humans. Virtues then represent for him what these innate qualities develop into when people are cultivated by the Way. One of the central points Sorai makes in relation to virtues is that different people should cultivate different virtues, a view that derives from his denial of a single universal human nature: "The inborn nature differs from person to person. Therefore virtues as well differ from person to person."[53] Another reason he gives for why people should only cultivate certain virtues is that the Way is too multifaceted to be grasped in its entirety by ordinary people: "The Way is vast, so if one is not a sage, how can one possibly unify oneself with the vastness of the Way? For this reason the ancient kings established the names of virtues, and caused scholars to take that which is close to their own particular inborn natures, base themselves on this and maintain it, and cultivate and elevate it."[54] The function of virtues, then, is to provide concrete goals that people can aspire to that allow them to participate in and contribute to the Way, which it would be impractical and counterproductive for them to attempt to grasp in its entirety.

For Sorai there are many different particular virtues, but there is no abstract, totalizing concept of virtue that either underlies or encompasses these. This aspect of his philosophy is tied to his rejection of Zhu Xi's idea that sages are those who have achieved complete virtue, and that to become such a sage is the ultimate goal of self-cultivation. First of all, Sorai argues, "The ancient kings' virtues of intelligence and wisdom are received in their Heaven-ordained nature, and are not things that ordinary people can attain. For this reason, the theory that by studying one can become a sage did not exist in the past."[55] On top of this, he denies that even sages possess the totality of virtues, and says that their status as sages comes from their act of creating the Way, and not from their attainment of any perfect and total virtue: "Sages are simply humans. People's virtues differ according to their inborn natures. How could even sages all have the same virtues? The reason they are all called sages is because of their creations."[56] Zhu Xi makes a double error, then, in that not only does he try to force people to attain the impossible by exhorting them to become sages, he does not even understand what it is that makes a sage a sage in the first place.

One aspect of people's natures that Sorai emphasizes is the diversity of talents they are born with: "'Talent' (Ch. *cai*, Jp. *sai*) is the same as 'capability' (Ch. *cai*, Jp. *zai*). People have capabilities in the same way that trees do.[57] Some trees are appropriate for being made into crossbeams, while others are appropriate for being made into rafters. In the same way, by following that which is different in their inborn natures, humans each have things they can do well. These are capabilities."[58] The specific goal of developing talents is so that they can be put to use in government: "When virtue is established and talent is brought to completion, then this is put to use in an official post."[59]

The cultivation of diverse talents is important to Sorai because, just as a building is constructed from different components that each play a critical role, he sees the governance of society as requiring the coordination of different skills and aptitudes. In *Bendō* he writes:

> The governance of the realm is not something that can be done by a single person alone. Its accomplishment necessarily requires many abilities. This can be compared to how it is only when spring, summer, autumn, and winter are combined that a year is brought to completion, or how carpentry can only be practiced when hammer, chisel, blade, and saw are all possessed together.[60]

The function of the ruler in such a system is not to be a perfect individual, but to be a skillful manager of others, able to identify, cultivate, and employ the talents latent in them.

Another implication of what Sorai is saying is that people are not good or bad in the abstract, but only in relation to the specific roles they are to perform. In a continuation of his metaphor of carpentry, he notes, "An awl is good if it is sharp, while a hammer is good if it is dull."[61] In *Seidan* we can see an application of this idea when Sorai describes how, for example, those entrusted with conveying reports to rulers must be good at carefully passing on information in an objective manner, while military captains in charge of many subordinates must be good at managing people fairly, and police need to be sticklers for rules.[62] The specific problem he is dealing with in this passage is that the first two classes of officials tended to be promoted from the ranks of police officers, with the result that these posts were carried out in the manner characteristic of police officers. His point is not that there is anything wrong per se with the strict disposition of police officers; it is precisely the kind of quality required of those whose job it is to combat crime. When people of this disposition are assigned to other offices, though, they become unable to carry out their duties effectively.

In addition to the attention he gives to the differences in people's natures, Sorai argues that all people share a basic instinct toward sociality, which is the ultimate basis upon which the Way is built: "Although the inborn natures of people are different, people are all alike in that whether wise or foolish, superior or inferior, they all have a heart of mutual love, nourishment, aid, and accomplishment, and a capacity for work and production.

Therefore we rely on rulers for government, and on the common people for nourishment, and the farmers, artisans, and merchants all work together to make their livelihoods. It is simply in the inborn nature of humans that they cannot live all by themselves in a deserted village."[63] While this assertion of a set of common human inclinations may seem to contradict Sorai's view that each person's inborn nature is different, his emphasis on the diversity of human nature is only meant to combat the view that human nature as a whole is universal, not to deny that there may be universal elements to human nature.[64] In the same way, he believes that human nature has a general inclination toward goodness, but unlike such philosophers as Zhu Xi he does not take this to the degree of saying that human nature contains within it the totality of goodness.[65]

Just as Sorai sees certain aspects of the inborn nature to be universal, he sees a certain set of virtues as being appropriate for all people to pursue. This least common denominator of virtue is represented by the Mean (Ch. *zhongyong*, Jp. *chūyō*), which for Sorai refers to "virtues that are not lofty and are easy to perform, such as filial piety (Ch. *xiao*, Jp. *kō*), brotherly obedience (Ch. *ti*, Jp. *tei*), loyalty (Ch. *zhong*, Jp. *chū*), and faithfulness (Ch. *xin*, Jp. *shin*)."[66] The difference between the Mean and other virtues is that the Mean plays the role of a kind of everyday morality, while the virtues developed in accordance with people's individual talents are to be put to use in government office. There is a clear mapping onto social class lines here, as the virtues of the Mean are all that is required of the common people, while the ruling class of gentlemen (Ch. *junzi*, Jp. *kunshi*) are expected to study and develop themselves on a higher level. As Sorai writes in *Benmei*, "even though you may have filial piety and brotherly obedience, if you do not study you cannot escape being a rustic,"[67] and "even though you may have the virtues of the Mean, if you do not study the Way it is not enough to make you a gentleman."[68]

This is not to say that gentlemen are not required to pursue the Mean as well, just that the Mean itself is not sufficient for them, as expressed in his comments on *Analects* VI.16, which states, "When substance (Ch. *zhi*, Jp. *shitsu*) exceeds culture (Ch. *wen*, Jp. *bun*), then one will be a rustic. When culture exceeds substance, then one will be like a scribe. It is only when substance and culture are in balance that one is a gentleman." Sorai interprets the difference between "substance" and "culture" in terms of the distinction between the basic virtues of the Mean and the more elevated teachings that gentlemen must pursue: "'Substance' is basic behavior. This refers to such things as filial piety, brotherly obedience, loyalty, and faithfulness. 'Culture' refers to studying the *Odes*, the *Documents*, ritual, and music, so that one's words are dignified and splendid. . . . Those who have culture, but not basic activities, are unable to achieve virtues with their studies, and instead merely memorize. That is why they are compared to scribes."[69] While it is cultural attainments that distinguish the gentleman from the common people, then, these studies can only play their appropriate role in the formation of the gentleman when they are combined with the practice of everyday morality.

The idea of diverse virtues mobilized toward a common end is expressed in Sorai's interpretation of "harmony" (Ch. *he*, Jp. *wa*), which he defines in *Chūyō kai* by explaining, "'Harmony' refers to when things are different but do not contradict each other. This is like the harmony of the eight notes of the scale, or the harmony of the five flavors, or Yanzi's discussion in the *Zuo zhuan* of harmony versus 'sameness' (Ch. *tong*, Jp. *dō*)."[70] In the passage Sorai cites here, Yanzi explains to the Lord of Qi that his subject Ziyou, who obeys him completely, is in fact the "same," and not truly in "harmony." Describing a "harmonious" relationship between lord and subject, Yanzi says, "When the lord says something is correct, but there are faults in it, then the subject should put forth these faults, so that the part that is correct can be achieved. When the lord says something is incorrect, but there are good points in it, then the subject should put forth these good points, in order to do away with the bad points. Through this, government becomes peaceful and nothing is amiss, and the people do not have disputatious hearts." He then contrasts Ziyou's behavior, which he characterizes as "sameness": "What you say to be correct, he also says to be correct, and what you say to be incorrect, he also says to be incorrect. This is like adding water to water. Who would want such a thing? It is like a single-stringed lute. Who could bear to listen to it? This is what is wrong with sameness."[71] Sorai cites this same *Zuo zhuan* episode in *Rongo chō* to explain *Analects* XIII.23, which states, "The Master said, 'The gentleman harmonizes but is not the same. The petty man is the same but does not harmonize.'" In his commentary on this passage, what Sorai particularly objects to is the idea that "harmony" refers to a pacification of the individual's heart, rather than a relationship between different individuals. This relational aspect, the intermixture and mutual nourishment of things that remain distinct from each other, is essential to Sorai's notion of harmony, and without it there is nothing but "sameness."[72]

In *Seidan*, Sorai cites these passages from the *Analects* and the *Zuo zhuan* to support the idea that successful government relies on the "harmonization" of diverse talents. He compares the mixture of different talents among government officials, which complement each other and make up for what is lacking in the ruler, to the mixture of flavors in cooking. He describes sameness, on the other hand, as being when "everyone matches themselves to the heart of the ruler, not differing a bit from his preferences," and compares this to "adding sugar to sweet miso, and then on top of this adding honey, and then adding syrup on top of that."[73]

For Sorai, the question of how to develop different talents is related to the problem of sycophancy and conformity of opinion (as presented in the *Zuo zhuan* passage), in that when people's individual talents are not recognized, they are forced to conform to arbitrary standards, and to falsify themselves in order to gain favor with their ruler. In *Taiheisaku* he writes, "People's material natures are each different, so even if the ruler tried to make them conform to his own preferences, who could make themselves the same? When the ruler wields his authority and treats people in such a manner, though, those below will try to conform to the ruler's heart. This is the source of flattery and obsequiousness, and it causes human talents to fail to develop."[74] This idea can also be seen in terms of Sorai's critique of the subjectivism of Song Confucians, which he sees as leading them to fail to see the complexity and richness of the world outside them, and instead to try to force it into the mold of their own personal prejudices. In *Sorai sensei tōmonsho*, Sorai admonishes the addressee of one letter for complaining about a lack of talented people, and explains that his inability to locate talented people stems from a refusal to recognize anything outside of his own rigid preconceptions of what constitutes talent, an attitude that Sorai compares to the narrowness of perspective of Zhu Xi's historical work the *Tongjian gangmu* (Outline of the *Comprehensive Mirror*), in which "not a single person in the realm, in the past or present, is satisfactory to Zhu Xi."[75] It is this kind of attitude, Sorai believed, that was leading to an underutilization of talent in the Japan of his day, and preventing effective rulership by the samurai class.

Ritual, Music, and the Cultivation of Virtues and Genuineness

For Sorai, the most important tools for the achievement of virtues are ritual and music. One passage he cites to explain how ritual and music relate to the accomplishment of virtues is *Analects* XIV.13, which states, "Zilu asked what it means to be an 'accomplished person' (Ch. *chengren*, Jp. *seijin*). The Master replied, 'Take for example the wisdom of Zang Wuzhong, the lack of avarice of Gongchuo, the bravery of Zhuang of Bian, and the arts of Ran Qiu—embellish (Ch. *wen*, Jp. *bun*) these with ritual and music, and this will suffice to make one an accomplished person." Zhu Xi interprets an "accomplished person" to mean a "fully-rounded person" (Ch. *quanren*, Jp. *zenjin*), which one can only become by combining the virtues of the four people listed in the passage. He explains the significance of ritual and music in the passage by saying, "When we regulate these with ritual, and harmonize them with music, we cause virtue to be completed within, and embellishment will be visible on the outside."[76] Jinsai, in contrast, does not read the passage as implying that the virtues of all four people are combined. Instead, he writes, "The strong points of these four people are sufficient to establish themselves in the world and make a name for themselves. Then when these are embellished with ritual and music, these people's unbalanced aspects are brought in line, and that which they lack is made up for, and through this they become worthy of being called 'accomplished people.'"[77] Sorai agrees with Jinsai in rejecting the idea that the "accomplished person" described in this passage has to have all of the virtues listed, but he disagrees with both Zhu Xi and Jinsai in their interpretations of what it means for virtues to be "embellished" by ritual and music.

In *Benmei*, Sorai explains the function of ritual and music in the above passage by writing, "This says that when they study ritual and music, and accomplish their virtues, then these four can all be accomplished people. An 'accomplished person' is one who has accomplished virtue. To 'embellish' this refers to how virtue is accomplished and is splendid. This does not refer to painting something on from the outside."[78] What he objects to in both Zhu Xi's and Jinsai's interpretations of this passage is how they take ritual and music to be something added on to virtues as a kind of embellishment or refinement of them. He argues instead, in his commentary on this passage in *Rongo chō*, "The phrase 'embellish these with ritual and music' refers to bringing these into the Way."[79]

Sorai's argument here can be situated in the context of the distinction we saw in Chapter 1 between two Confucian paradigms for defining the term *wen* in relation to the Way, one of which sees *wen* as an external embellishment to the Way, and the other of which sees *wen* as itself constitutive of the Way. It is the second of these paradigms that Sorai is working within, so that the *wen* of ritual and music is not an external embellishment to virtue, but rather is what allows virtue, as that which each individual "attains in the Way," to come to completion (or be "accomplished") in the first place. It is this that distinguishes his reading of this *Analects* passage from that of Zhu Xi, who defines the "accomplishment" of the virtues listed in the passage in terms of an additive aggregation of them, and Jinsai, who interprets this "accomplishment" as a kind of polishing up of rough spots.[80]

Earlier we saw how Sorai argues that it is only really possible to speak about the Way to those who understand it, and that the function of the teacher should be to transform the student in such a manner that the student comes to inhabit the Way, only after which it will become possible to speak to that student about specific matters of the Way. The importance of ritual and music for Sorai lies in how they are able to effect such a transformation, and teach the Way in a manner not possible with mere verbal explanations and argumentation. In *Benmei* he writes:

> When you say things to people they understand, and when you say nothing then they do not understand. Why is it, then, that although ritual and music say nothing, they are superior to language in instructing people? The reason is that they transform people. When people practice these and become fully immersed in them, then even though they may not yet understand them, their hearts and bodies have quietly been transformed by them. Therefore, do they not ultimately understand?[81]

Within the context of a given sphere of understanding, people come to grasp things by having them explained verbally, but such verbal explanations alone can never allow them to make the radical leap from being outside to being inside a sphere of understanding such as the Confucian Way. It is only ritual and music that can effect such a leap, which is described in the above passage as a "transformation" (Ch. *hua*, Jp. *ka*) of the self.

Another way that Sorai describes the accomplishment of virtue is as the attainment of genuineness (Ch. *cheng*, Jp. *sei/makoto*). His discussion of this term in *Benmei* begins, "'Genuineness' refers to that which comes straight from the heart, and requires neither thought nor effort."[82] He argues, for example, that the inborn nature can be described as "genuine" because "even though common men and women may be foolish and inferior, that which they receive in their inborn natures they know without consciously thinking, and perform without effort."[83] The issue that arises here, given Sorai's denial of the innate goodness of human nature, is that genuineness itself becomes normatively empty. Because people can be genuine even when doing the wrong thing, he writes, "genuineness was not originally something that the sages made part of their teachings."[84]

Why, then, does he speak of the accomplishment of virtues in terms of "genuineness"? The answer lies in how he uses the term "genuine" to refer not just to that which arises from the raw natural state of humans, but to anything that people do spontaneously, including things that are learned and internalized to the point that they become *as if* natural and innate. For example, he interprets the phrase from the *Doctrine of the Mean*, "one who attains genuineness," as referring to how "when one studies the Way of the ancient kings, and is transformed by it over a long period of time, so that learned customs become as if they were the Heaven-endowed inborn nature, then that which at the beginning could not be known or done can now be achieved without conscious thought, and be correct without effort."[85] He relates this to the cultivation of virtue when he writes in *Chūyō kai*, "When virtue is accomplished, then the inside and outside are united. This is what is called 'genuineness.'"[86] Because the Way is a cultural product, and is not inherent in human nature, in the beginning of people's studies it will appear artificial, and they can only follow it by making conscious efforts. When they truly have been educated in the Way, though, it will become second nature, and when they act in keeping with the Way this will be "genuine," in that it will come to them completely automatically.

Sorai argues that the only reason that genuineness came to be spoken of in Confucian texts in the first place was as a defense against the Daoist advocacy of unfettered naturalness, a naturalness that for Sorai represents an abandonment of all normative standards, which for him must necessarily be humanly created. The description of the cultivation of the Confucian Way in terms of genuineness, he claims, is meant to demonstrate that even though this Way is a human creation, it does not, as the Daoists charged, corrupt people's natural state. As he argues in *Chūyō kai*, "If the Way of the former kings contradicted the inborn nature of humans, then it would always just be forced. How could there be genuineness?"[87] The fact that the Way can indeed become completely internalized, though, "clarifies that ritual and music are not false."[88]

Conclusion

For Sorai the Confucian Way consists of institutions and cultural norms, initiated by the sage kings of ancient China, that subsequent ages must follow if they are to create peaceful and prosperous societies. He sees the problems of his own age, in particular the spread of commercial culture since the Genroku period, as stemming from the Tokugawa founders' failure to establish proper institutions based on the creations of the sages, and his proposals for political reform are designed to bring Tokugawa Japan back in line with the Way of the sages. While he depicts the Way as something that acts on people by transforming them from within, he is also careful to point out that the Way must always respond to the empirical reality of human nature, which puts an outer limit on what the Way can require of people. A crucial aspect of human nature for Sorai is that it is different for every person, an idea that leads him to advocate the need for leaders to develop the distinct talents of each person. This in turn gives rise to a vision of social cohesion as "harmony," a concept that he defines in terms of a unity in diversity, allowing for individuals to be integrated into an organic social whole that exceeds the sum of its parts, without demanding that they sacrifice the particularities of the natural qualities that they are born with. Sorai's policy proposals, though, are sometimes at odds with his theoretical openness to the empirical world. His proposal for a massive reorganization of Japanese society shows a reluctance to accept the reality of historical change, and he is driven to resort to authoritarian regulations in order to enforce the supposedly gentle and nurturing teachings of the sages. The next chapter turns to Sorai's views on poetry as a component of the education of the Confucian gentleman, examining how he values poetry as a method for learning the ancient language in which the creations of the sages have been transmitted, as well as for giving us knowledge of the human emotions that the Way is built upon and must respond to.

THREE

Poetry and the Cultivation of the Confucian Gentleman

The Literary Thought of Ogyū Sorai

Ogyū Sorai was a prolific kanshi poet, and his private academy was notable for the central role that poetry played in its educational and social life, such as the monthly gatherings he hosted called the Sōdō Shōshū (Little Society of the Grassy Hall), which combined drinking, poetry, and music in a re-laxed atmosphere.[1] This emphasis on poetry is reflected in the careers of his disciples, most of whom were known more for their literary output than their achievements as philosophers or textual commentators. In his writings he describes a wide variety of functions for poetry, presenting it as a way to cultivate elegance in expression, master the ancient Chinese language of the Confucian classics, and gain access to the nuances of human nature and human emotions. While he never provides a single unified theory of poetry, with his remarks on poetry scattered among various treatises, prefaces, let-ters, and commentaries produced at different stages in his career, his ideas on poetry are brought together by a common focus on its role in cultivating the Confucian gentleman (Ch. *junzi*, Jp. *kunshi*).

In his discussion of the term "gentleman" in *Benmei* (On Distinguishing Names), Sorai notes that it can be used in the context of social rank, to in-dicate those who hold positions as officials, as well as in reference to virtue, to describe those who possess surpassing virtue, even though they may be of lower rank. He gives precedence to the first of these uses, though, writing that the achievement of the virtue of the gentleman is meant to be followed by actual service as a governing official: "People of the past achieved virtues through study, then advanced to being scholars (Ch. *shi*, Jp. *shi*), and then arrived at being ministers (Ch. *daifu*, Jp. *taifu*)."[2] He criticizes those who would define the gentleman apart from humaneness, which for Sorai is a virtue specifically of rulers: "Later Confucians were permeated to the marrow with Laozi and Zhuangzi's theory of 'inner sageliness and outer kingliness,' and in the end forgot that the Way of the ancient kings is a Way for bringing peace to the people. Therefore what they call a 'gentleman' is often discussed apart from humaneness."[3] Instead of simply trusting that good government will spontaneously result from the achievement of inner purity, he emphasizes the need for elites to actively pursue the practical business of government.

In keeping with his emphasis on government service, rather than abstract moral purity, in his definition of the gentleman, Sorai sees the education of the gentleman as necessarily based on the artifacts left by the sages of ancient China, and not something that can be achieved simply through an extension of the "heart" (Ch. *xin*, Jp. *kokoro*) or "principle" (Ch. *li*, Jp. *ri*), concepts that were prominent in Song and Ming Confucianism:

> Generally speaking, ancient learning consists of the *Odes*,[4] the *Documents*, ritual, and music. Gentlemen thus cultivate their language, become accomplished in government, and embellish these with ritual and music. This is called accomplishing virtue. To speak of accomplishing virtue apart from this, instead speaking in terms of the heart and principle, is at odds with how the gentleman was discussed in the Three Dynasties.[5]

Here he brings up the *Odes* as a fundamental component of the education of the gentleman, and this chapter explores the multiple ways he sees the study of both the *Odes* and later poetry as contributing to the formation of an ideal member of the governing elite.

Ancient Phraseology and the Cultivation of Language

Sorai's early views on poetry were deeply colored by his encounter with the Ancient Phraseology (Ch. *guwenci*, Jp. *kobunji*) movement of the Ming, from which he inherited a poetic canon focused on the poets of the High Tang, as well as a methodology for composing poetry that stressed the imitation of classical models. He played an active role in promoting the works of the Ancient Phraseology movement by editing such anthologies as *Tōgo shi* (Poetry after the Tang), a collection of Ancient Phraseology poetry published in 1720, and *Zekku kai* (Explanation of Quatrains), published in multiple editions after his death, which includes poems by Li Panlong and Wang Shizhen, the Ming poets he looked up to the most. Sorai was more than just a passive follower of Ancient Phraseology, though, as he applied its ideas not only to literary composition, but also to the conceptualization and study of the Confucian Way. This appears most notably in his extension of the Ancient Phraseology movement's studies of ancient Chinese into a methodology for the exegesis of the Confucian classics, but we can also see other parallels between Sorai's reception of Ancient Phraseology and his later philosophy, such as in his idea of culture as a kind of organic wholeness through which things become intelligible and take on meaning, and his view of education as the transformation of the self through the internalization of cultural models.

THE MING ANCIENT PHRASEOLOGY MOVEMENT

The Ancient Phraseology movement dominated the Chinese literary scene in the sixteenth century. Literary historians often divide its leading practitioners into two generations, the Former Seven Masters (*qian qizi*), centered on Li Mengyang (1475–1529) and He Jingming (1483–1521), and the Later Seven Masters (*hou qizi*), the most prominent of whom were Li Panlong and Wang Shizhen.[6] The figures in this movement were by no means uniform in their views, but in general they were committed to the imitation of a narrow canon of classical models. They favored the prose of the Qin (221–207 B.C.) and Han (206 B.C.–A.D. 220) dynasties, particularly the *Shi ji* (Historical Records) of Sima Qian (c. 145–c. 85 B.C.), while for poetry their canon was centered on the verse of the High Tang, with the *yuefu* ballads of the Han and Wei serving as a secondary source of inspiration.

The poetic canon of Ming Ancient Phraseology has its origins in *Canglang shihua* (Canglang's Talks on Poetry), by the late Song author Yan Yu.[7] Yan Yu was instrumental in establishing a view of Chinese literary history that remains influential even today, in which the High Tang is seen as the pinnacle of Chinese poetry, with earlier poetry playing the role of a gradual development up to this peak, and later poetry representing a degeneration and vulgarization of the tradition. Yan Yu was concerned with establishing the idea of orthodoxy in poetry, which he developed by borrowing from the contrast between orthodox and heterodox transmissions in Zen Buddhism, comparing Han, Wei (220–265), Jin (265–420), and High Tang poetry to orthodox Zen, and later poetry to heterodox Zen.[8] Some of his harshest criticisms were directed toward writers of his own time, the Song, who "make poetry out of erudition and argumentation," in contrast to the poets of the High Tang, whose poetry "has a limpidity and clarity that resists fixed interpretation; like tones in the air, or the expression on a face, or the moon in the water, or a reflection in a mirror, its words may be limited but its meaning is inexhaustible."[9]

Ancient Phraseology eventually came under attack by Yuan Hongdao (1568–1610) and other members of the so-called Gongan school for its lack of individuality and originality.[10] The Gongan poets argued that poetry should arise spontaneously from within the poet, and that it should focus on "spirit" (*xingling*) rather than the "form and rhythm" (*getiao*) valued by Ancient Phraseology. They also criticized Ancient Phraseology for fixating on a narrow set of models, and presented a view of literary history that did not privilege any one particular period. In the face of such criticisms from the Gongan school and others, Ancient Phraseology fell out of favor in China in the seventeenth century, but this did not prevent it from later finding followers in Japan such as Sorai.[11] In a letter responding to a contemporary Japanese critic of Li and Wang, Sorai defends their approach to poetry by explaining that all study involves imitation, giving examples of how we learn things like ritual, music, and calligraphy by copying certain set forms. Much as in his discussion of how we learn the Way, he argues that when we learn things like poetry, the forms that we imitate eventually are internalized to the point that they come to seem natural to us:

> In the beginning of study, it can be called plagiarism and imitation. After a long period, when one becomes transformed by it, then learned customs become as if they were the Heaven-endowed inborn nature. Although they come from the outside, they become one with the self. This is why Zisi speaks of the Way of uniting the inner and outer. To complain about imitation, then, is to fail to know the Way of study.[12]

ANCIENT PHRASEOLOGY
AND THE PATTERNING OF LANGUAGE

One of Sorai's reasons for valuing the poetry of the Ancient Phraseology movement is because of how it allows people to cultivate the cultured language appropriate to the Confucian gentleman. The specific quality he identifies in such language is "patterning" (Ch. *wen*, Jp. *bun*), which is what he describes in a letter to one of his disciples as being the quality that distinguishes "phraseology" (Ch. *ci*, Jp. *ji*) from mere "words" (Ch. *yan*, Jp. *gen*): "Phraseology and words are not the same. . . . Phraseology is the patterning of words. . . . The reason that words seek out patterning is because they are the words of gentlemen."[13]

In Chapter 1 we saw the contrast in Confucian philosophy between those who view *wen*, taken in the sense of cultural artifacts such as ritual and music, as a means of expressing a Way that exists autonomously as an abstract principle, and those who maintain that such cultural artifacts are actually constitutive of the Way itself. These methods of relating *wen* to the Confucian Way reflect a more general difference between seeing *wen* as a decorative embellishment to something that is already complete in and of itself, and seeing it as a "patterning" through which something gains coherence and comes to completion to begin with. Much as Sorai sees the cultural artifacts of the sage kings as themselves making up the Way, in his writings on language he describes *wen* as a kind of organic coherence of language that allows for the compact expression of complex meanings. In this way, the "patterning" of elevated forms of language actively facilitates expression, rather than merely being an embellishment added on to language that already serves as a neutral and transparent conduit for meaning. In *Yakubun sentei* (A Guide to Translation), one way Sorai discusses this issue is through the paired terms *tatsui* (conveying intentions) and *shūji* (cultivating phraseology): "In the Way of literary writing, beginning with the words of the sages there have arisen two traditions, that of 'conveying intentions' and that of 'cultivating phraseology.' In reality, though, they are interdependent. If one does not cultivate one's phraseology, then one cannot transmit one's intentions."[14] He then goes on to specifically use the term *wen* to indicate a refined terseness in language, which he contrasts with vulgar prolixity to map out a hierarchy of linguistic forms arranged along the three axes of ancient versus modern, elegant versus common, and Chinese versus Japanese: "Ancient phraseology is terse and has *wen*; modern writing is prolix and vulgar. Elegant (*ga*) language is terse and has *wen*; common (*zoku*) language is prolix and vulgar. The language of China is terse and has *wen*; the language of our country is prolix and vulgar."[15]

While ancient phraseology has special expressive capacities, it at the same time makes extraordinary demands on the reader. For Sorai, the difficulty of reading ancient language has much to do with how its economy of expression can only be navigated by a reader who has cultivated an intuitive sensibility for the subtleties of language. In *Yakubun sentei* he writes:

> The language of ancient texts has many implicit meanings and resonances. Later language lays its meaning completely bare, and lacks profundity. Therefore those who are accustomed to reading writings of later times only look at a single strand of meaning. Those who are deeply versed in ancient phraseology, though, are able to keep many strands of meaning clearly in front of themselves simultaneously, without losing track of the logic of the text. As they continue reading, they gradually set aside these various meanings, and by the time they reach the end of a text, they arrive at a single meaning.[16]

The emphasis on implicit knowledge overlaps with the attitude of Sorai's discussed in Chapter 2 in which he privileges communication between insiders (such as those who share a set of cultural assumptions) over that with outsiders. Just as he looks down on attempts to explain the Way discursively, instead arguing that it must be internalized in order to be truly understood, he describes ancient phraseology as requiring that we negotiate it from within, in contrast to later language, which clearly spells out its meaning for the benefit of the reader. This does not mean, though, that for Sorai ancient phraseology is merely a self-enclosed world of language; rather, he values it for its capacity to record and transmit facts, specifically the historical reality of the creations of the ancient sages, and contrasts this capacity with the empty argumentative language of Song philosophers, which describes nothing more than their own subjective mental constructs.[17]

Literary composition is important to Sorai in part because of how he believes that actively producing ancient language is the only way that we can truly inhabit its world from within. He sees this as doubly important for Japanese scholars, as Chinese is a foreign language for them to begin with. In *Sorai sensei tōmonsho* (Master Sorai's Responsals) he explains,

> Because the sages were Chinese, and classical texts are written in the Chinese language, without a good grasp of Chinese characters it is difficult to understand the Way of the sages. It is not possible to gain such knowledge of Chinese characters unless you are able to grasp the mindset of the ancients when they wrote these texts, so without composing poetry and prose yourself there will be much that will remain beyond your understanding.[18]

Here we can see how Sorai took an approach to ancient language inspired by Ming Ancient Phraseology, and extended it from a technique for composing poetry to a methodology for understanding the Confucian classics.[19]

For Sorai, then, the linguistic sensibility acquired through composing poetry was not only a marker of one's elevated status as a cultured gentleman, but was also an important element of learning to read the ancient texts through which gentlemen were meant to gain knowledge of proper techniques of governance.

Sorai's Poetry in Chinese

Soraishū, the posthumously published collection of Sorai's poetry and prose, contains over 700 poems in Chinese. These include 32 five-character quatrains (Ch. *jueju*, Jp. *zekku*), 331 seven-character quatrains, 124 examples of five-character regulated verse (Ch. *lüshi*, Jp. *risshi*), 143 of seven-character regulated verse, 42 ancient-style poems (Ch. *gushi*, Jp. *koshi*), 14 imitation *yuefu* poems (Ch. *nigu yuefu*, Jp. *giko gafu*), and several poems in miscellaneous forms. Through these poems we can see how he attempted to access and reproduce the Chinese past, specifically through applying the neoclassical poetics he inherited from Ming Ancient Phraseology.[20]

One manifestation of Sorai's neoclassicism appears in poems that present vignettes based on Chinese literary models. An example of this is his seven-character quatrain "Shōnen kō" (Song about a Young Man):

猟罷帰来上苑秋	Returned from the hunt, autumn in Shanglin park
風寒憶得鸛鶒裘	Chilled by the wind, he longs for his feather robe of turquoise kingfisher
分明昨夜韋娘宿	Clear in his memory—last night at the house of pleasure of Weiniang
杜曲西家第二楼	The second house to the west in Duqu

The "Song about a Young Man" was a common poetic topic (Ch. *ti*, Jp. *dai*) used in *yuefu*, and it became popular among Tang poets as well. The typical treatment of the topic is to depict a wealthy young man pursuing the pleasures of the capital Chang'an, a practice followed in Sorai's poem with its descriptions of hunting in Shanglin park (a royal park in Chang'an), the man's luxurious feather robe, and his visit to the house of pleasure of Weiniang, a reference to the famous Tang courtesan Duweiniang. Sima Xiangru (179–117 B.C.) is described as wearing a feather robe of turquoise kingfisher in the *Xijing zaji* (Miscellaneous Records of the Western Capital), and the garment is also mentioned in "Baitou yin" #2 (White Hair Song #2) by Li Bo (701–762): "A feather robe of turquoise kingfisher over a brocade screen."

Duqu is a scenic spot near Chang'an, and the "du" of Duweiniang's name derives from this place name. Duweiniang is mentioned in "Zeng Li sikong niang" (To the Courtesan of Minister Li), by Liu Yuxi (772–842): "A song in the spring breeze—Duweiniang." While the content of this poem has little to do with the practice of government, it resonates with Sorai's philosophy of the Confucian Way in how it constructs a fantasy world based on the Chinese past, and on an identification with social elites from that past.

Another example of this type of vignette is Sorai's five-character quatrain "Kyōkaku" (The Knight-Errant):

飯罷溧陽媼	Fed by the old woman of Liyang
前途日欲斜	On the road ahead, the sun is setting
茫茫城市裡	Vast and wide is the city
莫有魯朱家	A Zhu Jia of Lu is nowhere to be found

This poem alludes to the story of the knight-errant Wu Zi Xu, whose biography in the *Shi ji* describes how he was forced to beg for food while fleeing to Wu from his native state of Chu, whose king was planning to put him to death together with his father and brother (he eventually achieved revenge against the king of Chu, for which he is praised by Sima Qian).[21] The detail about him receiving food from a woman in Liyang is not included in the *Shi ji* biography, but appears in the account of Wu Zi Xu in volume 1 of the *Yue jue shu*, a history of the state of Yue by the Han scholar Yuan Kang. The second line is taken verbatim from the five-character quatrain "Feng xiazhe" (Encountering a Knight-Errant) by Qian Qi (722–c. 780). This poem is included in the *Tangshi xuan*, an anthology of Tang poetry, compiled by Li Panlong, that was highly popular in Tokugawa Japan and was especially revered by the Sorai school.[22] This line also is similar to the line in the *Shi ji* where Wu Zi Xu states, "The day is growing dark on me, and the road is long," although this comes from a later episode in the biography, and not the section dealing with his escape to Wu. The final line is a reference to the "Biographies of Knights-Errant," a book of the *Shi ji* that tells the stories of various such figures, one of whom is Zhu Jia of Lu, who was famous for providing generous assistance to those in hiding from their enemies.[23] This poem, like the previous one, enters into the world of the Chinese past through the medium of a specific character who is at the center of the vignette.

Another common form of neoclassical composition practiced by Sorai involved mapping Chinese place names onto Japan, thus elevating Japan by incorporating it into the cultural and aesthetic sphere of the land of the sages. An example of this is his seven-character quatrain "Shinsai no gūsaku" (Composed on the New Year):

江城初日照芙蓉	New Year in the riverbank city, the sun shines on Lotus Peak
西望函関白雪重	Looking west to Han barrier, piled with white snow
無限武昌郡中客	Limitless are the throngs within Wuchang
陽春一曲少相逢	Yet few can be met with the song "Bright Spring"

The "riverbank city" refers to Edo, and Lotus Peak, a name used for a number of mountains in China, refers to Mt. Fuji. In addition to the basic comparison between Chinese and Japanese mountains, this name for Mt. Fuji comes from how its summit is said to resemble a lotus flower. In the next two lines, Han barrier corresponds to Hakone (which also had a famous customs barrier), and Wuchang to Edo. Besides being analogous places (barriers in the first case, cities in the second), these correspondences are based on wordplay with the characters, as the character for "Han" 函 can be read as "hako" in Japanese, thus connecting Han with Hakone (even though the "hako" of Hakone is written differently, with the character 箱), and the "Wu" of Wuchang is written with 武, which is one of the characters used to write Musashi 武蔵, the name of the province where Edo was located. The final line alludes to an episode in a piece in the *Wen xuan* by Song Yu (290–223 B.C.) entitled "Dui Chu wang wen" (Responding to the King of Chu), which tells of a traveler who gains a large audience when he sings common songs, but has his audience dwindle when he sings the difficult songs "Bright Spring" and "White Snow." "Bright Spring," then, indicates a particularly elevated, refined song, and the fact that it is mentioned together with the song "White Snow" in the *Wen xuan* piece creates a linkage in Sorai's poem between the fourth line and the second line, which mentions the white snow in Hakone. A line similar to Sorai's final line appears at the end of a poem by Cen Shen (715–770) that is included in the *Tangshi xuan*: "It is difficult for anyone to harmonize with the song 'Bright Spring.'"[24] Cen Shen's poem was written in response to the work of another poet, and the closing line is a polite expression of humility toward that poet. Sorai's poem, though, is less an expression of humility than a statement about how the speaker belongs to a select group of the highly cultured and literate, so that there are few people who can relate to him on his level. This idea matches closely with his view that Chinese poetry and Confucian studies should be pursued only by educated elites, and with his effort to create an exclusive cultural community through the activities of his private academy.

Sorai also often composed poetry in the context of social interactions, such as the seven-character regulated verse "Uhōshū ni towaruru o shasu" (Expressing Thanks upon the Visit of Amenomori Hōshū). Amenomori Hōshū (1668–1755) served Tsushima domain as a Confucian scholar and diplomat, in which capacity he spent time at the Japanese diplomatic mission in Pusan, and was famous for his studies of the Korean language. Sorai composed the following poem on the occasion of Hōshū's visit to his house in Edo to enroll his son Ken'in in Sorai's school:

客有乘槎北海来	My guest sailed from the North Sea
壮游曾使三韓廻	With great purpose he has gone as emissary to the three Korean kingdoms
携将紫気行相映	Cradling purple vapors, he illuminates the way
弾罷朱絃歌自哀	When he finishes strumming the vermilion strings, his song is plaintive
千里山川誰並駕	Who would journey with you in a carriage over a thousand *li* of mountains and rivers?
百年天地此銜杯	To exchange cups with you here is a chance that comes once in a hundred years
看君匣裏芙蓉色	Seeing the lotus in your sword case
不但翩翩書記才	You do not merely have a talent for elegant writing

The "North Sea" is another name for the Bohai Sea, the gulf of the Yellow Sea surrounded by the Shandong and Liaodong peninsulas, so the first two lines refer to Hōshū's activities as a diplomat. "Purple vapors" are a sign that a valued guest is coming, a reference that derives from the story of how when Laozi approached Han barrier on his way west to become immortal, the barrier guard recognized his impending arrival by the purple vapors he saw in the east. This story is alluded to in "Qiu xing" #5 (Autumn Stirrings #5), by Du Fu (712–770), included in the *Tangshi xuan*: "from the east come purple vapors / and fill Han Pass."[25] The reference to vermilion strings is from the "Record of Music": "The zithers (Ch. *se*, Jp. *shitsu*) in the pure ancestral temple had vermilion strings and widely spaced holes. One would sing and three would be moved with admiration."[26] The *se* is an example of the refined music of the sages, so this line is praising the cultivation of the addressee. The plaintive quality of the *se* is mentioned in a story cited in the *Shi ji*, which tells of how it originally had fifty strings, but the legendary emperor Fu Xi found it excessively sad and so broke it in half, making it into an instrument of twenty-five strings.[27] A lotus refers to a precious sword, as in Lu Zhaolin's "Chang'an guyi" (Ancient Thoughts on Chang'an), included in the *Tangshi xuan*: "The knights-errant meet with their lotus swords." The use of *pianpian* to describe elegant writing derives from "Yu Wuzhi shu" (Letter to Yu Wuzhi), by Cao Pi (187–226), included in the *Wen xuan*: "Yu Wuzhi's writing is elegant, and its grace offers pleasure." The term also appears in "Zeng Su Wan shuji" (To Secretary Su Wan), by Du Shenyan (d. c. 705), in the *Tangshi xuan*: "I know that your writings are truly elegant." The last two lines, taken together, are saying that Hōshū fulfills the ideal of combining skill in both the civil and the military arts. The poem, then, is what we might expect given the context of Sorai and Hōshū's interaction, with Sorai praising his guest extravagantly and expressing gratitude for his good fortune in being able to meet Hōshū.

The densely allusive quality of Sorai's poetry reflects his emulation of Ming Ancient Phraseology, as does his heavy reliance on the *Shi ji*, the *Wen xuan*, and High Tang poetry (especially the *Tangshi xuan*) for source poems and stories. At times this even takes the form of lifting entire lines directly from source poems, leading to a kind of patchwork approach to composition. Sorai's imitative approach to poetry is accompanied by a strong fictional element, both in poems that present scenes conjured out of the world of Chinese literature and in those where Sorai's own world is transformed by being mapped onto Chinese literary references. In this way, poetry becomes a way to enter into the Chinese past and to lift up the vulgar world of contemporary Japan by passing it through the filter of this past. Moreover, Sorai's poetry is intelligible only to those with a solid grounding in classical Chinese literature, so it serves to confirm the membership of both poet and audience in an elite community of gentlemen versed in the culture of the land of the sages.

Poetry and Knowing Human Emotions

In his philosophical writings and policy proposals, Sorai's comments on poetry stress how its essence lies in emotional expression, as conveyed in the following description of the nature and function of the *Book of Odes*:

> Among the Five Classics is included the *Book of Odes*. This is simply something along the lines of the waka poetry of this country. It is not something

for discoursing upon the principles of governing the heart or the self, nor is it something for discoursing upon the Way of governing the provinces and the realm. The Odes consist of the words produced by the sighs of people of ancient times when they felt joyful or sad, so they include words that accord well with human emotions, and they allow one to know of the customs of the period and province in which they were produced. For this reason, the sage Confucius collected them and taught them to people. Although studying them does not serve to help one grasp principle, they use language skillfully and express human emotions well, so they have the power to permeate the heart naturally and temper principle, and to make understood the customs of different countries and ages, which are difficult to perceive through principle alone. They allow our hearts to reach out naturally and grasp human emotions, so they have the benefit of allowing those of lofty station to know matters of the lowly, men to know the disposition of women, and the wise to know the mindset of the foolish.[28]

When Sorai argues that the emotional value of the Odes lies outside principle, he is implicitly targeting Zhu Xi, for whom the emotions expressed in the Odes, whether manifestations of virtue or of vice, are ultimately subordinated to the moral principle that they allow the reader to perceive. Sorai upholds the idea that the Odes constitute a form of Confucian teaching, but he presents this as an emotional teaching, and denies that the Odes speak of either morality ("governing the heart or the self") or the practice of government.[29] Although he is commenting specifically on the Odes here, we can interpret his comments as a more general theory of poetry, given how he compares the Odes to waka, and elsewhere writes, "The poems of the *Odes* are in no way different from the poetry of later ages."[30]

Sorai's refusal to read the emotional content of poetry in terms of underlying moral values is similar to what we saw in Chapter 1 with Itō Jinsai. Also like Jinsai, he rejects the attempt to reduce the Odes to any single meaning in the first place, commenting on the prefaces produced by the Mao tradition of *Odes* commentary, "The Odes originally have no fixed meanings. Why should we necessarily have to uphold what the prefaces say, and make these out to be immutable explanations?"[31] Sorai's emphasis on emotionality in poetry, I will argue, was motivated by a concern for social relationships similar to that which informed Jinsai's critique of Zhu Xi, but was distinct from Jinsai's view in that Sorai situated emotionality within a different set of assumptions about how such social relationships are to be governed by the Confucian Way.

SORAI'S CRITIQUE OF "APPROVING
VIRTUE AND CHASTISING VICE"

In Chapter 2 we saw how Sorai criticizes Zhu Xi for locating norms within
the self, leading to a narrow subjectivism that fails to engage with external
reality in its full complexity. He often presents study, especially the study
of poetry and history, as a way of broadening people's perspectives by
allowing them to see beyond their own limited sphere of personal experience. We saw this above in his discussion of the Odes, and he characterizes historical study as having a similar broadening effect when he writes:

> Xunzi called learning the Way of "flying ears and long eyes." The fact that
> while remaining in this country one can hear things of unseen countries is
> like having the ears sprout wings and fly. The fact that while being born in
> this age one can see things of thousands of years ago as if before one's very
> eyes is what is meant by "long eyes." Because learning consists of having
> one's sight and hearing extend widely across empirical facts, the pinnacle of
> learning lies in history. If one is not familiar with past and present, and Japan
> and China, then one will only see things within the confines of the customs
> of the present age and our own country, and will truly be like the proverbial
> frog in the well.[32]

Sorai sees poetry as offering certain historical knowledge as well, as poetry
"makes understood the customs of different countries and ages,"[33] but he
distinguishes the roles of poetry and history in that he sees poetry as unique
in the insight it provides into the most intimate aspects of human nature
and human emotionality.

Study needs to be carried out with the proper hermeneutic stance,
though, if it is to fulfill this purpose. In *Sorai sensei tōmonsho*, he describes
the harm that comes from the Song Confucian doctrine that knowing
things involves knowing their principle, a principle that is presumed to exist
also within the self:

> The Song Confucian practices of "investigating things" and "extending
> knowledge" involve deciding for themselves that such-and-such must be this
> way, and such-and-such must be that way, and that this must certainly be
> the Way of the sages. But this is just personal opinion. Because they follow
> along with what they themselves decide ahead of time that something must
> be like, they are unable to realize that many things actually end up not being
> like what they had thought.[34]

In other words, even when Song Confucians look outside themselves, they see everything through the lens of their own prejudices and preconceptions, making it impossible for them to gain any genuinely new knowledge.

From this standpoint, Zhu Xi's theory of "approving virtue and chastising vice" (Ch. *quanshan cheng'e*, Jp. *kanzen chōaku*) is a flawed mode of reading in that moral categories function as a perceptual apparatus that mediates and limits the reader's encounter with the text. In one passage in *Sorai sensei tōmonsho*, Sorai critiques the use of "approving virtue and chastising vice" in Zhu Xi's *Tongjian gangmu* (Outline of the *Comprehensive Mirror*), a commentary on the historical work by Sima Guang (1019–1086) entitled the *Zizhi tongjian* (Comprehensive Mirror for Aid in Government). Sorai argues that Sima Guang's original work captures historical reality in its full vitality and complexity, while Zhu Xi's commentary filters this reality through a reductionist conceptual framework: "The arguments of the *Tongjian gangmu* are like a woodblock print—they have a fixed form and a predetermined logic, and apply this method to everything. But Heaven-and-Earth is dynamic, as are humans. When we view these as if they were tied up with rope, then this is truly a useless form of study."[35] As with his critique of the idea of "investigating things," Sorai sees Song Confucians as approaching the world through a set of subjective blinders; even though they may look out into the external world, they do so through the lens of what they already think to be the proper way things should be, with the result that this external experience (such as the material encountered through historical study) does nothing to increase their knowledge, and only reinforces their preexisting prejudices through a solipsistic feedback loop.

A similar contrast in methods of reading can be seen in commentaries on the *Analects* passage that states, "[With the Odes] one can observe."[36] Zhu Xi interprets this as meaning "to consider one's merits and faults,"[37] but Sorai criticizes this reading for grasping only a narrow conception of what it means to "observe":

> "To consider one's merits and faults" is only to look at right and wrong. How could this exhaust the meaning of "to observe"? When it comes to the various types of governments and customs, the vicissitudes of the fortunes of the world, and people's situations, while in the court one can know the villages, while in prosperous times one can know of fallen times, as a gentleman one can understand petty men, as a man one can understand women, in ordinary times one can know of chaos, and the affairs of the realm are all gathered in oneself—this is the benefit of "observing."[38]

Again, he sees the rigid dualism of right and wrong as limiting our field of vision, and undermining the capacity of poetry to give us insight into the experiences of others. Sorai's rejection of moral readings of poetry, then, is more than a simple affirmation of the autonomy of literature, as his goal is not just to liberate poetry in an abstract sense, but to free it from one role so that it can be mobilized to play a different one. His notion of poetry as a vehicle for understanding the emotions of others is closely tied to his formulation of humaneness, which, as discussed below, is key to his vision of the ideal ruler.

HUMANENESS AND EMPATHY

Sorai opens the section of *Benmei* on "humaneness" (Ch. *ren*, Jp. *jin*) by calling it "the virtue of being the leader of others and bringing peace to the people."[39] By defining humaneness specifically in terms of rulership, he is rejecting the equation of the term with a generalized notion of benevolence or compassion, an idea he sees as a product of the admixture of Confucianism with Buddhism. While he recognizes that humaneness has something to do with love and compassion, he maintains that the love and compassion involved in humaneness need to be understood in the context of the active practice of governance, explaining, "When Confucius speaks of 'loving others,' this refers to being the father and mother of the people. If one does not bring peace to the people, then how can one be the father and mother of the people?"[40]

In the discussion in Chapter 2 of Sorai's and Jinsai's commentaries on the "Four Beginnings" passage in *Mencius*, we saw how Sorai agrees with Jinsai that the cultivation of proper social norms requires the active exercise of human nature through relationships with others, and can never be achieved through a retreat into any kind of static inner purity. At the same time, Sorai rejects the idea that activity and social interaction can by themselves lead to the establishment of successful interpersonal relationships, without these being mediated through proper external norms derived from the historical sages. Among the four virtues discussed in the *Mencius* passage, he particularly takes Jinsai to task for claiming that humaneness, which for Sorai is "the virtue of being the leader of others and bringing peace to the people," can be achieved by extending outward the heart of compassion. He writes, "Jinsai [defines humaneness as] 'the virtue of benevolent love (Ch. *ciai*, Jp. *jiai*) reaching far and near, within and without, filling and penetrating everything.' Here he is confused by Mencius, and tries to achieve humaneness by extending outward the heart of compassion. He makes humaneness belong not to the ancient kings but to people in general."[41] From this perspective, Jinsai's flaw is that he sees humaneness as something that can be achieved from the bottom up, a process that in Sorai's view leads to nothing more than an aimless sympathy without any regulating norms.

Sorai makes a similar point in his criticism of Jinsai's reading of the statements in *Analects* IV.15 that Confucius' Way "has one thing running through it," and that this Way "consists simply of loyalty (Ch. *zhong*, Jp. *chū*) and considerateness (Ch. *shu*, Jp. *jo*)." Sorai interprets the "one thing" running through the Way as humaneness, but denies that loyalty and considerateness can lead directly to humaneness, an idea that Jinsai expresses when he writes that "when we establish loyalty and practice considerateness, then our hearts broaden and we practice the Way, and humaneness is attained."[42] In *Rongo chō* (Clarification of the *Analects*), Sorai writes:

> "Loyalty" refers to having consideration for others, extending broadly and in great detail, and not failing to exhaust one's own heart. "Considerateness" refers to "not doing to others what you do not want done to yourself." All of this refers to interacting with other people. The relation of humaneness to the Way also lies in interactions with other people, and is what leads them and nurtures them, corrects them and brings them to completion, and allows each of them to achieve their livelihood. However, the Way of humaneness is vast, and is not something that [Confucius'] disciples can achieve. Therefore he uses loyalty and considerateness to suggest it.[43]

Again, Sorai finds fault with the idea that humaneness, which for him is a virtue of rulers, can be achieved simply through the mutual goodwill of ordinary people. He does not deny that ordinary people should reach out to each other, but he sees this as providing a lower level of social unity than that provided by the humaneness of rulers, which always comes from above, and provides the cultural framework within which the everyday interactions of the ruled take on value.

Although Sorai defines humaneness as a virtue that is necessarily embedded in social hierarchies, and refuses to reduce it to a simple extension of compassion or considerateness, he still sees it as requiring an emotional understanding of others. To begin with, he believes that the Way was created in response to human nature, a key element of which is emotionality, meaning that an understanding of human emotions is important for those who, as members of the governing class, are responsible for enacting the Way. More specifically, as we saw in Chapter 2, he idealizes feudal social relationships rooted in feelings of mutual affection and obligation between rulers and ruled. It is poetry that, as we saw him argue above, allows "those of lofty station to know matters of the lowly," making it indispensable to the practice of humane government. In this way, he follows Jinsai in placing great importance on understanding others, especially on understanding their emotions, but redefines the interpersonal space in which this understanding is practiced from the symmetrical relationship between fellow commoners to the asymmetrical relationship between the rulers and the ruled. At the same time, the ultimate purpose of this understanding shifts from the achievement of specific moral virtues in everyday life to the effective governance of society, which for Sorai includes the promotion of everyday morality, but is by no means limited to it.

The Odes among the Four Teachings and Six Classics

As we saw in his description of the content of "ancient learning," Sorai often situates the *Odes* among the "Four Teachings" (Ch. *sijiao*, Jp. *shikyō*) or "Four Techniques" (Ch. *sishu*, Jp. *shijutsu*)—the *Odes*, the *Book of Documents*, ritual, and music. The Four Teachings are associated with a subset of the Confucian Six Classics (Ch. *liujing*, Jp. *rikukei*), which consist of the *Odes*, the *Book of Documents*, the *Record of Ritual* (*Li ji*), the *Book of Music* (*Yue jing*), the *Book of Changes* (*Yi jing*), and the *Spring and Autumn Annals* (*Chunqiu*).[44] Sorai sees the Six Classics as the foundation of Confucian government due to their unique role in transmitting the culture of the sages, and defines the Four Teachings more specifically as the core of the education of the Confucian gentleman. One thing he stresses about the Four Teachings and the Six Classics is that each of them plays a distinct and necessary role. In his discussion of the Four Teachings in *Bendō* (On Distinguishing the Way) he writes, "What each of these teaches differs from Classic to Classic. Later Confucians interpret them through one general theory. But then why would there need to be four of them?"[45] This is a reference to such theories as Zhu Xi's idea that each of the Six Classics is a different expression of a unitary principle, with the corollary that any of them taken alone can suffice as a vehicle for grasping the Way in its entirety. This attitude of Zhu Xi's can be seen in the closing words of the preface to his *Shi jizhuan* (Collected Transmissions on the Odes), where he writes that if one studies the *Odes* in the proper manner, then "without needing to seek elsewhere, it will be sufficient to achieve the Way of cultivating the self and the household, and regulating the realm."[46] The Mao tradition of *Odes* interpretation reaches a similar conclusion from a different standpoint, presenting the study of the *Odes* as sufficient in itself for the internalization of the culture of King Wen. In his discussions of the Four Teachings and Six Classics, though, Sorai emphasizes the interdependence of their constituent elements, an idea that I will argue is related to his conception of how the Confucian Way can only achieve a coherent unity within the active practice of government.

THE *ODES* AND THE *DOCUMENTS*

An example of how Sorai sees the Four Teachings as complementing each other is his interpretation of the phrase from the *Zuo zhuan* that states, "the *Odes* and the *Documents* are the repository of rightness (Ch. *yi*, Jp. *gi*)."[47] In *Benmei* he writes that this label applies rather straightforwardly to the *Book of Documents*, in that it passes on the teachings of the ancient kings of China, which provide us with examples of what we should do, in other words "rightness." Describing the Odes, though, he writes, "Their words are based in human emotions. How can they be spoken of with reasoning? Those later Confucians who set up theories of 'approving virtue and chastising vice' all failed to understand this."[48] He then goes on to argue that the relationship of the Odes to rightness lies in how they provide a kind of background knowledge of the human emotionality upon which the Way is based, without which it is impossible to truly grasp the teachings of the *Book of Documents*: "The Way of the ancient kings was constructed by relying on human emotions. If one does not understand human emotions, how can one extend through the realm, with nothing in one's way? It is only when scholars understand human emotions that the rightness in the *Book of Documents* becomes clear. Therefore when the *Odes* is spoken of as a storehouse of rightness, this is always meant to be understood in conjunction with the *Book of Documents*."[49]

Taken alone, neither the *Odes* nor the *Book of Documents* can provide a knowledge of rightness. It is only when the records of the government of the sages described in the *Book of Documents* are understood in the context of the human emotionality to which they are responding that we can grasp their true significance, and learn how to apply them to the practice of governance today. For Sorai, it is specifically feudal government that is made possible by this complementary relationship between the *Odes* and the *Book of Documents*, as he argues that in feudalism rulers empathetically understand their subjects, which allows these rulers to apply the Confucian Way to government in a humane and nuanced manner, as opposed to the mechanistic legalism that he sees as characteristic of centralized bureaucracy.

THE *ODES* AND MUSIC

Sorai showed a strong scholarly interest in music, producing a number of treatises that combine technical discussions of musical theory with philosophical remarks on the function of music as an element of the Confucian Way. These include *Gakuritsu kō* (Reflections on Musical Pitches), *Gakusei hen* (On Musical Systems), and *Kingaku taiishō* (A General Study of the Koto). The music that interests Sorai is specifically that created by the ancient Chinese sages, and the first two works mentioned above examine the historical transformations of this music, arguing that in Japanese court music there still exist traces of the original court music of the Zhou and Han, which had been completely lost in China by the beginning of the Tang. In keeping with his view of the Way as a historical creation, he believes that the proper standards for music of today are rooted in concrete historical fact, such as in the specifications for the original "yellow bell" (Ch. *huangzhong*, Jp. *kōshō*), which he sees as the basis for recovering Zhou court music.[50] He also describes music as a crucial component of the cultivation of the gentleman, commenting in *Kingaku taiishō* that in ancient times "there were no gentlemen who did not play the koto."[51] This ideal was reflected in Sorai's own pursuit of not only the koto, but also the shō, as well as in the social life of his academy, where music played an important role in social gatherings, and was practiced in tandem with poetry in Chinese.[52]

Sorai describes distinct roles for the *Odes* and music and, to the extent that the Odes are viewed as a combination of words and musical tones, he differentiates between the functions of the lyrics of the Odes and the tones with which they were once accompanied. Poetry and music do have a certain connection for Sorai, in that "in ancient times, the inborn nature and emotions were only discussed in relation to the *Odes* and music."[53] The difference he describes between them, though, is that the role of the *Odes* is to depict emotionality in its natural state, while music is meant to regulate the emotions.[54] Describing the need for music, he writes, "Joy, anger, sorrow, and pleasure are things that all people have. But when the movements of these go too far in one direction and they lose their proper measure, then the spirit of centrality and harmony is damaged, leading to a loss in the constant inborn nature. This makes it difficult to achieve virtue. Therefore music was established in order to instruct these [emotions]."[55] This separation of words and tones can be contrasted with the view of the Mao tradition, which, as we saw in Chapter 1, grew out of an application of musical discourse to poetry, ascribing to lyrics themselves a moral role that had previously been seen as belonging to music. While the Mao tradition did make a distinction between expressing emotions and regulating them, it saw poetry and music as working together to play both of these functions. Moreover, it saw the knowledge of emotionality gained through the expressive powers of poetry and music in terms of the moral values that underlie these emotions, as well as what these emotions reveal about the quality of the government in a particular time and place. Sorai's view of poetry, in contrast, is based on the idea that rulers need to understand emotions in order to become familiar with the nuances of human nature, a process that he sees as undermined by the reduction of emotions to moral judgments.

Sorai's description of the relationship of music to the emotions parallels his more general discussion of how the Way responds to natural human emotions, while not being simply an extension of these emotions. In *Kingaku taiishō* he contrasts music with laws and punishments as methods of correcting people's hearts, explaining that laws and punishments may be easy to understand, but run counter to human emotions, and therefore are not as effective as music, which cannot be grasped intellectually and yet "in bringing pleasure to people's hearts, leads them to the correct Way."[56] At the same time, he cautions against music that simply panders to people's emotions. When discussing how music accompanies song, for example, he draws a distinction between "responding" (*ō*), in which music exactly matches the song that it accompanies, and "harmonizing" (*wa*): "Responding is human emotion, and harmonizing is the Way. Therefore, when [song and music] are matched, it is close to human emotions, and so it is easy to listen to. However, things like the shamisen and the common sort of zither are not conversant with the Way" (pp. 22–23).[57] The reason that people prefer these instruments over the music of the sages is that in recent times "people's hearts have become degraded, and so they find it pleasing when tones are closely matched" (p. 23). He explicitly relates harmony in music to his idea, discussed in Chapter 2, of the need to "harmonize" different talents in society: "When people do not know the Way, they only employ people who catch their fancy, and only do what they like, so people all become selfish, giving rise to chaos" (p. 23). The music of the sages, then, much like the Way as a whole, draws us outside the narrow subjectivism into which we fall when left to our own devices.

The difference between how poetry and music relate to human emotions means for Sorai that when the Odes are described in moral terms, this needs to be understood as referring to their tones, not their semantic content. In his commentary on *Analects* III.20, which describes "Guanju," the first poem in the *Odes*, as "joyful without being debauched, and sorrowful without causing harm,"[58] Sorai argues that this "speaks of its [musical] sounds," and criticizes Zhu Xi for instead focusing on "the meaning of the words."[59] He makes a similar point in his commentary on the portion of *Analects* XV.10 that states, "Banish the sounds of Zheng, and distance yourself from clever talkers. The sounds of Zheng are debauched, and clever talkers are dangerous."[60] He takes this as referring solely to the sounds of the music of Zheng, and not to the lyrics of the poems of Zheng, and goes on to cite approvingly the argument of the Ming poet Yang Shen (1488–1559) that "it is wrong how those in later times take all the poems of the Airs of Zheng to be debauched poems."[61]

The proper differentiation of the roles of words and tones is particularly important to Sorai because of how, as we saw in Chapter 2, he describes ritual and music as having the capacity to move us in a way that language cannot. One implication of this for Sorai is that music does not enjoy the same exemption from moral judgment that poetry does; just as the right music is necessary to regulate people's emotions properly, the wrong music has the potential to cause harm. In his commentary on the *Analects* passage cited above on the sounds of Zheng, he explains, "The sounds of Zheng harm proper music, and clever talkers harm ritual. . . . When the sounds of Zheng are present in the world, then the people will not take pleasure in proper music. This is the reason for banishing [the sounds of Zheng]."[62] This concern for protecting the people from the pernicious influence of debauched music shows that Sorai does not simply advocate a liberated attitude toward human emotions. While he refuses to apply moral judgments to the emotions expressed in the lyrics of the Odes, this is because he sees such judgments as inappropriate to the specific role of the *Odes* in Confucian education, which is to give us an understanding of the full range of human feeling.

THE WAY AS A "COMPOSITE NAME"

Sorai's argument for the distinct functions of each of the Four Teachings and Six Classics reflects a broader belief of his that the Confucian Way consists of an aggregation of institutions and cultural artifacts that cannot be reduced to any kind of unifying principle. In *Bendō* he writes, "'The Way' is a composite name. It brings together under a single name ritual, music, punishments, political administration, and in general all the things established by the ancient kings. Apart from ritual, music, punishments, and political administration, there is nothing that can be called the Way."[63] In other words, the Way is not an underlying principle that then takes form in things like ritual and music, but rather is these things themselves. If all these things were rooted in a single principle (as Zhu Xi asserts), then it would be possible for any one of them to play the role of any other, as the principle uncovered through the *Odes*, for example, would be identical to the principle uncovered through ritual. For Sorai, though, each one of the Six Classics plays a unique role, making it impossible to replace one with another and still maintain the Way in its entirety.

Sorai explains what unifies these diverse elements in his commentary on the statement in *Analects* IV.15 that Confucius' Way "has one thing running through it." Sorai takes this "one thing" to be humaneness, which he defines as the virtue of rulers in bringing peace to the people. He takes great pains, though, to distinguish the kind of unity provided by humaneness from that provided by Zhu Xi's principle. He explains, "Humaneness is one virtue of the ancient kings. Therefore if we were to say that humaneness exhausts the Way of the ancient kings, this would be wrong. However, the Way of the ancient kings is united in bringing peace to the people. Therefore humaneness is the great virtue of the ancient kings."[64] He goes on to explain why the *Analects* passage specifically mentions "one thing *running through*" the Way, instead of simply "one thing," by using the metaphor of a string of coins: "Humaneness is like the string, and the Way of the ancient kings is like the coins. How could we say that the string is the same thing as the coins? This is what it means for 'one thing to run through it.'"[65] The coins here represent the various creations of the sages that make up the Way, such as ritual, music, and punishments. The humaneness of rulers is what unifies these diverse components of the Way toward a common goal, but humaneness itself can never replace them, just as a string holding together coins cannot stand in for the coins themselves.[66]

Sorai's description of humaneness as the force that unifies the Way reflects his concern for the active application of the Way to government, and his criticism of interpretations of Confucianism, like Zhu Xi's, that he believes try to define the Way in abstraction from its actual practice. For Sorai, the creations of the sages are united not by what they are, but by what they do. That is, their commonality lies not in a shared underlying essence or principle, but rather in how they can all be harnessed to the single goal of governing the realm, a goal that is achieved through the virtue of humaneness. At the same time, the various creations of the sages contribute to this governance in distinct ways, which Sorai describes in a manner analogous to his idea of how diverse talents need to be "harmonized" so that people can contribute to the social whole in the capacity most appropriate to them. In his discussions of both the Six Classics and talent, Sorai conceives of unity as a unity in diversity, with the need to recognize the existence of diverse capacities (whether in the sages' creations, or in individual people) being specifically related to the need to uphold the practical orientation of the Way.

REASSESSING THE AUTONOMY OF POETRY IN SORAI

If we saw Sorai's role in the history of Tokugawa literary thought in terms of his contribution to the separation of literature from politics, then there would seem to be a contradiction in the inclusion of the *Odes* among the Six Classics, which Sorai sees as the basis of Confucian government. We can see this in the assessment of Sorai's literary thought by Wakamizu Suguru that was quoted in the Introduction, where he concludes, "As Sorai was unable to separate the *Odes* from the 'Classics,' and see it purely as a text of human emotionality, it was ultimately not possible for him to break free of the fetters of the past, in other words to separate literature from Confucian thought."[67] The assumption here is that there is an inherent conflict between valuing the *Odes* as emotional expression and valuing it for its political usefulness, and that Sorai manages to discover the *Odes* as a text of emotionality to the extent that he moves away from viewing it as a political text, a process that Wakamizu sees Sorai as having begun but not carried through to its proper conclusion. I see the importance that Sorai puts on the *Odes* as emotional expression, however, as in fact the product of new ways of imagining the political role of the *Odes*, as well as the role of the *Odes* as a Confucian Classic, making it misleading to see him as simply making inroads on a preexisting Confucian view of literature.[68]

Both the Mao tradition and Zhu Xi were concerned with the danger to the social order posed by unregulated human emotions, and saw poetry as a way of educating the emotions morally. For the Mao tradition this education involved internalizing the culture of King Wen by studying poems that expressed the emotions of those influenced by this culture. For Zhu Xi, in contrast, the proper regulation of emotions came from uncovering the a priori moral faculty possessed by all humans as part of their inborn nature, and he saw the exposure to correct and incorrect emotions in poetry as a way of bringing forth this faculty. Sorai does not see poetry as a tool for achieving correctness in one's emotions in order to cultivate virtues, a role he argues belongs properly to music, not poetry. He does, however, show a certain continuity with the Mao tradition and Zhu Xi to the extent that he still sees poetry as a device for mediating the particularity of human emotions with the universality of the social totality instituted through the Confucian Way. For Sorai, this mediation takes place through having poetry reveal human emotions to the ruling class, who then apply this knowledge by formulating government policies that respond to the reality of these emotions, thus ensuring a prosperous and harmonious society. Sorai's demand that poetry be read as pure emotional expression, then, is premised on a very specific vision of Confucian government, namely that of an empathetic paternalism practiced within the context of feudal social relationships.

It could be argued that Sorai does not connect poetry to the Confucian Way as directly as the Mao tradition or Zhu Xi, but it is important to keep in mind that for Sorai this indirectness is itself essential to how the Confucian Way is constituted, and thus does not represent a movement toward making poetry autonomous from the Way. More specifically, by separating out the functions of the Six Classics, and describing how they complement each other in the practice of Confucian government, Sorai makes these each contribute to the Way without individually embodying the entirety of the Way.[69] In other words, *all* of the Six Classics, not just the *Odes*, can be said to contribute to the Way "indirectly." This opens up the possibility for the emotional expression and refined language of the *Odes* to play a necessary role in the Way, without any demand that these qualities of the *Odes* be directly translated into a moral or political message. It is in the broader context of the interaction of the Six Classics that these qualities of the *Odes* contribute to government, so it is unnecessary that they do so on the level of the *Odes* taken as an isolated text. Not only is it unnecessary, it would actually undermine the unique and essential role of the *Odes* as a Confucian Classic. While on the one hand it seems as if Sorai is making the *Odes* more autonomous as a literary text by refusing to make it into a direct vehicle for the Way, he is at the same time making it more essential to the study of the Way than Zhu Xi and the Mao tradition had, for whom studying the *Odes* was one out of a number of possible ways to, in the former case, cultivate a single principle, and in the latter, internalize the culture of King Wen. The emotional and political roles of the *Odes* are for Sorai interdependent, then, and cannot be understood simply as a modernizing movement toward aesthetic autonomy awkwardly juxtaposed with the remnants of earlier Confucian traditions. Or, to the extent that we define the indirect relationship of the *Odes* to the Way as a kind of aesthetic autonomy, this autonomy needs to be considered as itself inscribed within a particular political configuration.

Conclusion

The variety of roles that Sorai ascribes to poetry reflects the multifaceted nature of his conception of the Confucian gentleman, who is meant to be simultaneously a master of the literary arts, a scholar of the Confucian classics, and a government official who formulates policy and relates empathetically to the governed. Moreover, he presumes that such a figure will operate within a community of similar gentlemen who form the ruling class of a society, bound together by their internalization of a common cultural and literary canon. Despite the range of ways that poetry contributes to the formation of the gentleman, Sorai's discussion of the mutual interdependence of the Six Classics makes it clear that poetry alone is never sufficient to create a gentleman, and that for poetry to fulfill its proper role, it must be integrated into both a broader program of Confucian education and a world of political practice.

Sorai's vision of poetry as contributing to the formation of a ruling elite of scholar officials remained, however, an unfulfilled ideal, as the role of poetry in his academy was essentially that of a literary pastime and a vehicle for elegant and cultured socializing. Moreover, his theoretical writings on poetry leave relatively unexplored certain questions that later writers would subject to much greater scrutiny, especially with regard to the relationship between the roles of poetry as a vehicle for cultural knowledge and as a means for knowing the authentic emotions of others. In the first of these roles, poetry is valued for its embodiment of the cultural allusions and elegant language that are essential to the cultivation of the gentleman, while in the second it is looked to as a source of insight into unadulterated human nature, prior to its cultural formation through the Way of the sages. He explains, for example, that both authentic emotions and elegant language are present in the *Book of Odes*, arguing that Confucius' editing of the Odes consisted of polishing their language, and that "if this were not so, then how could the words of farm inspectors and weaving women be so beautiful?"[70]

The idea that the Odes do not literally consist of the words of the common people, but have been reworked to make their language more refined, does not prevent Sorai from seeing these poems as providing insight into the experiences and emotions of people from all levels of society. His confidence in the capacity of the language of the Odes to express unaltered their original emotional content reflects his optimism regarding a Confucian cultural world that enhances and draws out the natural traits of the material that it works upon, bringing it into a world of humanly created value without compromising its original being. His disciples, though, did not always share this optimism, and in the following chapter we will explore the different solutions they offered to the contradictions they found between authentic emotions and highly formalized modes of literary expression.

FOUR

The Fragmentation of the Sorai School and the Crisis of Authenticity

Hattori Nankaku and Dazai Shundai

After Ogyū Sorai's death, the leadership of his academy was passed on to his nephew and adopted heir Ogyū Kinkoku (1703–1776). Kinkoku played mainly a preservationist role, however, and did not display the kind of strong leadership and scholarly originality that, for example, Itō Tōgai had in carrying on his father Itō Jinsai's school. Instead, it was Sorai's disciples who became the primary vehicle for the dissemination and development of his ideas. Two of his most prominent students, Andō Tōya and Hirano Kinka (1688–1732), died before or soon after Sorai, and the activities of a third, Takano Rantei (1704–1757), were limited by the fact that he went blind at age seventeen. Sorai's followers most active in propagating his teachings were Dazai Shundai and Hattori Nankaku, both of whom operated in Edo, and Yamagata Shūnan (1687–1752), who spread Sorai's teachings to the far west of Japan, to present-day Yamaguchi prefecture and Kyushu. This chapter focuses on Nankaku and Shundai, as they were the two figures most influential in developing different aspects of Sorai's teachings, with Nankaku carrying on Sorai's literary ideals based on the Ming Ancient Phraseology movement, and Shundai developing his views on Confucian philosophy and political economy in new directions.

Nankaku was born in 1683 into a Kyoto merchant family, giving him a background unusual within the Sorai school and contributing to his lack of interest in the aspects of Sorai's philosophy related to the practice of government. A number of his family members were active as waka and renga poets, and he received training in waka from an early age. He moved to Edo in 1696, after the death of his father, and in 1700 was brought into service as a waka poet with Yanagisawa Yoshiyasu, who, as discussed in Chapter 2, employed a large number of literary and intellectual figures, including Sorai, and regularly held events such as poetry gatherings and public lectures on Confucian texts. Yoshiyasu went into retirement in 1709 upon the death of Tokugawa Tsunayoshi, the shogun he had served, but Nankaku remained in Yoshiyasu's service, and continued to serve the Yanagisawa house after Yoshiyasu died in 1714. While he had been devoted to Yoshiyasu and grateful for his patronage, he did not get along with Yoshiyasu's successor, and ended up resigning from his position with the Yanagisawa house in 1718.

Nankaku never served again in an official capacity, and supported himself by teaching poetry in a series of private academies he operated in Edo. He had already enrolled as a disciple of Sorai in 1711, and his stature within Sorai's circle gradually grew, with his specialty now being poetry in Chinese, rather than waka. In 1727 Nankaku published *Nankaku sensei bunshū* (The Collected Writings of Master Nankaku), a collection of his poetry and prose. Such collections were usually issued posthumously by a prominent figure's disciples, so it was rather ambitious of Nankaku to publish this during his own lifetime. He continued to publish collections of his work periodically, with a second installment of *Nankaku sensei bunshū* coming out in 1737, a third in 1745, and a fourth in 1758, just a year before his death. He wrote little in the way of theoretical works, and the closest thing he wrote to an exposition of literary theory was *Nankaku sensei tōka no sho* (Master Nankaku's Jottings under the Lamplight), published in 1734. Another work of his is *Daitō seigo* (Stories of the East), published in 1750, a collection of setsuwa from such collections as the *Konjaku monogatari* and the *Uji shūi monogatari*, rendered into kanbun by Nankaku. He also exercised considerable influence on the literary world through his publication in 1724 of the *Tangshi xuan* (Jp. *Tōshisen*), an anthology of Tang poetry edited by the Ming Ancient Phraseology poet Li Panlong. Sales of the work, which due to its popularity was reissued in 1743, 1745, and 1753, helped Nankaku financially, and the collection was also responsible for establishing a certain canon of Tang poetry in Tokugawa Japan, with over thirty editions of the work appearing in print by 1868. These came in a wide variety of formats and with different types of annotations, and included *Tōshisen kokujikai* (An Explanation in Japanese of the *Tangshi xuan*), published in 1791, which contained Japanese commentaries on the poems that were said to be based on Nankaku's lectures.[1]

Shundai, unlike Nankaku, came from a samurai background, but he remained on the margins of official life, in part because of circumstances beyond his control, but also because of his refusal to compromise his ideals. He was born in 1680 in Iida domain in Shinano province, but due to an incident where his father caused offense to the daimyo of Iida, the family was expelled and forced to move to Edo in 1688. Reduced to rōnin status, they lived in poverty in the midst of the flourishing urban culture of the Genroku period (1688–1704). To help out with family finances, in 1694 Shundai took up a post as supervisor of pages for the daimyo of Izushi domain. Soon after, in 1696, he began studying Zhu Xi Confucianism under Nakano Kiken (1667–1720). In 1700, after the death of his mother, he resigned from his post with Izushi domain in order to pursue scholarship more deeply, an act that enraged his employer, who punished him by issuing a ban on his employment with any domain for the next ten years. He spent much of this time in Kyoto and Osaka, and developed his skills composing poetry in Chinese and playing the flute (*fue*). In 1711, after his ban was over, he returned to Edo and was employed as a secretary by the daimyo of Oyumi domain. In the same year he met Sorai for the first time, through the introduction of Andō Tōya, with whom Shundai had earlier studied under Kiken. Shundai resigned his new post after only four years, and did not serve in an official capacity again for the rest of his life, instead pursuing scholarship while receiving income from operating a private academy.

Shundai's scholarship was wide-ranging, covering such topics as political economy, Confucian philosophy, linguistics, and poetry. His main work on political economy is *Keizairoku* (A Record of Political Economy, 1729), which he supplemented later with a brief addendum entitled *Keizairoku shūi* (Gleanings from *A Record of Political Economy*, 1744). In *Bendōsho* (A Treatise on the Way), written in 1732 and published in 1735, he argues for the superiority of Confucianism over Shinto and Buddhism, a position that earned him many enemies among nativists. Other of his works on Confucian philosophy include *Seigaku mondō* (Dialogue on the Learning of the Sages, 1736), which includes detailed expositions on such topics as the relationship between human nature and the Way, and *Rikukei ryakusetsu* (A General

Outline of the Six Classics, 1745), which discusses the role of each of the Confucian Six Classics in the practice of the Way. His linguistics studies focus especially on how to read Chinese characters in Japanese, with one of his most important works in this field being *Wadoku yōryō* (Guidelines for Reading in Japanese, 1728). His two main general works on literary theory are *Bunron* (A Discourse on Literary Writing) and *Shiron* (A Discourse on Poetry), which were published together in 1748. *Shushi shiden kōkō* (The Fatal Errors of Zhu Xi's *Transmissions on the Odes*), written in 1730 and published in 1746, deals more specifically with refuting Zhu Xi's reading of the *Book of Odes*, and is preceded by an introductory essay entitled *Doku Shushi shiden* (Reading Zhu Xi's *Transmissions on the Odes*). Comments on poetry also appear in two pieces that cover a variety of miscellaneous topics, *Sekihi* (Pointing out Errors), published in 1745, and *Dokugo* (Solitary Ramblings), which remained unpublished, but circulated widely in manuscript form.

One of Shundai's most famous traits was his demand for strict adherence to ritual propriety in all matters, which led him to sabotage his own official career by refusing to engage with anybody who did not conform to his rigid standards. After leaving service with Oyumi domain, he announced that he would not take a post for less than two hundred koku, which had been his father's stipend, and which Shundai declared was the minimum necessary to maintain the affairs and rituals appropriate to a scholar-official (*shi*). Three daimyo who admired his scholarship arranged to support Shundai by sending him rice, without his even having to take up an official post, but Shundai was offended when one of the daimyo wrote a letter to him that did not follow the prescribed forms of salutation, and ended up refusing the rice as a consequence. In an even more shocking example, after the publication of *Keizairoku*, Shundai refused a request to present a copy of it to the shogun, on the grounds that the request had been made through an inappropriate intermediary.[2] His difficult personality contributed to a contentious relationship with Sorai, and he was always something of an outsider within Sorai's school, even more so after Sorai's death, when Shundai entered into a heated rivalry with Nankaku.[3]

In very different ways, then, both Nankaku and Shundai shifted away from the political engagement that Sorai had seen as the proper application of Confucian learning. They instead retreated into idealized worlds of their own making, in Nankaku's case by constructing a literary and aesthetic sphere removed from politics, and in Shundai's by creating an image of the Confucian scholar-official that was too rigid and purist to survive an engagement with reality. Although Shundai did, as we will see, develop a pragmatism in his writings on political economy, he did so by declaring the impossibility of practicing Confucian government in the society of his day, a stance that can be contrasted with Sorai's optimistic faith in the potential to revive the organic community that he believed was made possible through the institutions of the sages. The more skeptical attitudes of both Nankaku and Shundai toward Sorai's vision of Confucian culture are reflected in their literary thought, I contend, in a questioning of the notion of authenticity in poetry. Sorai had been able to accept unproblematically that authentic emotions could be expressed through imitative modes of composition, an idea that was part of a broader tendency of his to see Confucian culture as cultivating human nature without coming into conflict with it. Both Nankaku and Shundai subjected the notion of authenticity to greater scrutiny, though, with Nankaku responding by embracing the idea of poetry as fiction, and Shundai taking the opposite approach, demanding that poetry be returned to authenticity so that it could play its proper role in Confucian governance.

Nankaku on Poetic Elegance

In a letter, Nankaku sums up his approach to composing poetry: "The words I use have already been used by the ancients, and the conceptions I express have also been expressed by the ancients. When I try comparing my own poetry with the poetry of the ancients, they are so similar that it is difficult to tell them apart. It is like this not because I imitate the ancients, but, rather, because my very self is a product of their writings."[4] The idea expressed here of the transformation of the self through the study and internalization of cultural models is similar to what we have seen in Sorai. Nankaku differs from Sorai, though, in that he does not discuss poetry as a way to gain access to the authentic emotions of people from all elements of society. Instead, he presents poetry as something explicitly fictional, and argues that the classical Chinese poetic canon that both he and Sorai idealize is simply an expression of the cultured world of an educated elite, rather than a window onto a broader social reality.

In *Nankaku sensei tōka no sho*, Nankaku emphasizes how poetry needs to be elegant, and maintain a certain distance from the ordinary and everyday. He describes this on the level of linguistic expression by drawing a distinction between elegant (*ga*) and vulgar (*zoku*) language, writing, "Beginning with the Six Classics, elegant language is all embellished, and is not the language in ordinary use in the common world."[5] As examples of vulgar language, he lists statutes (*ritsuryō*), collected sayings (*goroku*), textual explanations in colloquial language (*chokkai*), popular historical tales (*engi*), and fictional tales (*shōsetsu*) (p. 49). He explains that the study of vulgar language is a useful adjunct to the study of elegant language, as vulgar language allows people to understand the customs of China in more detail, as well as helping them grasp what makes elegant language distinctive. He warns, though, against the dangers of studying vulgar language exclusively, and argues that it is only people who already have some learning who should study vulgar language (p. 50). He describes elegance not only in terms of language, but also in relation to emotions, giving a history of Chinese poetry in which the poetry of different periods is judged based on whether it expresses "elegant emotions" (*fūga no jō*). He sees these elegant emotions as existing in poetry from the earliest times until the late Tang, when poetry became excessively detailed, and began to veer toward the narrow rationalism of Song poetry (p. 58). He sees this process of decline as having been reversed in the Ming, although he cautions that not all Ming poetry is the same, and says to study only Ming poetry that takes after the Tang, a reference to the Ancient Phraseology movement (p. 65).

To illustrate "elegant emotions," Nankaku writes, "For example, when parting from a friend, we recall the pleasures that we have had and lament the sorrows that will follow our parting, and together with our friend we shed tears and speak of our pathos (*aware*). In the eyes of those of the Song and later, attuned only to the study of principle, such behavior appears like that of undisciplined women and children, but in reality these are the emotions of elegant people (*fūjin no jō*)" (p. 59). The reference to the "emotions of elegant people" (in the same section he also expresses this as the "emotions of poets" [*shijin no jō*]) suggests that the emotions expressed in poetry are those of a cultured elite. This idea is reinforced by how he describes these emotions as something that do not come naturally, but need to be learned and internalized through study: "At first the emotions of elegant people will be very unclear, and it will certainly be difficult to make them one's own. Therefore it is good to start by taking after the ancients" (p. 61). He connects this cultivation specifically to the figure of the gentleman (*kunshi*) when he writes, "All poetry and literary writing are the words of gentlemen, so they are not something for communicating to common men and women. . . . They are truly the words of gentlemen, and it is likewise gentlemen who listen to them."[6] He even goes so far as to repudiate the idea that the Odes provide access to the emotions of the common people, commenting, "What does it refer to when [the "Great Preface"] speaks of 'chanting the inborn nature and emotions' and 'putting primacy on patterning' (Ch. *wen*, Jp. *bun*)? These refer to the intentions of gentlemen. How could they be the songs of rural villages?"[7]

For Sorai, the usefulness of poetry to rulers was tied to its ability to provide a window onto the emotions of the governed, a knowledge of which he considered necessary for the practice of humane governance. It is not surprising, then, that Nankaku's abandonment of the idea of poetry as a depiction of authentic emotionality was accompanied by a retreat from the kinds of political claims Sorai had made for poetry. For Sorai, the presence of both cultural forms and natural emotions in poetry reflected his view of the Confucian Way as political practice, in which the culture of the sages must interact with the natural raw material that it works upon. Nankaku, though, moves away from Sorai's view of poetry as encompassing both natural and cultural elements, instead making poetry into something purely cultural, going so far as to say that even the emotions expressed in poetry are cultural constructs.

Nankaku does carry on Sorai's idea of poetry as a tool for bonding together a community of similarly educated elite gentlemen, but unlike Sorai he does not insist that the gentleman's literary and artistic accomplishments be combined with government service. He instead looks down on service in an official post as a "vulgar" (*zoku*) activity, and thus incompatible with the gentlemanly ideal. After leaving his post with the Yanagisawa house in 1718, he wrote in a letter to Andō Tōya, "You always say that official service (*kan*) is a vulgar thing, and now I have come to the same conclusion. . . . Letting our hair hang freely and sitting with legs outstretched, in a reverie we will forget each other on the rivers and lakes, and after that we will more and more come to realize how vulgar was our dragging of official robes in former days."[8] Nankaku alludes here to the "Dazongshi" (Great and Venerable Teacher) chapter of *Zhuangzi*, in which a rather un-Confucian Confucius appears in conversation with his disciples, where he praises the Daoist Way as a higher level of understanding than that provided by his own philosophy. Regarding those who "pay no attention to proper behavior and disregard their personal appearance," Confucius says, "Such men as they wander beyond the realm; men like me wander within it."[9] He later declares, "Fish thrive in the water, man thrives in the Way. . . . For those that thrive in the Way, do not bother about them and their lives will be secure. So it is said, the fish forget each other in the rivers and lakes, and men forget each other in the arts of the Way."[10] Nankaku, then, is suggesting that his abandonment of service will lead him into a higher realm than the mundane strictures of propriety would allow, an attitude in stark contrast to that of Shundai, whose refusal to serve was motivated by a quest for a purer adherence to Confucian ritual than he thought possible within the compromised environment of an official post.

Nankaku's use of poetry to create a community united through a world of fictional elegance is characteristic of the *bunjin*, a term that can be translated as "literati" or "people of culture," and that is used in the context of the Tokugawa period to refer to educated individuals who turned their backs on contemporary society, instead using poetry, painting, and other elegant pursuits to create alternative worlds in which they could craft new identities and communities.[11] *Bunjin* culture became especially prominent in Japan during the late eighteenth century, and representative *bunjin* include the painter and haikai poet Yosa Buson (1716–1783), Takebe Ayatari (1719–1774), famous particularly for his poetry and fictional prose writings, and the painter Ike no Taiga (1723–1776).[12] While *bunjin* were by no means all followers of Sorai, they shared with him an interest in the formative power of culture, while restricting, as we saw with Nankaku, the social sphere in which such culture is meant to hold sway.

Nankaku's Poetry in Chinese

Many of Nankaku's poems follow practices that we saw in Sorai's poetry in Chapter 3. For example, Nankaku presents a fictional vignette based on a traditional *yuefu* topic in his five-character quatrain "Chōan dō" (The Chang'an Road):[13]

躍馬長安道	Galloping along the Chang'an road
春風向冶遊	In the spring breezes, heading to the brothels
五陵花落尽	In Wuling the blossoms are scattered
公子不知愁	But the young lord knows no sorrows

Much like the "Song about a Young Man" topic, an example of which we saw from Sorai in Chapter 3, the "Chang'an Road" topic typically depicts a wealthy, pleasure-seeking young man. In Nankaku's poem, this association is strengthened by the reference to Wuling, an area in the north of Chang'an that was home to many aristocrats during the Western Han. The

Tangshi xuan contains the following poem on the "Chang'an Road" topic by Chu Guangxi (fl. 742): "Cracking his whip on the way to the drinking house / Splendidly dressed, he amuses himself at the brothel / Although he spends a million in a single instant / None grant him a word spoken with true feeling." Nankaku's poem also shows similarities to Li Bo's "Song about a Young Man" #2: "The young man of Wuling, east of the golden city / Silver-tipped saddle on a white horse, traversing the spring breezes / Stepping across fallen blossoms, off somewhere for amusement / With laughter he enters the drinking house of the women from the west." Like Sorai's "Song about a Young Man" poem, Nankaku's "Chang'an Road" provides a fictional character for poet and audience to identify with, and allows them to imagine themselves as members of the ruling class of China's past.

In one of his most famous poems, the seven-character quatrain "Yoru, bokusui o kudaru" (Going down the Sumida River at Night), Nankaku takes the mundane world of Edo and transforms it into an otherworldly setting:

金龍山畔江月浮	On the banks by Golden Dragon Mountain, the moon floats on the river
江揺月湧金龍流	The water is rippled, the moon springs forth, the golden dragon flows on
扁舟不住天如水	My skiff keeps moving, sky and water merge
両岸秋風下二州	Autumn winds on both shores, I float down between the two provinces

"Kinryūsan" (Golden Dragon Mountain) is a poetic name for Matsuchi-yama, a small hill located within the grounds of Honryūin in the Asakusa Kannon temple complex, on the west bank of the Sumida River. The final line refers to how the Sumida River forms the boundary between Musashi and Shimōsa provinces. Nankaku draws on two poems from the *Tangshi xuan*; the second line borrows from the line "The moon springs forth, the great river flows on," in Du Fu's "Lüye shuhuai" (Writing My Feelings while Traveling at Night), and elements of Nankaku's poem also overlap with Li Bo's "Emeishan yue ge" (Song on the Moon at Mount Emei): "At Mount Emei, the autumn half moon / Its light reflects on the Pingqiang River and follows its current / At night I depart Qingqi and head for the Three Gorges / I think of you but cannot see you, floating down toward Yuzhou." By mediating his description of contemporary Edo with poetry from the Chinese past, Nankaku affirms the cultural authority of China, while also suggesting that other countries can, by assimilating themselves to the proper cultural norms, participate in Chinese civilization.

In the next poem, the seven-character regulated verse "Hito no kyō ni yuku o okuru" #2 (Sending Someone off to the Capital #2), Nankaku maps ancient China onto modern Japan more explicitly by comparing Kyoto to the capital of the Zhou dynasty:

好向西京試遠游	Make your way to the western capital on your distant journey
巍巍文物満宗周	The flourishing artifacts of culture fill the Zhou capital
前王清廟迎琴瑟	In the pure and still ancestral temple of the former kings, they play lutes and zithers
中士明堂擁冕旒	In the Illumined Hall, the middle officials surround the ones wearing crown gems
正朔従来臨万国	The ruler issues the calendar as always to the many provinces
干城猶自錫諸侯	He charges the feudal lords with duties to protect the land
請看永鎮南山色	Observe the color of the southern hills, long at peace
不改千秋古帝州	Unchanged for a thousand years, in the ancient imperial capital

"Pure and Still Ancestral Temple" (Mao #266) is the title of the first poem in the "Zhou song" (Hymns of Zhou), a category within the "Song" (Hymns) section of the *Book of Odes*. Another *Odes* reference is the phrase "southern hills," which is used in the poem "Tian bao" (Heaven Protects; Mao #166) as a symbol of longevity. The Illumined Hall was a palace building where the ruler carried out affairs of state in the Zhou dynasty. The Zhou was traditionally seen as a time of ideal government, and the historical models provided by Zhou government were particularly important to the Sorai school. Nankaku follows this idea by describing the rituals of Zhou government in idealized terms, from the elegant music of the sages to the ruler's performance of acts through which his authority is symbolically manifested, such as the promulgation of the calendar. The comparison of Kyoto with the Zhou capital is transparently fictional, though, especially in the description of it as a political center, which did not reflect any actual advocacy on Nankaku's part for the restoration of imperial rule.

Nankaku's use of fiction in the above poems suggests a desire to escape into alternative worlds, and many of his other poems present more explicitly escapist ideals, especially his many poems that draw upon the works of Tao Qian (365–427), whom Nankaku valued for his ideals of freedom and simplicity, as well as his enthusiasm for using alcohol as a means of liberation. An example of a poem that references Tao Qian is the seven-character regulated verse "Kyo o kōhoku ni utsusu" (Moving to the North of the City):

十載衡門赤水西	For ten years my humble gate has stood west of the red river
移居仍自傍幽渓	I have moved house, and still am within the secluded valley
犬鶏不隔知窮巷	The nearby dogs and chickens know the shabby streets
燕雀相随安旧棲	Swallows and sparrows follow along, yet roost in my former home
欲避風塵難遠跡	I want to escape the dust of the world, but it is hard to avoid company
羞栽桃李易成蹊	I am chagrined that by planting peaches and damsons, the path has become easy to pass
只憑春樹漸遮断	If the spring trees would just gradually block it off
定似花源使客迷	It would surely be like how the blossom spring confounded its visitor

The "red river" mentioned in the first line refers to the Akabane River in the northern part of Edo. This poem draws especially on Tao Qian's "Taohua-yuan ji" (Record of Peach Blossom Spring), which tells of how a fisherman wanders through a peach grove and finds a utopian society made up of the descendants of people who had fled the chaos of an earlier dynasty. After returning home he tries to find his way back to the world he had discovered, but despite carefully marking his way, he is unable to find it again. In the final two lines of Nankaku's poem, then, the speaker is expressing his desire to be closed off in an isolated, ideal world. Nankaku's borrowing of specific words and phrases reinforces the ideal of reclusion. The word used for "humble gate" comes from a poem in the *Book of Odes*, itself called "The Humble Gate" (Mao #138), that describes the pleasures of the simple life, and the sounds of dogs and chickens are mentioned in descriptions of ideal societies in both "Peach Blossom Spring" and the *Dao de jing* (chapter 80). The reference to planting peaches and damsons alludes to a saying, "With peaches and damsons, even without saying anything, a path will naturally form," meaning that a person of virtue will attract admirers even without seeking them out. Nankaku is not necessarily boasting of his own virtue here, though, as the phrase is simply a way of describing how people have come to invade his private space, and of setting up the reference to "Peach Blossom Spring" that follows in the next two lines.

Another poem that makes reference to utopian ideals is the seven-character regulated verse "Kajitsu no kankyo" (Idleness on a Summer Day):

夏日清風臥草堂	On a summer day, lying down amidst the cool breezes in my thatched hut
無端牽睡到羲皇	I chanced to drift off to sleep, and came upon Emperor Fu Xi
思玄昔夢崑崙上	Pondering mysteries, long ago I dreamt of the summit of Mt. Kunlun
遺世還遊華胥鄉	Leaving the world behind, I amuse myself in the land of Huaxu
窓下寤来仍撫枕	Waking up by the window, I lean on my pillow
庭陰浴罷更移牀	I bathe in the shadows of the garden, and move my bed
暑天不厭昏時促	I pay no mind as the warm day gives way to the gathering dusk
回首園林已夕陽	Turning my head toward the trees in the garden, the sun is already setting

The first two lines are a reference to Tao Qian's "Yu zi Yandeng shu" (Memorial for My Son Yan): "I lay down beneath the north window, and after the cool breeze came upon me for some time, I thought myself to be Emperor Fu Xi." The phrase "pondering mysteries" alludes to a piece from the *Wen xuan* entitled "Sixuan fu" (Fu on Pondering Mysteries), by Zhang Heng (78–139). The dream world described in Nankaku's poem begins with the legendary Emperor Fu Xi, who was said to rule over an ideal society of Arcadian simplicity. It then moves to the mythical Mt. Kunlun, which was associated with the mystical and supernatural. Finally, the speaker arrives at the land of Huaxu, which according to the *Liezi* was seen by the Yellow Emperor in a dream, and is a utopian land whose inhabitants are free of all greed or selfishness, where "there are no teachers and leaders; all things follow their natural course."[14]

Nankaku is similar to Sorai in taking an imitative and allusive approach to poetry, and he bases this approach in a literary canon that is also largely shared by Sorai. Nankaku is especially noteworthy, however, for the extent to which he uses poetry as a way to construct alternative worlds and turn his back on contemporary reality. Poetry for Sorai, even if not explicitly political in content, was meant to be integrated into a broader program of cultural education designed to prepare members of the elite to carry out the business of government, which was to be based on the models provided by the sage kings of ancient China. Nankaku, though, while using the government of the sage kings as a fictional device to elevate contemporary Japan aesthetically, does not accompany this with any program to transform the models of the sages into contemporary political practice. Nankaku's abandonment of politics is also evident in his frequent expression of escapist fantasies in his poetry, including the idealization of Daoist-inspired utopias.[15] Nankaku's poetics is not without a social element, as his emphasis on classical norms is tied to the construction of a community of educated gentlemen, but this community is in the end a self-enclosed one that avoids engagement with the broader society in which it is situated.[16]

Shundai's Moral and Political Philosophy

The broad outlines of Shundai's interpretation of the Confucian Way are inherited from Sorai. He echoes Sorai when he begins the introduction to *Keizairoku* by declaring, "The Way of Confucius is the Way of the ancient kings. The Way of the ancient kings is the Way of governing the realm. The Way of the ancient kings exists in the Six Classics."[17] Also like Sorai, he sees Song and Ming Confucians as having lost the true meaning of the Way: "When it came to the Song, the learning of the Chengs and Zhu explained the Way of the sages entirely in terms of methods of the heart. . . . At the same time as Zhu Xi there was Lu Xiangshan [1139–1192], and then in the Ming there was Wang Yangming [1472–1529]. Although their theories were different from Zhu Xi's, they were the same in how they focused on methods of the heart. Because of this, the Way of the sages became obscured."[18] Central to Shundai's criticism of Song and Ming Confucians is his belief that they are deluded in seeking norms in the self. According to Shundai, "ritual and rightness are the Way of the ancient kings, and are not something that is in the original heart of humans."[19] Because the Way has its origins outside of human nature, he writes, "Confucius did not particularly concern himself with the inborn nature, and just saw learned habits as important."[20] Shundai was more than just a passive transmitter of Sorai's philosophy, though, as he developed some of his teacher's ideas in directions that differed in meaningful ways from Sorai's original formulation of these issues.

One of Shundai's departures from Sorai is his more pessimistic view of human nature. On the most basic level he agrees with Sorai that it is wrong to define the inborn nature as either good or bad, arguing that "although Mencius and Xunzi are at odds with each other in their explanations of the inborn nature, they are alike in violating the intentions of the sages."[21] As we saw in Chapter 2, though, this refusal to define human nature as purely good or purely bad does not prevent Sorai from asserting that people have a certain innate disposition toward cooperation. Shundai, however, emphasizes the negative aspects of human nature, describing the world before the emergence of the sages as a brutal Hobbesian state of nature in which "people were human in form, but their hearts were no different from beasts,"[22] and "the strong seized the food and clothing of the weak."[23] The Confucian Way then appears more as a disciplinary mechanism for saving people from their worst instincts than as the gently nourishing force envisioned by Sorai.

The difference between their views of human nature is reflected in how Shundai shows less faith than Sorai in the ability of the Way of the sages to transform people from within, instead emphasizing how the Way allows people to maintain social harmony even in the absence of such a transformation. In a metaphor that Shundai uses to describe the functioning of ritual, he writes, "Controlling the people with ritual and rightness is like holding back water with a levee."[24] His use of this image is telling when contrasted with how Sorai employs a similar metaphor in *Taiheisaku* to illustrate the futility of trying to control people with laws, without changing the underlying customs (*fūzoku*) through which their behavior is generated in the first place. Sorai writes, "This is like not stopping a flow of water at its source, and instead putting a levee downstream. The water will grow higher and higher, and in the end the levee will surely collapse."[25] From Sorai's perspective, Shundai would appear to be simply setting up piecemeal measures, without getting at the root of the problem by changing people's attitudes and consciousness.

The same logic that underlies Shundai's metaphor of the levee appears in how, in *Seigaku mondō*, he famously defines the gentleman according to strictly external criteria: "One who upholds the rituals of the ancient kings in his actions, and makes use of the rightness of the ancient kings in handling affairs, and has the appearance of a gentleman in his external aspect, is called a gentleman. There is no concern for the state of such a person's internal heart."[26] It is this ability to conceptually separate human emotions and desires from the actions that arise from them that he sees as the key to the superiority of Confucian over Buddhist moral philosophy. While the Buddha "even took it to be a sin to have [desirous thoughts] arise in the heart," he explains, "in the Way of the sages, even if one looks at another's wife, and thinks in one's heart about how beautiful she is, and takes pleasure in her appearance, as long as one does not violate ritual then one is considered a gentleman who upholds ritual. This is what is meant [in the *Book of Documents*] by the phrase 'with ritual control the heart'" (p. 126). The "control" that ritual exercises over the heart does not involve any inner transformation of the heart; the heart is controlled simply to the extent that we do not act on any immoral desires we may have.[27] It is this distinction that allows Shundai to combine a seemingly permissive acceptance of the reality of human emotions with a strong demand for moral uprightness, arguing that "to be without emotions is not to be human" (p. 74), and that the "great desires [for food, drink, and sex] are no different between sages and ordinary people" (p. 106), while at the same time warning that if people's true emotions "are not suppressed, and are just left as they are, then there will be no end to chaos in the realm" (p. 80).

Shundai does, however, see the following of external norms as ultimately leading to an internalization of correct attitudes. He follows Sorai in defining "genuineness" (*sei/makoto*) as when "the outer and inner are matched" (p. 99), and in seeing such a state as arising from the inborn nature, as well as from habits that are learned to the point where they become as automatic as the inborn nature. The fact that human nature is not inherently good or bad, though, and that people can moreover learn either good or bad habits, means that "there is genuineness in the good, and there is also genuineness in the wicked"(p. 101), making genuineness itself a normatively empty concept. Genuineness is only valuable when people do the proper things genuinely, which is the goal of cultivation in the Way: "The teachings of the sages come from the outside and enter into the inside. When these teachings have been completely absorbed, then the outer and inner are matched. This is considered accomplishment, and is called the 'attainment of virtue'" (p. 95). Shundai, then, is not as unconcerned with the internal as he appears at first glance. We can see further evidence of this in how, despite his statement that the Way of the sages "does not question whether the emotions are virtuous or wicked" (p. 95), he argues elsewhere that the sages created music in order to give order to the emotions, "suppressing what is in excess, aiding what is lacking, and making human emotions be in keeping with centrality and harmony."[28]

The difference between how Shundai and Sorai view the internalization of the Confucian Way is to a large degree a matter of emphasis. Shundai agrees that the ultimate goal is to make the Way permeate our interior, to the point that we do not even recognize it as something foreign to our inborn nature, but he also calls attention to how it is possible to follow the Way even in the absence of such complete internalization, when the conflict between desires and moral duties persists. This focus on the internal conflicts people experience in following the Way suggests a certain loss of faith in Sorai's optimism regarding the possibility of re-creating the Way in Tokugawa Japan. Rather than seeing the transformation of people by the Way as an automatic process that results from immersing them in the proper institutions of sagely government, Shundai stresses the need for individual cultivation through intense personal effort.[29] In this way, his turn to a more problematic vision of Confucian cultivation is accompanied by a shift from society as a whole to the individual as the locus of this cultivation.[30]

This is not to say that Shundai is unconcerned with the application of Confucianism to governing society, but he also argues for the need to be open to non-Confucian methods of governance.[31] The ideal society he describes in *Keizairoku* is very similar to that envisioned by Sorai, with a feudal (rather than centralized) government, and a four-class system of samurai, farmers, artisans, and merchants. He has an agrarian focus, arguing that although all the classes are necessary, "in the tasks of the common people there is the root and there are branches; farming is the root task, and the activities of artisans and merchants are branch tasks."[32] He is critical of the practice of samurai living in castle towns, writing, "The Way of governing the common people is based in being attached to the land," and complaining that in his own day, "the only people who are attached to the land are farmers, while all others are separated from the land, and are like guests at an inn" (p. 260). Shundai also echoes Sorai when he emphasizes how "in governing the realm and provinces, in all matters the foremost task is to establish institutions (*seido*) in all matters" (p. 248), and how ritual and music move people on a much deeper level than mere verbal teachings or laws, so that "the Way of ritual and music is how [the ancient sages] united the hearts of the people of the realm" (p. 33).

While he holds up these ideals, he argues that when it is impossible to practice the Way of the sages in its pure form, it is acceptable to make use of other Ways, such as Legalism and Daoism. In *Keizairoku* he explains this by comparing the Confucian Way to the five grains, and other Ways to medicines. Although normally people are nourished by the five grains, he writes, when they become ill they need to rely on medicines, which achieve results precisely because of their unbalanced, poisonous character:

> Such medicines are not things that one ought to consume ordinarily, but their effectiveness in curing illness is something that the five grains cannot achieve, so doctors make use of these. The Ways of people like Laozi are like this. They are not the ordinary Way for governing the realm and provinces, but in later ages, when various illnesses have arisen in the land, the Ways propounded by the various philosophers, including Laozi's non-action, Mozi's universal love, and Shen Buhai's and Hanfeizi's punishments and laws, all have their uses. When these are used well, they are all good medicines, and will not fail to cure the illnesses of the country. (p. 287)

An example of this is his qualified embrace of Legalism: "The Way of Lord Shang uses laws in order to govern the country, so it is called Legalism. Although it is at odds with the Way of the sages, it can be useful in governing in later ages" (p. 220). This is because even though "the government of the ancient kings entrusts things to people, and not to laws," in later times "it is very difficult to find talent" (p. 221). In the final book of *Keizairoku*, he presents an even more radical position on the usefulness of "medicines." Describing the role of Daoism, he writes, "With the non-action of Laozi, neither those above nor those below carry out any actions, and they leave everything to the natural course of Heaven-and-Earth. They do not meddle at all in matters of the realm, and just let things run their course. From the point of view of Confucians, this seems to lack humaneness, but in fact this is not the case. This is the Way appropriate for a decayed age" (p. 283). Later he argues that his own time is precisely such an age: "In the present age, since Genroku, both the samurai and the common people have become impoverished throughout the realm, and the vitality of the country has decayed, so now is a time when we should stop everything, and entirely practice non-action" (p. 287).[33]

In *Keizairoku shūi*, though, he uses the notion of "medicines" in a more positive, proactive way. One section of this text is an addendum to book five of *Keizairoku*, which dealt with food and money as the basis for the economy. The specific problem taken up in *Keizairoku shūi* is the impoverishment of the samurai class, which he attributes to the fact that they live in cities and are forced to purchase things in a currency economy. Ideally these problems should be resolved through the creation of institutions, without which "customs will decline, and the country's finances will be in the red."[34] He notes, though, that "it is beyond the power of a single domain to transform the institutions of the entire realm" (p. 300). Therefore, he argues, "just as in an emergency a doctor cures only the symptoms, one should look at what is critical in the illness of the present, and seek deliverance from this" (p. 301). The way to do this, he proposes, is for the samurai class to earn money through trade: "When it comes to techniques for amassing gold, nothing is better than to profit through trade. As a feudal lord, to seek profit through trade is not the optimal policy for governing the country, but it is one technique for finding salvation from the current emergency" (p. 305). Specifically, he advocates cultivating the products that the climate and other characteristics of a particular domain make it most suited for, and trading these with other domains. While he still casts such activities in somewhat negative terms, he shows a greater willingness than Sorai to flexibly adapt the Confucian Way to respond to the economic and social changes of his day.

This pragmatic approach to economic problems ended up becoming central to certain later thinkers inspired by Sorai, most notably Kaiho Seiryō (1755–1817), who studied under Sorai's disciple Usami Shinsui (1710–1776). For Seiryō, trade is not just a necessary evil, a second-best solution when the ideal society of the sages is not possible, but is rather the very essence of the teachings of the sages. In his *Keikodan* (Conversations about Learning from the Past, 1813), he argues that the denunciations of profit (Ch. *li*, Jp. *ri*) by Confucius and Mencius need to be understood in the context of the chaos of their times, when profit-seeking was giving rise to various problems.[35] He maintains that in a peaceful age like the Tokugawa, though, profit is perfectly acceptable. He describes the relationship between rulers and subjects as at root a relationship of market exchange, in which "[rulers] give salaries to subjects and make them work, and subjects sell their labor to rulers and collect rice" (p. 222), and argues that "when the calculations of buying and selling are achieved to the utmost, then the realm will be in a peaceful age of the sages" (p. 224). While such a vision is sharply at odds with how Sorai lamented the decline of organic feudal social relationships and their replacement by relationships of market exchange, this does not stop Seiryō from seeing Sorai as one of his intellectual forebears, praising him and Arai Hakuseki for being "people who argued by putting real things in the forefront," and for "putting methods of achieving profit first" (p. 230).[36]

Shundai on Poetry and the Confucian Way

Much of what Shundai has to say about poetry echoes Sorai's views on the role of poetry in the education of the ruling class. First of all, he sees the Odes as providing a model of the refined language appropriate to the gentleman, writing in *Rikukei ryakusetsu*, "The words of the Odes are correct and gentle, so those who study them naturally have beautiful language and attain the style of the gentleman. This is what Confucius meant when he told Boyu, 'If you do not study the Odes, then you will not be fit to speak.'"[37] His explanation of why the Odes, many of which are the products of common people, can serve such a purpose, is that they were created by "collecting the poems of the various provinces, taking them to the Music Bureau of the royal court, and choosing from among them those whose expression was refined and not vulgar."[38] The idea that the Odes literally contain the words of the common people is clearly distinct from Nankaku's view that the Odes are all the words of gentlemen, and also subtly different from Sorai's interpretation of the editing of the Odes, which he argues involved not selecting a subset of a larger corpus of source material, but actually beautifying the phrasing of the poems, albeit in a way that did not compromise their capacity to communicate the original sentiments of their creators. Shundai's difference from Sorai here is relatively minor, but it takes on greater significance in light of how, as we will see later, Shundai was much more adamant than Sorai about the need for poetry to be truly authentic.

Another way Shundai sees the Odes as contributing to the education of the governing class of gentlemen is by allowing them to understand the emotions and experiences of people from all levels of society. He describes how people's emotions differ according to their individual experiences, social status, gender, and position within such relationships as father and son, or elder and younger brothers. The Odes serve to overcome these differences, he argues, because they "contain all the matters of the realm, the external and internal and public and private deeds of everyone from the ruler down to the common people."[39] Shundai gives particular attention to how it is difficult for people of the highest levels of the ruling class to know the emotions of the lower classes, and how poetry can help to overcome this gap in knowledge:

> When one lives deep within the palace, how can one know the emotions of common men and women? Yet if one blindly issues proclamations without knowing the emotions of the common people, then there will be things that

go against the emotions of the people, and when this is the case such orders will not be carried out. Therefore those who govern must make an effort to know the emotions of the people. For those who occupy a lofty place in the realm, and who want to know the emotions of the people, there is nothing better than to study poetry.[40]

This is very similar to the idea we saw in Sorai that poetry allows rulers to move beyond the confines of their own subjective experience, which makes possible not only empathy but also the effective practice of government.

This concern for understanding the emotions of the governed is part of a broader idea of Shundai that rulers need to respond to the dynamic conditions of society. In the first volume of *Keizairoku*, he includes human emotions among a list of four things that need to be known in order to govern, the other three being "the times" (*toki*), "principle" (*ri*), and "force" (*ikioi*).[41] He discusses "the times" in terms of the changes in systems of political organization throughout history, particularly the shifts between feudal and centralized institutions, cautioning, "If you do not know [of these changes], and indiscriminately try to carry out the ancient Way today, it will clash with the times and not work" (p. 24). Unlike Zhu Xi, Shundai does not raise "principle" to the level of a metaphysical norm, and instead sees it simply as the regularities existing in things. An example he gives of this is the grain of wood, and he explains that all things have a "grain" that is difficult to cut against. This applies not only to material objects, he goes on, but also to "affairs of the realm," and he argues that "the people, no matter how lowly they may be, will always refuse to follow government that goes against principle" (p. 25). He then describes "force" as a temporary overcoming of ordinary principle, such as how water puts out fires, but a small amount of water will be overwhelmed by a large fire, or how wind generally fans flames, and yet will blow out the small flame of a candle (pp. 25–26).

Shundai describes human emotions in an analogous manner to the times, principle, and force, in that he sees human emotions as a raw state of affairs that rulers need to respond to in order to be effective, such as when he comments, "In enacting matters of government, if one is in keeping with human emotions then it will be easy to get people to follow, while if one runs counter to human emotions, then the people will not follow" (p. 26). In his discussion of human emotions, as well as the times, principle, and force, Shundai echoes Sorai in emphasizing how the norms of the Confucian Way can only be put into practice by interacting with a complex empirical reality. What sets apart human emotions from the other elements of this reality is that "the times, principle, and force are easy to know, while human emotions are difficult to know; the reason for this is that human emotions have elements that lie outside of ordinary reasoning" (p. 27). While the likes of principle can be known through the study of ordinary books, he goes on to argue, the complexity and diversity of human emotions do not lend themselves to such analysis, and require instead that people put themselves in the place of others to understand what they feel, something that only the Odes make possible.

Shundai attacks Zhu Xi's reading of the *Odes* directly in *Shushi shiden kōkō*, which consists of line-by-line refutations of specific passages in Zhu Xi's *Shi jizhuan*, and in *Doku Shushi shiden*, which deals with Zhu Xi's commentary as a whole. Shundai is especially critical of Zhu Xi's division of poems into right and wrong, which is the basis for reading the Odes in the mode of "approving virtue and chastising vice." One of his objections to such a reading is that "the Odes have no fixed meaning, so if you take them to be encouragements to virtue, then all three hundred can be encouragements to virtue, and if you take them to be condemnations of vice, then all three hundred can be condemnations of vice."[42] Shundai also argues that Zhu Xi does not realize that when lewdness is discussed in relation to the Odes, this properly applies to the music of the Odes, and not their lyrics: "Even the poems of the 'Zhounan' and 'Shaonan' sections would become lewd music if they were sung in lewd voices and accompanied by lewd instrumental sounds. And if we were to take the poems of Zheng and Wei, and give them correct tones, then they would become proper music."[43] Like Sorai, he does not deny that certain Odes may have lewd words, but he sees the application of moral judgments to the words of the Odes as a distortion of their real function, which is to allow us to understand human emotions.

This distinction between the roles of poetry and music is related to the broader point that each of the Six Classics plays a distinct and necessary function, an idea we also saw in Sorai. In a discussion of the role of the *Odes* among the Six Classics, Shundai criticizes Zhu Xi for failing to recognize that each Classic has a unique use, and for claiming that any one Classic is sufficient for achieving the Way, an error that Shundai says derives from the Buddhist idea that enlightenment can be gained through any one of the sutras:

> Song Confucians believe that if one masters any one of the Six Classics, then this one Classic alone, without any of the others, will be sufficient to achieve everything from cultivating the self, to ordering one's household, to govern-

ing the provinces and realm. Such a theory can be seen in the preface to Zhu Xi's *Shi jizhuan*. . . . This is like how with those who establish Buddhist sects, those who make use of the *Lotus Sutra* say that the *Lotus Sutra* exhausts the law of the Buddha, and those who make use of the *Kegon Sutra* say that the *Kegon Sutra* exhausts the law of the Buddha.[44]

Shundai actually does not see such an approach as inappropriate to Buddhism: "The law of the Buddha is a law for governing a single heart, so if one studies and masters any one of the sutras, this will be sufficient to govern the heart."[45] For Shundai the Confucian Way, in contrast, needs to be able to govern a complex social reality that can never be reduced to a single principle, or be achieved through the outward emanation of a single inwardly cultivated heart.

This concern that the ruling class not become isolated is also reflected in his criticism of those who pursue poetry at the expense of government, retreating into a self-enclosed aesthetic world rather than confronting the problems of their society. Although he sees poetry as an essential element in the cultivation of the Confucian gentleman, he maintains that a focus on poetry alone detracts from such cultivation. In *Keizairoku* he writes, "The Way of the sages has no purpose other than governing the realm and provinces. . . . Those who discard this and fail to study these matters, instead passing their lives occupied pointlessly with literary writings, are not true scholars. They are no different from the practitioners of such minor arts as the lute, *go*, calligraphy, or painting."[46] We can also see this attitude reflected in his assessment of Du Fu in *Shiron*. He singles out Du Fu as the best of the Tang poets, but expresses some ambivalence about him because of how he made poetry his sole occupation: "Although Du Fu is considered the saint of poetry, poetry is all he did. He spent his entire life without engaging in any other activities. . . . Therefore he cannot escape being a narrow-minded person (*kyokushi*). How could he aspire to be a 'gentleman who is not a utensil'?"[47] Shundai's comment on being a "gentleman who is not a utensil" is a citation from the *Analects* (II.12), and his assessment of Du Fu reflects a belief that the Confucian gentleman is defined through his role in government, so that even the best poets fail as gentlemen if they never put their learning to use in government service. He is making these comments at a time when Sorai's followers had largely turned away from the study of government and the economy in favor of such pursuits as poetry and painting, so he is denying his contemporaries the status of gentleman, and accusing them of having lost sight of the true meaning of Confucian scholarship.

Shundai on Music

Shundai was an accomplished flutist, and also gave considerable attention to music in his philosophical writings. On a theoretical level his views on music are similar to Sorai's, in that he situates music among the creations of the sages, and sees it as having the power to transform people in a way that verbal teachings cannot. In *Rikukei ryakusetsu* Shundai describes the unique function of music by writing, "It is music alone that can regulate and improve the heart; other techniques cannot do this."[48] The transformative powers of music can work toward either good or bad ends, though, and the use of music as a civilizing force requires, he argues, that this music be "proper music" (*gagaku*) and not "lewd music" (*ingaku*): "When proper music is practiced, then the customs (*fūzoku*) of the people will improve, but when lewd music is practiced, the customs of the people will grow worse. This is something that is beyond the power of people to control."[49] It is because of how music functions on a level that is beyond our control, then, that it is so important to have the right music and not the wrong music, with the right music defined as that created by the ancient sage kings of China.[50]

Shundai locates the origins of music in sung poetry, but sees the music of the sages as providing a normative correctness that is absent from spontaneously produced song. He begins the section of *Rikukei ryakusetsu* on the *Odes* by drawing on the "Great Preface" to describe poetry as the spontaneous outburst in song of emotions inspired by our encounters with external stimuli: "Poetry is something sung. . . . When people feel in response to things, in accordance with various events they feel joy, or anger, or sadness, or pleasure, or love, or dislike. Joy, anger, sadness, pleasure, love, and dislike are the emotions of humans. When these emotions arise inside, they take shape in words and are released in the voice."[51] He then argues that the reason the sages created music was to give order to this song. As he writes in *Dokugo*:

> When people are born, while they are still infants they cry out. From the age of two or three they scream, and from the age of four or five, even without being taught, they at some point learn songs, and chant clumsy children's ditties. This is all natural (*shizen*), as people could not get by without having a way to release their voices to speak of their sorrows. . . . But if this were just left as it is, then it would naturally tend toward the vulgar, and end up descending into disgracefully lewd sounds. The ancient sages foresaw this and created music, so that song and dance comfort the heart with the rhythm of musical instruments, allowing people to let out their pent-up feelings of sorrow.[52]

Much as Sorai sees the Confucian Way as nurturing and cultivating the inborn qualities of humans, which without this Way would lack proper direction, Shundai describes the music of the sages as a civilizing influence that elevates natural song and brings it in line with a normative world of cultural value.

In *Rikukei ryakusetsu* Shundai gives a brief outline of the history of music, told as the story of the gradual loss of the proper music of the sages. In the case of China, he writes that the ancient music of the sages was lost by the Qin dynasty (221–207 B.C.), but that elements of it were preserved until the beginning of the Sui dynasty (581–618), when music changed drastically and the ancient music was lost completely. Japan imported Chinese music prior to the Sui, he explains, and in early times in Japan people from all levels of society practiced proper music. During the Kamakura and Muromachi periods, though, new forms of music such as *dengaku* and *sarugaku* emerged, first among the lower classes, and then spread to the warriors who governed Japan at the time.[53] Finally, he laments that in the most recent times (that is, the Tokugawa period), lewd music has spread completely among both the common people and the samurai. There is still a note of optimism in this narrative of the decline of music, though, in that Shundai (like Sorai) argues that because the musicians of the imperial court in Kyoto have passed on the music originally imported to Japan from China prior to the Sui, it is possible to gain access to the remnants of the sages' music through these court traditions.[54]

Where Shundai departs from Sorai most sharply is in his translation of this theoretical framework into actual policies for reforming society. While Sorai had acknowledged the moral effects of music, this never featured prominently in his political writings. Shundai, however, shows a deep concern for the social disintegration that he believed to be the result of improper music. In *Dokugo* he launches into a full-scale attack on the popular music of his time, declaring, "Among the many types of lewd music in the world today, among instruments it is the shamisen, and among sung genres it is jōruri, that have the lewdest sounds."[55] While he sees both the shamisen and jōruri as definitively cut off from the music of the sages, he does concede that in their original forms they were not deeply lewd, and only became so through a period of decline during the Tokugawa period, in which the Genroku period represents a kind of tipping point, after which both the shamisen and jōruri became irredeemably lewd. He sees the popularity of such degraded forms of music as directly related to a decline in morals in recent times: "Ever since this kind of jōruri began to flourish, there have been countless cases of lascivious relations between men and women in Edo. By the time of the Genbun period [1736–1741], there have come to be innumerable incidents of adultery, theft of others' wives, and incestuous relationships. . . . This is truly the harmful effect of lewd music."[56] The solution Shundai proposes to this is to ban lewd music. Or, if it is impossible to ban it entirely, he suggests that its damage could be minimized by limiting its performance to outcasts, and thus driving it to the margins of society.[57]

Shundai's Critique of Ancient Phraseology

Shundai's main departure from Sorai's literary thought is his criticism of the imitative approach to composition derived from Ming Ancient Phraseology. While Sorai had emphasized the capacity of poetry to manifest authentic emotions, Shundai shows much more concern for the potential ways in which this authenticity can be compromised. In *Shiron*, for example, he tells the history of Chinese poetry as the story of a gradual loss of genuineness, and the rise of poetry as a specialized profession. This narrative can be contrasted with Nankaku's, where it is the loss of poetic elegance, which he explicitly identifies as the purview of a class of specially cultivated poets, that he blames for the decline of poetry.

In the Three Dynasties, Shundai begins, "those who composed poems always had thoughts; those who did not have thoughts did not compose."[58] He drives this point home by reminding us that there are only two instances recorded of Confucius bursting into song, and no record of any poetry having been produced by any of his disciples. In the Han, he continues, there began to be professional poets, but they were limited in number, so the situation was not that different from the Three Dynasties. He argues that a more important turn came with Cao Cao (155–220) and his sons Cao Pi (187–226) and Cao Zhi (192–232), who "because they took pleasure in composing poetry, did not wait to have thoughts before composing" (p. 6). From the Wei (220–265) and Jin (265–420) dynasties on, he writes, people took after the Caos and composed more and more poetry, a development that culminated in the flowering of poetry in the Tang.

He gives a generally positive evaluation of Tang poetry, saying that it is "inspired without using poetic topics (*dai*), and emerges out of actual events, and because of this has a wondrous natural quality" (p. 7). He passes over Song poetry as being beneath mention, and moves on to Ming poetry (especially that of Ancient Phraseology), which he describes as artificial and forced, a pale imitation of the poetic models it strives to emulate. He sums up the difference between Tang and Ming poetry with the following metaphor:

> The poetry of the High Tang is like the flowers in the garden of the emperor. There are precious specimens of different varieties, and their brilliance dazzles the eye. The poetry of the Middle Tang is like the flowers in the garden of a wealthy man. Although they do not attain the level of those of the emperor's garden, they still each have their particular attractions. The poetry of the Late Tang is like wildflowers. Although they do not catch the eye, they have a natural beauty. All three of these are produced by nature, and do not rely on human artifice. Ming poetry, though, is like cut flowers. Although their brilliance dazzles the eye, they are lacking in vitality. This is because they are created through human artifice. (p. 8)

The Ming poetry that he attacks here was idealized by the Sorai school, so he is very consciously breaking ranks on this point. He insists, though, that his views are a logical extension of Sorai's philosophy, declaring at the end of *Shiron*, written eleven years after Sorai's death, "Alas! If Master Sorai had lived ten years longer, he surely would have come to despise Ming poetry. . . . I am not establishing deviant theories that go against our teacher" (p. 29).

He develops these ideas further in *Bunron*, where he emphasizes the need for writing to have an organic wholeness, a quality he finds lacking in the works of Ancient Phraseology. Describing how texts are built up of progressively greater units, he writes, "Those who produce literary writing assemble characters to make phrases, assemble phrases to make chapters, and assemble chapters to make a work. All four of these [characters, phrases, chapters, and works] have their methods, and if any one of these methods is lacking, a piece of writing will remain incomplete."[59] Judging the Ancient Phraseology writers according to these criteria, he concludes, "Although their writing is not without craft, they only use appropriate methods with words and phrases, and lack proper methods for chapters and works" (p. 10). Where Ancient Phraseology falls short, then, is in the higher levels of unity required to create a literary work, a failure that he attributes to its collage-like approach to composition.

He sees this lack of unity as ultimately caused by the absence of an underlying intentionality on the part of the poet. Describing how characters, phrases, sections, and chapters are integrated in properly composed literary works, he explains, "A single intentionality permeates [these works], so they have no gaps. This can be compared to the human body. Although it has joints and articulations, its blood vessels are not disordered, as a single life force permeates them" (p. 10). He does not object to emulating the poetry of the past, but draws on the ideas of Han Yu (768–824) to argue that people should model themselves on the methodologies of these poets, rather than just copying the words of their poems. He compares this acceptable form of imitation to weaving cloth on a loom used by people in the past; although you are using the same methods, you are creating something new and distinctly your own. He compares the methods of Ancient Phraseology, in contrast, to clothing that is made by sewing together fragments of discarded garments (p. 7). As with his metaphor of the single life force that animates the body, his emphasis here is on the need for a literary work to constitute an organic whole.

When we consider Shundai's critique of Ancient Phraseology together with his assertions about the importance to rulers of knowing human emotions, we can see the fundamentally political character of his concern for authenticity in poetry. If poetry becomes a self-enclosed world, referring to nothing but poetic traditions themselves, then it can provide no insight into the empirical reality of human nature, knowledge of which is essential to the formulation of effective government policies. The fact that Shundai associates the loss of genuineness in poetry with the rise of the specialized poet also connects his critique of Ancient Phraseology to his political philosophy, as he views specialized poets as problematic specifically because of how they pursue poetry at the expense of government service.

Conclusion

As discussed in the Introduction, Maruyama Masao claims that Sorai made the Confucian Way something entirely political and external, thus liberating the interior, emotional lives of people, which found expression in literature. He then explains the split in the Sorai school by saying that Shundai inherited the political and external half of this division, and Nankaku the interior and emotional half. While the idea of a split between politics and literature in the Sorai school is valid on the level of the general emphasis of Shundai's and Nankaku's teachings, I see it as misleading to frame this in terms of a philosophical distinction between politics as the sphere of the external and public, versus literature as interior, private emotionality. One thing that Maruyama's analysis fails to account for is that it was actually

Shundai who insisted most strongly on emotional authenticity in poetry, while Nankaku openly embraced poetry as fiction. In this way, Nankaku's undoubtedly greater interest in the activity of composing poetry was in fact accompanied by a movement away from Maruyama's characterization of pure literature as the expression of natural emotions.

Shundai's greater emphasis on genuine emotions makes more sense, though, when we consider the interdependence of the Six Classics in Sorai's philosophy. This interdependence means that the valorization of the Odes as authentic emotional expression is inseparable from their position within a broader matrix of cultural practices designed to "bring peace to the realm"; rulers are meant to use the Odes to understand the emotions of the people they rule, and this understanding is compromised when the emotions expressed in the Odes are not authentic. The idea that the Six Classics perform distinct but complementary functions is what makes it possible, for example, for Shundai to combine a strong demand that poetry express authentic emotions with an equally strong demand that deviant emotions be brought under control with proper music. In this way, the "modern" demand for emotional authenticity is intertwined with "premodern" ideas of the political uses of literature, and of the need for people's private emotions to be subject to government regulation. When we turn to Nankaku, it makes sense that his isolation of the Odes from the other cultural practices represented by the Six Classics would be accompanied by an abandonment of the idea that the Odes must represent human emotionality in its unadulterated state. For Nankaku, the Odes and other poetry play an important role in the formation of community, but this is a community of literati who are united by the elevated sentiments and linguistic elegance they have internalized through the study and composition of poetry. Such literati keep aloof from society at large, unlike Sorai's and Shundai's image of the gentleman, who is meant to achieve a certain elegance through poetry, but also apply this to governing the realm.

A key aspect of Sorai's philosophy had been his focus on society as a whole as the proper field in which to practice Confucianism, an idea he presented in opposition to the focus on individual cultivation that he believed to be a flaw of Song and Ming Confucianism. With Nankaku and Shundai, though, there is a shift back to more individual-centered notions of cultivation, which they present in the context of a skepticism toward the practice of Confucian government as envisioned by Sorai. Nankaku rejects government service in favor of constructing a fictional self through poetry and other elegant pursuits, which he defines as the purview of an educated elite that remains at a distance from mundane society. Shundai, while acknowledging Sorai's model of government as an ideal, sees this ideal as impossible to practice, and instead favors a more flexible and pragmatic approach to government, while insisting on a rigid adherence to Confucian ritual in one's personal life. In the following chapters we will see how eighteenth-century nativists reintegrated, albeit in a different form from Sorai, many of the elements of his philosophy that had become fragmented with Nankaku and Shundai, presenting personal cultivation through poetry as seamlessly connected to broader social ends, a unity they achieved by imagining the Japanese past as a world in which emotional authenticity, classical poetic elegance, and proper government are mutually reinforcing rather than contradictory.

Kamo no Mabuchi and the Emergence of a Nativist Poetics

When Tokugawa Confucian scholars discussed poetry in relation to political and ethical philosophy, they did so for the most part with reference to poetry in Chinese. A similar interest in the philosophical significance of poetry can be seen, however, in eighteenth-century discourse on waka.[1] A growing number of scholars in this period idealized Japanese culture and the Japanese past, and rejected Chinese culture, especially Confucianism, which they charged with corrupting Japan and leading it astray from its original virtue. They saw waka not only as the purest form of the Japanese language, but also as uniquely suited to the expression of authentic emotions, and argued that the emotional communication made possible by waka gave rise to a form of harmonious community unique to Japan. These scholars also articulated their views in opposition to earlier interpretations of the Japanese classics, particularly those produced by the schools of aristocratic court poets in Kyoto. This chapter examines how a new discourse on waka emerged in the eighteenth century, and how this discourse defined itself in relationship to both Confucianism and court poetics. It focuses on the work of Kamo no Mabuchi, who was a pivotal figure in the systematization of ideas about waka and its relationship to Japanese identity. While the notion of waka as distinctively Japanese was not new, eighteenth-century writers like Mabuchi took this idea in a new direction with their theories of waka as a vehicle for the formation of interpersonal relationships marked by complete transparency, which they believed would spontaneously give rise to the virtues that Confucianism unsuccessfully tried to impose through artificial rules and rationalistic modes of thinking.

Mabuchi was born in Hamamatsu into a family with close connections to Shinto; although his immediate family appears to have been engaged in farming, they were descended from the Kamo family that served as hereditary priests at the Kamo shrine in Kyoto (Mabuchi's family name at birth was Okabe, but he later changed it to Kamo). His family associated with local shrine priests, and these connections were instrumental in determining the course of his education and scholarly career. In 1707 he started lessons in reading and writing with Sugiura Masaki (1690–1754), niece of the Shinto scholar Kada no Azumamaro (1669–1736) and wife of Sugiura Kuniakira (1678–1740), a local shrine priest in Hamamatsu who was a student of Azumamaro. The Sugiura house was a center of scholarly and literary activity in Hamamatsu, with a focus on Shinto studies and waka. Mabuchi received instruction in Chinese studies from a member of Sugiura's circle, Watanabe Mōan (1687–1775), who had studied together with Dazai Shundai under Nakano Kiken.[2] At a poetry gathering at Kuniakira's house in 1722 Mabuchi met Azumamaro for the first time, and he gradually deepened his relationship with Azumamaro, formally enrolling as his student in 1728 and going to Kyoto to study with him on a more long-term basis in 1733.

Azumamaro's intellectual heirs, his younger brother Kada no Nobuna (1685–1751) and his adopted son (Nobuna's biological son) Kada no Arimaro (1706–1751), were living in Edo at the time, and Mabuchi moved there to join them in 1737 after Azumamaro's death. Mabuchi had lectured on the *Hyakunin isshu* (Hundred Poems by a Hundred Poets) at Azumamaro's house in 1735, and continued lecturing on the Japanese classics while in Edo. In addition to the Kada family, other important contacts Mabuchi made in this period were Katō Enao (1692–1785), a samurai employed by the *machi bugyō* (Edo city magistrate), and Murata Harumichi (?–1769), a wealthy merchant. Both of these men had an interest in classical Japanese literary studies, and their sons, Katō Chikage (1735–1808) and Murata Harumi (1746–1811), both tutored by Mabuchi from a young age, would become two of the most influential inheritors of Mabuchi's teachings after his death.

Mabuchi's reputation as a scholar was growing in this period, as evidenced, for example, by his taking on his first formal student, Ono

Furumichi (1697–?), in 1738, and his serving as judge for a poetry contest at Arimaro's house in 1741. In 1742 he produced his first studies of poetry, *Man'yōshū Tōtōmi uta kō* (Reflections on the Tōtōmi Poems in the *Man'yōshū*) and *Kokin wakashū sachū ron* (A Study of the Marginal Notes in the *Kokinshū*). He wrote the second of these in response to a request from Tayasu Munetake (1715–1771), the second son of the shogun Tokugawa Yoshimune, and Munetake's patronage was to play a key role in advancing Mabuchi's career. At the time Arimaro was serving Munetake as an official scholar of Japanese studies (*wagaku goyō*), and in 1742 he wrote a text entitled *Kokka hachiron* (Eight Essays on Japanese Poetry) which, as discussed below, gave rise to a debate between Arimaro and Munetake, with Mabuchi eventually called in to provide his own views. It became clear that Mabuchi had more in common with Munetake than Arimaro did, and in 1746 Arimaro resigned his post and was replaced by Mabuchi. Mabuchi carried out various scholarly projects for Munetake, as well as completing a number of important works of his own conception, including an influential work on *makurakotoba* (poetic epithets) entitled *Kanjikō* (Reflections on Poetic Epithets, 1758), and textual commentaries such as *Man'yō kai* (Explanation of the *Man'yōshū*, 1749), *Ise monogatari ko'i* (Ancient Meanings of the *Tales of Ise*, 1753), and *Genji monogatari shinshaku* (New Interpretation of the *Tale of Genji*, 1758).

Mabuchi retired from service with Munetake in 1760, and the next decade, until his death in 1769, was his most productive in terms of scholarly output. He also continued to be active teaching in his private academy, which eventually enrolled over three hundred students. His students came from a wide variety of backgrounds, including samurai, merchants, Buddhist monks, and Shinto priests, and about a third of them were women. His most significant works from the 1760s are *Ka'ikō* (Reflections on the Meaning of Poetry, 1764) and *Niimanabi* (An Introduction to Learning, 1765), both treatises on Japanese poetry, *Kokuikō* (Reflections on the Meaning of Our Country, 1765), which attacks Confucianism and argues for the superiority of Japan's native values, *Man'yōkō* (Reflections on the *Man'yōshū*, 1768), another commentary on the *Man'yōshū*, *Noritokō* (Reflections on *Norito*, 1768), a study of *norito* (Shinto prayers), and *Go'ikō* (Reflections on the Meaning of Language, 1769), a linguistics treatise. His writings from this period were important in giving a systematic philosophical expression to his views on ancient Japan, with Mabuchi arguing that ancient Japanese language and literature were manifestations of a native Japanese Way, which made possible the ideal government and society that he claimed had existed in ancient Japan and could be revived in the present.[3]

The Kokka hachiron Debate

The question of the relationship of poetry to politics and ethics was at the core of the debate over Arimaro's *Kokka hachiron*, a work that gave rise to one of the most significant literary controversies of the eighteenth century, or for that matter the Tokugawa period as a whole. This debate began in the eighth month of 1742, when Munetake asked Arimaro to write a treatise explaining his views on waka. Arimaro responded with *Kokka hachiron*, which, as the title implies, consists of eight sections, each dealing with a different aspect of poetry, entitled "Kagenron" (On the Origins of Poetry), "Gankaron" (On Taking Pleasure in Poetry), "Takushiron" (On Selecting Words), "Hishiron" (On Words to be Avoided), "Seikaron" (On Correcting Errors), "Kankaron" (On Court Nobles), "Kogakuron" (On Ancient Learning), and "Junsokuron" (On Poetic Standards). Arimaro's work sparked a critical response from Munetake, who eventually called upon Mabuchi for his opinion on the issues brought up in *Kokka hachiron*, leading to a series of rebuttals and counterarguments between the three figures that lasted until 1746.[4]

The *Kokka hachiron* debate continued and developed two tendencies that had been gaining prominence in discourse on waka throughout the early Tokugawa period. One of these was the idea that waka is the expression of a universal human nature, and the other was the belief that waka from the past can be understood by anyone who applies the proper scholarly methodologies. The second of these assertions was specifically a challenge to the Kyoto court nobles (*tōshō*) who had dominated the world of waka up to that time. These figures belonged to various poetic houses, such as the Reizei, Karasumaru, and Asukai, which constituted exclusive societies within which waka was composed and taught. These houses had their origins in the competing heirs to the medieval poet Fujiwara no Teika (1162–1241), and each of the houses claimed to be the orthodox bearer of Teika's teachings. They only deigned to teach poetry to an exclusive circle of insiders, and knowledge of poetry was passed on from master to disciple in the form of jealously guarded "secret transmissions" (*hiden*).[5]

In the seventeenth century a number of scholars, such as Toda Mosui

(1629–1726) and Keichū (1640–1701), began to question the validity of these secret transmissions, arguing that knowledge of poetry could be pursued by anyone who applied the proper techniques of philological analysis, and that there was no need to receive the esoteric teachings of any secretive poetic cult. At the same time there was a growth in interest in the eighth-century *Man'yōshū*, which fell outside the purview of the court poets' secret teachings. A key factor in the development of these new scholarly approaches was the spread of printing in Japan from the beginning of the seventeenth century, which allowed texts on poetry to circulate independently of the institutional structures and master-disciple relationships of the poetic houses, creating a new reading public that soon began to make its own claims to interpretive authority.[6]

Arimaro carried on the skeptical attitude of Mosui and Keichū toward the court poets, complaining in *Kokka hachiron* about those who "arbitrarily use their courtier status to lord it over commoners,"[7] and "do not understand the nature of poetry, and so consider it something for courtiers to compose, and that commoners couldn't possibly grasp" (p. 555). Criticizing the secret transmissions of poetic houses, he writes that in judging poetry, "it is unnecessary to refer to who we take our founder to be, or what school we belong to; instead, we can pursue this simply through natural principle (*tōzen no ri*)" (p. 549).[8] Arimaro's attacks on the court poets were met with approval by both Munetake and Mabuchi, but other of his assertions, especially about the role of poetry in promoting proper social and political relationships, were more controversial. The ensuing debate on this issue supplemented the new philological approaches to waka with a variety of more systematic accounts of its philosophical significance, explaining its role in promoting good government and cementing interpersonal relationships.

ARIMARO ON THE POLITICAL USELESSNESS OF POETRY

The section of Arimaro's essay that would generate the greatest disagreement was the one entitled "On Taking Pleasure in Poetry." Arimaro opens this section by arguing, "Because poetry does not belong among the six arts, it is by nature of no use in governing the realm, nor is it of any aid in everyday life" (p. 540).[9] He specifically takes aim at the preface to the *Kokinshū*, in which the function of poetry in governance is described in terms of its ability to "effortlessly move Heaven-and-Earth (*ametsuchi*), cause invisible spirits to feel deep emotions, moderate the relations between men and women, and calm the hearts of fierce warriors."[10] Arimaro counters this by saying,

"When the preface to the *Kokinshū* speaks of 'moving Heaven-and-Earth' and 'causing spirits to feel deep emotions,' this comes from believing in baseless theories. Although poetry may do something to calm the hearts of fierce warriors, how could it do this as well as music? And though poetry may moderate the relations between men and women, does it not also serve to encourage licentiousness?" (pp. 540–41). Therefore, he concludes, "poetry is not something to be revered" (p. 541). The "baseless theories" that Arimaro speaks of are a reference to the "Great Preface" to the *Book of Odes*, and while the *Kokinshū* preface is less strictly moral than the "Great Preface" in its definition of the social and political functions of poetry, Arimaro criticizes the idea that such functions should be attributed to poetry at all.[11]

Arimaro does grant that poetry can serve as a personal consolation, and he connects this idea specifically to the sung character of poetry. He begins the section entitled "On the Origins of Poetry" by declaring, "Poetry is something in which words are lengthened and the heart is cleared" (p. 533), and says that "truly if one does not sing it is impossible to clear the heart" (p. 534). He argues that although poetry originally came into being as song, a process of historical change has resulted in the transformation of poetry from song into "playing with words," with a corresponding loss in its capacity to console the heart. Already in the time of the *Man'yōshū*, "there were some poems that were sung and some that were not sung; those that were not sung just played with words" (p. 539). By the time of the *Kokinshū*, "apart from the Poetry Bureau Songs (*Ōutadokoro no uta*) and the Songs of the East (*Azuma uta*), none of the poems appears to have been sung" (p. 539).[12] After the *Kokinshū*, he writes, poetry became more and more occupied with skillful expression, and finally the style of the thirteenth-century *Shinkokinshū* "brought to an extreme this flowering beauty" (p. 540).

Arimaro's literary historical narrative is the story of the loss of a certain authenticity, but he does not portray this in negative terms, or try to turn back the clock and recover an idealized past. He accepts the fact that in his own time poetry consists of "playing with words," and extols the *Shinkokinshū* as the most appropriate poetic model, writing, "There are many scholars who consider the *Shinkokinshū* to be excessively decorative and to lack substance, but I disagree. Literary language should by nature value decorativeness. Therefore I cannot see why one would make the criticism of this poetry as being too decorative" (p. 564). Today poetry mainly functions as a source of pleasure, he argues, and when we compose a skillful poem this gives us a kind of pleasure similar to that we get from "producing a good painting, or winning a game of *go*" (p. 541). He does concede that there is good reason for scholars to devote themselves to poetry, as "poetry alone uses the natural sounds of our country" (p. 541), preserving something purely native even after all other aspects of Japanese culture have been influenced by China. He criticizes those scholars, though, who elevate waka to the status of "the Way of Japan" (*Shikishima no michi*), arguing that "not only does this fail to recognize the nature of poetry, but it is an absurdity that comes from not understanding the meaning of the term 'Way'" (p. 542).[13]

THE DEBATE BETWEEN ARIMARO AND MUNETAKE

In *Kokka hachiron yogen* (My Views on the *Eight Essays on Japanese Poetry*, 1742), his rebuttal to Arimaro's piece, Munetake begins his critique of Arimaro's position on the social function of poetry by asserting that poetry belongs within the rubric of music, and therefore of the "ritual and music" (*reigaku*) that the ancient Chinese sage kings employed to rule the realm:

> It is said that King Shun strummed the five-stringed lute, sang the song "Nan feng" (Southern Wind), and governed the realm. It is truly the Way of poetry that serves to moderate people's hearts. Therefore in the reigns of the sage kings, they valued ritual and music. Within the category of music are included poetry/song,[14] dance, stringed instruments, wind instruments, and percussion instruments. Therefore splendid poetry aids people, and bad poetry harms people.[15]

Munetake acknowledges Arimaro's point that poetry is no longer joined to music, but he uses Zhu Xi's theory of "approving virtue and chastising vice" (Ch. *quanshan cheng'e*, Jp. *kanzen chōaku*) to argue that poetry can exercise a positive moral influence even in the absence of any musical qualities: "However, when we recognize that bad poems are bad, then they can serve as an admonition. Therefore even after the decline of proper music, the sage [Confucius] edited the *Book of Odes* in order to guide people. Even though in later times these may not be sung, they are vastly superior to ordinary language in moderating people's hearts" (pp. 99–100). For poetry to serve this function, Munetake stresses that it must be genuine, a quality that he finds lacking in Chinese poetry of the Tang dynasty and later, as well as in recent Japanese poetry. He sees Japanese poetry as inherently "not as profound in meaning as that of other countries," but still sees it as having some value in that it "has a rhythm that can gently communicate with people's hearts" (p. 100). The latest Japanese poetry, however, "is composed without any significance at all, simply taking pleasure in being unusual and decorative, so that in the end it cannot serve as a guide to good and bad at all, and even leads to licentiousness" (p. 100). This is the very kind of poetry that Arimaro had praised in his judgment of the *Shinkokinshū*, but Munetake instead seeks a return to the poetry of the *Man'yōshū*, saying that "by following the ancient style, and learning from the ancient style of other countries, poetry can be made into something that truly aids people" (p. 100).

Arimaro responded to Munetake's criticisms in *Kokka hachiron sairon* (A Restatement of the *Eight Essays on Japanese Poetry*, 1742). His criticism of Munetake's attempt to include poetry among the "ritual and music" of the ancient Chinese sage kings is that Munetake fails to distinguish between the words of poetry and the tones with which it was once accompanied, an argument that echoes the comments we saw Ogyū Sorai and Dazai Shundai make in Chapters 3 and 4:[16]

> The reason the sages valued ritual and music is that they used ritual to regulate, and music to harmonize. There is nothing better than tones when it comes to harmonizing the human heart. Therefore when people speak of music it is its tones that they refer to, and poetry/song and dance accompany this music. With such poetry/song as well, it is the tones that matter, and not the words. And yet when you speak of splendid poetry aiding people, and bad poetry harming people, you seem to be indicating that it is the words that do this.[17]

In his original essay Arimaro had already made the point that music and poetry play different functions, but here he clarifies further what kind of relationship poetry has to music. From his original statement on this issue it seemed that Arimaro saw music simply as having nothing to do with poetry, but here he says that music indeed is connected to sung poetry. He maintains, however, that this connection lies in the tonal aspect of sung poetry, not its words, thus upholding the idea that poetry, taken in the sense of the words alone, has no social or ethical role.

KAMO NO MABUCHI'S RESPONSE TO *KOKKA HACHIRON*

In Mabuchi's first statement on *Kokka hachiron*, his *Kokka hachiron yogen shūi* (Gleanings from *My Views on the "Eight Essays on Japanese Poetry,"* 1742), he describes three basic ways in which poetry aids governance. First of all, poetry can be used to make people willingly submit to the ruler, a function that relies on the ability of poetry to reach deep into people's hearts and change their behavior. Poetry "not only comforts one's own heart; the heart of the one who listens is touched as well."[18] He sees poetry and music functioning similarly in this regard: "In government it is important to make the people spontaneously follow. Therefore when the sages governed in China, they took into consideration that which cannot be reached by principle and rules, and so created music, and used it among the households and among the feudal states in order to change the customs of the people and harmonize their hearts" (p. 117).[19] The second function he attributes to poetry is its ability to allow the ruler to know the feelings of the ruled. The ruler "usually does not directly witness the conditions within society and the various provinces, much less is he conversant with the emotions of the people" (p. 117), but because poetry directly expresses emotions, it can serve as a substitute for the ruler actually observing the situation of the ruled with his own eyes. The third function of poetry he lists is its ability to regulate people's emotions. He argues that people naturally have a tendency to let their emotions get out of control, leading to strife and chaos, but that by composing and listening to poetry these desires can be moderated (pp. 117–18). What all of these political functions that Mabuchi describes have in common is that they are rooted in the special relationship of poetry to emotionality, which he sees poetry as able to both express and control in a way not possible with the Song Confucian "principle" that Munetake saw as at the root of poetry.

In one of his later contributions to the debate over *Kokka hachiron*, *Futatabi kingo ni kimi no kotaematsuru fumi* (Another Reply to Tayasu Munetake, 1744), Mabuchi frames his position in relation to the two paradigms for reading the *Odes* that were discussed in Chapter 1, the "old commentaries" (*kochū*), in other words the Mao tradition, and the "new commentaries" (*shinchū*), that is Zhu Xi's *Shi jizhuan* (Collected Transmissions on the Odes).[20] Mabuchi sees both of these as offering inadequate solutions to the problem posed by the disappearance of the music of the Odes: "The old commentaries are excessive in their glorification of the Odes, leading to many things that are difficult to believe. The new commentaries cling to the idea of principle in everything, so many of their explanations do not make sense, and ruin the flavor of the poems."[21] As we saw in Chapter 1, the *Correct Significance* saw the music of the Odes as guaranteeing perfect transmission of the intentions inscribed in the Odes, and argued that once this music was lost, its function was taken over by the Minor Prefaces, which explained the moral import of each Ode (the goal of these prefaces specifically being to show that all of the Odes, even the seemingly immoral ones, were in fact expressions of morally correct intentions). In the passage quoted here, Mabuchi charges that these prefaces distort the Odes by providing exaggerated and implausible claims about their moral significance. We also saw in Chapter 1 how Zhu Xi attempted to do away with the need for these prefaces by claiming that all humans possess the "principle" within themselves that allows them to make moral judgments about the Odes, but Mabuchi rejects this view as well.

Like Arimaro, Mabuchi criticizes Zhu Xi for attempting to locate the moral function of poetry in its semantic rather than its musical qualities: "In ancient times when people discussed poetry they did so only in relation to the tones, but Song Confucians speak of it with respect to the words. It seems that they were forced to rely on the words because the ancient melodies have been lost. Therefore what emerged from this was very different from what the meaning of poetry was in ancient times" (p. 155). Mabuchi goes beyond Arimaro, though, in making the additional criticism that Zhu Xi fails to see that human experience cannot be reduced to a morally defined "principle": "When it came to the Song Confucians, they discussed poetry entirely with reference to principle, and said that it was solely for the purpose of approving virtue and chastising vice. But even though principle is what generally holds sway in the world, the world cannot be governed through principle alone. Poetry speaks the truth (*makoto*) of humans, so can we expect that all of these real emotions (*jitsujō*), expressed just as they are felt, will be in keeping with principle?" (p. 155). What poetry is uniquely suited to expressing, he writes, are "irrepressible yearnings" (*warinaki negai*): "If such an unbearable heart were just stated outright, who would take it to have pathos (*aware*)? It is by singing with gentle words and with pathos in the voice that it is possible to go outside principle and make human emotions felt" (p. 155). Zhu Xi, as we saw in Chapter 1, did not claim that the emotions expressed in poetry had to be in keeping with principle in order for this poetry to serve an ethical function. He did, however, argue that emotions should be cultivated so that they harmonize with principle, and that poetry that expresses emotions contrary to principle is only useful to the extent that the reader of such poetry, by exercising the power of moral judgment represented by the original inborn nature, recognizes that this poetry violates principle. Mabuchi's difference from Zhu Xi, then, is not so much that Zhu Xi fails to recognize that humans are emotional beings, but rather that he uses a morally defined principle as the norm according to which emotions are to be regulated and judged. Mabuchi does see poetry as having various regulative functions, but he defines such regulation as occurring on the level of emotionality itself, not through the conformity of emotions to a moral principle that exists outside of them.

Mabuchi on Poetry and the Ancient Way

In a series of works he produced in his final years, Mabuchi articulated a vision of a native Japanese Way through which he believed ancient Japan had been governed prior to the introduction of corrupting foreign value systems, especially Confucianism. He saw this Japanese Way as rooted in the natural workings of Heaven-and-Earth, which he contrasted with the humanly constructed character of Confucianism. Moreover, he maintained that Japanese forms of literary expression, as well as the Japanese language itself, were manifestations of Heaven-and-Earth, and that it was through literature, specifically ancient Japanese poetry, that people of the present could regain touch with Japan's Ancient Way. He expressed this philosophy of a natural Japanese Way in opposition to the Sorai school's view of the Way as a cultural construct, as well as charging that the Sorai school obscured Japan's native virtues with its doctrine that only ancient China, and not Japan, could serve as a source of norms.

MABUCHI'S *KOKUIKŌ* AND THE CRITIQUE OF CHINESE CULTURE

In *Kokuikō*, Mabuchi depicts Japanese culture as in harmony with the workings of Heaven-and-Earth, and contrasts this with Confucianism, which he sees as trapped within the limitations inherent in human creations and human reasoning. One way Mabuchi characterizes this quality of Confucian thought is by how it reduces the fluidity of natural phenomena to a set of rigid categories. He writes, "Just as in the progression of the seasons, spring gradually becomes mild and summer likewise gradually turns hot, the workings of Heaven-and-Earth are gradual and smooth. If it were to be as the Chinese say, on the first day of spring it should suddenly become warm and on the first day of summer immediately turn hot."[22] He also depicts this kind of reasoning as sapping the world of vitality: "To try to define things unequivocally in terms of principle is to treat them as dead objects. It is the things that occur naturally (*onozukara*), in accordance with Heaven-and-Earth, that are alive and active" (pp. 377–78).

He argues that the vastness of Heaven-and-Earth makes it unfathomable by the human intellect, and attributes the spread of Confucianism in Japan to its seductive promise of an easily comprehensible worldview: "The learning of China is from the beginning something created by humans on the basis of their own hearts, so it is fabricated with sharp, square angles and is easy to grasp. The Ancient Way (*inishie no michi*) of our Imperial Land is round and smooth in accordance with Heaven-and-Earth, and it cannot easily be described exhaustively with the meanings and words of humans, so it is difficult for people of later times to understand it" (p. 384). He is critical of the human tendency to try to understand things through reasoning, arguing that this alienates people from the spontaneous workings of nature: "In China they place great value on humans as the loftiest of all things, but in my opinion humans should be considered the worst of all things. Just as Heaven-and-Earth, and the sun and moon, continue on unchanged, birds, beasts, fish, plants, and trees all remain as they were in the past. Humans, however, with their half-baked understanding of things, pursue their own reasoning. As a result, various wicked intentions arise between people, and the world becomes disordered" (p. 379). Mabuchi's arguments show similarities to Daoist critiques of Confucianism, and despite his antipathy toward things Chinese, he acknowledges the general validity of Daoist ideas when he writes, "Laozi's saying that one should simply act in keeping with Heaven-and-Earth surely accords better with the Way of the world" (p. 382). Mabuchi's description of how Heaven-and-Earth exceeds the powers of human reasoning is similar to Sorai's view that Heaven is unknowable, a view that represented a denial of Zhu Xi's equation of Heaven with principle. Sorai and Mabuchi have very different attitudes, though, toward how such an unknowable realm should connect with the human world; while Sorai sees the sages as having used Heaven's authority to create the human cultural institutions of the Way, Mabuchi rejects such human culture, instead seeking an immediate communion of humans with Heaven-and-Earth through the abandonment of rational modes of thinking. Even though Sorai and many other Tokugawa Confucians shared Mabuchi's misgivings about Song Confucianism, Mabuchi saw Song Confucianism not as a departure from the authentic Confucian tradition, but instead merely as the deepening of an overreaching of human reason that was already present in earlier forms of Confucianism, making "the already extremely narrow Confucian Way even narrower" (p. 382).

The specific Tokugawa Confucian whom Mabuchi targets most directly is Dazai Shundai. *Kokuikō* is made up of a series of answers to questions from an imaginary interlocutor, and many of the questions represent ideas put forth in Shundai's *Bendōsho* (A Treatise on the Way, 1735). One of Shundai's most controversial claims in *Bendōsho* is that Japan was originally a primitive and barbaric country, and that it was only rescued from this state when "the Way of the Chinese sages came to be practiced in this country, and in all things in the realm they learned from China. From that point on people in this country knew ritual and rightness, became aware of the Way of human ethics, and did not commit the acts of beasts."[23] Shundai gives a prominent position to the role of Prince Shōtoku (Shōtoku Taishi) (574–622) in this process, describing his activities as analogous to the acts of cultural creation carried out by the sage kings of ancient China: "He established court offices and regulated dress, promoted ritual and music, governed the country and led the people, and carried out a civilizing transformation in the realm. The achievements of Umayato [Shōtoku] in our country can be considered acts of creation by a sage" (p. 204).

One of Shundai's examples of what Japan gained from China is moral values: "Proof that there was originally no Way in Japan can be seen in the fact that there are no native Japanese readings (*wakun*) for the Chinese characters 'humaneness,' 'rightness,' 'ritual,' 'music,' 'filial piety,' and 'brotherly obedience'" (pp. 223–24). In *Kokuikō* Mabuchi responds, "A certain person scorned our country, saying, 'In ancient times humaneness, rightness, ritual propriety, and wisdom did not exist in our country, so there were no Japanese words for them.' This is an immature argument. In China they established these five virtues, and declared that anything that diverged from these was wicked. These five virtues exist naturally in the world, though, just like the four seasons" (p. 383).[24] He goes on to say that the creation of names for virtues actually backfires, arguing, "Things end up becoming constrained because humans . . . create particular names such as humaneness, rightness, ritual propriety, and wisdom. It is better to do without such names and just go along with the heart of Heaven-and-Earth" (p. 384).

Mabuchi argues that the ancient Japanese acted in accordance with Heaven-and-Earth, and thus were able to achieve a kind of natural morality, even without elaborate moral teachings. The quality of the ancient Japanese that made this possible, he maintains, is that they were "straightforward" (*naoshi*), but he is careful to explain that straightforwardness is not an absolute moral perfection. Instead, he sees it as defined by a complete transparency, in which people are exactly what they seem to be: "When people are straightforward, occasionally there are those who do bad things or want to seize power, but because these desires arise out of a straightforward heart, they are not concealed. Because they are not concealed, they are quickly stamped out and do not result in any serious disturbance" (p. 386). He sees this transparency as having been obscured in Japan by the introduction of Confucianism, after which "on the surface everything became elegant, [while] there came to be many people with wicked hearts" (p. 377).

Another example Mabuchi gives of the harm caused by Confucian ideals is the idea that rulers should be chosen based on their virtue, a virtue determined by human judgment. He argues that this idea, while superficially attractive, is in fact responsible for Confucianism's failure to provide a lasting basis for government in China. Going back to the earliest Chinese sage kings, he criticizes how Yao passed on the throne not to his own son, but instead to Shun, whom Yao selected for his virtue. He sees this as having set a dangerous precedent by making the throne into something to be contested, rather than being determined through a fixed and stable hereditary succession. He goes on to note how every Chinese dynasty eventually descended into chaos, and surveying the pantheon of Chinese sage rulers, he finds flaws even in such revered figures as the Duke of Zhou, whom he depicts as a ruthless seeker of power. He concludes that in China, "the world was disordered in every generation and was never governed well" (p. 376). He writes that in contrast to the political disorder of China, Japan "was originally governed well in accordance with the heart of Heaven-and-Earth" (p. 377). He maintains that after the introduction of Confucianism, though, Japan began to experience various political disturbances, leading him to assert that Confucianism "has not only brought about disorder in China, but has also done the same in this country" (p. 377).

Mabuchi discusses not only the proper basis for choosing rulers, but also how to make people follow them. He argues that rulers who lead simple lives inspire reverence, and influence the ruled as well to have few desires, a line of reasoning that again echoes certain Daoist ideas.[25] Rulers who flaunt their wealth and status, though, give rise to envy among their subjects, which inspires rebellious sentiments. He presents an idealized image of the emperors of ancient Japan, writing that "the emperor's dwelling had a shingled roof and earthen walls, and he went out hunting with a bow and arrow, wearing mulberry fiber and hempen clothes" (p. 385). This is in contrast to

China, where "those in high positions make a display of their power and status" (p. 385), a tendency that he claims spread in Japan with the introduction of Chinese court practices in the Nara period, precipitating political strife and corrupting the original good government of the emperors.

Despite his praise for ancient imperial rule, his discussions of government in the Japan of his own day focus not on any form of imperial restoration, but on rule by the warrior class. He is quite blunt about the origins of the Tokugawa ruling class, pointing out that people's current rank is a function of how successful they were at killing during the period of warfare that preceded the Tokugawa peace. He values warrior rule, though, writing, "As a means of showing authority, nothing surpasses the Way of the warrior (*mononofu no michi*) " (p. 385).[26] He describes this not as the ostentatious display of wealth and status that he decries as a Chinese trait, but as a kind of upright martial valor through which warriors inspire both gratitude and fear in those they govern. The Way of the warrior does not rely on discursive teachings that instruct people in right and wrong, as "however reasonable people may find this, unless there is some promise of return, such teachings will not penetrate to the depths of their hearts and draw them in" (p. 391). Earlier we saw how Mabuchi distinguishes between rationalistic Confucian morality and the Japanese ethic of "straightforwardness," and he applies this distinction to his discussion of warrior rule as well, arguing, "Being straightforward, the true Way of the warrior (*bu no michi*) is not lackadaisical or selfish, so it allows one to govern both house and realm effortlessly" (p. 391). This warrior government is different from the imperial rule that he idealizes in his discussions of ancient Japan, but we can see an overlap in the qualities of honesty and directness that he attributes to both forms of government. His praise of warrior rule does not mean that he sees the contemporary political situation as ideal, as at the end of *Kokuikō* he discusses the need for reform. He argues that "the multitudes are governed according to the heart of the ruler" (p. 392), and all that people can do is hope for the emergence of a good ruler, after which, he optimistically predicts, "all the world would become straightforward within the space of ten or twenty years" (p. 393).

The main objects of Mabuchi's scholarship were ancient Japanese language and literature, and in *Kokuikō* he connects these topics to the harmonious society of ancient Japan and its corruption by foreign influences. The contrast he draws between the duplicity of Chinese civilization and the original straightforwardness of Japan is mirrored, for example, in how he contrasts Chinese characters with Japanese phonetic writing. One problem he points out with Chinese characters is simply that there are so many of them, making them unnecessarily burdensome, and he notes that China is the only country that uses such a system, while India and Holland use phonetic writing systems. He then describes the adoption of Chinese writing in Japan through a narrative of infiltration and corruption, in which Chinese characters were first used only for their phonetic value, serving as a transparent medium to represent the existing Japanese language, but eventually came to change the language itself from the inside, a process he likens to political usurpation: "[At first] the words were the masters and the characters were the servants, so people used characters as they saw fit. Later, though, it was as if the words, which had been the masters, lost their position and were replaced by the characters that had been the servants" (p. 381).[27] He relates this process to his earlier discussion of China's political instability, commenting, "Such a development shows the influence of the wicked Chinese custom of lowly people becoming the ruler" (p. 381). Here we can see how Mabuchi discusses language and politics through a common discourse, and we will turn next to how poetry is incorporated into this discourse as well.

POETRY AND THE RECOVERY OF THE STRAIGHTFORWARD HEART

In his discussions of poetry in his later writings, Mabuchi continues to argue for many of the functions of poetry that he had brought up in his contributions to the *Kokka hachiron* debate two decades earlier, but develops these in new directions. For example, in *Kokuikō* he presents poetry as offering an understanding of society useful to rulers, commenting that "when one understands poetry, one will also naturally understand the causes of peace and disorder" (p. 377). He acknowledges the overlap of this with Confucian theories of poetry when he goes on to say, "It must have been for this reason that even Confucius did not discard the *Odes*, but made it first among the books" (p. 377). This idea of poetry as providing a special kind of knowledge about society bears some resemblance to the idea, which he had expressed in the *Kokka hachiron* debate, that poetry allows rulers to understand the emotions of the ruled, and thus govern them properly.

Another role for poetry Mabuchi had presented in the *Kokka hachiron* debate was its ability to regulate people's emotions. He continues this idea in his later writings, describing in *Kokuikō* how poetry promotes a gentle, magnanimous disposition that facilitates proper interpersonal relationships: "The human heart is selfish, so people quarrel with others and judge things on the basis of reasoning (*kotowari*), but when they possess the spirit of poetry, they go beyond reasoning and employ gentleness, so the world is governed well and people are at peace" (pp. 391–92). He depicts the self-cultivation achieved through poetry not only as a moderation of the emotions, but also in terms of achieving the ideal of "straightforwardness." He begins *Ka'ikō* by declaring:

> In ancient times, people's hearts were direct and straightforward. Because their hearts were direct, their actions were few, and because there were few things, the words they spoke were also few. When feelings arose in their hearts they would put them into words and sing, and they called this "poetry" (*uta*).[28] When they sang they did so directly and with a single heart. Their words were in straightforward ordinary language, so they flowed and were rhythmical without any conscious effort to make them so.[29]

The pristine simplicity of ancient poetry, in which things were stated exactly as they were, was then destroyed by the introduction of foreign thought:

> But then the ideas and words of China and India were blended together and introduced to our country, where they mixed in with our own ideas and words. Things became complex, so the hearts of those here who used to be straightforward were blown by a wind from the shadows and turned wicked. Their words became disordered like dust on the road, and grew innumerably diverse. Thus in the most recent times the feelings and words of poetry have come to differ from ordinary feelings and words. In poetry people distort the proper heart, and seek out words to express such a distorted heart.[30]

Here again we see the idea of Chinese thought as introducing a duplicity that sullies an original Japanese honesty and transparency. He also describes the corruption of poetry in gendered terms, as a shift from the "manly" (*masurao*) to the "feminine" (*taoyame*) style.[31] Mabuchi offers hope to poets of his own day, though, by arguing that people can recover the straightforward heart by composing in the style of the *Man'yōshū*: "Because people of today are in their essence the same as people of the past, when they carry out such practice their hearts become polished mirrors."[32]

A new element we see in Mabuchi's later discussions of poetry is his argument that the study of poetry provides us with the tools to investigate the Japanese past. In *Kokuikō* he writes, "Through ancient poetry we come to know the ancient meanings and words, and through these we can then know the state of the world in ancient times. From knowing the conditions of ancient times, we can go back further and consider matters of the

Age of the Gods."[33] He contrasts this method of knowing, which relies on inhabiting linguistic and cultural worlds, with the theoretical knowledge of Confucians (especially followers of Song Confucianism), who try to use their individual powers of reasoning to "construct theories about everything and give things deep meaning."[34] He specifically targets those, like Yamazaki Ansai, who used the Song Confucian categories of principle (Ch. *li*, Jp. *ri*) and material force (Ch. *qi*, Jp. *ki*) to explain the *Nihon shoki* and other texts from ancient Japan.[35] Mabuchi criticizes this interpretive methodology for how it "explains [matters of the Age of the Gods] as if they could be determined exhaustively by the human heart."[36] So while on one level poetry helps people understand ancient texts by providing them with the necessary linguistic knowledge about ancient Japanese, on a deeper level poetry cultivates in them the proper hermeneutic stance, one in which they open themselves up to entering the mindset of the ancient Japanese, rather than judging things from within the confines of their subjective prejudices, which have been shaped by the degraded age they live in.

The ultimate source of the value of ancient Japanese poetry for Mabuchi is that it connects people to the governing forces of nature. He maintains the sounds of the Japanese language are the "natural fifty sounds of Heaven-and-Earth,"[37] and that the rhythm of Japanese poetry is the "natural rhythm (*shirabe*) of Heaven-and-Earth."[38] Moreover, he emphasizes that the rhythm of Japanese poetry is something that emerges specifically when people sing, opening *Niimanabi* by declaring, "In ancient poetry it is rhythm that is primary, and this is because it is sung."[39] As we have seen in the "Great Preface" and elsewhere, the idea that the sung character of poetry is a product of its emotional authenticity is an idea with a long history in Confucian discourse on poetry. These Confucian theories, however, see this song as needing to be integrated into either a metaphysical system (in the case of Zhu Xi) or a broader structure of cultural value (in the case of the Mao tradition and the Sorai school) in order for it to play a normative function. Shundai, the target of Mabuchi's harshest criticisms, is deeply suspicious of the unstructured and vulgar character of natural song, contrasting it with the correctness of the music of the sages. For Mabuchi, though, it is through the spontaneous act of singing itself that people gain access to and reproduce the normative forces of Heaven-and-Earth. Song not only transparently expresses feelings, then, but also unites the singer with a universal natural order, an order that is in turn reflected in the harmonious social relationships that the transparent communication of feelings makes possible.

SITUATING MABUCHI'S ANCIENT WAY THOUGHT

Mabuchi produced his later writings at a time when philosophies that seriously challenged the legitimacy of Tokugawa rule were beginning to emerge. The most radical of these was the utopian agrarianism of Andō Shōeki (1703?–1762?), who was active in the Tōhoku region and directed himself toward a rural audience. Shōeki shared Mabuchi's view that people originally lived in peace and harmony, and that this natural state was disrupted by the political institutions and culture created by the Chinese sages, a process that Shōeki describes as a movement from the "living truth" (kasshin) of nature to the humanly created "world of law" (hōsei). Shōeki's idealization of nature over culture is similar to Mabuchi's Ancient Way thought, but Shōeki goes a step further in that he points to the emergence of economic inequalities as a key element of the culture of the sages. In their natural state, Shōeki argues, humans all cultivated the land, and there were "no divisions of high and low, noble and base, or rich and poor."[40] He then describes how the exploitative economic relations of feudalism emerged as part of the larger matrix of cultural institutions promoted by the sages: "[The sages] lived idly without engaging in cultivation of the land. They stole and greedily devoured the products of the right cultivation of the Way of natural processes and the Way of humanity. . . . They established the distinctions between the king and the common people and the high and the low. They also established the five relationships, the four classes, and systems of governing through rewards and punishments. In their arrogance they placed themselves above others, making those below envy them."[41] He proposed a radical restructuring of society to reverse the effects of the creations of the sages, arguing that all people should be made to engage in the labor of cultivating grains, the use of currency should be eliminated, and such luxuries as alcohol, tobacco, meat-eating, and artistic entertainments should be banned.

While Shōeki presented his ideas from the perspective of the ruled, Yamagata Daini (1725–1767) approached the weaknesses of the Tokugawa regime from the side of the rulers. Born into a samurai family, Daini served in the bakufu garrison in Kōfu, but lost his post in 1751 because he was suspected of aiding the escape of his brother, who had committed a murder. In 1754 he was hired by Ōoka Tadamitsu (1709–1760), junior councilor of the shogun Tokugawa Ieshige (1711–1761, r. 1745–1760), for whom he served as a physician and scholar until 1760.[42] It was during this period that Daini wrote Ryūshi shinron (Master Ryū's New Thesis, 1759), his most important treatise on government. In this work, Daini describes the need for government in terms similar to Sorai, and is particularly close to Shundai in his emphasis on the brutal and chaotic state of humans prior to their transformation through proper cultural institutions. Writing of humans in the state of nature, Daini comments that "lacking distinctions of noble and base, they scramble for food and give free rein to their desires, and as such are no different from beasts."[43] To give order to human society, "rituals were instituted to create distinctions in rank, duties were decreed to establish official posts, and clothing was made so there would be gradations in court caps and dress; those who created all these are called 'sages'" (p. 396). Like Shundai, Daini praises the accomplishments of Prince Shōtoku, but Daini differs from Sorai and Shundai in attributing sagely rule to the Japanese imperial line from the earliest times, even before the importation of Chinese teachings, such as when he comments that "[Emperor Jinmu's] radiant virtue illuminated the four quarters for over a thousand years." (p. 392). He writes that after the establishment of the military government of the Kamakura shogunate in the late twelfth century, though, "the ancient kings' ritual and music were cast aside" (p. 392), and applies the same judgment to the military government of the Tokugawa period, lamenting the loss of the proper ritual and music of sagely government. He is similar to Mabuchi, then, in idealizing the government of the ancient Japanese emperors, but the similarity stops there, as he values this government for achieving the kind of cultural transformation of the realm that is central to Sorai's conception of sagely government.

Daini was writing at a time of increased government concern over social unrest, and suspicions of rebellious intent eventually led to his downfall. One manifestation of anti-bakufu sentiment was a growth of interest in imperial restoration. In the 1750s, Takenouchi Shikibu (1712–1767) taught in his school in Kyoto that the emperor should have precedence over the shogun, and he was banished from Kyoto in 1758 when it came to light that some younger court nobles had been inspired by his teachings to start training in the military arts, with the presumed aim of rebelling against the bakufu.[44] Another significant incident was the so-called "post-horse rebellion" (tenma sōdō) of 1764, which stemmed from dissatisfaction with the increased demands placed on "assisting villages" (sukegō), villages along major highways that were required to provide porters and horses for travelers as a form of corvée duty. The post-horse rebellion arose from requirements for sukegō duty in relation to a shogunal pilgrimage to Nikko, and the protest eventually grew to include around two hundred thousand people. The protesters marched on Edo, and were only stopped when the bakufu agreed to rescind the requirements for extra *sukegō* duty. This did not put a stop to the disturbance, though, as the assembled mob proceeded to attack various other perceived enemies, such as wealthy peasants and moneylenders.[45] Daini was not directly involved in the post-horse rebellion, but he was indirectly tied to it by the fact that a number of his students were vassals of Obata domain, where it had occurred. There were massive bakufu crackdowns in the wake of the incident, and soon after, in 1766, accusations of plotting rebellion were leveled against Daini and a student of his, who was also a disciple of Shikibu. They were found innocent of the original charges brought against them, but were found guilty of discussing strategies for attacking shogunal castles, leading to death sentences for both of them.[46]

Mabuchi's contemporaries positioned themselves in relation to the kind of ideal of sagely rule that had been promoted by Sorai, and by critiquing this view of the sages—in Shōeki's case by denying the legitimacy of the sages entirely, and in Daini's case by claiming that the emperors were the true bearers of sagely rule in Japan—envisioned alternatives to the Tokugawa system. Sorai too had been critical of many aspects of the Tokugawa system, but he presented his proposals for reform less as challenges to the Tokugawa regime itself than as ways for this regime to more perfectly realize its true essence, which he equated with the feudal government of the sages of ancient China. Mabuchi's critique of Sorai's Way of the sages was, like Shōeki's, based on a utopian ideal of a society rooted in the processes of nature, but unlike Shōeki he did not deny the legitimacy of social hierarchy, instead simply arguing over its proper basis, claiming that the Confucian virtues, most notably the proper relationship between ruler and ruled, had existed naturally in ancient Japan. In his idealization of ancient imperial rule Mabuchi overlapped with Daini, but he did not present the kind of harsh criticism of the Tokugawa regime that Daini had, instead finding a way to define warrior rule as a manifestation of the "straightforwardness" that he idealized in ancient Japan. Mabuchi's philosophy of the Ancient Way, then, while growing out of a similar sense of dissatisfaction with the contemporary world that had motivated figures like Shōeki and Daini, represented a comparatively tame political vision when compared with these other thinkers.

Mabuchi as Poet

Mabuchi produced waka throughout his adult life, and his career as a poet was closely tied to his participation in scholarly and literary circles whose activities included both public lectures on the Japanese classics and the composition of waka in a group setting. While still in Hamamatsu, Mabuchi was a regular participant in monthly waka gatherings that Sugiura Kuniakira began hosting in 1720, and after moving to Kyoto in 1733, he participated in similar events held by Azumamaro.[47] In Edo, Mabuchi himself began holding waka gatherings in 1740, shortly after starting a study group on the *Tale of Genji*.[48] Such waka gatherings were a regular feature of Mabuchi's life in Edo, and in addition to hosting them himself, he attended those held by other prominent scholarly and literary figures, such as Arimaro and Munetake. Looking at the various groups within which Mabuchi composed waka, we can see continuity not only in the association that many of his fellow poets shared with Azumamaro, but also in the basic form of the social space in which waka was composed, in which groups of disciples gathered regularly to compose poetry at the private home of a teacher or other respected figure. The composition of waka for these figures went hand in hand with their study of classical Japanese literary texts, and waka gatherings were also often convened to mark significant events, such as to celebrate the construction of a new house or mourn the passing of a friend. Mabuchi also presented waka in the context of a poetic travel diary with his *Okabe no nikki*, an account of a trip he took from Edo to Hamamatsu and back in 1740 that combines prose sections discussing the famous places he visited with thirty-three tanka and chōka.[49] After his death Mabuchi's waka were published by his disciples in a number of anthologies. In 1790 Ueda Akinari (1734–1809) arranged for the publication of two such anthologies, *Agatai no kashū*, edited earlier by Katō Umaki (1721–1777), and *Agatai no shūi*, edited by Akinari himself. Another important anthology was *Kamo-ō kashū*, published in 1806 and edited by Katō Chikage and Murata Harumi.

Azumamaro showed a strong scholarly interest in ancient Japanese texts, and like such earlier figures as Keichū and Toda Mosui produced a number of studies of the *Man'yōshū*. His own poetry, though, drew on the waka of the Heian period and later, and Mabuchi initially followed him in this. Mabuchi's poetry took a major turn, though, after he began his employment with Munetake in 1746. From this time on he began to emulate the style of the *Man'yōshū* in much of his poetry, a tendency shared by Munetake, who, as we saw earlier, had promoted the *Man'yōshū* as an ideal in his contributions to the *Kokka hachiron* debate. While earlier Tokugawa figures had pioneered the use of new methodologies in their scholarly commentaries on the *Man'yōshū*, then, Mabuchi was revolutionary in the extent to which he made the *Man'yōshū* into a model for his actual poetic compositions. Because it is Mabuchi's poetry from 1746 on that played the greatest role in his reputation as a poet and his impact on later Tokugawa poets, this is the poetry of his that I will focus on here.[50]

One example of a poem from Mabuchi's period of employment with Munetake is "Arashi" (The Storm), composed in 1752:

Shinano naru / Suga no arano o / tobu washi no
tsubasa mo tawa ni / fuku arashi kana

[The raging storm strains even the wings of the eagle that soars over the rugged moor of Suga in Shinano][51]

The exclamatory ending *kana* is characteristic of poetry of the *Kokinshū* and later, but the strong images of the raging storm, the soaring eagle, and the rugged moor combine to create the kind of "manly" style that Mabuchi idealized in the *Man'yōshū*, and found lacking in later poetry. Also, the poem references a specific *Man'yōshū* poem from the "Azuma uta" section, which makes up book 14 of the anthology: "When I hear the cuckoo cry on the rugged moor of Suga in Shinano, I feel the passage of time."[52]

Some of Mabuchi's best-known poems from his later years are a sequence of five poems he composed at a moon-viewing party held on 1764.9.13 to celebrate his moving to a new house. The final poem of the sequence is:

niodori no / Katsushika wase no / niishibori
kumitsutsu oreba / tsuki katabukinu

[While drinking the freshly brewed sake, made from the early rice of Katsushika of the grebe, the moon has set]

Niodori (grebe) is a *makurakotoba* used with Katsushika (located in Shimōsa province), a connection based on how the grebe dives (*kazuku*). Mabuchi borrows specifically from a poem in the "Azuma uta" section of the *Man'yōshū*: "Though it is the night for making offerings of the early rice of Katsushika of the grebe, I will not keep you, my poor love, standing outside."[53] The final line is taken from another *Man'yōshū* poem: "On the eastern plain, the light of dawn becomes visible; looking back, the moon has set."[54]

An important aspect of Mabuchi's promotion of the *Man'yōshū* style was his revival of the chōka form, such as in the poem "Yoshino no hana o mite

yomeru" (Composed on Viewing the Blossoms in Yoshino), from a trip he
took to Yoshino in 1763:

	kotosaegu	Even in babbling
	hito no kuni ni mo	foreign countries
	kikoekozu	it is unheard of.
	waga mikado ni mo	Even in our emperor's realm
5	taguinaki	it is without parallel.
	Yoshino takane no	When the cherry blossoms
	sakurabana	of the high peak of Yoshino
	saki no sakari wa	are in full bloom,
	uma nabete	taking a horse
10	tōku mo misake	and gazing at it from afar,
	tsue tsukite	aided by a walking stick,
	mine ni mo nobori	climbing up to the peak,
	miru hito no	the one who sees it
	katari ni sureba	speaks of it,
15	kiku hito no	so the one who hears of it
	ii mo tsugaite	passes on word of it.
	amagumo no	To the edge of the heavenly clouds
	mukabusu kiwami	that stretch out in the distance,
	taniguku no	even as far as
20	sawataru kagiri	the toad ranges,
	medenu hito	there were none who
	koinu hito shimo	did not love
	nakarikeri	or yearn.
	shika wa aredomo	And yet
25	yo no naka ni	old men
	sakashira o su to	within the world
	hokoraeru	who pride themselves
	okina ga tomo wa	on their cleverness,
	yaoyorozu	always reject
30	yorozu no kotora	all the
	kikishi yori	myriad things,
	mi no otoru zo to	going on and on about
	iizurai	how they suffer in comparison
	arinami suru o	to what they have heard.
35	mine mireba	But upon seeing the peak,
	yae shirakumo ka	and seeing the eight-fold white clouds
	tani mireba	or the valley,
	ōyuki furu to	it looks like a great snowfall.

	ametsuchi ni	Within Heaven-and-Earth,
40	kokoro odoroki	hearts are astonished;
	yo no naka ni	within the world,
	koto mo taetsutsu	words cannot do it justice.
	yuku ushi no	The old man,
	osoki okina ga	plodding like a walking cow,
45	utsuyū no	with a heart that is hemmed in,
	sakarishi kokoro	like hollow-spun silk,
	kui mo kuitaru	piles regret upon regret.

Lines 17–20 borrow from a chōka in the *Man'yōshū* by Yamanoue no Okura (660–733?): "On earth, our great lord rules. Beneath this shining sun and moon, to the edge of the heavenly clouds that stretch out in the distance, even as far as the toad ranges, is the great land he rules over."[55] Lines 33–34 borrow from another *Man'yōshū* poem, which contains the lines "*iizurai / arinami suredo*" ("although they go on and on, and go on rejecting").[56] Mabuchi uses the *makurakotoba* "*kotosaegu*" ("babbling"), usually attached to such names of foreign countries as "*Kara*" and "*Kudara*," in line 1, and "*utsuyū no*" ("like hollow-spun silk"), typically used with phrases indicating narrowness or confinement, in line 45. He also shows his linguistic inventiveness with the phrase "*yuku ushi no*" ("like a walking cow"), in line 43, which he uses much like a *makurakotoba*. Although this is not an established *makurakotoba*, it is similar to such *makurakotoba* as "*yuku kawa no*" ("like a rushing river") and "*yuku tori no*" ("like flocking birds").[57] On one level, this chōka is a kind of linguistic exercise, demonstrating Mabuchi's virtuosity in ancient Japanese. It also communicates his philosophy of the Ancient Way, criticizing those who are narrow-minded and incapable of opening up their hearts to aesthetic wonder. The poem contains a strong element of nativist pride, which is continued in the envoy:

Morokoshi no / hito ni misebaya / Miyoshino no
Yoshino no yama no / yamazakurabana

[I'd like to show it to people from China—the mountain cherry blossoms of Mount Yoshino in fair Yoshino]

Yoshino was the most famous place for viewing mountain cherry blossoms, and here the blossoms are presented as a supreme symbol of Japan's beauty, which, as Mabuchi describes in the opening lines of the chōka, is "unheard of in babbling foreign countries."

An extreme example of Mabuchi's archaism is his "Umazake no uta" (Poem on Delicious Sake):

umara ni oyarafuru kaneya / hitotsuki futatsuki
eraera ni tanasoko uchiaguru kaneya / mitsuki yotsuki
koto naoshi kokoro naoshi mo yo / itsutsuki mutsuki
ama tarashi kuni tarasu mo yo / nanatsuki yatsuki

[Drinking it tastily—one cup, two cups
Laughing and clapping hands—three cups, four cups
Words and heart are straightforward—five cups, six cups
Heavenly and earthly realms are at ease—seven cups, eight cups]

The praise of drinking in this poem overlaps thematically with the series of poems on drinking by Ōtomo no Tabito (665–731) in the *Man'yōshū* (book 3, poems 338–50). Mabuchi evokes the even earlier forms of verse of the *Kojiki* and *Nihon shoki*, though, such as by not always adhering to the standard 5/7 meter that developed in later poetry. He alludes specifically to a song attributed to Emperor Kenzō (r. 485–487) in the *Nihon shoki*, which contains the lines, "We have brewed sake. / With gusto let us drink it. . . . To the clear ring of hand-palms / Ye will revel."[58] Also, the uncomplicated sentiments and repetitive phrasing reinforce the ideal of artlessness associated with Mabuchi's notion of being "straightforward."

Mabuchi's poetry at times provides a rather direct expression of certain ideas from his philosophy of the Ancient Way. More significantly, though, his poetry represents an attempt to reproduce the world of ancient Japan on an aesthetic and linguistic level, and to bring it to life again in his contemporary world. The fact that he saw it as important to actually compose poetry in the *Man'yōshū* style, rather than just make the *Man'yōshū* into an object for scholarly exegesis, reflects his idea that the recovery of the Way is a form of active self-cultivation in which, through continued effort and practice, we recover the original straightforward heart. His neoclassical style of composition, which not only drew upon poetic forms and vocabulary from earlier poetry, but at times even involved lifting entire sections out of other poems, is very similar to what we saw earlier in Sorai's and Nankaku's poetry. This imitativeness was rooted in a belief that the spirit of ancient Japan was connected to specific literary and linguistic forms that people of the present must reconnect with in order to create a harmonious society. If people followed their own personal inclinations in composing poetry, without relying on forms inherited from the past, they would remain mired in the degraded present. It was only by copying the forms of ancient language and literature, Mabuchi believed, and allowing them to permeate and transform one's heart, that it was possible to recover the Ancient Way and reenact it in the present.

Conclusion

Mabuchi shared many of Sorai's views on the role of poetry, valuing it not only as a manifestation of human emotions, but also as a way to achieve the knowledge of ancient language needed to decipher ancient texts, which both Mabuchi and Sorai saw as the source of the political norms necessary to bring order to Tokugawa society. Also like Sorai, Mabuchi stressed the need for scholars to compose poetry themselves, and strove to create poems that resembled his idealized poetic models, liberally borrowing words and phrases from source poems.

One way Mabuchi differed from Sorai and his followers was in looking to ancient Japan, rather than ancient China, as his source of literary and political norms. Moreover, he rejected the artifice of humanly created culture, which Sorai had seen as necessary in order to raise people up from their natural state and unite them in a harmonious society. He instead idealized an immediate communion with the primal simplicity of nature, claiming that the introduction of the kinds of human cultural constructs promoted by Confucians like Sorai only served to generate social discord. He was deeply committed to specific cultural forms derived from ancient Japan, but he insisted that these were in fact manifestations of nature, in contrast to the artificiality of both Chinese culture and later Japanese culture. Many Confucians too, of course, had seen the Way as existing in nature, and Mabuchi's ideal of the self as a "polished mirror" that is united with Heaven-and-Earth has similarities with Zhu Xi's vision of self-cultivation, the goal of which is a purified original nature that perfectly manifests the universal principle of the cosmos. Mabuchi differs from Zhu Xi, though, in that he refuses to define the purified heart in terms of a set of defined moral values, leaving him closer, as he himself acknowledges, to a Daoist ideal of self-cultivation.

Another way of thinking about the differences between Mabuchi and Sorai is in terms of how they conceived of the relationship of the individual to the Way. Sorai criticized Zhu Xi for defining the Confucian Way as something that could be attained on the level of the individual, and stressed that the Way of the sages was a method for coordinating the social interactions of people with diverse inborn characteristics, uniting them into a social whole without sacrificing their particular individual natures. In Chapter 4 we saw how this vision of the Way began to break down among Sorai's students, as they questioned the ability to maintain both individual authenticity and a holistic vision of the culture of the sages. For Mabuchi, though, the purification of the individual heart through poetry allows for perfect sincerity, while at the same time uniting the individual with the universality of Heaven-and-Earth. Moreover, social harmony comes not from the active engagement of individuals with people different from themselves, but from the common cultivation of a single straightforward heart. Mabuchi, then, shows a certain backing off from the interest in active social and political engagement that had dominated the philosophy of not only Sorai, but also Jinsai. While he espoused the superiority of Japanese imperial rule, for example, he showed no interest in actually pursuing any kind of imperial restoration. In the next chapter we will see how Mabuchi's follower Motoori Norinaga presented a more complex vision of poetic authenticity, one that revealed more concern than Mabuchi had with the difficulties of connecting to other people, while still ultimately finding a way to use Japanese culture, more specifically Japanese poetry, to eliminate interpersonal conflicts.

Motoori Norinaga and the Cultural Construction of Japan

Motoori Norinaga is one of the most influential as well as most controversial figures in Japanese literary and intellectual history. His textual commentaries established paradigms for understanding the Japanese classics that continue to exercise a role in interpretations of these texts today, and his linguistics treatises were instrumental in systematizing the study of Japanese grammar. At the same time, his proclamations on the superiority of Japan to all other countries and his advocacy of total obedience to the Shinto gods and Japanese emperors can make him appear more like an extremist ideologue than a careful scholar. As discussed in the Introduction, many have found a more humanistic side to Norinaga in his writings on waka and monogatari, in which he rejects a moral approach to literature in favor of an emphasis on human emotionality. In this chapter, though, I argue that his writings on literature, while less blatantly ideological than his works on Shinto and the emperor, nevertheless share with them certain ideas about how cultural forms inherited from the Japanese past should structure and mediate interpersonal relationships in the present.

Norinaga was born into a family of cotton merchants in Matsusaka in Ise Province, a regional city famous for its merchants, who exercised a powerful influence not only locally but also through their branches in the shogunal capital of Edo. When Norinaga was eleven his father died, and when he was nineteen he was sent to be the adopted son of a local family of paper merchants. He found he did not enjoy the work of a merchant, preferring to spend his time composing poetry and reading, and he soon returned to his original family. Norinaga had been sent out for adoption because it was his elder brother who was the designated heir of the family business, but when Norinaga was twenty-two his brother unexpectedly died of illness, thrusting Norinaga into the position of head of the family. His mother recognized, though, that he was not suited to take over the family business, and instead sent him to Kyoto to study to be a doctor.

Norinaga stayed in Kyoto from 1752 to 1757, where he studied not only medicine but also the Chinese and Japanese classics. His Chinese studies teacher Hori Keizan (1688–1757) introduced him to the work of Ogyū Sorai and Keichū, who were to be important influences in the development of Norinaga's own scholarship. Norinaga had enjoyed composing waka since his teens, and while studying in Kyoto he continued to study and compose waka, often in the context of poetry gatherings that were as much social as literary occasions.

After returning to Matsusaka in 1757, Norinaga set up a medical practice where he worked by day, while in the evenings he lectured to audiences, made up mostly of local merchants, on texts such as the eighth-century poetry anthology the *Man'yōshū*, Heian prose writings such as the *Tales of Ise* and *Tale of Genji*, and the *Hyakunin isshu* (Hundred Poems by a Hundred Poets), an anthology compiled in the thirteenth century that was one of the most widely read collections of waka in the Tokugawa period. He produced two major treatises on waka during this time, *Ashiwake obune* (A Small Boat Punting Through the Reeds), written around 1757, and *Isonokami sasamegoto* (Ancient Whisperings), written in 1763.[1] In 1763 he also wrote *Shibun yōryō* (Essentials of the *Tale of Genji*), an analysis of the *Tale of Genji*.

Norinaga soon shifted his focus from Heian literature to the most ancient Japanese texts, a move that owed much to his meeting in 1763 with Kamo no Mabuchi. Mabuchi encouraged Norinaga to work on the *Kojiki* (Records of Ancient Matters), the eighth-century mythohistory that describes the creation of Japan by the gods and the descent of the Japanese imperial line from these same gods. Norinaga made the study of the *Kojiki* his main scholarly pursuit for the rest of his life, and spent thirty-five years on a massive commentary called the *Kojikiden* (Transmission of the *Records of Ancient Matters*), which he finally completed in 1798. Norinaga believed that the *Kojiki* contained the key to understanding and recovering a native Way bestowed by the Japanese gods, which he presented as an alternative to such foreign Ways as Confucianism and Buddhism. He thought that the *Kojiki* had been made obscure by the Chinese characters in which the text had been recorded, and devoted much of his commentary to attempting to uncover the original phonetic text, in pure ancient Japanese, that he saw as lying underneath these Chinese characters.

Norinaga also produced a number of important works on Japanese linguistics, such as *Kotoba no tama no o* (Words on a String of Jewels, 1771), a grammatical study, and *Kanji san'on kō* (Reflections on the Three Modes of Pronouncing Chinese Characters, 1784), a work on phonology. Other important texts of Norinaga's include *Genji monogatari tama no ogushi* (*The Tale of Genji*, A Small Jeweled Comb, 1796), an expansion and revision of the earlier *Shibun yōryō*, and *Uiyamabumi* (First Steps in the Mountains, 1798), a pedagogical essay that puts forth the philosophical principles and habits of scholarship for making the study of the Japanese classics into a lifetime pursuit.[2]

This chapter focuses primarily on Norinaga's theoretical writings on waka. These have received considerable attention from modern scholars, but they were rather marginal to his reputation in his own time, which was rooted more in his interpretation of the *Kojiki* and his studies of the Japanese language. One of his two major poetics treatises, *Isonokami sasamegoto*, was not published until 1816, when the first two volumes of it appeared in a woodblock edition, and the other, *Ashiwake obune*, was not even discovered until 1916.[3] I focus on these early works because of how they develop the discourse on poetry and emotionality described in the previous chapters. I am not claiming to present a comprehensive account of Norinaga's philosophy or his influence within the intellectual world of the late eighteenth century. It should be noted, though, that his interest in waka was by no means limited to his early years, as he was an active waka poet throughout his life, and helped promote waka among non-specialists with his *Kokinshū tōkagami* (A *Kokinshū* Telescope), a vernacular translation of the *Kokinshū* published in 1797. Also, his views of waka overlapped considerably with his framework for interpreting the *Tale of Genji*, which he did present in a work published in his own lifetime, *Genji monogatari tama no ogushi*. Beyond the fact of Norinaga's continued involvement with the composition and interpretation of literary texts, his theoretical writings on poetry are significant for how they outline a vision of Japanese cultural identity that I will contend carried over into his studies of Japan's native Way. While in one sense I am concentrating on a rather narrow aspect of his output, then, I see his early writings on waka not merely as an abandoned direction in his scholarship, but rather as very much of a piece with his later work.

Communicating Emotions through Patterned Language

In the opening section of *Isonokami sasamegoto*, Norinaga defines song (*uta*) according to two basic characteristics: first, it must be based in emotions (*jō*), and second, it must possess "patterning" (*aya*). He argues that song can be produced by any animate being (*ujō no mono*), not just humans, but that only their patterned sounds can properly be considered song; the unpatterned utterances of humans, for example, are merely "ordinary language" (*tada no kotoba*).[4] Inanimate things (*hijō no mono*), in contrast, cannot be said to produce song, even if the sounds that come from them do indeed have patterning. As examples of such inanimate things, he lists not only phenomena of nature, such as wind and water, but also musical instruments, thus drawing a clear line separating song from music (p. 254).

Although Norinaga notes that birds, insects, and other animals can produce song, he is primarily concerned with the song produced by humans, namely poetry, which is defined by the forms of emotionality and patterning particular to humans.[5] In examining the emotional basis of poetry, he argues that humans are at root emotionally weak and fragile, and that to deny this fact is to lose touch with our true human nature. In *Isonokami sasamegoto* he writes, "No matter how intelligent people may be, when we look into the depths of their hearts, they are no different from women and children" (p. 408). In response to the observation that fathers appear stoic upon the death of a child, he notes, "The way that fathers are respectably calm indeed appears manly and splendid, but this is an outward appearance they put on by suppressing their feelings of sadness and forcefully making things seem fine, which they do because they hesitate before the eyes of others, and are ashamed of how they would appear to the world. The way that mothers pay no heed to the eyes of others, drenching themselves with tears, may appear to be womanly and shameful, but it is this that constitutes unadorned, true emotions" (p. 412). For Norinaga, the role of poetry is to express these fragile emotions: "Poetry, unlike other writings, is not something that should posture about everything, saying it should be like this or that. Instead, it should simply be the feelings in the heart just as they are, whether good or bad" (p. 413). He praises Japanese poetry for having remained true to the essential character of poetry as emotional expression, in contrast to Chinese poetry, which has descended into argumentation and didacticism. He writes, "When we look at the three hundred poems of the *Book of Odes*, although the words are Chinese, their spirit is not a bit different from the poetry of our country" (p. 403). In later times, though, Chinese poetry came to be transformed by the character of the Chinese, whose "hearts all revere cleverness, and in all matters make bothersome arguments about people being good or bad" (p. 404).

Norinaga describes the emotionality that gives rise to poetry most famously with the term *mono no aware*.[6] His earliest statement on this idea came in a short piece entitled *Aware ben* (An Explanation of *Aware*), dating from 1758, in which he explains how the terms *aware* and *mono no aware* indicate a form of emotionality that is at the core of waka and monogatari: "The Way of poetry has no significance apart from the single word '*aware*.' All the waka that have been composed from the Age of the Gods down to the present, reaching even to the latest days, can be summed up by the single word '*aware*.' Therefore the only way to inquire into the true meaning of this Way is through the word '*aware*.' Also, when we look into the essence of the *Tales of Ise*, the *Tale of Genji*, and other monogatari, this essence comes down to the single word '*aware*.'"[7] He also draws a connection to Confucian views of poetry, commenting, "When Confucius says, 'The three hundred Odes can be summed up by a single phrase: no crooked thoughts,'[8] this is similar to what I am talking about here."[9] In *Isonokami sasamegoto*, he goes through an extensive list of appearances of *aware* in a variety of Japanese poetry and prose texts, and sums up these examples by commenting, "In this way, the word '*aware*' has had various different usages, but their meaning is all united in how they refer to feeling deep emotions in response to things seen, heard, or done."[10] He presents *aware* as a primal form of emotionality by noting that it derives etymologically from the sound of a sigh, and is similar in this regard to such exclamatory words as *ana*, *aya*, and *aa* (p. 285). Also, he maintains that the later usage of *aware* to refer specifically to sadness is a narrowing of the word's original meaning, which encompassed all types of emotions (p. 284).

Poetry is not just emotional expression for Norinaga, though, but also emotional communication. In *Isonokami sasamegoto*, he describes how whenever people feel deep emotions, this creates a kind of blockage in the heart that can only be relieved by expressing these deep emotions in poetry and having them be understood by another. He describes the indispensability of the listener to the cathartic process of poetic composition as follows:

> Poetry is not just something that we compose when we are unable to bear *mono no aware*, and that naturally relaxes the heart. When we feel *aware* very deeply, just by composing by ourselves our heart cannot be satisfied, so we have a person listen to us and are comforted. When another hears this and feels *aware*, it greatly clears the heart. . . . For example, if a person feels deeply about something that is difficult to keep bottled up in his heart, even if he talks to himself about it in great detail his heart is not cleared, so he tells it to someone else and has them listen, and then his heart is cleared. And if the person who hears agrees with what he says and commiserates, the poet's heart will be cleared even more. . . . Having someone listen is truly the essence of poetry, and is not an accidental aspect of it. (pp. 312–13)

Emotional expression must always be directed toward another, and the listener described here is more than just a passive object at which the poet directs himself; the listener must understand the poet and respond on an emotional level, providing the poet with some confirmation that a successful act of communication has taken place.

Norinaga later goes on to explain that the communication of emotions serves not only to comfort the poet, but also has broader social benefits due to the emotional connections it creates between people. One of these benefits is that poetry allows rulers to understand the emotions of their subjects. In *Isonokami sasamegoto* he describes, in terms very similar to Sorai and Shundai, how those of high status lead sheltered lives, which makes it difficult for them to understand the sufferings ordinary people must endure. This leads rulers to lack empathy for the common people, and to enact unnecessarily harsh and cruel policies. By studying poetry, though, rulers can understand the needs and desires of the common people, giving rise to empathy for the ruled and leading to a more humane form of governance (p. 444). He then argues that poetry can also improve relations among commoners themselves:

> This does not pertain only to those who govern, though. In people's everyday dealings with one another as well, those who do not know *mono no aware* show no considerateness in anything and are often hard-hearted and cruel. Because they have no encounters with various matters, they do not understand them. The rich do not know the hearts of the poor, the young do not know the hearts of the aged, and men do not know the hearts of

women. . . . But when people deeply understand the hearts of others, they naturally act so as not to harm society or other people. This is another benefit of making people know *mono no aware*. (pp. 444–46)

As an example, he explains how children are only unfilial because they fail to understand the emotions of their parents, but when emotions are perfectly communicated between parents and children, unfilial behavior will disappear (p. 445). The communication of emotions gives rise not only to empathy, then, but also to ethical behavior.

The reason Norinaga sees it as necessary that poetic language be "patterned" is, first of all, because it is only with such language that it is possible to fully express emotions. In *Isonokami sasamegoto* he writes, "There are deep emotions that cannot be exhausted with ordinary language, no matter how lengthy and detailed it may be. However, when we give patterning to our words and sing in a drawn-out voice, then due to the patterning of the words and the patterning of the voice, even such depth of emotionality will be manifested" (p. 307). He also relates the need for patterning to the communicative function of poetry. Following the passage quoted earlier on the need for poetry to be directed toward a listener, he continues, "People who do not understand this say that a true poem consists of simply saying what one feels just as it is (*ari no mama*), whether well or poorly, and that the aspect that relates to the listener is not true poetry. Although this seems true as first glance, it fails to understand the true principle of poetry. . . . Because it is important that another hear poetry and feel *aware*, it is the nature of poetry to create patterning in one's words" (p. 313). The distinction between direct, spontaneous expression and crafted language, then, is made not only out of an aesthetic consideration for what constitutes beautiful poetry, but is also connected explicitly to the issue of how to make others understand what we feel.

The "Patterning of Language"

When Norinaga brings up "patterning" as an essential characteristic of song in the opening section of *Isonokami sasamegoto*, he at first simply describes song as having "words that are well ordered and have patterning" (p. 251), without indicating what exact qualities of language this refers to. Elsewhere, though, he is more specific. One way he describes the "patterning" that makes the communication of deep emotions possible is in terms of certain rhetorical techniques commonly used in waka, such as the *makurakotoba* (pillow word, or poetic epithet), which he notes is used "for the purpose of making words patterned and rhythm well ordered" (p. 314), and the *jokotoba* (poetic preface), of which he provides the following love poem from the *Kokinshū* as one of a series of examples:

> Shikishima no / Yamato ni wa aranu / karakoromo
> koro mo hezu shite / au yoshi mogana[11]

> [I long for a way to meet you constantly, as constant as the Chinese robes that do not exist in Japan]

Commenting on this poem and those like it, he writes, "These speak what the heart feels in only two lines, and the remaining three lines are all the patterning of words. There are some who would therefore say that those three lines are superfluous, but through such 'useless' patterning of words, the *aware* of the other two lines is given greater depth" (p. 315). The two lines that he refers to as "speaking what the heart feels" are the final two lines of the original, "I long for a way to meet you constantly." The first three lines then function as a *jokotoba*, or poetic preface, that connects to the phrase "*koro mo hezu shite*" (constantly) and presents an image of something else that is constant. The poem also uses a *makurakotoba*, "*Shikishima no*," to modify "Yamato" (Japan) (I have left the *makurakotoba* untranslated). Such techniques as *makurakotoba* and *jokotoba* have a special power for Norinaga in that even though they add nothing to the semantic message of a poem, they are able to make a poem communicate deep emotions more effectively than even the most exhaustive description of the poet's feelings in ordinary, non-poetic language.

While these techniques are only used in certain poems, a more fundamental aspect of "patterning" for Norinaga is the adherence of poetic language to a specific meter, namely that of alternating lines of five and seven syllables. After bringing up in the first section of *Isonokami sasamegoto* the requirement that the words of poetry be well ordered and have patterning, he opens the next section by further clarifying this point:

> Question: What are you referring to when you speak of "words that are well ordered and have patterning"?
> Answer: I am speaking of when, in singing, the number of words is appropriate, and the words sound appealing and flow unhindered. "Having patterning" is when words are arranged well and not disordered. In both past and present, and in both the elegant (*ga*) and the common (*zoku*), the arrangement of five and seven syllables is appropriate. Therefore both the poetry of

the past and the popular ditties of today are all in patterns of five and seven syllables. This is a wonder of nature. (p. 255)

Here we can see a narrowing of the definition of the patterning of language, from a general idea of being well put together to the specific pattern of alternating phrases of five and seven syllables. This focus on the five/seven meter makes the "patterning" of language rely on adherence to a particular cultural form, in that this meter is that of Japanese forms of song.[12]

For Norinaga, then, certain formal structures connected to Japanese poetic traditions have an a priori validity, and are not merely contingent products of history. This attitude is reflected in his interpretation of the irregular syllable patterns of the most ancient Japanese poetry, much of which did not follow a five/seven meter. This would seem to make it difficult to argue for the transhistorical nature of the five/seven meter, but Norinaga claims that even when these ancient poems are recorded in writing in what appears to be an irregular meter, when they were originally sung the lines were lengthened or shortened to make them conform to the five/seven meter (pp. 255–56). Or, because Norinaga sees the oral song itself as primary, and the written recording of it as secondary, it would perhaps be more accurate to say that when the words were recorded in writing, these words were lengthened or shortened from the original five/seven pattern in which they had been sung. In this way, the five/seven meter ceases to be something arrived at through a long period of refinement and poetic practice, and instead comes to function as a transcendent norm that precedes any historically specific instances of its manifestation. It is a cultural form, but one that is at the same time natural and universal. As we saw earlier, Norinaga links the need for "patterning" in poetic language to his assertion that we cannot just express ourselves as we please and expect to be understood, but must make conscious efforts to reach out to others. He thus suggests that communication (and by extension, the connection between self and other) is something inherently problematic, whose success cannot be taken for granted.[13] In this light, his emphasis on "patterning" as involving certain stable, universal norms of expression can be seen as an attempt to overcome this uncertainty in a way that would not be possible if poets merely relied on their own personal ideas of what constitutes properly ordered language.[14]

The notion of the stabilizing powers of the formal properties of waka is presented more explicitly in Norinaga's description of the ability of waka to preserve the Japanese language in its pure state. He argues that the formal

characteristics of Japanese song, particularly its meter, are unsuited to foreign words, so that as long as one follows this meter there will be no danger
of incorrect foreign sounds infiltrating the Japanese language:

> In later times everything in Japan has ended up becoming more and more
> like China, and yet poetry alone even today retains the natural heart and
> words of our august country from the Age of the Gods just as they were,
> without the slightest admixture of anything foreign. Is this not terrifically
> splendid? The reason for this is that if one composes song with the bother-
> some and muddled heart and sounds of foreign countries it will be very
> unbecoming. It will grate upon the ear and sound strange, so if even a single
> Chinese sound is introduced to a poem, it will always sound filthy. This is a
> sign of how the heart and words of the language of our august country are
> upright and elegant, and supremely wondrous. (p. 416)

Chinese sounds produce a dissonant effect when people try to fit them
into Japanese poetry, so even if people have a tendency to allow them to
slip into their everyday speech, as long as they are expressing themselves in
the form of Japanese poetry these sounds will instantly make themselves
known, allowing people to purge them from their language. Japanese poetry, then, plays the role of a kind of disciplinary mechanism, preserving
the unique characteristics of the Japanese language from the pull of external
forces that would draw it away from its true essence.

For Norinaga, threats to the purity and correctness of the Japanese language come not only from foreign cultures, but also from the unreliability
of people's own subjective inclinations. He pursues this idea in his writings
on linguistics, such as in his famous debate with the fiction writer, waka
poet, and scholar Ueda Akinari, who had studied under Mabuchi's disciple
Katō Umaki. In a discussion of historical changes in the pronunciation of
Japanese, Norinaga concedes that such changes are natural, but cautions
Akinari against taking their natural character as evidence of their normative
correctness: "The modification (namari) of sounds and words is something
entirely natural. There is a principle that determines how modification oc-
curs, and thus modifications occur naturally. However, it is a great error to
say that, just because there is a natural principle to this, the corruption and
modification of pronunciation is something correct."[15] Norinaga describes
the kana syllabary as providing objective evidence of proper pronunciation
from the past, and denounces as unreliable subjectivism the idea that people
can use the natural inclinations of the organs of speech as evidence for how
words should be pronounced. Criticizing Akinari's use of such a methodol-

ogy, he argues, "It is extremely subjective (*watakushi*) not to believe in *kana*, and to try to establish ancient sounds through your own mouth and tongue. The mouth and tongue are things that are easy to draw astray and change, so they cannot serve as a standard" (p. 389). Norinaga describes *kana* as providing a kind of ritual correctness, and attributes the natural tendency toward drift in pronunciation to a laziness akin to that which makes people abandon proper modes of dress: "The ancient pronunciation *kamukaze* is like sitting upright in court dress with cap, while the later pronunciation *kankaze* is like lying down in ordinary clothes. Lying down in ordinary clothes is comfortable, but how can it be said to be correct?" (p. 389).

Norinaga's emphasis on the need for reliable standards from the past, and his skepticism regarding people's ability to use their own personal reasoning or inclinations as a basis on which to seek knowledge, is very similar to what we saw with Sorai, and Norinaga echoes Sorai in his criticism of Song Confucians' use of a subjective "principle," to which he compares Akinari's attempt to use the organs of speech as a basis for knowledge:

> There is no way to know the sounds of ancient language apart from through *kana*. To try to determine these by extending the "principle of how things should be (*tōzen no ri*)" and using one's own mouth and ears is the method of the Song Confucians of China, and is completely at odds with the essence of the ancient learning of this Imperial Land. On what standard is the "principle of how things should be" established? It is nothing but pursuing things based on one's own heart, and all such efforts to determine things with one's own heart are subjective. (p. 396)

Norinaga is critical of the use of Chinese characters to record ancient Japanese texts, but he does not merely discard writing in favor of natural speech, as he sees phonetic writing as important for how it preserves the proper forms that speech must follow.

Norinaga's description of the role of patterned language in poetry has parallels to certain Confucian views on *wen* (written with the same character that Norinaga uses for the Japanese term *aya*), in that he sees patterning not only as an aesthetic quality of language, but also as representing both a unique capacity for the expression of emotion and a normative correctness that integrates such expression into a sphere of social value. His assertion that patterning makes it possible to express emotions that cannot be exhausted in ordinary language is similar to how the "Great Preface" states, "Emotions move on the inside, and take form in words. When words are insufficient, then we sigh our emotions. When sighing is insufficient, then we lengthen and sing them. Emotions are released in sounds (*sheng*). Sounds form patterning (*wen*), and this is called tones (*yin*)." Norinaga presents a similar idea of patterning as a spontaneous outgrowth of deep emotions when he writes, "When expressing things that are difficult to bear, we naturally have patterning in our words, and draw them out."[16] Moreover, much as the Mao tradition sees tones as necessary to reliably convey the intentions of the Odes, Norinaga argues that it is only through patterning that the emotional content of poetry can be effectively communicated to a listener. Norinaga sees the benefits of such communication in less explicitly moral terms than the Mao tradition, but still argues that patterned language is crucial in the formation of social bonds. Closer to his own time, he shows similarities to Sorai, for whom *wen* is the quality that gives ancient phraseology its capacity to convey profound meanings with an economy of words.

Norinaga shares with both the Mao tradition and Sorai a concern for the distance that separates people of the present from the cultural forms that provide normative standards for linguistic patterning, and like them sees the investigation of texts from the past as a necessary means for recovering this language. He differs from them, though, in that he defines the linguistic patterning embodied in these texts as in fact a spontaneous product of the timeless and universal emotional nature of humans, rather than as a historical creation of sagely rulers. In effect, he merges the expressive and normative notions of pattering, arguing that when emotions are sufficiently profound, then these emotions are themselves capable of engendering the patterning necessary to bind people together in a properly governed society. In *Ashiwake obune* he argues, "In the past, even ordinary language had ancient elegance. Moreover, when they composed poetry it was well ordered, so it was naturally beautiful. Also, people's hearts were full of genuineness and their human emotions were profound, and on top of this their words were beautiful, so their poetry was deep and full of meaning, and naturally achieved an indescribable effect. But as times changed, ordinary language changed greatly and became filthy."[17] In the past, then, people naturally produced appropriately patterned language, but today they must actively give poetic qualities to their language to achieve the same effect. While this kind of conscious creation of poetic language is acceptable to Norinaga as a provisional solution, his ultimate goal is to make such language come about spontaneously by reuniting people with their authentic emotional nature. He defines such an emotional nature through the term "knowing *mono no aware*," which we turn to next.

"Knowing Mono no Aware*" and Emotional Correctness*

One of the most striking aspects of Norinaga's writings on poetry, especially when compared to the naïve naturalism of Mabuchi, is his exploration of the multiple ways that poetry can be defined as emotionally genuine. The complexity of the notion of genuineness is one of the main issues he explores in *Ashiwake obune*, where he acknowledges that, contrary to his assertion that the essence of poetry lies in spontaneous emotional expression, people of his own time do not compose simply by blurting out whatever they feel. He explains, though, that as long as people compose what they intend to compose, this qualifies as the "genuine emotions" (*jitsujō*) that poetry is supposed to express: "For example, suppose you see blossoms, and even though you do not find them particularly striking, you go ahead and compose a poem about them as if they in fact were striking, because it is the custom to do so in poetry. Even though it is false (*itsuwari*) to say that they are striking, the desire to compose on them as if they were striking represents genuine emotions."[18] Here he decouples the intentionality of the poet from the spontaneity of natural emotions, and asserts that either of these can be legitimately labeled "genuine."

Although Norinaga's discussion of the genuineness of poetic intentionality at first makes it seem as if anything we desire to compose can be considered genuine, later in *Ashiwake obune* he argues that it is only certain sentiments, namely those present in the waka of the past, that can be considered genuine. He discusses this when he contrasts the falseness of waka with that of Chinese poetry:

> Waka since middle antiquity does not contain genuine emotions; it is all false. But this falseness is different from that of Chinese poetry, as the falseness of waka is composed from learning the genuine emotions of the past. While it is false, then, it is the truth of human emotions (*hito no jō no makoto*). . . . The falseness of Chinese poetry does not learn from the genuineness of the past, and simply speaks the poet's own falsehood, and so is false from beginning to end, and insipid. (pp. 350–52)

The emotions expressed in classical Japanese poetry represent for Norinaga the truth of human nature, a truth that people have become alienated from over time. In the past, "genuine emotions" in the sense of what people spontaneously felt were united with "genuine emotions" in the sense of the truth of human nature. Today, though, there is a discrepancy between these kinds of "genuine emotions," and the task of students of poetry is to eliminate the gap between what they express in poetry and what they spontaneously feel. The way to do this is to "immerse our hearts in the poetry composed by the ancients, and become accustomed to it on a daily basis, so that our emotions will naturally be transformed, and the elegant intentions of the ancients will arise in our own hearts" (p. 306). He maintains that poetry needs to be learned primarily through the imitation of classical models; it is pointless to simply try to be sincere, as if people of today "just composed based on the state of their own heart, this would create extremely vulgar poetry" (p. 303). The imitation of models will at first be a mechanical exercise in academic correctness, but in time the sentiments expressed in the poems people imitate will be internalized and come to inhabit their own hearts. This is similar to Sorai's description of how people learn the Confucian Way, and Sorai likewise warned against a sincerity practiced without reference to any set of normative standards. For Sorai, though, the Way that is internalized through this process is a human construct, and not an a priori human nature.

This conception of how people should learn poetry is reflected in Norinaga's idealization of the *Shinkokinshū*, which he praises in *Ashiwake obune* for how "its poems are composed by immersing the heart in the style of the past" (p. 267). In keeping with this reason for valuing the *Shinkokinshū*, he actually does not advocate directly copying it, instead arguing that the proper way to emulate its poetry is by reproducing the methodology through which it was produced, specifically by immersing oneself in the poetry of the first three imperial anthologies, the *Kokinshū*, *Gosenshū*, and *Shūishū* (p. 267). An example of what he is referring to is the technique of *honkadori* (allusive variation), commonly employed in the *Shinkokinshū*, in which the experience of the poet is not stated directly, but instead is expressed through quoting and referencing earlier poetry. On a more general level, Norinaga's views overlap with those of Fujiwara no Shunzei (1114–1204), a compiler of the *Shinkokinshū*, who writes in *Korai fūteishō* (Selections from Poetic Styles from Ancient Times to the Present, 1197), "When visiting spring blossoms and viewing autumn leaves, were it not for poetry none would know of their beauty and fragrance."[19] In other words, people's appreciation of beauty is always mediated through the expectations and aesthetic preferences generated by their knowledge of poetry. "Genuine experience" itself therefore involves an element of fictionality. Norinaga similarly sees the poetry of the past as a device that mediates people's experience of the world, and for him the goal of studying poetry is to learn the set of approved responses to the world that are embodied in a certain canon of poetry.[20]

In *Shibun yōryō* and *Isonokami sasamegoto*, Norinaga further develops this idea of learning emotions from the poetry of the past through his explanation of what it means to "know *mono no aware*" (*mono no aware o shiru*). Earlier we saw him use *mono no aware* to refer broadly to deeply felt natural emotions, but he introduces a normative element to this emotionality when he writes about what it means to "know" *mono no aware*. In *Shibun yōryō* he describes "knowing *mono no aware*" as involving "knowing the essence of things (*mono*) and knowing the essence of events (*koto*)."[21] Knowing the essence of things refers to an ability to respond in the proper way to objects of beauty in the natural world: "For example, when seeing beautiful cherry blossoms in full bloom, to appreciate the blossoms as beautiful is to know the essence of the thing. Discerning that the blossoms are beautiful, we feel how beautiful indeed they are. This is *mono no aware*. But not to feel that the blossoms are beautiful, no matter how beautiful they may be, is to fail to know the essence of the thing. Such a person is not affected by the beauty of the blossoms at all. This is to fail to know *mono no aware*" (p. 125). Knowing the essence of events, on the other hand, is an ability to respond appropriately to events in the human world, in particular to respond empathetically to the sufferings of others: "When encountering the deep grief of others and witnessing their great sorrow, it is because we know about the events that ought to make one sad that we realize that they must be sad. This is to know the essence of events. . . . Those who do not know *mono no aware* do not feel anything and do not discern the essence of events that ought to make one sad. Therefore no matter how much they witness the sorrow of others, they see it as unconnected to their own heart, so their heart is entirely unmoved" (p. 126). Empathy is seen here as rooted in the fact that all humans are made sad by the same events (such as the death of a loved one), which makes it possible to compare the experiences of others with their own. Central to Norinaga's idea of "knowing *mono no aware*," then, is the need for people to align themselves with a universal human emotionality. He argues, for example, that monogatari value following human emotions, but immediately goes on to clarify, "Following human emotions is not the same as just acting according to what one feels oneself. . . . To see how another is sorrowful and to feel sorrow oneself, or to see how another is delighted and to feel delighted together with him—this is namely to be in keeping with human emotions, and to know *mono no aware*" (p. 84). Much like Jinsai and Sorai, Norinaga is concerned with escaping a narrow subjective standpoint, and sees a connection with the emotions of others, which poetry can provide, as a means to this end.

In light of the normative approach that Confucianism typically takes toward emotions, it is significant that Norinaga borrows heavily from Confucian sources, specifically Confucian discussions of the need to regulate emotions, when he discusses "knowing *mono no aware*." He explains that all living things have emotions, and because they have emotions, feelings are aroused in them upon encountering things in the external world. Because these feelings are aroused, all living things produce song (*uta*) (p. 281). This account of how song comes about echoes the "Record of Music," which states, "[The human heart] feels in response to things and moves, and therefore takes form in sound."[22] He continues to draw on the "Record of Music" when he frames his discussion through the vocabulary of emotions being "at rest" or "in motion," and connects this with the idea that emotions need to be guided in certain directions, so that people feel what they *should* feel on the appropriate occasions:

> Because there are many events in the world, whenever people encounter these events their emotions are put in motion and do not remain at rest (*kokoro wa ugokite shizuka narazu*). As for the emotions moving, this comes from feeling various things, such as sometimes feeling joyful, sad, aggravated, delighted, pleased, diverted, fearful, distressed, affectionate, hateful, fond, or repelled. This is namely moving because of knowing *mono no aware*. Moving because of knowing *mono no aware* is, for example, feeling joyful upon encountering an event that should make one feel joyful—one is joyful because of discerning the essence of the event that should make one feel joyful. Or feeling sad because of encountering an event that should make one feel sad— one is sorrowful because of discerning the essence of the event that should make one sad. So knowing *mono no aware* refers to discerning the essence of events that should make one feel joyful or sad upon encountering these events. (pp. 281–82)

The idea of emotions being "at rest" or "in motion" appears in the "Record of Music" passage that begins, "Humans are born at rest; this is the Heavenly nature. They feel in response to things, and their nature is put into motion; these are the desires of the inborn nature."[23] As discussed in Chapter 1, this passage goes on to describe the social chaos brought about when there is nothing to regulate the emotions that arise in people upon contact with external things, and presents the ritual and music of the sages as regulatory mechanisms with which to remedy this chaos.

Norinaga rejects the creations of the sages as means to regulate emotionality, but as his concept of "knowing *mono no aware*" indicates, he does see emotions in terms of some kind of correctness and incorrectness. Norinaga borrows from the same "Record of Music" passages that Zhu Xi had alluded to in the preface to his *Shi jizhuan* (Collected Transmissions on the Odes), and in his description of emotional correctness as well, he speaks in terms similar to the summary of Zhu Xi's idea of emotions "attaining their proper measure" given by his follower Chen Chun. The passage below was already quoted in Chapter 1, but it is worth repeating here to call attention to Norinaga's similarities to it:

> Emotions are the activity of the heart. They are something that humans cannot do without, and are not something bad. However, when it comes to the causes of emotions, they each have their proper norms. For example to feel joyful when one should feel joyful, to feel angry when one should feel angry, to feel sad when one should feel sad, to feel happy when one should feel happy, to feel compassion when one should feel compassion, to feel shame and disapproval when one should feel shame and disapproval, to feel deference when one should feel deference, and to feel right and wrong when one should feel right and wrong—this is in accord with proper norms, and is what is meant by emotions "being manifested and attaining their proper measure."[24]

There is an important difference between Zhu Xi and Norinaga in that Norinaga rejects the idea that such emotional regulation should be seen explicitly in terms of morality. Still, as we saw earlier, he sees the communication of emotions as leading to a natural morality, in which people treat each other ethically because they empathize with each other. Although on one level Norinaga defends human emotions against Confucian moralism, we should keep in mind that in Confucian ethical philosophies it is common for morality and emotionality to go together, in that being a moral person is defined in terms of having the right moral sentiments. By appealing to both emotionality and its proper regulation as essential to human social interactions, then, Norinaga is very much on a continuum with Confucian views of emotionality.

Another way Norinaga overlaps with Confucian traditions of thinking about emotionality is the distinction he makes between "emotions" (*jō*) and "desires" (*yoku*). In *Isonokami sasamegoto*, he writes that "feelings of pity or tenderness for others, or feelings of sadness or pain, are called 'emotions,'" while "feelings of coveting wealth are 'desires,'" and then goes on to say that it is emotions, and not desires, that give rise to poetry (p. 421).[25] His description of "emotions" as involving reaching out to others, and "desires" as a mere quest for selfish gain, echoes the distinction that Confucians often make between those forms of emotionality that are publicly acceptable and contribute to the social good, and those that harm society.

Some of what Norinaga calls "emotions" can be socially disruptive, but his acceptance of these emotions in poetry and monogatari is premised on their being fictional. On the one hand, he argues that the emotions that come from "knowing *mono no aware*" are not to be subject to moral judgment, and even goes so far as to say that immorality, particularly illicit love, is particularly conducive to bringing out deep feelings of *mono no aware*. While this would appear to suggest that Norinaga's idea of "knowing *mono no aware*" represents a negation or inversion of Confucian morality, in *Shibun yōryō* he defends himself against charges that he is promoting immoral amorousness, writing, "I do not value amorousness as something wonderful, but rather value knowing *mono no aware*" (p. 159). He explains this by comparing the *mono no aware* that arises from amorousness to a lotus that grows in a muddy pond: "One keeps a muddy pond because it is the material in which one plants lotuses in order to look at their flowers. Although one does not value the muddy pond, one values the great purity of the lotus flowers, so one sets aside the fact that the muddy pond is clouded" (p. 159). The muddy water is still muddy, just as the amorousness depicted in the *Tale of Genji* is still immoral. The *Genji* is fiction, however, and Norinaga is not suggesting that people behave like *Genji* characters in their real lives. What he wants them to do is to cultivate their emotional sensibilities, including a sensitivity to the emotions of others, by reading the *Genji*, which will then lead them naturally to behave properly.

Norinaga on the Autonomy of Poetry

In a letter from his student days in Kyoto, Norinaga writes to a friend, "You reject my taste for waka, and I reject your taste for Confucianism. The reason I reject Confucianism is that it is the Way of the sages. The Way of the sages is a Way for governing the country and realm, and bringing peace to the people. It is not something for private pleasure. Now, we are not ones to govern the country or bring peace to the people. So what use can we make of the Way of the sages?"[26] Norinaga's characterization of Confucianism is taken from Sorai, who describes the Way in *Bendō* (On Distinguishing the Way) by stating, "The Way of Confucius is the Way of the ancient kings. The Way of the ancient kings is a Way for bringing peace to the people."[27] For Norinaga this association of Confucianism with rulership makes it irrelevant to those, like himself, who by birth are precluded from holding government office. He then suggests that waka is an alternative to Confucianism, and belongs to a realm separate from that of the public business of government. This dissociation of waka from government is also expressed in the opening section of *Ashiwake obune*, where he writes, "The essence of poetry is not to aid in governance, nor is it for personal cultivation. Rather, it consists of nothing but simply expressing what is felt in the heart" (p. 245).

As we saw earlier, though, Norinaga does see poetry as having certain social and political benefits. Although this may seem to contradict his insistence that poetry is simply something for expressing emotions, he reconciles his different statements about poetry by drawing a distinction between the "essence" of poetry and its "applications": "In all things there is a distinction between their essential character and the benefits that come from their use. This is what is referred to in Chinese writings as 'essence' (Ch. *ti*, Jp. *tai*) and 'application' (Ch. *yong*, Jp. *yō*).[28] If we look into the original character of poetry, it is nothing more than something to express *mono no aware*. I have already explained this in great detail. But when it comes to its application, it has many applications for both oneself and others."[29] He then describes how these "applications" of poetry include its ability to console the heart of the poet, to allow rulers to know the hearts of their subjects, and to give rise to empathy, which causes people to spontaneously treat each other in an ethical manner.

Although poetry has these various applications, Norinaga insists on the autonomy of its "essence" from its "applications." In *Ashiwake obune* he writes that "waka is not created with a mind to being applied to major or minor, or good or bad purposes" (p. 340), and explains this through a comparison with the difference between a tree itself and the uses to which it can be put:

Although trees do not grow out of any intention to be useful to humans, once large trees have grown in the mountains, people see them, realize that they will make good lumber, and so cut them down to use them. The use of this lumber lies in various major and minor, and good and bad things. When one makes a house, it becomes material for a house. When one makes a vessel, it becomes a vessel. But at the time they stand in the mountains, a pine is simply a pine, and a cypress is simply a cypress. . . . Waka is like this as well. To use it for government is a major application, like using cypress as material for a house. But cypress is not limited to being used as material for houses, nor did it originally grow as something that was to be used as such. Still, when we use it this way it is beautiful, so we use it. The use of poetry as an aid to governance is also like this. (pp. 340–41)

In this way, Norinaga maintains the notion of poetry as the spontaneous expression of emotion, while still allowing for the possibility that the products of such expression may happen to serve political ends.

One reason Norinaga sees it as so important to keep emotional expression independent of its applications is that these applications are themselves dependent on the truthful depiction of emotions. If poetry is composed with the explicit intent of being useful, then it is no longer a spontaneous expression of emotion, thus undermining the usefulness that it aspires to. In his *Kokka hachiron sekihi hyō* (A Critique of *A Rejection of the "Eight Essays on Japanese Poetry,"* 1768),[30] he describes this dilemma through a framework similar to the distinction between "essence" and "application" that he had employed in *Ashiwake obune*: "The displaying of human feelings is not the original character (*honbun*) of poetry, but rather how it is applied. The application comes last. The original character of poetry consists merely of singing in a lengthened voice the overflowing feelings in one's heart. One never sings poetry with the intention of applying it to something. If one sings with the intention of applying it, it will not be one's true feelings, and will just be a false front. Thus it will be of no use in knowing human feelings. Confucians do not understand this, and simply take the application to be the original character."[31] Somewhat paradoxically, then, we can only achieve the applications of poetry by temporarily suspending our interest in these applications. For Norinaga, the problem with Confucian views of poetry is not that they put poetry to political use, but that they demand that poetry be composed for the purpose of being useful from the outset. Although he simply speaks of "Confucians" in general here, his criticism is most directly applicable to Zhu Xi's Confucianism, particularly the idea, discussed in Chapter 1, that poetry should "transmit the Way."

Despite Norinaga's insistence that emotional expression be kept separate from its political and social applications, a closer look at how he conceives of this expression gives us reason to question whether he is really making it as autonomous from its applications as he claims. When we consider that the essence of poetry consists of simply expressing emotions, while its applications involve benefits that come from making these emotions understood by others, we can see that it is specifically communication that provides the link between essence and application. This applies not only to the empathy that poetry gives rise to, but also to the personal consolation that poetry provides for the poet, which only comes when the poet has been understood by another. Norinaga's assertion that the essence of poetry is independent of its applications then implies that communication is extraneous to the original act of expression. As we have seen, though, he takes great pains to show how people's deepest, most authentic emotions are in fact the manifestation of universal norms of feeling, and how the patterned language that emerges spontaneously from such deep emotions is structured according to universal norms. In this way, the forms of feeling and expression that guarantee transparent communication are already inscribed within people's spontaneous expression from the outset, provided that they are properly cultivated through immersion in classical Japanese poetry. Translated into Norinaga's schema of "essence" and "application," we could say that the applications of poetry, which are a product of its ability to communicate emotions to others, are already inscribed in its essence, which lies in spontaneous expression.

This unity of essence and application is connected to Norinaga's merging of expressive and normative conceptions of linguistic patterning, which, as I noted earlier, removes the mediating role played by sagely rulers in certain Confucian philosophies. The Mao school and Sorai do not use the terms "essence" and "application," but they are similar to Norinaga in seeing poetry as at core a spontaneous outgrowth of emotionality, which then can be put to various social uses. They insist on the need for rulers as a link in this process, though, as rulers observe the emotional expression of ordinary people, and then use the knowledge gained from this to put into practice policies or teachings that will properly socialize the people on an emotional level. Norinaga, however, eliminates the need for such a mediating role by defining cultural norms as constitutive of human nature itself.

When Norinaga declares that the applications of poetry are independent of its essence, this suggests a gap that must be overcome between the poet and others; poetry is simply the expression of emotions, and this may or may not lead to any kind of connection to others. But by defining the cultural norms of classical Japanese poetry as themselves natural, he implies that those who do not understand them are not fully in touch with their authentic human nature, and absolves the poet of the responsibility to reach beyond these norms. This attitude can be contrasted with Sorai's description of the Confucian Way, as discussed in Chapter 2, where he argues that the Confucian Way must be taken on faith, but at the same time emphasizes that this Way needs to respond to an external reality that exists prior to its structuring by the Way. This helps Sorai avoid, I argued, a view of the culture of the sages as a closed world that answers to nothing but itself. Norinaga, though, by equating the cultural norms of Japanese poetry with human nature, does fall into such a self-referential vision of culture. As a consequence, despite his concern for reaching out empathetically to others, he ultimately places limits on how far this empathy extends.

Norinaga's Way of the Gods and Its Critics

Norinaga's turn to the study of the *Kojiki* in the 1760s was accompanied by an effort to articulate the philosophical foundations of the Ancient Way (*kodō*), or Way of the Gods, that he believed was transmitted by this text. He refined his ideas on the Way of the Gods through a series of works that, despite their different titles, can essentially be thought of as drafts of a single work in progress. The first of these, *Michi chō mono no ron* (A Treatise on the Thing Called a Way), was written before 1767, and the second, *Michi chō koto no ron* (A Treatise on the Matter Called a Way), was produced sometime between 1767 and 1771, when the third version, *Naobi no mitama* (The Upright Spirit), appeared. An only slightly modified version of *Naobi no mitama* was then used as part of the introduction to Norinaga's *Kojikiden*, the first part of which was published in 1790.[32]

In *Naobi no mitama*, Norinaga argues that the Way is the creation of the Japanese gods, and is "not the natural Way of Heaven-and-Earth . . . nor is it a Way created by humans."[33] The first of these views he rejects is meant to refer to Daoism, as he comments, "Do not mistakenly think [this Way] to be the same as the ideas of those such as Laozi and Zhuangzi in China" (p. 57). He does not give any examples of proponents of the second view, but given the historical context in which he is writing, it is safe to assume that he is targeting Ogyū Sorai and his followers. Following the *Kojiki*, Norinaga sees the Japanese emperor as descended from the gods, specifically Amaterasu, and based on this divine descent posits the emperor as the supreme earthly political authority. The only limit imposed on the emperor is that he must obey the gods, as they are the ultimate source of authority: "In all matters, the emperor does not act according to his own august heart, but carries things out and governs according to how things were in the Age of the Gods. When he has doubts, he inquires by means of august divination into the august hearts of the Heavenly gods" (p. 49).

A central tenet of Norinaga's vision of the Way of the Gods is that humans must passively accept whatever the gods do, whether good or bad. He writes, "All affairs in Heaven-and-Earth are in accordance with the will of the gods. All affairs in this world, such as the changing of the seasons, the falling of the rain, and the gusting of the wind, as well as the various good and bad things that happen to countries and people, all are entirely the works of the gods. Among the gods there are good ones and bad ones. Their works are in accordance with their different natures, so they cannot be understood with ordinary reason" (pp. 53–54). Any attempt to understand the works of the gods is for Norinaga a manifestation of the "Chinese heart" (*karagokoro*), which tries to extend human reasoning to all matters.

An example he gives of such a "Chinese heart" is the idea of rulership being based in a "mandate of Heaven" (Ch. *tianming*, Jp. *tenmei*). While the mandate of Heaven, which can be lost by rulers who are unjust, is supposed to provide a moral basis for government, Norinaga cites the idea of the mandate of Heaven to depict Confucianism as nothing more than an ideology to mask the exercise of power: "The mandate of Heaven is a pretext concocted by the sages of ancient China in order to be absolved of their crime of killing rulers and seizing countries" (p. 54). While he concedes that the kings of ancient China had special skills, he sees these as operating purely on the level of a crude realpolitik, and denies that they can provide normative standards for people today. More specifically, he sees the skills displayed by the Chinese kings as having value only in the context of a degraded country like China:

> [In foreign countries] there were some who displayed authority and intelligence, won over the people, seized countries held by others, took successful measures to avoid being overthrown themselves, governed well for some time, and served as models for later ages. In China they refer to such people as "sages." In times of chaos, people become practiced at war, and therefore it is only natural that many great generals emerge. In the same way, when people make great efforts to govern a country that has wicked customs and is difficult to govern, in each generation they devise various methods and become practiced in them, leading to the emergence of clever rulers. But it is mistaken to imagine these so-called sages to be as superior as the gods, and to possess miraculous powers. (pp. 50–51)

In the end, he concludes, "When one considers the essence of what is called a 'Way' in China, one finds that it consists of nothing more than the two elements of trying to seize others' countries, and trying to keep one's own country from being seized" (p. 51).

Much like Mabuchi in *Kokuikō*, Norinaga argues that Japan has been drawn away from its original goodness by the corrupting influence of Chinese culture. He writes, "In ancient times in our Imperial Land, even though there were no such bothersome teachings, there was no disorder at all, and the realm was governed peacefully" (p. 52). He notes, for example, "Such things as humaneness, rightness, ritual propriety, deference, filial piety, brotherly obedience, loyalty, and faithfulness are all things that humans necessarily possess, and therefore without needing teachings, people naturally know them" (p. 59). The natural morality and good government of ancient Japan were disrupted, he maintains, when Chinese books were imported, and came to influence the customs and government of Japan: "Abandoning the splendid Way of our august country, they valued the clever and bothersome ideas and actions of other countries. Because they took after these, the hearts and actions that had been straightforward and pure became entirely filthy and twisted" (p. 53).

Norinaga's attack on the notion of a humanly created Way originating in ancient China is clearly opposed to Sorai's view of the Way. While the Sorai school was considerably weakened by the time Norinaga wrote *Naobi no mitama*, a follower of Sorai's philosophy, Ichikawa Kakumei (1740–1795), wrote a refutation of Norinaga's ideas entitled *Maganohire* (Dispelling Delusions, 1780).[34] Kakumei attacks from the angles we would expect given his affiliation with Sorai, criticizing Norinaga for believing that norms can exist in the absence of the creations of the sages. Kakumei sees Norinaga's heresy as the same as that of the Daoists, whom he claims Norinaga takes after with his view that Confucian virtues are something that are forced on people artificially, and that they were only given names in the first place because of the breakdown of an original spontaneous goodness.[35] Kakumei goes after a number of other ideas of Norinaga's, and takes aim at his idealization of the *Kojiki* as oral tradition, arguing that oral traditions are actually less reliable, and that it is only with the invention of writing that there came to be accurate historical records (p. 183). Another way he casts doubt on the veracity of the *Kojiki* is by arguing that it was simply written to suit the political needs of the emperor at the time (p. 184). Norinaga then penned a rejoinder to this critique, entitled *Kuzubana* (Arrowroot, 1780), in which he defends himself against Kakumei's charges, particularly stressing how the inventions of the gods differ from the pure naturalism of Daoism.[36]

Chapter 2 discussed how Sorai's demand that the Way respond to empirical reality, particularly the reality of human nature, prevents the Way from becoming a completely self-enclosed and self-validating sphere of cultural value. This method of relating the Way to empirical reality is connected to his emphasis on "harmony" (Ch. *he*, Jp. *wa*), defined as the coexistence of dissimilar things, as the diversity and complexity of reality can never be forced into a single uniform mold. Sorai warns against the reduction of harmony to "sameness" (Ch. *tong*, Jp. *dō*), and interprets this pair of terms with reference to a *Zuo zhuan* passage in which the terms are applied to the relationship between lord and subject, with the unreflective agreement of "sameness" contrasted with the productive criticism of rulers that is possible when subjects "harmonize" with their lords. Norinaga, in contrast, advocates unconditional obedience to the emperor: "In the true Way, one discards arguments over whether [the emperor] is good or bad, and instead completely fears, reveres, and obeys him."[37] In *Maganohire*, Kakumei criticizes this attitude of Norinaga, writing, "The role of the ruler is to care for the people, but if he neglects this role, this is a selfish act. Ancient people said that subjects should not follow a ruler's selfishness. . . . To dismiss questions of whether the ruler is good or bad, and simply to stand in awe of him, is like being a serving woman."[38]

Both Norinaga and Sorai see earthly rulers as subject to a higher authority; this authority is represented by the Japanese gods for Norinaga, and by Heaven for Sorai. Unlike Norinaga's view of the indissoluble link between the emperors and the gods, though, Sorai sees it as possible for people to bypass earthly rulers and connect directly to Heaven: "Mencius speaks of the 'officer of Heaven (Ch. *tianli*, Jp. *tenri*).' This term is used in the context of times of chaos. When there is a [true] ruler in the realm, then the people treat the ruler as Heaven, and the ruler alone serves the Heavenly mandate and carries it out. When there is no [true] ruler in the realm, though, then there is nobody to receive the mandate. Therefore the gentleman directly serves the mandate of Heaven. This is called being an 'officer of Heaven.' This is why when Tang attacked King Jie, and when Wu attacked King Zhow, they invoked Heaven."[39] The primary unit of Chinese historiography is the dynasty, and Sorai accepts the idea of the replacement of one dynasty with the next when the old dynasty has lost the mandate of Heaven. For Norinaga, however, the only acceptable dynasty is an eternal one, specifically the Japanese imperial line. While he offers a legitimate critique of how the idea of the mandate of Heaven can be used to mask the exercise of power, the force of this critique is weakened by the fact that he at the same time abandons the very real critical potential of the mandate of Heaven. A world governed by Norinaga's Way of the Gods, then, is one in which both conflict and political subjectivity have been eliminated, rendered unnecessary by the fact that people live in a society uncorrupted by the strife and selfishness that he believed to be the product of foreign cultures.

Contemporary opposition to Norinaga's Ancient Way thought came not only from Confucians, but also from others who, like Norinaga, were trying to define a place for the study and cultivation of Japanese culture, but objected to his absolute elevation of Japan above all other countries. Akinari, for example, attacked Norinaga's idea that the sun goddess Amaterasu is a universal source of light to all countries of the world, and that the fact she is native to Japan means that Japan is superior to all other countries. After describing a Dutch map of the world that portrays countries according to their true relative sizes, Akinari argues:

> If we were to look for where our country was on this map, we would see that it is merely a small island, like a tiny leaf fallen onto a large pond. If we told people of other countries that this tiny island came into existence before all other countries, and that it is the country in which the sun and moon that illuminate the entire world first appeared, and that for this reason all other countries benefit from the illumination of our country, and that they should therefore pay tribute to our court, there is not a single country that would be convinced by this. Not only this, but they would doubt this because in response to the ancient legends of our country, they would say that they have the same kind of legends in their countries. When people engage in disputes, each saying that it was in the ancient times of their own country that the sun and moon first appeared, then who can adjudicate among these claims?[40]

He then goes on to describe myths from India and China that are similar to those of Japan, and argues that such myths belong only to the countries from which they derive, and cannot be used to make arguments about other countries. Norinaga responds by charging Akinari with seeking refuge in a noncommittal skepticism, rather than seeking the truth: "All countries have their own legends, and these all have elements that resemble each other, but among these there can only be one ancient legend that is true. The rest are all false. But in the argument that Ueda Akinari is making, he says that these legends are all false. . . . Although it appears clever to know that they are all false, and thus not be fooled, he fails to realize that out of all of them one must be true."[41]

Another of Norinaga's critics was Murata Harumi, who together with Katō Chikage formed the core of the "Edo school" (Edo-ha) of Mabuchi's disciples. In contrast to Norinaga, the members of the Edo school were primarily devoted to literary activities, which they saw as the true essence of Mabuchi's legacy, and did not occupy themselves with Shinto myth or with elucidating a uniquely Japanese Ancient Way.[42] In a debate between Harumi and Norinaga's follower Izumi Makuni (?–1805) in 1803–1804, later collected by Makuni under the title *Meidōsho* (A Clarification of the Way, 1804), Harumi mocks the myths of the *Kojiki* and *Nihon shoki*, writing, "The traces of the Age of the Gods that are the basis [of Norinaga's theories] are all nonsensical, or were added on from elsewhere. The many writings Norinaga creates that argue about the Way of our country, then, all ought to be regarded as a fool speaking of his dreams."[43]

In his debate with Makuni, Harumi even refers to himself as a Confucian (*jusha*) (p. 139), but this by no means amounts to a rejection of the study of Japan. In a short piece entitled *Wagaku taigai* (An Outline of Japanese Learning, 1792), he criticizes Japanese Confucians of his day for concerning themselves only with Chinese matters, but sees this as a failure to grasp what Confucianism is really about, rather than an inevitable outgrowth of their Confucianism: "The occupation of Confucians consists entirely of methods of governing the country, so such learning cannot be practiced without knowing about the general outlines of the establishment of government in this country from ancient times, as well as the vicissitudes in institutions and the changes in human emotions and social conditions. Therefore, Japanese learning (*wagaku*) is an urgent task."[44] He then goes on to describe a division of "Japanese learning" into three main categories: national history, the study of laws, and the study of ancient language. While Harumi is critical of the sinophilia of the Sorai school, he still adopts certain of its premises. He takes Confucianism in the Sorai school's sense of a tool for governance (rather than just personal moral cultivation), and accepts the importance of such an endeavor, but seeks to make it more applicable to the particular circumstances of Japan. His emphasis on the study of history and laws is very much in line with Sorai's idea of the need for people to broaden their perspective through the empirical study of the past, but Harumi is saying that this is incomplete if people arbitrarily limit this study only to one country, which is not even their own country. What distinguishes figures like Akinari and Harumi from Norinaga, then, is that while they value Japan and what is distinctive to Japan, they see Japan merely as one country among many, each of which has its own customs and culture, rather than as a divine country superior to all others.

Norinaga on Contemporary Society

For the most part Norinaga stayed away from commenting on contemporary politics and society, but his fame as a scholar led him to be called upon in 1787 by Tokugawa Harusada (1728–1789), the daimyo of Kii, to present his views on political reform, a request that Norinaga responded to with *Hihon tamakushige* (The Secret Jeweled Comb Box). One of the most basic problems that daimyo had always faced was how to extract maximum tax revenue from the peasants without driving them to revolt, but this issue took on a new urgency in the 1780s, as crop failures between 1782 and 1787 resulted in a period of widespread starvation known as the Tenmei famine. The desperate conditions of the time led to levels of peasant protest unprecedented in the Tokugawa period, as well as riots in Edo, Osaka, and other major cities. The shogunate was in upheaval as well, as 1786 saw the final downfall of Tanuma Okitsugu (1719–1788), who had dominated the shogunal government during the 1770s, but was notorious for his corruption, and faced increasing opposition as he failed to deal adequately with fiscal problems that arose in the 1780s. There was also turnover in the office of the shogun, as Tokugawa Ieharu (1737–1786, r. 1760–1786) was succeeded by the teenaged Tokugawa Ienari (1773–1841, r. 1787–1837), after which Tanuma's remaining followers contended with the adherents of Matsudaira Sadanobu (1758–1829) for control within the new administration.

One of the fundamental principles of governing that Norinaga lays out is the need to go beyond surface measures and deal with problems at their source: "The ideas of those without learning often deal just with what is close to them and right before their eyes at the moment. They make schemes based on this, and often do not give attention to the root. . . . If one does not correct the root, then no matter what schemes one comes up with, and even if one has good ideas, it will be like, as the proverb says, brushing away flies from rice."[45] He also warns against becoming caught up in theories that have little correspondence to reality, a quality he sees as characteristic of Confucian ideas about government. He acknowledges that Confucian learning is better than none at all, especially when it goes beyond the study of the Four Books and Five Classics, and extends broadly to history and other matters. Still, he cautions, "Confucians have a certain type of Confucian-like thinking, and while the theorizing they employ in their arguments may sound reasonable, when they actually try to apply their ideas to government, many bad things come about that run counter to their expectations" (p. 330). Because of Confucians' failure to engage with reality, "During the many ages of China when people carried things out with clever arguments, there was no instance of peaceful government lasting long" (p. 330). Much of his characterization of Confucianism overlaps with ideas we saw Mabuchi express in *Kokuikō*, where Mabuchi depicts Confucians as offering superficially enticing but ultimately useless theories, which gain much of their power from how they appeal to people's desire for easy, logical explanations.

Norinaga's more concrete comments on Tokugawa society focus on economic issues, particularly changes brought about by the spread of a currency economy. He is critical of the increasing luxury that he sees around him, writing, "People buy useless things that they should not buy, and do useless things that they should not do, so they naturally become practiced in extravagance, which becomes the cause of impoverishment. All people, both high and low, only set their sights on money, so the warriors, farmers, and priests of today have all come to have the base hearts of merchants" (p. 353). He also comments on how the prevalence of moneylending exacerbates the gap between the rich and the poor: "There are many people who borrow money, so the rich often lend money and receive profits, while the poor borrow money and pay out interest, and suffer more and more" (p. 346). To avoid this, "In all matters, people should act in accordance with their station" (p. 348). Despite his concern about the gap between the rich and the poor, then, he is not so much interested in bringing about equality as he is in maintaining people in their preexisting status relationships. He also proposes that rulers should do their best to reduce people's use of currency, after which "people's base hearts, as well as frivolous customs, will surely be corrected" (p. 353).

Certain of Norinaga's ideas are similar to Sorai's, such as his criticism of spending on luxuries, his desire to maintain fixed social hierarchies, and his belief in the importance of paying attention to the underlying habits and customs that lie at the root of social problems, rather than just pursuing surface remedies. He is critical of the application of Chinese learning to governing Japan, but even here he shares certain attitudes with Sorai, as Norinaga's objection to Confucians is that they base their ideas in empty theories, and fail to engage with reality, a criticism Sorai himself made of Song Confucians (although not, of course, of Confucianism as a whole).

One important point where Norinaga differs from Sorai, though, is in his reluctance to recommend an active program of political reform. Sorai had urged a radical restructuring of Japanese society, and laid out detailed plans for how to go about this. Norinaga, in contrast, writes, "However clever people may be, affairs of the world are generally things that are difficult to grasp with human intelligence and efforts, so one should not hastily institute new ways of doing things. In all affairs, if one does not go against how things are done in the world, and governs by preserving the rules that have been passed down, then even if there are some minor bad things, there will be no great harm" (p. 332). He contrasts this attitude with that taken by Chinese, who "just think about things with their own private intelligence, and change everything" (p. 331).

An example of this attitude toward change is Norinaga's position on the taxation of the peasants. He expresses concern for the suffering of the peasants, and judges the tax rates levied on them to be too high, but he argues that any abrupt lowering of rates would cause too much disruption to the samurai who rely on these taxes for their income (p. 339). Commenting on how the peasants would be impacted by keeping the existing rates of taxation, he concludes, "This is the annual tax that the peasants have grown accustomed to over many years. They believe that it will certainly go up, so they do not find it excessive. Therefore, miserable as they may be, the annual tax should remain where it is fixed now. Still, you should at least consider what I said earlier, and day and night never fail to remember that the peasants of today exert themselves in body and spirit more than in the past, and suffer greatly from the annual tax" (pp. 339–40). Moving on to the specific problem of how to avoid peasant revolts, he argues that current policies fail because they do not address the root of the problem. He continues, "To fix the root is namely to stop unreasonable treatment, and have pity on the common people. However much they may be suffering, as long as those above treat them well, these [revolts] will not arise" (p. 342). While his demand to get to the root of social problems may seem to promise radical change, his actual proposals are tamer, as putting a stop to "unreasonable treatment" does not involve alleviating the burden of taxation. Norinaga's less proactive approach to political reform is in line with his view that the existing state of the world should simply be accepted as the will of the gods, who are both good and bad, and whose actions cannot be fathomed by human reasoning, or subjected to human judgments of right and wrong.[46]

Norinaga as Poet

In *Tamagatsuma* (The Jeweled Basket), a collection of brief essays on a wide range of topics written during his final years, Norinaga describes his early attraction to waka: "From my seventeenth or eighteenth year, a desire arose in me to compose poetry. I began to compose, but I did not learn by following a teacher, and did not show my poems to anyone, but rather simply composed by myself."[47] His first formal instruction in waka came in 1749, when he began to have his poems evaluated and corrected by a Buddhist priest from a local temple who was trained in court poetics. During his time in Kyoto, he began studying waka in 1752 with Morikawa Akitada (1670–1762), a shrine priest and student of the court poet Reizei Tamemura (1712–1774), and attended monthly poetry gatherings at Akitada's for about a year. For a while Norinaga was more devoted to Chinese poetry than waka, but in 1756 he took up waka in earnest again, this time under the guidance of Aruga Chōsen (1717–1778), a follower of the teachings of Matsunaga Teitoku (1571–1653), who had spread court poetics to a commoner audience. Norinaga participated in monthly poetry gatherings held by Chōsen, and continued to send his waka to Chōsen for corrections even after returning to Matsusaka. His early education in waka, then, was carried out within a world strongly influenced by court poetics.[48] Like Mabuchi and the other participants in the *Kokka hachiron* debate, he was critical of the secret teachings of the court poets, invoking the basis of poetry in natural emotion to deny the court poets' claims to special authority: "Poetry is not like the various other arts (*gei*). It is something that emerges from one's own heart, so there should not be any such thing as poetic houses (*ie*)."[49] However, unlike Mabuchi's and Munetake's attempts to define a new aesthetic based on the *Man'yōshū*, Norinaga, even as he expanded his poetry to include the *Man'yōshū* style, continued to value the conservative aesthetics of the Tokugawa court poets, whose poetry adhered to a narrow range of language and subject matter.[50]

After returning to Matsusaka and opening his medical practice, Norinaga continued to be devoted to waka. In addition to waka gatherings at his own academy, he was a member of many local groups that met regularly to compose waka. In 1758 he joined the Reishōin poetry group, which had been in existence since 1723 and included a number of his relatives. This group met twice a month to compose poetry, and some of its members were among Norinaga's earliest students at his lectures on the *Tale of Genji*. Other waka groups that he participated in regularly included one held from 1764 at the Henjōji, a local Buddhist temple, and one held from 1765 at the home of Suga Naoiri (1742–1776), a student of Norinaga and a member of the Reishōin group.[51]

Norinaga, unlike Mabuchi, is rarely judged to have been anything more than a mediocre waka poet, but he was certainly prolific, with his largest collection of waka, *Isonokami kō*, containing almost eight thousand poems. This collection was not published, but the *Suzunoya shū*, a collection of his poetry and prose published between 1798 and 1803, contains over twenty-five hundred waka. His interest in poetry was a constant throughout his career, even as the main focus of his scholarship shifted from literary studies to the Ancient Way. In *Uiyamabumi*, written just three years before his death, he argues for the importance of studying both poetry and the Ancient Way, and not neglecting one at the expense of the other. On the one hand, he comments disapprovingly that "some people compose poetry and prose and have a fondness for the past, but are simply caught up in surface elegance, while neglecting the Way and paying no attention to it."[52] On the other hand, he criticizes those who "concentrate on studying the Way," but "dismiss the composition of poetry, considering it a mere frivolity" (p. 539).

Although Norinaga maintained an interest in waka throughout his life, he defined the function of poetry in new ways as he developed his scholarship on the Ancient Way. First of all, he argued that the elevated emotional and aesthetic sensibility learned through poetry was valuable not only, as he had argued in his early works, because of how it allows people to empathize and communicate with others, but also for how it is a precondition for grasping the Ancient Way. In *Uiyamabumi* he writes, "All people should know the elegant style. Those who do not know it do not know *mono no aware* and are heartless people. Such knowledge of the elegant style comes from composing poetry and reading monogatari. Knowledge of the elegant emotions of the ancients and of everything about the elegance of the world in ancient times is a stepping-stone to knowing the Ancient Way" (p. 539). He sees the most ancient Japanese poetry as providing people with the knowledge of ancient language necessary to decipher the texts in which the Ancient Way is transmitted, in particular the *Kojiki* and *Nihon shoki*. Describing the importance of studying the *Man'yōshū*, he writes, "When one has grasped ancient language and ancient poetry, and then reads [the *Kojiki* and *Nihon shoki*], the meaning of their Way will naturally become clear" (p. 527). Moreover, he emphasizes that we must actually compose in the ancient style ourselves to achieve such knowledge: "In all matters, there is a difference between matters that we think of in relation to others, and matters that we think of as our own. This is a difference of depth. . . . Poetry is also like this. No matter how deeply we ponder ancient poetry, it is an affair of others, and so still there are points where it does not reach deeply. When we come to compose ourselves, though, it becomes our own affair. Therefore we give particular attention to it, and grasp its deep meaning" (p. 528). Much as we saw in Norinaga's earlier writings on poetry, he stresses the importance of fully internalizing the norms embodied in poetry, a process that involves being transformed by poetry, rather than merely contemplating it from a distance. His attitude toward the *Man'yōshū* has changed, though, as in his earlier writings he had argued that "the *Man'yōshū* comes first in poetic studies (*kagaku*)," and yet had warned that "it is a grave error to attempt to compose by imitating the *Man'yōshū*."[53]

One of the distinguishing features of Norinaga's waka, at least in the later part of his career, is how he self-consciously pursues two distinct styles, one modeled after the *Man'yōshū* and the other after later waka. He is critical of those who adhere only to the *Man'yōshū* style, and argues that each style should be appreciated for what it has to offer: "The ancient style is like white robes, and the later style is like robes dyed with crimson and purple. White robes are splendid for how they are white, but dyed robes are also splendid in various ways depending on how they are dyed. So just because white robes are splendid, this does not mean that we should take dyed robes all to be bad."[54] At the same time, he is adamant that each style be kept distinct: "While composing the ancient style and the later style side by side, I cleanly separate these, and do not confuse them with each other."[55] This division of styles is apparent in the *Suzunoya shū*, where the poetry sections are labeled as either the "recent style" (*kinchō*) or the "ancient style" (*kofū*).

The following example of a recent style poem reflects Norinaga's ideal of mediating expression through canonical poetic models:

kore ya kono / haru tatsu kyō no / toshi no kure
yuku mo kaeru mo / Ōsaka no seki

[On this first spring day, which comes within the old year, is this the barrier of Osaka, where people meet coming and going?]

The idea of spring beginning during the old calendar year is most famously expressed in the opening poem of the *Kokinshū*: "Springtime has come within the old year; what of the year then—are we to speak of 'this year,' or are we to say 'last year'?"[56] Not only is the basic theme of Norinaga's poem borrowed, but four of its five lines are taken directly from other poems. The second line comes from the second poem of the *Kokinshū*: "On this first spring day, are warm breezes melting the frozen waters I scooped up in my hand, soaking my sleeves?"[57] The first, fourth, and fifth lines are then from the *Gosenshū* poem: "Is this Osaka barrier, where strangers and friends meet, while those coming and going separate?"[58] This kind of borrowing from earlier poems is known as *honkadori*, or "allusive variation," a technique common in the *Shinkokinshū*, and Norinaga's poem can be seen as an attempt to emulate the *Shinkokinshū*, which, as we saw earlier, he values for how its poetry is the product of an immersion in the earliest imperial anthologies. Still, even Fujiwara no Teika, an editor of the *Shinkokinshū* and an advocate of *honkadori*, decrees, "When composing a new poem by borrowing from old ones, it is excessive when as many as three of the five lines are borrowed."[59]

An example of one of Norinaga's ancient style poems, composed on the topic of travel, is:

ōkimi no / mikoto kashikomi / tamamo nasu
nabiki neshi ko o / okite kinikeri

[The emperor's command is awe-inspiring, so I came, leaving behind the girl I slept with, she yielding like jeweled seaweed]

Like the preceding poem, this uses allusive variation, drawing on a poem from the *Man'yōshū* by Kakinomoto no Hitomaro (7–8th c.), composed when he left his wife behind in Iwami to go to the capital: "because I came, leaving my wife behind, she who slept yielding to me like jeweled seaweed,"[60] Once again, Norinaga's use of allusive variation takes on something of the form of an academic exercise, as he adds little to the source poem. The third through fifth lines of Norinaga's poem are borrowed more or less verbatim from Hitomaro's poem, and the first two lines express the same idea as the source poem, as travel to the capital implies government business, and hence an imperial command.

In addition to seeing poetry as a medium for internalizing the linguistic and aesthetic worlds that allow us to grasp the Ancient Way, Norinaga composed poems that directly express his views on the Way. His most notable example of this is *Tamaboko hyakushu* (A Hundred Poems on the Jeweled

Sword), a collection of poems on the Ancient Way that was published in 1787.[61] Some examples of poems from this collection are:

ametsuchi no / kiwami miterasu / takahikaru
hi no ōkami no / michi wa kono michi

[This Way is the Way of the great Sun Goddess, who shines from on high, augustly illuminating the farthest reaches of Heaven-and-Earth]

momoyaso to / kuni wa aredomo / hi no moto no
kore no Yamato ni / masu kuni wa arazu

[Although there are many countries, there is no country that surpasses this Japan, which lies at the origin of the sun]

Karazama no / sakashiragokoro / utsurite zo
yohito no kokoro / ashiku narinuru

[It is after the importation of the crafty heart of the Chinese that the hearts of people in the world have become wicked]

Norinaga's records these poems in *man'yōgana*, lending them an aura of archaism that is in keeping with the message they are meant to convey. Taken as a whole, *Tamaboko hyakushu* constitutes a kind of primer on the Way, presenting Norinaga's central ideas about the Way in easily digestible snippets.

Norinaga's most famous poem presents his ideal image of Japan in less prosaic terms than the poetry of *Tamaboko hyakushu*:

Shikishima no / Yamatogokoro o / hito towaba
asahi ni niou / yamazakurabana

[If I were asked to explain the Japanese spirit, I would say it is wild cherry blossoms, glowing in the morning sun][62]

Norinaga affixed this poem to a self-portrait, suggesting that he saw it as summing up the meaning of his scholarship. Cherry blossoms were one of his favorite topics for poetry, and in 1800 he composed a series of 315 poems on cherry blossoms, which was entitled *Makura no yama*, and was published in 1802, the year after his death.

Norinaga's basic approach to composing poetry is similar to that of figures like Sorai and Mabuchi, who composed by emulating classical models, sometimes essentially patching together lines from earlier poems and rearranging them into a new poem. Also like Sorai and Mabuchi, Norinaga's imitative approach is based on a belief that immersion in canonical poetic models from the past can cultivate people in such a way as to allow them to form a more perfect society in the present. Norinaga went further than these earlier figures, though, in his willingness to use poetry as a vehicle for the direct expression of his philosophical views. Also, while he was not the only one to compose in a variety of styles, he was notable for the explicit division he made between "ancient style" and "recent style" poetry, each of which was meant to put the poet in touch with a certain aspect of the Japanese past.

Conclusion

Norinaga's literary thought provides a certain resolution to problems raised by earlier thinkers. Sorai had linked the political importance of poetry to its ability to provide access to the unadulterated state of human nature and human emotions, and assumed that this function of poetry was in no way compromised by its adherence to culturally prescribed norms of expression. His disciples Nankaku and Shundai, though, problematized the relationship of cultural norms to natural emotions. Nankaku made poetry into something that was first and foremost cultural, and defined the community created through poetry as an elegant cultural elite that remained aloof from society at large. Shundai, in contrast, in order to uphold the political role of poetry as defined by Sorai, was led to denounce Sorai's imitative neoclassicism. Mabuchi then criticized Sorai and Shundai by appealing to a primitivist naturalism that was meant to avoid the duplicity of humanly constructed culture altogether. Norinaga, though, grapples with the contradictions that Nankaku and Shundai saw between human nature and culture, and synthesizes their positions by declaring that the waka tradition's norms of feeling and expression are in fact natural and universal, and that people's failure to perceive them as such is a result of having lost touch with their original human nature. This synthesis allows Norinaga to advocate the cultural construction of the self through poetry, like Nankaku, while at the same time denying that poetry is merely an elegant game, and instead, like Shundai, seeing it as offering the access to human nature needed to uphold a political role for poetry.

The vision of politics that emerges from Norinaga's resolution of these issues, though, brings with it a loss of Sorai and Shundai's efforts to engage actively and critically with society. Sorai and Shundai had valued the study of poetry for how it allows us to reach outside ourselves and encounter the full diversity and complexity of human nature. Norinaga also values poetry as a way to form interpersonal bonds, but by demanding that such relationships be based on common adherence to the emotional norms of a canon of Japanese poetry, he ultimately backs away from seeing poetry as a way to engage with others as people truly different from ourselves. For Sorai, the demand that we deal with others as they are, rather than through the projections of our own subjective viewpoints, is rooted in the idea that people's inborn natures are bestowed by Heaven, so that to ignore their natures is to show disrespect for Heaven. Heaven also played a much broader role for Sorai, as he saw it as the ultimate source of political authority, and argued that in times of bad government, it was acceptable to disobey existing rulers and connect directly with Heaven to institute a new government. For Norinaga, though, it is the Japanese gods that are the highest authority, and he takes a very different stance toward them than Sorai had toward Heaven, advocating absolute obedience to the gods, and to the emperors as their descendants. While Norinaga had not yet fully developed his theory of the gods at the time he produced his early works on poetics, we can see a certain continuity between his early and late work, in that they both create a self-validating sphere of culture, one that provides a normative structure for social relationships while denying people the right to step outside of or reflect upon the validity of such norms.

Epilogue

In this study I have reexamined eighteenth-century Japanese theories of poetry by bringing to the forefront their treatment of poetry as a means for the formation of communities held together by cultural norms, an approach that is meant as an alternative to the more common view of eighteenth-century poetics as a quest for free emotional expression. I recognize the importance of emotions and their expression in discourse on poetry from this time, but I see this interest in emotionality as inseparable from a concern for the integration of emotions into various structures of cultural value that were thought to give order and harmony to society. By appealing to classical linguistic and aesthetic standards as prerequisites for proper poetic composition, and demanding that poets internalize these standards through long study and practice, eighteenth-century writers presented the spontaneous expression of emotions in poetry as at the same time the reproduction of a poetic tradition. They also argued that the expression of emotions only takes on its full meaning through the interpersonal bonds it generates by inspiring empathy in a reader or listener. The importance of communication in their theories was connected to their idealization of classical norms of expression and feeling, as the cultivation of both poet and audience in these shared norms was what made such communication possible.

By exploring how an emphasis on both emotions and their cultural regulation arose out of a single coherent discursive field, I have presented an alternative to seeing the coexistence of these elements merely as a contradiction, or an intermediate stage in the achievement of modernity. Given the common association of nativism with pure emotionality, and Confucianism with political and moral views of literature, my approach also implies a questioning of the boundary between Confucian and nativist approaches to poetry. Moreover, this questioning does not just involve arguing that figures like Sorai were moving away from Confucianism by valuing emotions, or that nativists showed lingering remnants of Confucian views by finding poetry socially useful; my point, rather, is to question the dichotomy that such judgments are based on in the first place.

Viewing conceptions of cultural norms as central to eighteenth-century discourse on poetry is particularly relevant to assessing Norinaga's place in relation to Confucian views of poetry, especially his relationship to Sorai. If we were to see Sorai as having freed emotions from Confucian moralism, then Norinaga's extolling of fragile human sentiments would appear as a deepening of Sorai's liberated attitude toward emotions, and his declarations about the social benefits of poetry would seem, like Sorai's, to be little more than a holdover from stubborn Confucian traditions. Comparing these two figures' views by focusing on how they conceive of poetry as a cultural form, however, yields a different picture. Both Sorai and Norinaga connect poetry to visions of a communal cultural interiority, but Norinaga pulls back from certain methods that Sorai had theorized of maintaining a critical perspective on this interiority. The result, I have argued, is a more self-enclosed and self-validating ideal of culture as a force for socialization. While Maruyama and many other scholars have described the transition from Sorai to Norinaga as involving a foreclosure of possibilities for political subjectivity, I distinguish my interpretation from theirs in that I see this foreclosure as appearing in Norinaga's early literary writings, and not just in his formulation of his philosophy of the Ancient Way.

Another outgrowth of my approach, then, is a more sympathetic reading of Confucian literary thought, as I attempt to go beyond what I see as a common caricature of it as offering little more than a crude didacticism or utilitarianism. I have no intention of making nostalgic appeals to an essentialized image of Confucianism as a source of authentic East Asian tradition, but it is important to pay attention to how Confucianism has been constructed as a foil for narratives of both modernization and the unfolding of Japanese national identity. When we overlook how many Confucians viewed poetry not merely as a didactic tool, but also as a means for critically reflecting on social norms, this obscures how nativists like Norinaga turned away from certain possibilities that Confucians had found in poetry, even while these nativists discovered new ways of depicting poetry as a manifestation of emotionality.

Throughout this study, I have emphasized that the politicization of poetry by eighteenth-century Japanese writers is central to why they were so interested in poetry to begin with, and is not merely a sign of their imperfect grasp of poetry as "literature," a category that is itself problematic. To the extent that we judge poetry according to its success in achieving an ideal of the free emotional expression of the individual, then this study could perhaps come across as a downgrading of the importance of eighteenth-century theories of poetry. By exploring the complex ways in which writers of this time valued poetry, though, my goal has been to show that it in fact played a much richer and more integral role for them than has often been acknowledged.

Reference Matter

Character List

Agatai no kashū	県居歌集
Agatai no shūi	県居拾遺
Akabane	赤羽
Amaterasu	天照
Amenomori Hōshū	雨森芳洲
ametsuchi	天地
Andō Shōeki	安藤昌益
Andō Tameakira	安藤為章
Andō Tōya	安藤東野
Arai Hakuseki	新井白石
Arakida Hisaoyu	荒木田久老
"Arashi"	嵐
Aruga Chōsen	有賀長川
Asakusa Kannon	浅草観音
Ashiwake obune	排蘆小船
Asukai	飛鳥井
aware	哀れ
Aware ben	安波禮辨
aya	文
Azuma uta	東歌
"Baitou yin"	白頭吟
"Baizhou"	柏舟
bakufu	幕府
Beixi ziyi	北渓字義
Bendō	弁道
Bendōsho	弁道書
Benmei	弁名
benran zhi xing	本然之性
bi	比
bian	変
Bian	卞

Bian Gong	辺貢
Bohai	渤海
Bo Juyi	白居易
Boyu	伯魚
bun	文
bunjin	文人
bu no michi	武の道
Bunron	文論
cai (talent)	才
cai (capability)	材
Canglang shihua	滄浪詩話
Cao Cao	曹燥
Cao Pi	曹丕
Cao Zhi	曹植
Cen Shen	岑参
Chang'an	長安
"Chang'an guyi"	長安古意
Chen Chun	陳淳
cheng	誠
Cheng	程
chengren	成人
Chen Liang	陳亮
chi	智
Chikamatsu Monzaemon	近松門左衛門
"Chōan dō"	長安道
chōka	長歌
chokkai	直解
choku	直
chōnin	町人
Chu	楚
chū	忠
Chu Guangxi	儲光羲
Chunqiu	春秋
chūsei	中世
chūyō	中庸
Chūyō hakki	中庸発揮
Chūyō kai	中庸解
ci	辞
ciai	慈愛
dai	題
daifu	大夫
Daigaku kai	大学解
Daigaku teihon	大学定本
Daigaku wakumon	大学或問

Daitō seigo	大東世語
dao	道
Dao de jing	道徳経
"Daxu"	大序
Daxue zhangju	大学章句
"Daya"	大雅
Dazai Shundai	太宰春台
"Dazongshi"	大宗師
de	徳
dengaku	田楽
dō (Way)	道
dō (sameness)	同
Dōjimon	童子問
Dokugo	独語
Dokushi yōryō	読詩要領
Doku Shushi shiden	読朱氏詩伝
duan	端
Du Fu	杜甫
"Dui Chu wang wen"	対楚王問
Duqu	杜曲
Du Shenyan	杜審言
dushu fa	読書法
Duweiniang	杜韋娘
Edo	江戸
Edo-ha	江戸派
Eiga no taigai	詠歌大概
Emei	峨眉
"Emeishan yue ge"	峨眉山月歌
engi	演義
feng	風
fengjian	封建
"Feng xiazhe"	逢侠者
fu	賦
fue	笛
fūga	風雅
fūga no jō	風雅の情
fūjin no jō	風人の情
Fujiwara no Fuhito	藤原不比等
Fujiwara no Shunzei	藤原俊成
Fujiwara no Teika	藤原定家
fusokufuri	不即不離
Futatabi kingo no kimi ni kotaematsuru fumi	再奉答金吾君書
Fu Xi	伏羲

fūzoku	風俗
ga	雅
gagaku	雅楽
Gakuritsu kō	楽律考
Gakusei hen	楽制篇
Gakusoku	学則
ganbutsu sōshi	玩物喪志
"Gankaron"	翫歌論
gei	芸
gen	言
Genbun	元文
genbun itchi	言文一致
Genji monogatari	源氏物語
Genji monogatari shinshaku	源氏物語新釈
Genji monogatari tama no ogushi	源氏物語玉の小櫛
Genroku	元禄
getiao	格調
gewu	格物
gi	義
giko gafu	擬古楽府
Gion Nankai	祇園南海
giri	義理
Go'ikō	語意考
Gomō jigi	語孟字義
Gongan	公安
Gongchuo	公綽
goroku	語録
Gosenshū	後撰集
"Guanju"	関雎
Guanzi	管子
gunken	郡県
"Guofeng"	国風
gushi	古詩
guwenci	古文辞
Hachijōjima	八丈島
haikai	俳諧
Hakone	箱根
Hamamatsu	浜松
Han (dynasty)	漢
Han (school of *Odes* commentary)	韓
Han (name of barrier)	函
Hanfeizi	韓非子
Han shu	漢書
Han Yu	韓愈

Hattori Nankaku	服部南郭
Hayashi Gahō	林鵞峯
Hayashi Razan	林羅山
Hayashi Razan bunshū	林羅山文集
he	和
"He Gu Zhi sheren zaochao daminggong zhi zuo"	和賈至舍人早朝大明宮之作
Heian	平安
He Jingming	何景明
Henjōji	遍照寺
hiden	秘伝
Hihon tamakushige	秘本玉くしげ
hijō no mono	非情の物
Hikita Yakara	疋田族
Hino Tatsuo	日野龍夫
Hirano Kinka	平野金華
"Hishiron"	避詞論
hito no jō no makoto	人の情のまこと
"Hito no kyō ni yuku o okuru"	人の京に之くを送る
hōken	封建
honbun	本分
honkadori	本歌取り
Honryūin	本龍院
honzen no sei	本然之性
Hori Keizan	堀景山
hōsei	法世
hou qizi	後七子
hua	化
huangzhong	黄鐘
Huaxu	華胥
huowu	活物
Hyakunin isshu	百人一首
Ichikawa Kakumei	市川鶴鳴
ie	家
Iida	飯田
Ike no Taiga	池大雅
ikioi	勢
ingaku	淫楽
inishie no michi	古への道
Inoue Tetsujirō	井上哲次郎
Ise	伊勢
Ise monogatari	伊勢物語
Ise monogatari ko'i	伊勢物語古意
Ishikawa Jōzan	石川丈山

Isonokami kō	石上稿
Isonokami sasamegoto	石上私淑言
Itō Jinsai	伊藤仁斎
Itō Tōgai	伊藤東涯
itsuwari	偽り
Iwami	石見
Izumi Makuni	和泉真国
Izushi	出石
ja	邪
ji	辞
jiai	慈愛
Jie	桀
jikoteki kansei	自己的完成
Jin	晋
jin	仁
Jinmu	神武
jitsujō	実情
jo	恕
jō	情
jokotoba	序詞
jōruri	浄瑠璃
jueju	絶句
Ju Meng	劇孟
"Junsokuron"	準則論
junxian	郡県
junzi	君子
jusha	儒者
ka	化
Kada no Arimaro	荷田在満
Kada no Azumamaro	荷田春満
Kada no Nobuna	荷田信名
kagaku	歌学
"Kagenron"	歌源論
Kaibara Ekiken	貝原益軒
Kaiho Seiryō	海保青陵
Ka'ikō	歌意考
Kaiyuan	開元
"Kajitsu no kankyo"	夏日の閑居
Kakaika	呵刈葭
Kakinomoto no Hitomaro	柿本人麻呂
Kamakura	鎌倉
Kamo no Mabuchi	賀茂真淵
Kamo-ō kashū	賀茂翁歌集
kan	官

kana	仮名
kanbun	漢文
Kang Hai	康海
Kanjikō	冠辭考
Kanji san'on kō	漢字三音考
"Kankaron"	官家論
kanshi	漢詩
kanzen chōaku	勧善懲悪
Karasumaru	烏丸
kasshin	活真
Katō Chikage	加藤千蔭
Katō Enao	加藤枝直
Katō Umaki	加藤宇万伎
katsubutsu	活物
Kazusa	上総
Keichū	契沖
Keikodan	稽古談
Keizairoku	経済録
Keizairoku shūi	経済録拾遺
Ken'en zuihitsu	護園随筆
Ken'in	顕允
Kenzō	顕宗
ki	気
Kii	紀伊
kinchō	近調
Kingaku taiishō	琴学大意抄
Ki no Tsurayuki	紀貫之
Kinryūsan	金龍山
kinsei	近世
kō	孝
kobunji	古文辞
kochū	古註
kodō	古道
kofū	古風
Kōfu	甲府
kogaku	古学
"Kogakuron"	古学論
Kogidō	古義堂
Kojiki	古事記
Kojikiden	古事記伝
Kojima Yasunori	小島康敬
Kokinshū	古今集
Kokinshū tōkagami	古今集遠鏡
Kokin wakashū sachū ron	古今和歌集左注論

Kokka hachiron	国歌八論
Kokka hachiron sairon	国歌八論再論
Kokka hachiron sekihi	国歌八論斥非
Kokka hachiron sekihi hyō	国歌八論斥非評
Kokka hachiron yogen	国歌八論餘言
Kokka hachiron yogen shūi	国歌八論餘言拾遺
kokoro	心
kokoro wa ugokite shizuka narazu	情は動きて静かならず
koku	石
Kokugaku	国学
Kokugaku no hihan	国学の批判
Kokugaku seiji shisō no kenkyū	国学政治思想の研究
Kokuikō	国意考
Kong Yingda	孔穎達
Konjaku monogatari	今昔物語
Korai fūteishō	古来風躰抄
koshi	古詩
kōshō	黄鐘
koto (event)	事
koto (type of stringed instrument)	琴
Kotoba no tama no o	詞の玉緒
kotowari	理り
Koyasu Nobukuni	子安宣邦
Kumazawa Banzan	熊沢蕃山
Kunlun	崑崙
kunshi	君子
Kurozumi Makoto	黒住真
Kuzubana	くず花
Kyōchūkikō	峡中紀行
Kyōhō	享保
"Kyōkaku"	俠客
kyokushi	曲士
"Kyo o kōhoku ni utsusu"	居を巷北に移す
Laozi	老子
li (principle)	理
li (profit)	利
li (ritual)	礼
li (measurement of distance)	里
Liang Youyu	梁有誉
Li Bo	李白
Liezi	列子
Li ji	礼記
Li Mengyang	李夢陽
Li Panlong	李攀龍

liujing	六経
Liu Yuxi	劉禹錫
Liuyu yanyi	六諭衍義
Liyang	溧陽
Lu (state, school of *Odes* commentary)	魯
Lu (mountain)	廬
Lunyu jizhu	論語集注
lüshi	律詩
Lu Xiangshan	陸象山
"Lüye shuhuai"	旅夜書懐
Lu Zhaolin	廬照鄰
machi bugyō	町奉行
Maganohire	末賀乃比礼
makoto	誠
makurakotoba	枕詞
Makura no yama	枕の山
mana	真名
man'yōgana	万葉仮名
Man'yō kai	万葉解
Man'yōkō	万葉考
Man'yōshū	万葉集
Man'yōshū Tōtōmi uta kō	万葉集遠江歌考
Mao	毛
Maoshi	毛詩
Maoshi jian	毛詩箋
Maoshi xu	毛詩序
Maoshi zhengyi	毛詩正義
Maoshi zhuan	毛詩伝
Maruyama Masao	丸山真男
masurao	丈夫
Matsuchiyama	待乳山
Matsudaira Sadanobu	松平定信
Matsumoto Sannosuke	松本三之介
Matsunaga Teitoku	松永貞徳
Matsusaka	松坂
Meidōsho	明道書
Mengzi jizhu	孟子集注
michi	道
Michi chō koto no ron	道云事之論
Michi chō mono no ron	道テフ物ノ論
Ming	明
miyabi	雅
Mizuno Genrō	水野元朗

Momokawa Takahito	百川敬仁
mono	物
monogatari	物語
mono no aware o shiru	物のあはれを知る
Morikawa Akitada	森川章尹
Mōshi kogi	孟子古義
Motoori Norinaga	本居宣長
Mozi	墨子
Murata Harumi	村田春海
Murata Harumichi	村田春道
Muromachi	室町
Musashi	武蔵
Nakamura Yukihiko	中村幸彦
Nakano Kiken	中野撝謙
namari	訛り
"Nan feng"	南風
Nankai shiketsu	南海詩訣
Nankaku sensei bunshū	南郭先生文集
Nankaku sensei tōka no sho	南郭先生灯下書
Naobi no mitama	直霊
naoshi	直し
nigu yuefu	擬古楽府
Nihon seiji shisōshi kenkyū	日本政治思想史研究
Nihon shoki	日本書紀
Niimanabi	邇飛麻那微
Nijō	二条
ninjō	人情
ninjōbon	人情本
norito	祝詞
Noritokō	祝詞考
ō	応
Obata	小幡
Ogyū Kinkoku	荻生金谷
Ogyū Sorai	荻生徂徠
Okabe	岡部
Okabe no nikki	岡部日記
Ono Furumichi	小野古道
Ōoka Tadamitsu	大岡忠光
Ōsuga Nakayabu	大菅中養父
Ōtomo no Tabito	大伴旅人
Ōutadokoro no uta	大歌所の歌
Oyumi	生実
pianpian	翩翩
Pingqiang	平羌

qi	気
Qi	斉
Qian Qi	銭起
qian qizi	前七子
Qin	秦
qing	情
Qing	清
Qingqi	清溪
qing zhi zheng	情之正
"Qiu xing"	秋興
"Qiuzhong you ma"	丘中有麻
"Qiyu"	淇奥
quanren	全人
quanshan cheng'e	勧善懲悪
Ran Qiu	冉求
rei	礼
reigaku	礼楽
Reishōin	嶺松院
Reizei	冷泉
Reizei Tamemura	冷泉為村
ren	仁
renga	連歌
ri (principle)	理
ri (profit)	利
rikugei	六芸
rikukei	六経
Rikukei ryakusetsu	六経略説
risshi	律詩
ritsuryō	律令
Rongo chō	論語徴
Rongo kogi	論語古義
rōnin	浪人
Ryūshi shinron	柳子新論
sai	才
saidō	載道
Saigō Nobutsuna	西郷信綱
sakui	作為
Sakushi shikō	作詩志彀
"Sangzhong"	桑中
sankin kōtai	参勤交代
sarugaku	猿楽
se	瑟
sei (genuineness)	誠
sei (inborn nature)	性

sei (correctness)	正
Seidan	政談
seido	制度
Seigaku mondō	聖学問答
seijin	成人
"Seikaron"	正過論
Seikyō yōroku	聖教要録
Sekihi	斥非
sen'ō no hō	先王の法
sentei	筌蹄
setsuwa	説話
sewamono	世話物
shamisen	三味線
Shang	商
Shanglin	上林
"Shan you fusu"	山有扶蘇
"Shaonan"	召南
Shen Buhai	申不害
sheng	声
Sheng'an waiji	升菴外集
shi (poetry)	詩
shi (scholar-official)	士
Shibun yōryō	紫文要領
Shigaku hōgen	詩学逢原
Shigen	詩源
Shihō seigi	詩法正義
Shi ji	史記
Shi jing	詩経
shijin no jō	詩人の情
Shi jizhuan	詩集伝
shijutsu	四術
Shika shichiron	紫家七論
Shikishima no michi	敷島の道
shikyō	四教
Shimizu Yoshitarō	清水吉太郎
Shimōsa	下総
shin	信
Shinano	信濃
shinchū	新註
Shinkokinshū	新古今集
"Shinsai no gūsaku"	新歳の偶作
Shiron	詩論
shitsu (zither)	瑟
shitsu (substance)	質

shizen	自然
Shizen shin'eidō	自然真営道
shō	笙
Shōnai	庄内
"Shōnen kō"	少年行
shōsetsu	小説
Shōtoku Taishi	聖徳太子
shu	恕
Shūishū	拾遺集
shūji	修辞
Shu jing	書経
Shun	舜
"Shuoren"	碩人
Shushi shiden kōkō	朱氏詩伝膏肓
sijiao	四教
Sima Guang	司馬光
Sima Qian	司馬遷
Sima Xiangru	司馬相如
sishu	四術
si wu xie	思無邪
"Sixuan fu"	思玄賦
sobayōnin	側用人
Sōdō Shōshū	草堂小集
Sōju	宋儒
"Song"	頌
Song	宋
Song Yu	宋玉
"Soraigaku an"	徂徠学案
Sorai sensei tōmonsho	徂徠先生答問書
Soraishū	徂徠集
Sugagasa no nikki	菅笠日記
Suga Naoiri	須賀直入
Sugiura Kuniakira	杉浦国頭
Sugiura Masaki	杉浦真崎
Sui	隋
sukegō	助郷
Suzunoya shū	鈴屋集
Tabi no nagusa	旅のなぐさ
tada no kotoba	ただの詞
tai	体
taifu	大夫
Taigiroku	大疑録
Taiheisaku	太平策
Takano Rantei	高野蘭亭

Takebe Ayatari	建部綾足
Takenouchi Shikibu	竹内式部
"Takushiron"	択詞論
Tamaboko hyakushu	玉鉾百首
Tamagatsuma	玉勝間
Tamenaga Shunsui	為永春水
tan	端
Tang (king)	湯
Tang (dynasty)	唐
Tangshi xuan	唐詩選
tanka	短歌
Tanuma Okitsugu	田沼意次
"Taohuayuan ji"	桃花源記
Tao Qian	陶潜
taoyame	手弱女
tatsui	達意
Tayasu Munetake	田安宗武
tei	悌
ten	天
tenma sōdō	伝馬騒動
Tenmei	天明
tenmei	天命
tenri	天吏
ti (brotherly obedience)	悌
ti (poetic topic)	題
ti (essence)	体
tian	天
Tianbao	天宝
"Tian bao"	天保
tiandi zhi zhong	天地之中
tianli	天吏
tianming	天命
tianming zhi xing	天命之性
tian zhi xing	天之性
"Ti xishanbi shi"	題西山壁詩
Toda Mosui	戸田茂睡
Tōga	東雅
Tōgo shi	唐後詩
toki	時
toku	徳
Tokugawa	徳川
Tokugawa Harusada	徳川治貞
Tokugawa Ieharu	徳川家治
Tokugawa Ienari	徳川家斉

Tokugawa Ienobu	徳川家宣
Tokugawa Ieshige	徳川家重
Tokugawa Ietsugu	徳川家継
Tokugawa Ieyasu	徳川家康
Tokugawa Tsunayoshi	徳川綱吉
Tokugawa Yoshimune	徳川吉宗
tong	同
Tongjian gangmu	通鑑綱目
Tōshisen	唐詩選
Tōshisen kokujikai	唐詩選国字解
tōshō	堂上
tōzen no ri	当然の理
Tsushima	対馬
Ueda Akinari	上田秋成
"Uhōshū ni towaruru o shasu"	雨芳洲に訪わるるを謝す
Uiyamabumi	宇比山踏
Uji shūi monogatari	宇治拾遺物語
ujō no mono	有情の物
Umayato	厩戸
"Umazake no uta"	うま酒の歌
Usami Shinsui	宇佐美灊水
uta	歌
wa	和
Wadoku yōryō	和読要領
wagaku	和学
wagaku goyō	和学御用
Wagaku taigai	和学大概
"Waiwu"	外物
waka	和歌
Wakamizu Suguru	若水俊
wakun	和訓
Wang Jiusi	王九思
Wang Shizhen	王世貞
Wang Tingxiang	王廷相
Wang Yangming	王陽明
watakushi	私
Watanabe Mōan	渡辺蒙庵
Wei (state)	衛
Wei (dynasty)	魏
Weiniang	韋娘
wen	文
Wen	文
Wen xuan	文選
Wu (king)	武

Wu (state)	呉
Wuchang	武昌
Wu Guolun	呉国倫
Wujing zhengyi	五経正義
Wuling	五陵
Wu Zi Xu	伍子胥
Xi	僖
Xia	夏
xiao	孝
xiaoxu	小序
"Xiaoya"	小雅
xie	邪
Xie Zhen	謝榛
Xijing zaji	西京雑記
xin (faithfulness)	信
xin (heart)	心
xing (inborn nature)	性
xing (evocation)	興
xingling	性霊
xing zhi yu	性之欲
xue	学
Xunzi	荀子
Xu Zhenqing	徐禎卿
Xu Zhongxing	徐中行
ya	雅
yaku	訳
Yakubun sentei	訳文筌蹄
Yamaga gorui	山鹿語類
Yamaga Sokō	山鹿素行
Yamagata Daini	山県大弐
Yamagata Shūnan	山県周南
Yamamoto Hokuzan	山本北山
Yamanoue no Okura	山上憶良
Yamashiro	山城
Yamato	大和
Yamato shōgaku	大和小学
Yamazaki Ansai	山崎闇斎
yan	言
Yan	燕
Yanagisawa Yoshiyasu	柳沢吉保
Yang Shen	楊慎
Yan Yu	厳羽
Yanzi	晏子
Yao	堯

yi	義
Yi jing	易経
yin	音
Yin	殷
yō	用
Yodoya	淀屋
yoku	欲
yong	用
"Yoru, bokusui o kudaru"	夜、墨水を下る
Yosa Buson	与謝蕪村
Yoshikawa Kōjirō	吉川幸次郎
"Yoshino no hana o mite yomeru"	よし野の花をみてよめる
Yu	禹
Yuan Hongdao	袁宏道
Yuan Kang	袁康
Yuan Zhongdao	袁中道
Yuan Zongdao	袁宗道
Yue	越
yuefu	楽府
"Yue ji"	楽記
Yue ji dongjing shuo	楽記動静説
Yue jing	楽経
Yue jue shu	越絶書
"Yu Wuzhi shu"	与呉質書
Yuzhou	渝州
"Yu zi Yandeng shu"	与子儼等疏
zai	材
Zang Wuzhong	臧武仲
zekku	絶句
Zekku kai	絶句解
"Zeng Li sikong niang"	贈李司空娘
"Zeng Su Wan shuji"	贈蘇縮書記
zenjin	全人
Zhang Heng	張衡
Zhao	趙
zheng	正
Zheng	鄭
Zheng Xuan	鄭玄
zhi (substance)	質
zhi (intention)	志
zhi (wisdom)	智
zhi (direct)	直
zhong (loyalty)	忠
zhong (centrality)	中

zhongyong	中庸
Zhongyong zhangju	中庸章句
Zhou	周
"Zhounan"	周南
"Zhou song"	周頌
Zhow	紂
Zhuang	莊
Zhuang Jiang	莊姜
Zhuangzi	莊子
Zhu Jia	朱家
Zhu Xi	朱熹
Zhuzi yulei	朱子語類
Zigong	子貢
Zilu	子路
Zisi	子思
Zixia	子夏
Ziyou	子猶
Zizhi tongjian	資治通鑑
zoku	俗
zokugaku	俗樂
Zong Chen	宗臣
Zuo zhuan	左伝

Notes

Introduction

1. "Nativism" has often been used in English-language scholarship simply as a translation for the Japanese term "Kokugaku," but some recent scholars have sought to differentiate the terms. In *Proving the Way*, for example, Mark McNally draws a distinction between Kokugaku and nativism by using "Kokugaku" to "refer specifically to the scholarship of Atsutane and the members of the Norinaga School during the nineteenth century," as opposed to "nativism," which he uses "for classical literary studies prior to 1800, and for the various forms of Shinto scholarship of the nineteenth century other than Kokugaku" (McNally, *Proving the Way*, p. 1 n1). In a review article on *Proving the Way* and Susan Burns' *Before the Nation*, Mark Teeuwen takes a different approach to the term "nativism," defining it as "the ambition to revive or perpetuate aspects of indigenous culture in response to a perceived threat from other cultures" (Teeuwen, "Kokugaku vs. Nativism," p. 227). He argues that we need to "lay aside our own orthodoxy about Kokugaku: that Kokugaku is nativism, and that nativism is Kokugaku," and instead pay attention to the existence of non-nativist forms of Kokugaku, and non-Kokugaku forms of nativism (p. 240). Like Teeuwen, I use "nativist" to indicate those Tokugawa figures who sought to purify Japanese culture of foreign influences, whether or not they belong to what is normally labeled as "Kokugaku" (which is itself a category with flexible boundaries, defined variously by such factors as these figures' objects of study, scholarly methodology, or institutional affiliation). Although Mabuchi and Norinaga would fall within any modern scholar's conception of Kokugaku, I prefer to speak of their poetic theories as "nativist" rather than "Kokugaku" theories, as I am primarily interested in their development of ideas of Japanese superiority and cultural purity in their writings on poetry.

2. In describing Tokugawa figures as critics of Zhu Xi, I am not suggesting that they always presented a balanced picture of his philosophy, or that their interpretations were unaffected by later readings of Zhu Xi. To a certain extent, then, the "Zhu Xi" or "Song Confucians" (*Sōju*) criticized by the writers I discuss have to be considered a discursive construct that plays a particular role as a foil for philosophies being developed in Tokugawa Japan. While this is not an arbitrary construct,

as it is certainly based in the writings of Zhu Xi and other Song philosophers, it is not the only possible interpretation of them. The idea of Zhu Xi's Confucianism as a static and monolithic tradition plays a major role in Maruyama Masao's *Nihon seiji shisōshi kenkyū*, a work I discuss later. Maruyama has been criticized on this point by, among others, Wm. Theodore de Bary (see, for example, his Introduction to *Principle and Practicality*), and Maruyama himself acknowledges the validity of such criticisms in his introductory notes to the English translation of *Nihon seiji shisōshi kenkyū* (Maruyama, *Studies in the Intellectual History of Tokugawa Japan*, pp. xxxv–xxxvi).

3. At times they went so far as to accuse Zhu Xi of wanting to extinguish emotions altogether, a view that is, as I discuss later, an oversimplified interpretation of Zhu Xi's view of emotionality. Among Tokugawa followers of Zhu Xi, it was Yamazaki Ansai (1618–1682) whose reading of him most closely conformed to the Sorai school and nativists' picture of him as an extreme moral rigorist and opponent of emotionality. In his early years Sorai himself was a follower of Zhu Xi, and Wakamizu Suguru has noted that Sorai's reading of Zhu Xi's view of human emotions was much more nuanced in his earlier writings, suggesting that Sorai, once he developed his own philosophy in opposition to Zhu Xi, intentionally presented a polemical reading of him as simply hostile toward emotionality (Wakamizu, *Sorai to sono monjin no kenkyū*, pp. 37–45).

4. This aspect of the Sorai school and nativism has been brought up in a number of English-language studies. Norinaga's school is discussed in Rubinger, *Private Academies of Tokugawa Japan*, pp. 158–73. In *Bonds of Civility*, Eiko Ikegami explores the extension of aesthetic communities to a broad range of society in the Tokugawa period (see pp. 232–35 for her discussion of Kokugaku constructions of "Japaneseness"). Mark McNally's *Proving the Way*, which focuses on developments after Norinaga's death, applies Pierre Bourdieu's theories of the sociology of culture to analyze how competition between various schools and factions affected the development of nativism. Sorai's academy is the subject of Yamashita, "School Relations in Ogyū Sorai's Miscanthus Patch Academy."

5. The poetry of the Sorai school and nativism, and particularly that of Sorai and Norinaga themselves, has been relatively neglected by scholars, as it is generally seen as primarily of interest as an illustration of certain philosophical ideals, rather than for its literary merit. The poetry of Sorai's less philosophically minded disciples, such as Nankaku, has been given more attention than that of Sorai himself. For Parvulesco's discussion of the poetry of the Sorai school, see pp. 91–130. She translates and discusses a number of poems by members of the Sorai school, although she does not include any of Sorai's own poetry. There are numerous studies in Japanese of the poetry of the Sorai school, most notably Hino, *Sorai gakuha*. A work that situates Nankaku's poetry in a biographical context is Hino, *Hattori Nankaku denkō*. Turning to nativist poetry, Michael Marra's *The Poetics of Motoori Norinaga* contains, in addition to translations of Norinaga's essays on poetry, translations of a poetic travel diary of his, *Sugagasa no nikki* (The Sedge Hat Diary) (pp. 33–95), and selections from his poetry collection the *Suzunoya shū* (pp. 96–101).

Mabuchi enjoys a higher reputation than Norinaga as a poet, and many book-length studies of Mabuchi contain sections on his waka. The most comprehensive study devoted entirely to Mabuchi's poetry is Tabayashi, *Kamo no Mabuchi kashū no kenkyū*. Another book that focuses on Mabuchi's poetry is Okumura, *Kamo no Mabuchi: den to uta*, which presents his poetry in a biographical context. Within Mabuchi's school, like Sorai's, it is the less philosophically oriented figures, such as Murata Harumi (1746–1811) and Katō Chikage (1735–1808), the leaders of the so-called Edo school (Edo-ha) of Mabuchi's disciples, who have higher reputations today as poets. A pioneering work on the Edo-ha is Uchino, *Edoha kokugaku ronkō*. The Edo-ha has received increased attention in recent Japanese scholarship, and two major studies are Tanaka, *Murata Harumi no kenkyū*, and Suzuki, *Tachibana Chikage no kenkyū* (Tachibana Chikage is another name for Katō Chikage). The poetic activities of another follower of Mabuchi, Arakida Hisaoyu (1746–1804), are the focus of Teeuwen, "Poetry, Sake, and Acrimony." In this article, Teeuwen rightly stresses the role of poetic practice, rather than ideological theories about waka, in the growth in popularity of Kokugaku. While the philosophical concerns that I deal with were admittedly not of primary importance to many students of Kokugaku, I still do maintain that the theoretical writings on waka of figures like Mabuchi and Norinaga are significant as more than just outgrowths of their activities as poets.

6. Ogyū Sorai, *Bendō*, p. 14. Complete English translations of *Bendō* can be found in Lidin, *Ogyū Sorai's "Distinguishing the Way"*; Najita, ed., *Tokugawa Political Writings*; and Tucker, *Ogyū Sorai's Philosophical Masterworks*.

7. Sorai particularly singled out Zhu Xi and his Tokugawa followers for sacrificing pragmatic issues of government to the pursuit of individual moral purity. This criticism of Zhu Xi had precedents in Chinese Confucianism, most notably with Zhu Xi's contemporary Chen Liang (1143–1194). Imanaka Kanshi discusses the similarities between Sorai and Chen Liang in *Soraigaku no shiteki kenkyū*, pp. 253–65. For an account in English of Chen Liang and his relationship with Zhu Xi, see Tillman, *Confucian Discourse and Chu Hsi's Ascendancy*, pp. 145–86.

8. A classic study of this phenomenon, covering both Genroku literature and the philosophy of Itō Jinsai, is Nakamura Yukihiko's "Bungaku wa 'ninjō o iu' no setsu," in *Kinsei bungei shichō kō*, pp. 56–94. Hino Tatsuo's "'Mono no aware o shiru' no setsu no raireki" discusses how the emotionalism of Norinaga's literary thought relates to broader tendencies in Tokugawa literature and culture.

9. Kaibara Ekiken, *Taigiroku*, p. 17.

10. Itō Jinsai, *Gomō jigi*, p. 31. For an English translation of *Gomō jigi*, see Tucker, *Itō Jinsai's "Gomō jigi."*

11. Itō Jinsai, *Gomō jigi*, p. 53.

12. Zhu Xi's philosophy does allow for certain outward-oriented forms of cultivation, as principle can be found in external things. Such a process of investigating external things, however, is still oriented toward uncovering the principle that already exists in the self a priori, a notion that Jinsai found problematic.

13. Kumazawa Banzan, *Daigaku wakumon*, p. 411.

14. For a more detailed account of these and other issues in Banzan's thought, see

McMullen, "Kumazawa Banzan and *Jitsugaku*: Toward Pragmatic Action." Banzan also had a great interest in literature, specifically the *Tale of Genji*, as explored in depth in McMullen, *Idealism, Protest, and the "Tale of Genji."* For discussions of how Sorai's plans for reform compare to Banzan's, see McEwan, *The Political Writings of Ogyū Sorai*, pp. 27–28, and Koschmann, *The Mito Ideology*, pp. 14–15.

15. Yamaga Sokō, *Yamaga gorui*, p. 177.

16. Ibid., p. 27.

17. Ibid., p. 15.

18. While the term *kogaku* was in use in the Tokugawa period, it was in the Meiji period, with Inoue Tetsujirō's *Nihon kogakuha no tetsugaku*, that the term came to be used consistently to group together Sokō, Jinsai, and Sorai, and to present them as a single coherent movement in opposition to followers of Zhu Xi.

19. The "High Tang" refers specifically to the Kaiyuan (713–741) and Tianbao (742–755) eras.

20. This book, published as a single volume in 1952, consists of three essays originally published separately in *Kokka gakkai zasshi* between 1940 and 1944. It has been translated into English by Mikiso Hane as *Studies in the Intellectual History of Tokugawa Japan*.

21. Maruyama borrows this framework from the German sociologist and political scientist Ferdinand Tönnies (1855–1936).

22. Maruyama was innovative in granting positive value to a disinterest in personal morality. Earlier interpreters of Sorai had seen this exact same point as a significant flaw in his vision of Confucianism (Inoue, *Nihon kogakuha no tetsugaku*, pp. 509, 583; Iwahashi, *Sorai kenkyū*, p. 461).

23. Maruyama, *Nihon seiji shisōshi kenkyū*, p. 107. The philosophical significance Maruyama gives to the public/private distinction comes from Hegel. Maruyama follows the Hegelian view of China as representing a historical stage in which "the element of Subjectivity—that is to say, the reflection upon itself of the individual will in antithesis to the Substantial (as the power in which it is absorbed) . . . is not found. . . . The universal Will displays its activity immediately through that of the individual: the latter has no self-cognizance at all in antithesis to Substantial, positive being, which it does not yet regard as a power standing over it" (Hegel, *The Philosophy of History*, p. 120). This complete absorption of the individual into the powers by which it is dominated—so much so that domination is not even recognized as such—is the Hegelian background for Maruyama's discussion of the fusion of the public and private spheres in Zhu Xi. He then sees Sorai's separation of the public and private as the introduction of a "divided consciousness" that is aware of the opposition between itself and others. According to Hegel this recognition of opposition is the precondition for Spirit's forward movement, propelling it out of the stagnation characteristic of the historical stage represented by China.

24. This is a point that has been noted by a number of later interpreters of Sorai, such as Kojima Yasunori, who brings up Sorai's conception of Heaven specifically to counter Maruyama's reading of him as an advocate of a modern notion of political invention, and argues that while Sorai's Way was not itself metaphysical, it did

have to answer to a metaphysical source of legitimacy (Kojima, *Soraigaku to han Sorai*, pp. 5–25).

25. Ogyū Sorai, *Benmei*, p. 140. For a complete English translation of *Benmei*, see Tucker, *Ogyū Sorai's Philosophical Masterworks*. Portions of *Benmei* are translated in Najita, ed., *Tokugawa Political Writings*.

26. In his "Senchū • sengo Sorairon hihan" (pp. 81–98), Hiraishi Naoaki discusses these problems with Maruyama's dichotomies of public versus private and politics versus morality. Hiraishi argues that everyday morality is in fact very important for Sorai, and that the promotion of this morality is part of the broad sense of governance for Sorai (so governance is not limited to the restricted notion of "politics" that Maruyama attributes to Sorai).

27. de Bary, "Sagehood as Secular and Spiritual Ideal in Tokugawa Neo-Confucianism," p. 172.

28. Tucker, *Ogyū Sorai's Philosophical Masterworks*, p. 11. Tucker does allow that Sorai has a certain "modern" character to his philosophy, but defines this in terms of Sorai's interest in linguistic analysis as the key to solving philosophical problems (p. 1).

29. Sakai, *Voices of the Past*, p. 239.

30. Najita, ed., *Tokugawa Political Writings*, p. xxxvii.

31. Ansart, *L'empire du rite*, p. 24.

32. Yamashita, "Nature and Artifice in the Writings of Ogyū Sorai," p. 138.

33. My framework is related to the contrast between history and nature presented by Tetsuo Najita in "History and Nature in Eighteenth-Century Tokugawa Thought," but my use of "culture" is somewhat different from Najita's "history." Najita's categories are related to his focus on the epistemological question of how history and nature were looked to as sources of reliable knowledge in the eighteenth century. I use "culture," though, to refer not only to a concrete historical source of knowledge that can be put to use in the present, but also to a certain mode of structuring subjectivity and sociality.

34. I do not aim for a consistent translation of *wen*, as it takes on different meanings in different contexts, but I do make an effort to call attention to cases when this term, or the associated Japanese term *aya*, is being used. It should also be noted that both senses of "culture" that I describe here are normative, and not merely descriptive, for Sorai, in that there are correct and incorrect forms of social organization, music, language, etc. When discussing social practices in a purely descriptive sense, Sorai uses the term *fūzoku*, which I translate as "custom."

35. See, for example, Maruyama, *Nihon seiji shisōshi kenkyū*, p. 27, and Hino, "Jugaku to bungaku," p. 209.

36. Inoue, *Nihon kogakuha no tetsugaku*, pp. 492–93.

37. Hino, "Sorai gakuha no yakuwari," p. 66.

38. Hino, *Sorai gakuha*, p. 9.

39. Ibid., p. 28; Hino, "Jugaku to bungaku," p. 223.

40. This piece first appeared in volume 36 of the *Nihon shisō taikei*, and this is the source of my citations. It was later reprinted in Yoshikawa, *Jinsai • Sorai • Norinaga*.

41. Hino, *Sorai gakuha*, p. 8.

42. Yoshikawa, "Soraigaku an," p. 632.

43. The quoted phrase within this passage is from a 1712 letter of Sorai to a certain Tanabe in Nagasaki.

44. Nosco, *Remembering Paradise*, p. 170.

45. Maruyama, *Nihon seiji shisōshi kenkyū*, pp. 173, 178.

46. Matsumoto, *Kokugaku seiji shisō no kenkyū*, p. 146.

47. Saigō, *Kokugaku no hihan*, p. 89.

48. Harootunian, *Things Seen and Unseen*, p. 49.

49. Ibid.

50. Kojima, *Soraigaku to han Sorai*, p. 315.

51. Momokawa, *Uchi naru Norinaga*, p. 254.

52. Yoda, "Fractured Dialogues: *Mono no aware* and Poetic Communication in the *Tale of Genji*," p. 541.

53. Koyasu, *'Norinaga mondai' to wa nani ka*, p. 81.

54. Maruyama, *Nihon seiji shisōshi kenkyū*, p. 112.

55. Ibid., p. 111.

56. Wakamizu, *Sorai to sono monjin no kenkyū*, p. 80.

57. Kurozumi, *Fukusūsei no Nihon shisō*, p. 275.

58. References to the Confucian classics are common, as one would expect, in the writings of Sorai and his disciples, but also show up frequently in nativist waka poetics. A study that catalogues the many references to Confucian and other Chinese writings in Tokugawa waka poetics is Usami, *Kinsei karon no kenkyū*.

59. In scholarship on Tokugawa literary thought, a notable exception to this rather caricatured image of Confucian literary thought is McMullen, *Idealism, Protest, and the "Tale of Genji,"* which discusses how Kumazawa Banzan used the image of Heian Japan as an ideal Confucian society in order to cast a critical light on the regime of his own day.

60. Maruyama, *Nihon seiji shisōshi kenkyū*, p. 172.

61. The diversity of Confucian views on literature is explored in much scholarship on Chinese literary thought, such as Van Zoeren, *Poetry and Personality*. Scholarship on Tokugawa literary thought, however, tends to either refer to "Confucian views" without specifying which Confucians these come from, or else to take Zhu Xi as representative of Confucianism as a whole.

Chapter 1

1. "Bakusho Sōgakushatachi no bungaku kan," in Nakamura, *Kinsei bungei shichō kō*, pp. 1–31.

2. From *Hayashi Razan bunshū*. Quoted in Nakamura, *Kinsei bungei shichō kō*, p. 13.

3. From the preface to *Yamato shōgaku*. Quoted in Nakamura, *Kinsei bungei shichō kō*, p. 22.

4. Andō Tameakira, *Shika shichiron*, pp. 431–32.

5. The other three schools were the Lu, Qi, and Han schools. Their teachings have for the most part been lost.

6. Van Zoeren, *Poetry and Personality*, p. 52. I use *Book of Odes* or *Odes* to refer to the book itself, and "Odes" to refer to the poems that make up the book. At times the distinction is irrelevant, but sometimes it does matter, such as when it is a certain subset of the poems in the collection that is being referred to. Also, in the texts I deal with it is often ambiguous whether *shi* (Jp. *shi*) refers to the *Odes*/Odes, or simply to poetry in general. The ambiguity is rooted in the fact that Confucian scholars tend to see the *Odes* as the source of all later poetry, and as embodying the essence of poetry, with the result that the *Odes* is used to illustrate points about poetry in general. There is no way to make a clear distinction in meaning in all cases, and I have simply translated according to what the author seems to be emphasizing in a given passage.

7. Ibid., pp. 78–79.

8. The Mao text actually consists of a combination of three texts: the *Maoshi* (Mao Odes), which consists of the texts of the poems themselves, the *Maoshi xu* (Prefaces to the *Mao Odes*), and the *Maoshi zhuan* (Commentary on the *Mao Odes*). By describing the commentaries as explaining the meanings of the words of the poems, and the prefaces as explaining their moral significances, I do not mean to imply that these are completely separate interpretive tasks, as the Mao commentaries often attribute meaning to individual words and phrases in such a way as to generate a certain moral significance.

9. The Five Classics are the *Book of Odes*, *Shu jing* (Book of Documents), *Chunqiu* (Spring and Autumn Annals), *Li ji* (Record of Ritual) and *Yi jing* (Book of Changes).

10. Bol, *This Culture of Ours*, p. 79.

11. The "Great Preface" actually includes within it the Minor Preface to the first poem of the *Odes*, "Guanju," and there are numerous explanations as to the relationship between this Minor Preface and the "Great Preface."

12. Van Zoeren, *Poetry and Personality*, p. 133.

13. As indicated in my translation, the term *feng* can take on multiple meanings, and the rhetoric of the "Great Preface" relies on drawing connections between these different meanings.

14. Kong Yingda, *Maoshi zhengyi*, p. 36. I have benefited greatly from an annotated translation into modern Japanese of the *Maoshi zhengyi* commentary on the "Great Preface," in Okamura, *Mōshi seigi yakuchū*. I have also referred to Steven Van Zoeren's discussion of the first part of the *Maoshi zhengyi* commentary on the "Great Preface" in his *Poetry and Personality*, pp. 136–45, as well as the explanations of the "Great Preface" in Owen, *Readings in Chinese Literary Thought*, pp. 37–49, and in Saussy, *The Problem of a Chinese Aesthetic*, pp. 75–83. Saussy in particular focuses on the interpretations of Kong Yingda and Zheng Xuan.

15. The first of the quoted statements echoes the declaration in the *Book of Documents* that "Poetry speaks the intention" (Part 2, Bk. 1, paragraph 24). The third is related to the passage in the "Yue ji" (Record of Music) chapter of the *Record of Ritual* that states, "Emotions move on the inside, and so take form in sounds.

Sounds form patterning, and this is called tones" ("Yue ji," 558). The second is a modification of another "Record of Music" passage: "When we are joyful then we speak of it. When words are insufficient, then we lengthen our words. When lengthening words is insufficient, then we sigh it. When sighing is insufficient, then unconsciously our hands dance it and our feet tap it" ("Yue ji," p. 606).

16. Kong Yingda, *Maoshi zhengyi*, p. 38.

17. My analysis here owes much to Steven Van Zoeren's discussion of this section of the *Correct Significance* commentary. Van Zoeren describes how the commentary makes a distinction between what he calls the word-meanings and the music-meanings of the Odes; while word-meanings are provisional and opaque, music-meanings provide a perfect knowledge of the intentions inscribed in the Odes, as well as of the political circumstances that gave rise to these intentions (*Poetry and Personality*, pp. 139–45).

18. Bol, *This Culture of Ours*, p. 76.

19. For a discussion of developments in *Odes* interpretation between Kong Yingda and Zhu Xi, see Van Zoeren, *Poetry and Personality*, pp. 145–217.

20. Zhu Xi, *Shi jizhuan*, p. 1. A complete English translation of this preface is included in Lynn, "Chu Hsi as Literary Theorist and Critic," pp. 344–46.

21. Zhu Xi, *Yue ji dongjing shuo*, p. 94.

22. Zhu Xi is not completely consistent in his use of the terms "emotions" and "desires." Sometimes they are used as synonyms, while at other times the term "desires" is used to specifically denote those emotions that damage morality.

23. Chen Chun, *Beixi ziyi*, p. 57.

24. *Doctrine of the Mean* I.4.

25. Zhu Xi, *Zhongyong zhangju*, p. 18.

26. Chen Chun, *Beixi ziyi*, pp. 57–58. The emotions of joy, anger, sadness, and pleasure are mentioned in the *Doctrine of the Mean* passage cited earlier. The feelings of compassion, shame and disapproval, deference, and right and wrong come from *Mencius* Bk. 2, Pt. 1, Ch. 6, which will be discussed later in this chapter. Although Chen Chun lists the emotions from these two passages together, commentators have typically identified the *Mencius* passage with a more positive view of emotions, and the *Doctrine of the Mean* passage with a view of emotions as something that needs to be brought under control.

27. Zhu Xi, *Shi jizhuan*, pp. 2–3.

28. *Analects* II.2.

29. Zhu Xi, *Lunyu jizhu*, p. 53.

30. *Great Learning*, "The Text of Confucius," Sect. 5.

31. Zhu Xi, *Daxue zhangju*, p. 4.

32. Zhu Xi, *Zhuzi yulei*, p. 167.

33. Zhu Xi, *Shi jizhuan*, p. 3.

34. Itō Jinsai, *Gomō jigi*, p. 53. For a complete English translation of *Gomō jigi*, see Tucker, *Itō Jinsai's "Gomō Jigi."*

35. *Mencius* Bk. 2, Pt. 1, Ch. 6.

36. Zhu Xi, *Mengzi jizhu*, p. 238.

37. Itō Jinsai, *Gomō jigi*, p. 54.

38. Ibid., p. 43. Although Jinsai is critical of how Zhu Xi depicts emotionality in this *Mencius* passage, Zhu Xi's description of emotions as outward manifestations of virtue can be seen as a more affirmative stance toward emotionality than that taken by his commentaries on such texts as the *Doctrine of the Mean* and the "Record of Music," which focus more on how emotions can be either good or bad, and thus need to be regulated. How to conceive of the relationship between these two perspectives on emotionality became a topic of considerable debate among later followers of Zhu Xi, most famously in the so-called Four-Seven Debate in sixteenth-century Korea. The name of this debate refers to the Four Beginnings in *Mencius* and the seven emotions listed in the *Record of Ritual* (the emotions listed in the *Doctrine of the Mean* passage discussed earlier are a subset of these emotions). For a discussion of the Four-Seven Debate, see Chung, *The Korean Neo-Confucianism of Yi T'oegye and Yi Yulgok*. The main texts from the debate are translated in Kalton, *The Four-Seven Debate*.

39. This term appears most famously in *Analects* XV.23: "Zigong asked, 'Is there one word that one can act upon for one's entire life?' The Master said, 'Is not considerateness such a word? What you do not want done to yourself, do not do to others.'" This term is often rendered as "empathy" in English translations of Confucian texts. I avoid this translation here, despite its relevance to my argument, as *shu* can have a range of meanings, and I want to call attention to how Jinsai, by explicitly equating this term with the idea of accessing the experiences of others, is consciously steering its meaning toward a notion of empathy. In other words, I am trying to keep my translation itself as neutral as possible, so as not to obscure Jinsai's role in creating textual meaning as a commentator.

40. Itō Jinsai, *Gomō jigi*, p. 65.

41. Itō Jinsai, *Dōjimon*, pp. 154–55.

42. Itō Tōgai, *Dokushi yōryō*, p. 12. Lawrence Marceau discusses this text of Tōgai's in "*Ninjō* and the Affective Value of Literature at the Kogidō Academy," pp. 52–55.

43. Itō Jinsai, *Rongo kogi*, p. 15.

44. Itō Jinsai, *Gomō jigi*, p. 86.

45. Itō Jinsai, *Rongo kogi*, p. 191. From the commentary on *Analects* XIII.5.

46. Itō Jinsai, *Gomō jigi*, p. 86.

47. The *Mencius* passage is Bk. 7, Pt. 2, Ch. 19, which describes how superior men tend to be subjected to unfair criticism. The Ode quoted is "Baizhou" (Mao #45).

48. This poem does not appear in the *Odes*, but Jinsai is referring to *Analects* IX.30: "'The flowers of the plum tree flutter about. How could I not be thinking of you? Yet your house is distant.' The Master said, 'It is that one hasn't thought of it. How could it be distant?'"

49. The Airs, Elegantiae, and Hymns are categories of poems within the *Book of Odes*, while exposition, comparison, and evocation are rhetorical techniques used in the *Odes*. It is not entirely clear why the categories of poems in the *Odes* are listed

together with these rhetorical techniques as the six principles; commentators have given a variety of explanations for this.

50. The Odes that Jinsai discusses this point in relation to are "Sangzhong" (Mao #48), "Qiuzhong you ma" (Mao #74), and "Shan you fusu" (Mao #84).

51. My analysis here owes much to Noguchi Takehiko's discussion of this issue in "Itō Jinsai ni okeru bungakuron no seiritsu katei." Noguchi writes about how Jinsai started out as a follower of Zhu Xi, but then developed theories of human nature and self-cultivation based on the idea of virtue as something that needs to be actively developed, rather than simply uncovered. Noguchi then relates these views of Jinsai's to his idea of the active role of the reader in creating meaning in the Odes, and his rejection of Zhu Xi's interpretations of certain Odes as lewd.

52. It is actually only the first two lines in the quotation that are from "Shuoren." The source of the third line is not clear.

53. Itō Jinsai, *Rongo kogi*, p. 13.

54. Itō Jinsai, *Gomō jigi*, p. 31.

55. Itō Jinsai, *Rongo kogi*, p. 34.

56. Kurozumi Makoto describes this aspect of Jinsai's literary thought when he writes, in the context of a discussion of how Jinsai views the *Odes* as one of the Six Classics, "Jinsai recognizes in the Six Classics a certain dimension of expression that differs from disputation and proof, and that cannot be reduced to simple 'meanings' and 'arguments.' If we are to find in Jinsai the 'literary' or the 'poetic,' it is in this moment. When people move beyond the normative one-to-one correspondence between people and people, or people and things, then they arrive at an imaginative dimension. . . . It is in such a place that the literary and the poetic are manifested" (Kurozumi, *Kinsei Nihon shakai to jukyō*, p. 275).

Chapter 2

1. He came across their writings among a large collection of books that he purchased in 1705 (Hiraishi, *Ogyū Sorai nenpu kō*, p. 57).

2. For a discussion of Sorai's activities while working for Yoshiyasu, and how these tied in to the development of his new views on language, see Pastreich, "Grappling with Chinese Writing as a Material Language."

3. *Benmei* can be read as a response to Jinsai's *Gomō jigi* (The Meaning of Terms in the *Analects* and *Mencius*), which was in turn responding to Chen Chun's exposition of Zhu Xi's philosophy in his *Beixi ziyi* (Master Beixi's Lexicon). The relationship of *Benmei* to these earlier works is emphasized by John Tucker in the introduction to *Ogyū Sorai's Philosophical Masterworks*.

4. These works were written in secret, which makes it difficult to pin down precise dates for them. In *Ogyū Sorai nenpu kō*, Hiraishi Naoaki gives 1721 as a date for *Taiheisaku* (pp. 132, 229–39) and 1726 for *Seidan* (pp. 159, 254–63).

5. The officials are not mentioned by name in the letters, but were later identified as Mizuno Genrō and Hikita Yakara, both from Shōnai domain. For a discussion of Sorai's relationship with them, see Yamashita, *Master Sorai's Responsals*, pp. 8–16.

6. See Lidin, *The Life of Ogyū Sorai*, pp. 63–65, for a discussion of Sorai's pos-

sible role in two policies. The first was a system providing for temporary increases in stipends for lower-ranking samurai who took up positions that would normally be considered above their rank. Previously, offices that carried a certain stipend could only be filled by samurai who received an equivalent hereditary stipend, thus impeding the promotion of talented people from lower ranks. The new system allowed for greater flexibility, as people could be promoted and given a higher stipend during their time in office, without the need to make the new stipend a permanent hereditary right. The other policy Lidin brings up involved new measures for fire prevention in Edo. Lidin argues that Sorai probably did play a significant role in the first of these policies, but that his role in the latter has likely been exaggerated.

7. See Iwahashi, *Sorai kenkyū*, pp. 165–66.

8. For more detailed biographical information on Sorai, see Lidin, *The Life of Ogyū Sorai*, and Yamashita, "Compasses and Carpenter's Squares."

9. For a discussion of Hakuseki's political thought, see Nakai, *Shogunal Politics*.

10. Ogyū Sorai, *Bendō*, p. 28.

11. Ogyū Sorai, *Benmei*, p. 136.

12. Itō Jinsai, *Gomō jigi*, p. 39.

13. Ogyū Sorai, *Benmei*, p. 56.

14. Ibid., p. 43.

15. Ibid., p. 106.

16. Naoki Sakai uses this notion of framing to discuss Sorai's philosophy in *Voices of the Past*, especially with regard to Sorai's idea of inhabiting linguistic worlds, and I draw on Sakai's analysis here.

17. Ogyū Sorai, *Yakubun sentei*, p. 551. For an English translation of the introduction to *Yakubun sentei*, see Pastreich, "Grappling with Chinese Writing as a Material Language."

18. Not only does Sorai see the two languages as distinct in vocabulary and syntax, he also judges vernacular Chinese a superior language to vernacular Japanese. His emphasis on the vernacular, then, should not be confused with an approach that takes all natural languages to be equally valid.

19. Ogyū Sorai, *Yakubun sentei*, p. 549.

20. The metaphor of the fishtrap and rabbit snare comes from chapter 26 of *Zhuangzi*, entitled "Waiwu" (External Things): "The fish trap exists because of the fish; once you've gotten the fish, you can forget the trap. The rabbit snare exists because of the rabbit; once you've gotten the rabbit, you can forget the snare. Words exist because of meaning; once you've gotten the meaning, you can forget the words. Where can I get a man who has forgotten words so I can have a word with him?" (Translation from Watson, trans., *Chuang Tzu*, p. 140.) Based on its use in this passage, the term *sentei* came to have the meaning of a provisional tool used to achieve some goal, or an introduction or guide to something. Sorai is not really trying to "forget words" entirely, so he is borrowing somewhat loosely from the source passage, but he is adhering to it to the extent that he sees translation as a tool for the ultimate goal of mastering the Chinese original.

21. From Su Shi's "Ti xishanbi shi" (Poem on the Cliff of the Western Mountain): "They do not know the true character of Mount Lu / They only rely on their place within the mountain."

22. Ogyū Sorai, *Yakubun sentei*, p. 548.

23. Ogyū Sorai, *Taiheisaku*, pp. 448–49.

24. Ogyū Sorai, *Seidan*, p. 304. For an English translation of *Seidan*, see Lidin, *Ogyū Sorai's "Discourse on Government."*

25. Ogyū Sorai, *Taiheisaku*, p. 462.

26. Ogyū Sorai, *Seidan*, p. 304.

27. Ogyū Sorai, *Taiheisaku*, p. 459.

28. Ibid.

29. Ibid.

30. Ogyū Sorai, *Seidan*, p. 305.

31. Ibid., p. 311.

32. Ogyū Sorai, *Taiheisaku*, p. 475.

33. Ogyū Sorai, *Seidan*, pp. 290–91, pp. 267–69.

34. Sorai often uses the comparison to living in an inn to describe the life of the samurai in cities. See, for example, Ogyū Sorai, *Seidan*, pp. 305–6.

35. Ogyū Sorai, *Seidan*, p. 265.

36. Ogyū Sorai, *Bendō*, pp. 21–22.

37. Ogyū Sorai, *Seidan*, p. 276.

38. Ibid., p. 275.

39. Ibid., pp. 274–75.

40. Ogyū Sorai, *Bendō*, p. 25.

41. Ibid.

42. Ibid., pp. 25–26.

43. Ibid., p. 25.

44. Ibid.

45. Ogyū Sorai, *Sorai sensei tōmonsho*, p. 456. For an English translation of *Sorai sensei tōmonsho*, see Yamashita, *Master Sorai's Responsals*.

46. Ogyū Sorai, *Bendō*, p. 24.

47. *Doctrine of the Mean* I.I.

48. Zhu Xi, *Daxue zhangju*, p. 17.

49. Ogyū Sorai, *Bendō*, p. 14.

50. Ibid., pp. 14–15.

51. Ogyū Sorai, *Benmei*, p. 137.

52. Ibid., p. 48.

53. Ibid.

54. Ibid.

55. Ogyū Sorai, *Bendō*, p. 15.

56. Ogyū Sorai, *Benmei*, p. 67.

57. Sorai is playing on the multiple meanings of *cai/zai*, which can mean not only "capabilities," but also "lumber."

58. Ogyū Sorai, *Benmei*, p. 143.

59. Ibid., p. 49.

60. Ogyū Sorai, *Bendō*, p. 24.

61. Ibid.

62. Ogyū Sorai, *Seidan*, pp. 360–61.

63. Ogyū Sorai, *Benmei*, p. 54.

64. In *Japanische Anthropologie*, Gerhard Leinss focuses on the differences between the theories of the "inborn nature" put forth by Zhu Xi, Jinsai, and Sorai. He explains how Sorai denies the universality of human nature that is central to both Zhu Xi and Jinsai, but one thing lacking in his analysis of Sorai's view of human nature is that he does not discuss Sorai's idea of a universal human tendency to sociality and compassion.

65. Sorai's view of human nature as having certain good tendencies that were then harnessed and cultivated by the sages is an aspect of his philosophy that has sometimes been overlooked, especially in prewar interpretations of Sorai. Inoue Tetsujirō claims that Sorai has a bleak view of human nature, and compares him to Xunzi and Hobbes (Inoue, *Nihon kogakuha no tetsugaku*, p. 529). Inoue is critical of such a view of human nature, and argues that even in the state of nature humans have some basic altruistic tendencies, and that government is built on these tendencies (pp. 633–37). What he ignores, though, is that this is precisely the view that Sorai himself had put forth. Nomura Kanetarō makes an argument similar to Inoue's, claiming that Sorai followed Xunzi in seeing human nature as wicked, in contrast to Jinsai's view, following Mencius, that human nature is good (*Ogyū Sorai*, p. 53). Iwahashi Junsei, on the other hand, while noting certain similarities between Sorai and Hobbes, argues that Sorai sees human nature as neither entirely good nor entirely wicked, and points out how Sorai sees humans as inherently social beings (Iwahashi, *Sorai kenkyū*, pp. 268, 276). Maruyama Masao similarly rejects an equation of Sorai's and Xunzi's views (Maruyama, *Nihon seiji shisōshi kenkyū*, p. 86). I would agree with those who note that comparisons of Sorai to Xunzi and Hobbes fail to take into account his description of humans' social instinct and tendency toward mutual aid. Bitō Masahide contends that this emphasis of Sorai's on mutual aid and love represents a movement away from the Chinese Confucian emphasis on the individual as the primary unit of cultivation. Bitō sees Sorai's focus on the social whole over the individual as an adaptation of Confucianism to a Japanese mode of social consciousness, and claims that this distinctively Japanese aspect of Sorai is what led to him having such a great influence on nativism and Mito Learning ("Ogyū Sorai and the Distinguishing Features of Japanese Confucianism," p. 159). I do not see such a clear break, though, between Sorai (or nativism) and Chinese Confucianism.

66. Ogyū Sorai, *Chūyō kai*, p. 403.

67. Ogyū Sorai, *Benmei*, p. 85.

68. Ibid., p. 109.

69. Ibid., p. 174.

70. Ogyū Sorai, *Chūyō kai*, p. 408.

71. This passage is in the Duke Zhou, Year 20 section of the *Zuo zhuan*.

72. Ogyū Sorai, *Rongo chō*, vol. 2, pp. 176–77.

73. Ogyū Sorai, *Seidan*, p. 375. My discussion of Sorai's idea of "harmony" owes much to Kurozumi Makoto's "Nihon shisō ni okeru 'wa' no gainen." Kurozumi makes a point of stressing how the idea of "harmony" promoted by Sorai is very different from the common usage of "harmony" (*wa*) in modern Japanese to indicate a smoothing over of all differences in the interest of creating a homogeneous community (an idea that Sorai would see as "sameness," the opposite of "harmony").

74. Ogyū Sorai, *Taiheisaku*, p. 470.

75. Ogyū Sorai, *Sorai sensei tōmonsho*, p. 442.

76. Zhu Xi, *Lunyu jizhu*, p. 151.

77. Itō Jinsai, *Rongo kogi*, p. 208.

78. Ogyū Sorai, *Benmei*, p. 49.

79. Ogyū Sorai, *Rongo chō*, vol. 2, p. 190.

80. This discussion of *wen* is slightly different from Sorai's commentary on *Analects* VI.16, where he is concerned with *wen* as a quality that people possess as a result of training in such things as ritual and music (as opposed to *wen* as a quality of ritual and music themselves). There is a basic similarity, though, in how in his reading of *Analects* VI.16 as well he describes *wen* (or, at least, properly employed *wen*) as joined to some kind of raw material, while integrating it into a higher level of cultural value.

81. Ogyū Sorai, *Benmei*, p. 70.

82. Ibid., p. 92.

83. Ibid., p. 93.

84. Ibid., p. 94.

85. Ibid., p. 93.

86. Ogyū Sorai, *Chūyō kai*, p. 423.

87. Ibid., p. 424.

88. Ogyū Sorai, *Chūyō kai*, p. 403. He does explain elsewhere that it is possible for people to internalize bad things as well: "When one becomes accustomed to wickedness and makes it as if the inborn nature, then wickedness is also genuine" (Ogyū Sorai, *Benmei*, p. 94). Sorai's account of human nature (for example, his assertion that humans are naturally social beings) implies that there are certain limits to what we can internalize, but he does not see human nature as fully good or fully bad, which is why it is possible for both good and bad things to fulfill the minimal requirement of not contradicting human nature. The fact that ritual and music can be internalized is not meant to be final proof of their normative correctness, then, but rather a refutation of the specific Daoist criticism of ritual and music as a violation of the natural state of humans. This is why Sorai stresses that the discussion of genuineness only rose to prominence among Confucians within the context of their debates with Daoists. Ultimately what matters in Confucianism, according to Sorai, is that we internalize the right customs and norms rather than the wrong ones, and our ability to distinguish which are right can only come from following historical traditions, not merely by doing what feels right.

Chapter 3

1. Lidin, *The Life of Ogyū Sorai*, p. 128.

2. Ogyū Sorai, *Benmei*, p. 181.

3. Ibid., pp. 181–82. Sorai brings up the same Daoist phrase in *Bendō*, commenting that it "slights the external and values the internal" (Ogyū Sorai, *Bendō*, p. 12).

4. As in previous chapters, I use *Odes* (italicized) to refer to the *Book of Odes* as a text, and "Odes" to refer to the individual poems that make up the collection.

5. Ogyū Sorai, *Benmei*, p. 182.

6. In addition to Li Mengyang and He Jingming, the Former Seven Masters include Wang Jiusi (1468–1551), Bian Gong (1476–1532), Kang Hai (1475–1541), Wang Tingxiang (1474–1544), and Xu Zhenqing (1479–1511). The other of the Later Seven Masters are Xie Zhen (1495–1575), Xu Zhongxing (1517–1578), Liang Youyu (1520–1556), Zong Chen (1525–1560), and Wu Guolun (1529–1593). For an account in English of the Ancient Phraseology movement, see Yoshikawa, *Five Hundred Years of Chinese Poetry, 1150–1650*, pp. 137–76. The definitive treatment in Japanese of the relationship between Ming and Tokugawa theories of poetry is Matsushita Tadashi's massive *Edo jidai no shifū shiron*. The majority of the book is taken up by discussions of the influence of Ming poetics on individual figures from Tokugawa Japan, and the final part of the book contains an outline of the main poetic theories of the Ming and Qing. For Matsushita's discussion of Li Panlong and Wang Shizhen, see pp. 847–915.

7. A partial English translation of this text, with commentary, is included in Owen, *Readings in Chinese Literary Thought*, pp. 391–420.

8. This idea is developed in the opening section of the treatise. See Yan Yu, *Canglang shihua*, p. 21. This is part of a broader extended metaphor around which the treatise as a whole is structured, in which the mastery of poetry is compared to the quest for Zen enlightenment.

9. Ibid., p. 36. This judgment of High Tang poetry is repeated almost verbatim in Sorai's *Shigen* (Origins of Poetry), a collection of critical comments on poetry focused on the same distinction between High Tang and Song poetry that figures in Yan Yu's treatise (Ogyū Sorai, *Shigen*, p. 559). *Canglang shihua* was a major influence on Tokugawa poetics of verse in Chinese, and its appropriation was by no means limited to the Sorai school. Two authors who draw heavily on *Canglang shihua* in their poetics treatises are Ishikawa Jōzan (1583–1672), in his *Shihō seigi* (Correct Meanings of Poetic Methods), and Gion Nankai (1676–1751), in his *Nankai shiketsu* (Nankai's Principles of Poetry) and *Shigaku hōgen* (Encountering the Origins of Poetry).

10. The central figures of this school were Hongdao and his brothers, Yuan Zongdao (1560–1600) and Yuan Zhongdao (1570–1624). "Gongan" is the name of the place where they were from. The Gongan school is discussed in Yoshikawa, *Five Hundred Years of Chinese Poetry, 1150–1650*, pp. 181–84, and Matsushita, *Edo jidai no shifū shiron*, pp. 916–85.

11. It is no accident that when the poetics of the Sorai school eventually came under criticism in Japan in the late eighteenth century, the arguments against it

drew heavily on the writings of the Gongan school. The most notable example of this criticism of the Sorai school is *Sakushi shikō* (Thoughts on Composing Poetry, 1783), by Yamamoto Hokuzan (1752–1812).

12. Ogyū Sorai, *Soraishū*, p. 531. From a letter to Hori Keizan (1688–1757).

13. Ibid., p. 503.

14. Ogyū Sorai, *Yakubun sentei*, p. 563.

15. Ibid., p. 564. He repeats this point in a letter to Hori Keizan. See Ogyū Sorai, *Soraishū*, p. 530.

16. Ogyū Sorai, *Yakubun sentei*, p. 562.

17. For example, he comments in a letter to Hori Keizan that the ancient phraseology of Li and Wang "focuses on recording facts, and does not take pleasure in argumentation, and so corrected the flaw of Song [writers]" (Ogyū Sorai, *Soraishū*, p. 529). Yoshikawa Kōjirō discusses Sorai's idea of the capacity of ancient phraseology to record facts in "Soraigaku an," p. 675.

18. Ogyū Sorai, *Sorai sensei tōmonsho*, p. 460.

19. For Sorai's own description of how he extended the teachings of Li Panlong and Wang Shizhen to the interpretation of the Six Classics, see Ogyū Sorai, *Soraishū*, p. 530 and p. 537. Also, in the opening section of *Bendō* he credits Li and Wang with opening his eyes to ancient language and allowing him to grasp the Six Classics (Ogyū Sorai, *Bendō*, pp. 11–12).

20. My interpretations of Sorai's poems in this section have benefited from the notes in Ikkai and Ikezawa, eds., *Jusha*.

21. The biography of Wu Zi Xu is in book 66 of the *Shi ji*. An English translation is in Nienhauser, *The Grand Scribe's Records*, vol. 7, pp. 49–60.

22. The entire poem by Qian Qi is: "The gentlemen of Yan and Zhao sing many laments / I met Ju Meng in his home / I pour out my heart, but things remain unsaid / On the road ahead, the sun is setting."

23. The "Biographies of Knights-Errant" is book 124 of the *Shi ji*. An English translation is in Watson, *Records of the Grand Historian of China*, pp. 452–61. The section on Zhu Jia is on pp. 455–56 of the translation.

24. From "He Gu Zhi sheren zaochao daminggong zhi zuo" (Harmonizing with Retainer Gu Zhi's Work 'Morning Audience at the Palace of Great Light').

25. Translation by Stephen Owen, in Owen, *An Anthology of Chinese Literature*, p. 437.

26. "Yue ji," p. 560.

27. Watson, *Records of the Grand Historian of China*, vol. 2, p. 55.

28. Ogyū Sorai, *Sorai sensei tōmonsho*, p. 460.

29. It is difficult to accept Sorai's view that the *Odes* does not deal with governance, as many of the Odes in the Greater Elegantiae, for example, quite explicitly discuss the ideal government of King Wen. For our purposes, though, the scholarly accuracy of his account of the *Odes* is less important than the broader discourse on poetry that he is trying to promote.

30. Ogyū Sorai, *Sorai sensei tōmonsho*, p. 484.

31. Ogyū Sorai, *Bendō*, p. 31.

32. Ogyū Sorai, *Sorai sensei tōmonsho*, pp. 432–33. As Samuel Yamashita notes, the phrase that Sorai attributes to *Xunzi* is actually from *Guanzi* (Yamashita, *Master Sorai's Responsals*, p. 44 n18).

33. Ogyū Sorai, *Sorai sensei tōmonsho*, p. 460.

34. Ibid., p. 477.

35. Ibid., p. 432.

36. *Analects* XVII.9.

37. Zhu Xi, *Lunyu jizhu*, p. 178.

38. Ogyū Sorai, *Rongo chō*, vol. 2, p. 289.

39. Ogyū Sorai, *Benmei*, p. 53.

40. Ibid., pp. 55–56.

41. Ibid., p. 56.

42. Itō Jinsai, *Gomō jigi*, p. 68.

43. Ogyū Sorai, *Rongo chō*, vol. 1, pp. 165–66.

44. Because the *Book of Music* has been lost, these are sometimes referred to instead as the Five Classics. When Sorai discusses music as one of the Four Teachings, what he has in mind is the actual practice of music, not a text about music. This applies to ritual as well; the ritual that is one of the Four Teachings is for Sorai a form of practice, and does not just refer to the *Record of Ritual* as a text.

45. Ogyū Sorai, *Bendō*, p. 30.

46. Zhu Xi, *Shi jizhuan*, p. 3.

47. From the Duke Xi, Year 27 section.

48. Ogyū Sorai, *Benmei*, p. 80.

49. Ibid.

50. The yellow bell is the base tone in a Chinese scale, so the recovery of the original yellow bell used by the sages would make it possible to derive all the tones of their music.

51. Kawashima, "Ogyū Sorai cho 'Kingaku taiishō' honkoku," p. 18.

52. For a discussion of the role of music in Sorai's academy, see Chang, "Ken'en gakuha to ongaku," pp. 158–62.

53. Ogyū Sorai, *Benmei*, p. 140.

54. This is different from the view he put forth earlier in *Ken'en zuihitsu*, where he writes, "If you from time to time chant [poetry], it nourishes the inborn emotions. After music has disappeared, [poetry] takes on the role of music" (Ogyū Sorai, *Ken'en zuihitsu*, p. 181). While in his later writings he continues to imply a role for poetry in cultivating the emotions, as we are meant to internalize the elegant sentiments expressed by the poets of the past, this is different from the role that he describes music as playing in cultivating virtue.

55. Ogyū Sorai, *Benmei*, p. 140.

56. Kawashima, "Ogyū Sorai cho 'Kingaku taiishō' honkoku," p. 18.

57. This distinction between "responding" and "harmonizing" is discussed in Takahashi, *Edo no barokku*, pp. 149–50.

58. *Analects* III.20.

59. Ogyū Sorai, *Rongo chō*, vol. 1, pp. 131–32.

60. *Analects* XV.10. Also see *Analects* XVII.18: "The Master said, 'I dislike how purple takes away from the brilliance of vermilion. I dislike how the sounds of Zheng destroy correct music. I dislike how those clever of speech overthrow states and houses.'"

61. Ogyū Sorai, *Rongo chō*, vol. 2, p. 233. The passage that Sorai quotes is from Yang Shen's *Sheng'an waiji*.

62. Ogyū Sorai, *Rongo chō*, vol. 2, pp. 232–33.

63. Ogyū Sorai, *Bendō*, p. 13.

64. Ogyū Sorai, *Rongo chō*, vol. 1, p. 165.

65. Ibid.

66. Olivier Ansart makes a similar point when he notes that for Sorai, "A political capacity, humaneness, must secure the coherence and guarantee the sense of a system made of profoundly heterogeneous components." This is in contrast to Song Confucianism, in which "it is the mastery of one part, of one virtue, for example, that allows one to grasp the whole: coherence is given a priori when the smallest things of the world are impregnated with the immanent principles of the infinite natural order" (Ansart, *L'empire du rite*, pp. 81–82).

67. Wakamizu, *Sorai to sono monjin no kenkyū*, p. 80.

68. Although I develop this point in a different direction by emphasizing Sorai's view of the interrelationships between the Six Classics, my argument is similar to that made by Sawai Keiichi, who notes that while "Sorai's theory has generally been evaluated as having liberated the *Odes* from being an object of classical studies or politics, instead opening up the way for it to be perceived as 'literature' that expresses human emotions," in reality Sorai does not deny the status of the *Odes* as a Confucian Classic. Instead, Sawai notes, "Between Zhu Xi and Sorai a change came about in the understanding of both the Confucian Way itself and the significance of classical texts" ("'Giko' no sekai ninshiki," pp. 4–5).

69. Naoki Sakai makes a similar point when he writes of Sorai, "It was assumed that social and cultural institutions, of which the interior supposedly consisted, were regularities of a similar nature. Rites and the legal system were among them, as were poetry and music. Yet, none of these held overall supremacy. Together, they constituted a whole, and only in reference to the whole could each of them function as it ought" (Sakai, *Voices of the Past*, p. 233).

70. Ogyū Sorai, *Soraishū*, p. 503. He brings this up specifically in the context of rejecting the theory that the Odes were edited by selecting 300 from an original 3,000 poems.

Chapter 4

1. My source for biographical information on Nankaku is Tajiri and Hikita, *Dazai Shundai • Hattori Nankaku*.

2. My sources for biographical information on Shundai are Takebe, *Dazai Shundai* and Tajiri and Hikita, *Dazai Shundai • Hattori Nankaku*.

3. The tense, even bordering on hostile, relationship between Shundai and Sorai is discussed in Yamashita, "School Relations in Ogyū Sorai's Miscanthus Patch

Academy." Yamashita brings up an unsent letter from Shundai to Sorai, written just before Sorai's death, in which Shundai mentions that Sorai has accused him of being narrow and petty, and defends himself by saying that this is simply his nature bestowed by Heaven, and not something he should be expected to change.

4. Hattori Nankaku, *Nankaku sensei bunshū*, p. 227.

5. Hattori Nankaku, *Nankaku sensei tōka no sho*, p. 49.

6. Ibid., p. 61. Gion Nankai expresses a similar idea in his *Shigaku hōgen* (Encountering the Origins of Poetry) when he writes that "poetry is a vessel for elegance (*fūga*)," and goes on to criticize Bo Juyi (772–846) for trying to make poetry that even common people could understand: "Bo Juyi of the Tang believed that because poetry is a manifestation of human emotions, to do such things as refer to events from the past, use words skillfully, and make verses difficult by giving them mysterious depth, is to make poetry distant from the ears of the common people. He thought that the true essence of poetry was to be something that anyone could hear and understand, and that expresses well the emotions of common people. Every time he composed, he would strive to make it clear and easy to understand, so it could be grasped by vulgar people. If even the old woman who lived next door thought it interesting, then he would be pleased that he had succeeded, but if she did not understand it, he thought it was no good, and would discard it. Although this may sound reasonable, in fact it is ridiculous" (Gion Nankai, *Shigaku hōgen*, p. 247).

7. Hattori Nankaku, *Nankaku sensei bunshū*, p. 197. Asayama Yoshirō notes how Nankaku's description of the Odes as all being the product of gentlemen differs from Sorai's view of the Odes as coming from all levels of society (Asayama, "Hattori Nankaku no 'shi' no ishiki," p. 152).

8. Hattori Nankaku, *Nankaku sensei bunshū*, p. 202.

9. Translation adapted from Watson, trans., *Chuang Tzu*, p. 83.

10. Ibid., p. 84. The phrase that Nankaku cites also appears earlier in the same chapter of *Zhuangzi*: "When the springs dry up and the fish are left stranded on the ground, they spew each other with moisture and wet each other down with spit—but it would be much better if they could forget each other in the rivers and lakes. Instead of praising Yao and condemning Jie, it would be better to forget both of them and transform yourself with the Way" (ibid., p. 76). "Yao" refers to the sage king, and "Jie" to the famously cruel last ruler of the Xia dynasty.

11. A classic study of the role of Nankaku as a pioneering *bunjin* is Nakamura Yukihiko's "Bunjin Hattori Nankaku ron," included in *Kinsei bungei shichō kō*, pp. 155–91.

12. For a discussion of Takebe Ayatari as *bunjin*, as well as the *bunjin* phenomenon more generally, see Marceau, *Takebe Ayatari*.

13. In my interpretations of Nankaku's poems in this section, I have benefited from the notes in Yamamoto and Yokoyama, eds., *Hattori Nankaku, Gion Nankai*.

14. Graham, trans., *The Book of Lieh-tzu*, p. 34.

15. Hino Tatsuo discusses Nankaku's Daoist leanings in "Hattori Nankaku no shōgai to shisō," pp. 528–30. Olof Lidin has noted the presence of Daoist ideals

in Sorai's early writings, such as his travel diary *Kyōchūkikō* (Report from a Journey to Kai, 1710). This was before Sorai developed his own interpretation of Confucianism, which was critical of Daoism ("Ogyū Sorai's Place in Edo Intellectual Thought," p. 571).

16. Asayama Yoshirō, contrasting Nankaku's theory with the political role that Sorai finds for poetry, describes Nankaku as finding the purpose of poetry as lying in a kind of "self-completion" (*jikoteki kansei*) (Asayama, "Hattori Nankaku no 'shi' no ishiki," p. 147). I basically agree with this assessment, although with the added observation that self-completion for Nankaku is at the same time achieved through cultural completion, as the completed self is one that is constructed through culture. Asayama expresses ideas along these lines when he notes that Nankaku's poetics does not idealize a modern ideal of individual self-expression. Hino Tatsuo draws a similar contrast between Sorai's social orientation and Nankaku's individual orientation when he writes, "For Sorai, the ritual and music established by the sages were political forms for realizing order in society. Nankaku's ritual and music, though, were mediums for affirming the self" (Hino, "Hattori Nankaku no shōgai to shisō," pp. 524–25).

17. Dazai Shundai, *Keizairoku*, p. 9.

18. Ibid.

19. Dazai Shundai, *Seigaku mondō*, p. 82.

20. Ibid., p. 67.

21. Ibid., p. 71.

22. Dazai Shundai, *Bendōsho*, p. 215.

23. Ibid., p. 216.

24. Dazai Shundai, *Seigaku mondō*, p. 125.

25. Ogyū Sorai, *Taiheisaku*, p. 462.

26. Dazai Shundai, *Seigaku mondō*, p. 95. Inoue Tetsujirō criticizes Shundai strongly for this attitude, saying that it amounts to holding up hypocrisy as the ideal to which gentlemen are to strive (Inoue, *Nihon kogakuha no tetsugaku*, p. 692).

27. Maruyama Masao uses the passage I cite to support his idea of Sorai's modern liberation of the private interior sphere (Maruyama, *Nihon seiji shisōshi kenkyū*, p. 247). The problem with his explanation is that he conflates Shundai and Sorai by using a quote from Shundai to make a point about Sorai's philosophy, when in fact Sorai never presents such an idea himself.

28. Dazai Shundai, *Rikukei ryakusetsu*, p. 317.

29. This difference between Sorai's and Shundai's visions of cultivating the Way is discussed in Bitō, "Dazai Shundai no hito to shisō," p. 503, and Tajiri and Hikita, *Dazai Shundai • Hattori Nankaku*, pp. 58–59.

30. Kojima Yasunori, for example, argues that while Sorai sees the ritual and music of the sages as cultural and political mechanisms for regulating society as a unified whole, Shundai puts greater emphasis on their role as tools for regulating the individual heart (*Soraigaku to han Sorai*, p. 72). Bitō Masahide makes a similar point, noting that Sorai uses "ritual and music" as a broad term to refer to social institutions, while Shundai uses the term in a more concrete sense, to refer to specific

rules of propriety and the actual performance of music ("Dazai Shundai no hito to shisō," p. 504).

31. An account in English of Shundai's philosophy of political economy is Najita, "Political Economism in the Thought of Dazai Shundai (1680–1747)." Najita stresses the pragmatic character of Shundai's thought and his emphasis on economics above all else.

32. Dazai Shundai, *Keizairoku*, p. 115.

33. Shundai also notes here that Confucianism has its own kind of "non-action," but that it is distinct from that of Daoism. In Confucian non-action, according to Shundai, a political system is put in place, and then things are allowed to run their course within the bounds of this system.

34. Dazai Shundai, *Keizairoku shūi*, p. 300. For an English translation of *Keizairoku shūi*, see Najita, ed., *Tokugawa Political Writings*, pp. 141–53.

35. Kaihō Seiryō, *Keikodan*, p. 217.

36. For a discussion in English of Seiryō's development and transformation of the Sorai school's thought, see Najita, "Method and Analysis in the Conceptual Portrayal of Tokugawa Intellectual History," pp. 23–34. Najita argues that Seiryō took the instrumentalist political economy of Sorai and Shundai and shifted its focus from the samurai aristocracy to the merchant class, creating a vision of society as an economic union based not on hereditary class distinctions, but rather on proper calculation and measurement in economic exchange. He has also written about how Seiryō radically redefined the concept of virtue, casting it as a principle of economic calculation (Najita, "History and Nature in Eighteenth-Century Tokugawa Thought," pp. 647–48).

37. Dazai Shundai, *Rikukei ryakusetsu*, p. 310. The *Analects* quote is from XVI.13.

38. Dazai Shundai, *Rikukei ryakusetsu*, p. 308.

39. Ibid., p. 309.

40. Ibid., p. 310.

41. Dazai Shundai, *Keizairoku*, p. 21.

42. Dazai Shundai, *Doku Shushi shiden*, p. 2.

43. Dazai Shundai, *Shushi shiden kōkō*, pp. 17–18.

44. Dazai Shundai, *Rikukei ryakusetsu*, p. 305.

45. Ibid.

46. Dazai Shundai, *Keizairoku*, p. 19.

47. Dazai Shundai, *Shiron*, p. 7. Shundai's claim that Du Fu was solely occupied with poetry, and never became involved in official life, is an exaggeration.

48. Dazai Shundai, *Rikukei ryakusetsu*, p. 318.

49. Ibid. In modern Japanese, *gagaku* refers to the musical traditions of the imperial court in Kyoto, but Shundai also uses the term in a more philosophical sense, in which it denotes music that is "proper" in the sense of being in accord with the Way created by the sages of ancient China. As will be discussed below, though, he sees the court music of Kyoto as derived from the music of the sages, so there is ultimately an overlap between these two senses of *gagaku*.

50. Although Shundai has a reputation as a strict moralist, a reputation only

strengthened by his criticism of lewd music, we should not overlook that he saw music as potentially having a nurturing, uplifting potential as well. Noguchi Takehiko, for example, argues that Shundai's interest in music reveals a more passionate side to his character (Noguchi, *Edo bungaku no shi to shinjitsu*, p. 196).

51. Dazai Shundai, *Rikukei ryakusetsu*, p. 307.

52. Dazai Shundai, *Dokugo*, p. 279.

53. *Dengaku* ("field music") has its origins in music used in planting rituals. *Sarugaku* ("monkey music") began as a comic performing art and is the ancestor of Noh and Kyogen. Both *dengaku* and *sarugaku* involve dance and performance as well as music, but Shundai is particularly concerned with the musical aspects of them here. In *Dokugo* he goes into *sarugaku* in more detail, saying that even though it is "vulgar music" (*zokugaku*), it is not as bad as other vulgar music in that it is not lewd. He describes *sarugaku*, then, as a kind of intermediate stage in the degeneration of music (Dazai Shundai, *Dokugo*, pp. 277–79).

54. Dazai Shundai, *Rikukei ryakusetsu*, pp. 320–22.

55. Dazai Shundai, *Dokugo*, p. 273.

56. Ibid., p. 274.

57. Ibid., p. 276.

58. Dazai Shundai, *Shiron*, p. 6.

59. Dazai Shundai, *Bunron*, p. 10.

Chapter 5

1. The term "waka" refers most narrowly to the 31-mora form in classical Japanese verse. I use the term in this chapter and the next to refer not only to the 31-mora form, but also to other forms that appear in the *Man'yōshū* and the imperial anthologies, such as the chōka. Motoori Norinaga was actually opposed to the term "waka," which translates literally as "Japanese song," and argued that it is only from the standpoint of an outsider (such as a Chinese) that one would have to specify that it was *Japanese* song that was being referred to. Instead, he said that we should simply speak of "song" (*uta*) (*Isonokami sasamegoto*, p. 348). *Uta* is in fact the term most commonly used in the nativist writings on Japanese poetry that I discuss in this chapter and the next. I generally translate this term as "poetry," rather than "song," although I do call attention to places where it is specifically the sung character of poetry, rather than its semantic content, that is being emphasized.

2. Mōan wrote the preface for Shundai's *Shushi shiden kōkō* (The Fatal Errors of Zhu Xi's *Transmissions on the Odes*), which was discussed in Chapter 4.

3. My sources for biographical information on Mabuchi are Saigusa, *Kamo no Mabuchi*, and Nosco, *Remembering Paradise*.

4. A detailed account of the contributions to this debate can be found in Toki, *Tayasu Munetake*, vol. 1, pp. 509–754. Rather than presenting each text separately, Toki gives each segment of Arimaro's original text followed by the various responses to that specific portion of his essay, a format that is useful in showing how the debate on each particular point unfolded. A summary in English of each of the texts

of the *Kokka hachiron* debate can be found in Thomas, *The Way of Shikishima*, pp. 197–201.

5. The fact that the court poets continued to be influential well into the Tokugawa period is something that is downplayed in many modern literary histories. This omission owes much to the categories established in *Nihon kagaku shi*, by Sasaki Nobutsuna (1872–1963), originally published in 1910, which established a narrative of the history of waka poetics that continues to inform scholarship on the topic today. Sasaki uses the terms *chūsei* (medieval) and *kinsei* (early modern) not simply to designate historical periods, but to refer to particular attitudes toward waka. He defines early modern waka poetics through its spirit of free inquiry, versus the medieval conformity to rigid traditions such as secret transmissions. In this way, he classifies the court poets of the Tokugawa period as medieval, even though they were living within the historical period generally marked as early modern. While Sasaki's approach makes out Tokugawa court poets to be little more than an anachronistic holdover, in recent years scholars have given more serious attention to these poets and their role in Tokugawa literary culture. One major study is Suzuki, *Kinsei tōshō kadan no kenkyū*. Kinsei Tōshō Waka Ronshū Kankōkai, ed., *Kinsei tōshō waka ronshū* is a collection of articles by various scholars. A study focusing specifically on the Reizei house is Kubota, *Kinsei Reizeiha kadan no kenkyū*. In the English-language scholarship, discussions of Tokugawa court poetics can be found in Butler, *Emperor and Aristocracy in Japan, 1467–1680*, and Carter, *Householders: The Reizei Family in Japanese History*.

6. For an account in English of developments in Tokugawa poetics prior to the *Kokka hachiron* debate, see Thomas, *The Way of Shikishima*, pp. 1–44.

7. Kada no Arimaro, *Kokka hachiron*, p. 553.

8. The term "natural principle" comes from Song Confucianism. While Arimaro does not use it with the full philosophical baggage of Song Confucianism, there is a certain overlap to the extent that he uses it to suggest a universal capacity for reasoning that is inherent in human nature.

9. The "six arts" (*rikugei*) refers here to the six arts to be mastered by the Confucian gentleman: etiquette, music, archery, charioteering, calligraphy, and mathematics.

10. Although there are two prefaces to the *Kokinshū*, the *kana* (Japanese) and the *mana* (Chinese) prefaces, when I speak of the "*Kokinshū* preface," I am referring to the *kana* preface.

11. Peter Nosco discusses the different attitudes of the participants in the *Kokka hachiron* debate toward the political and moral role of poetry in "Nature, Invention, and National Learning." Nosco argues that Arimaro's position is similar to Sorai's view of poetry, which Nosco characterizes as valuing poetry as something artistic, rather than didactic and normative. Such a comparison of Arimaro and Sorai, though, does not take into account the strongly political character of Sorai's poetics. While Sorai does not take a strictly didactic approach to poetry, in the sense of viewing poems as moral teachings, neither does he see poetry as divorced from social concerns.

12. The Poetry Bureau Songs and the Songs of the East, both included in the twentieth and final book of the *Kokinshū*, consist of adaptations of folk songs and are thus somewhat at variance with the dominant aesthetic of the anthology.

13. The term *Shikishima no michi* was used by the court poets to refer to waka. *Shikishima no* is a *makurakotoba* for "Yamato" (Japan).

14. See Note 1, above, on the translation of *uta*. Here I use the translation "poetry/song" in order to highlight how the disagreements between Arimaro and Munetake are related to ambiguities in which aspects of *uta* allow it to be socially beneficial; as I discuss in what follows, Arimaro charges Munetake with failing to properly distinguish the roles of the lyrics of song and its tones, and as a result coming to faulty conclusions about the social role of poetry (taken in the sense of the words alone).

15. Tayasu Munetake, *Kokka hachiron yogen*, p. 99. The first part of this passage quotes the "Record of Music" chapter of the *Record of Ritual*: "In ancient times, King Shun strummed the five-stringed lute, and sang the song 'Nan feng'" ("Yue ji," p. 571).

16. Usami Kisohachi points out this aspect of the Arimaro/Munetake debate in *Kinsei karon no kenkyū: kangaku to no kōshō*, pp. 51–53, 82–83, 88–90. Usami sees Arimaro's position as influenced by the writings of Itō Jinsai and his son Itō Tōgai, and writes that the Sorai school did not pay that much attention to the issue of words versus tones in its critiques of Zhu Xi's reading of the *Odes*. Jinsai and Tōgai did, as Usami points out, criticize Zhu Xi for ignoring the words/tones distinction, but as I showed in Chapters 3 and 4, Sorai and Shundai put considerable emphasis on this issue as well. Moreover, I see this point as having deeper significance in the context of the Sorai school's critique of Zhu Xi, as Sorai (and especially Shundai) gave a more important place to music on a philosophical level than Jinsai and Tōgai did.

17. Kada no Arimaro, *Kokka hachiron sairon*, p. 108.

18. Kamo no Mabuchi, *Kokka hachiron yogen shūi*, p. 117.

19. The last part of this passage quotes from the "Great Preface." Usami Kisohachi comments on how Mabuchi explains the function of poetry in terms of musical discourse in *Kinsei karon no kenkyū*, pp. 180–82.

20. Mabuchi is specifically discussing *Odes* commentaries here, but the term "old commentaries" is used more generally to refer to Han and Tang commentaries on the Confucian classics, and "new commentaries" to refer to Zhu Xi's commentaries.

21. Kamo no Mabuchi, *Futatabi kingo no kimi ni kotaematsuru fumi*, p. 155.

22. Kamo no Mabuchi, *Kokuikō*, p. 383. For an English translation of *Kokuikō*, see Flueckiger, "Reflections on the Meaning of Our Country." There is also a German translation, in Dumoulin, "Kamo Mabuchi: Kokuikō—Gedanken über den 'Sinn des Landes.'"

23. Dazai Shundai, *Bendōsho*, p. 224. Mabuchi was one of a number of eighteenth-century figures to criticize Shundai along similar lines. I discuss the controversy brought about by *Bendōsho*, and Mabuchi's relationship to earlier critics of Shundai, in Flueckiger, "Reflections on the Meaning of Our Country," pp. 218–30.

See also Ogasawara, *Kokuju ronsō no kenkyū*, pp. 9–82, and Mogi, "Kokugaku to jukyō no ronsō," pp. 210–21.

24. Mabuchi only lists four virtues, even though he then refers to "these five virtues." I translate *rei* as "ritual" in *Bendōsho*, but "ritual propriety" in *Kokuikō*, because Shundai is pairing the term with music, implying that he is speaking of actual rituals themselves, while Mabuchi is using *rei* as one of a number of virtues. Mabuchi is not strictly quoting from *Bendōsho*, then, and he does not mention the text by name, but given the prominence of *Bendōsho*, it is safe to assume that this is the text Mabuchi has in mind.

25. For example, the *Dao de jing* states, "Not to honor men of worth will keep the people from contention; not to value goods which are hard to come by will keep them from theft; not to display what is desirable will keep them from being unsettled of mind" (translation from Lau, trans., *Lao Tzu: Tao Te Ching*, p. 7).

26. *Mononofu no michi* is one of a number of similar terms Mabuchi uses, all of which I translate as "the Way of the warrior."

27. Mabuchi's argument here is similar to a comment Arai Hakuseki makes in *Tōga*, where he writes, "The obscuring and disappearance of the meaning of the ancient words of our country appears to be largely due to how Chinese characters were used, and the ancient language was discarded. To explain this in more detail, the words from here [Japan] and the characters from there [China] are necessarily in a relationship of master to guest. The words of our country, as transmitted from earliest antiquity, are namely the master, and the words of foreign countries are namely the guest. When Chinese characters came to be commonly used, the meanings of the two were matched up with each other, and they always followed [the Chinese characters]. After that, the guests in the end became the masters, and the masters became the guests" (*Tōga*, p. 121). Kate Wildman Nakai discusses Hakuseki's views on ancient language in *Shogunal Politics*, p. 243, and brings up this passage from *Tōga* on p. 381 n17.

28. Although I translate *uta* as "poetry" here, the meaning of "song" is also crucial to Mabuchi, as I discuss below.

29. Kamo no Mabuchi, *Ka'ikō*, p. 349. Both *Ka'ikō* and *Niimanabi* have been translated into German, in Dumoulin, "Zwei Texte zum Kadō des Kamo Mabuchi."

30. Kamo no Mabuchi, *Ka'ikō*, p. 349.

31. Kamo no Mabuchi, *Niimanabi*, p. 358. In this passage he attributes the change in poetry from the Nara to the Heian period to the qualities of the regions in which the capital was located at these times, claiming that Yamato province has a manly character, while Yamashiro province has a feminine character.

32. Kamo no Mabuchi, *Ka'ikō*, p. 350. The language Mabuchi uses to describe the cultivation of an original nature has much in common with both Buddhist and Song Confucian descriptions of self-cultivation as the purification of the heart.

33. Kamo no Mabuchi, *Kokuikō*, p. 381.

34. Ibid., pp. 381–82.

35. For a discussion of Ansai's interpretation of the *Nihon shoki*, see Ooms, *Tokugawa Ideology*, pp. 227–44.

36. Kamo no Mabuchi, *Kokuikō*, p. 382.

37. Kamo no Mabuchi, *Goikō*, p. 395. The introductory portion of *Goikō* has been translated into German, in Dumoulin, "Zwei Texte Kamo Mabuchis zur Wortkunde."

38. Kamo no Mabuchi, *Kanjikō*, p. 1.

39. Kamo no Mabuchi, *Niimanabi*, p. 358.

40. Andō Shōeki, *Shizen shin'eidō*, p. 631. For a partial English translation of *Shizen shin'eidō*, see Yasunaga, *Ando Shoeki*. This book also includes biographical background on Shōeki and an introduction to his thought. A recent Western-language work on Shōeki is Joly, *Le naturel selon Andō Shōeki*, and an older study is Norman, "Andō Shōeki and the Anatomy of Japanese Feudalism."

41. Andō Shōeki, *Shizen shin'eidō*, p. 650.

42. Wakabayashi, *Japanese Loyalism Reconstrued*, pp. 30–31.

43. Yamagata Daini, *Ryūshi shinron*, p. 395. A complete English translation of *Ryūshi shinron* is available in Wakabayashi, *Japanese Loyalism Reconstrued*.

44. Webb, *The Japanese Imperial Institution in the Tokugawa Period*, pp. 248–50. He violated this ban, leading him to be exiled in 1767 to Hachijōjima, en route to which he died.

45. Totman, *Early Modern Japan*, pp. 325–28.

46. Ibid., p. 340.

47. Saigusa, *Kamo no Mabuchi*, pp. 83, 166.

48. Ibid., p. 187.

49. An earlier travel diary of his, *Tabi no nagusa*, which is based on a trip he took in 1736 from Kyoto to Hamamatsu, discusses many famous poetic places, but does not actually contain any poetry.

50. In my interpretations of Mabuchi's poems in this section, I have benefited from the notes in Takagi and Hisamatsu, eds., *Kinsei waka shū*.

51. Based on my translation in Shirane, ed., *Early Modern Japanese Literature*, p. 607.

52. MYS 3352: "Shinano naru / Suga no arano ni / hototogisu / naku koe kikeba / toki suginikeri."

53. MYS 3386: "niodori no / Katsushika wase o / nie sutomo / sono kanashiki o / to ni tatemeyamo."

54. MYS 48: "himugashi no / no ni kagiroi no / tatsu miete / kaerimi sureba / tsuki katabukinu."

55. MYS 800: "tsuchi naraba / ōkimi imasu / kono terasu / hitsuki no shita wa / amagumo no / mukabusu kiwami / taniguku no / sawataru kiwami / kikoshiosu / kuni no mahora zo."

56. From MYS 3300. This poem presents major problems of interpretation, and modern commentaries do not provide any consensus on how to read it. In Mabuchi's commentary on this poem in the *Man'yōkō*, he interprets *iizurai* as "difficult to say," and *arinami* as "to constantly be together," so that the borrowed lines mean, "although it is difficult to speak [of our love?], we are always together" (*Man'yōkō*, p. 232). Another meaning sometimes given for *iizurai* is "to go on and on," and

another possible reading of *arinami* is "to go on rejecting." The latter meanings make more sense in the context of Mabuchi's poem, so I have followed these in my translation, despite the fact that they are at odds with his commentary on the *Man'yōshū* poem itself.

57. Mabuchi discusses these two *makurakotoba* in *Kanjikō*, pp. 263–64.

58. Translation from Aston, trans., *Nihongi*, vol. 1, p. 381.

Chapter 6

1. Translations of excerpts from both of these works are included in Marra, *The Poetics of Motoori Norinaga*, pp. 136–200.

2. My sources for biographical information on Norinaga are Jōfuku, *Motoori Norinaga*, Nosco, *Remembering Paradise*, and Matsumoto, *Motoori Norinaga*.

3. *Ashiwake obune* was discovered among Norinaga's papers by the scholar Sasaki Nobutsuna, who introduced it in a piece entitled "'Ashiwake obune' to Norinaga no karon," included in Sasaki, *Kamo no Mabuchi to Motoori Norinaga*, pp. 225–48.

4. Motoori Norinaga, *Isonokami sasamegoto*, p. 254.

5. As in the preceding chapter, I generally translate *uta* as "poetry," rather than "song," but I do note where Norinaga is stressing the importance of the sung qualities of poetry.

6. I leave *mono no aware* (and *aware*) untranslated in this chapter because it is such a well-known term, and is so strongly identified with Norinaga.

7. Motoori Norinaga, *Aware ben*, p. 585.

8. *Analects* II.2.

9. Motoori Norinaga, *Aware ben*, p. 585.

10. Motoori Norinaga, *Isonokami sasamegoto*, p. 297.

11. KKS 697, by Ki no Tsurayuki (872?–945?).

12. Some forms of Chinese poetry also use lines of five or seven syllables, but Norinaga does not connect these to the Japanese forms that he writes about. A study that gives particular attention to Norinaga's view of *aya* as a fixed linguistic form uniquely capable of manifesting deep emotion is Kanno, *Motoori Norinaga*. See especially the discussion on pp. 143–68.

13. Momokawa Takahito points out how Norinaga and Mabuchi differ on this point. He writes, "For Mabuchi, the other is already given naturally as a self-evident existence that does not require any particular effort. Norinaga, on the other hand, lacks a certain confidence in the existence of the other. For him, the other is an existence that can only be believed in through a difficult process of mutual understanding, and is a goal that has to be consciously attained" (Momokawa, *Uchi naru Norinaga*, p. 92). Momokawa sees Norinaga's problematization of the other as reflecting an acceptance of the inevitability of mediation both in communication and in the formation of community, and interprets the difference between Norinaga and Mabuchi on this point in terms of a contrast between Mabuchi's ideal of the organic community of the village and Norinaga's orientation toward the mediated community of the city.

14. Michael Marra points out the role of linguistic patterning as a preexisting

structure, and the implications of such a structure for the imagining of interpersonal relationships, when he comments, "In a move reminiscent of the Derridean critique of Western phonocentrism, Motoori argued that the formation of the semantic field of 'pattern words' preceded the act of vocal articulation inasmuch as *aya* already structured the singing voice (*kowe*) of the living realm (*ujō*). This 'specialized' language—the language of creation spoken by all living creatures—provided a common, universal ground that tamed the violent threat of difference and brought the other back to the source of signification" (Marra, "Nativist Hermeneutics," pp. 24–25).

15. Motoori Norinaga, *Kakaika*, p. 381.

16. Motoori Norinaga, *Isonokami sasamegoto*, p. 306.

17. Motoori Norinaga, *Ashiwake obune*, p. 303. There is a complete translation into German of *Ashiwake obune* in Buck-Albulet, *Emotion und Ästhetik*, pp. 211–375.

18. Motoori Norinaga, *Ashiwake obune*, p. 248.

19. Fujiwara no Shunzei, *Korai fūteishō*, p. 273.

20. For a detailed account of Norinaga's appropriation of the *Shinkokinshū*, see Takahashi, *Motoori Norinaga no kagaku*, pp. 55–75.

21. Motoori Norinaga, *Shibun yōryō*, p. 125.

22. "Yue ji," p. 556.

23. Ibid., p. 561.

24. Chen Chun, *Beixi ziyi*, pp. 57–58.

25. In addition to this usage of "emotions" and "desires" as contrasting terms, Norinaga mentions in this section that "emotions" is sometimes used in a broader sense to describe everything felt in the heart, in which case "desires" would fall within the rubric of "emotions." In the writings of Confucians as well, the term "emotions" is not always used consistently, and can take on either the broad or the narrow senses described by Norinaga.

26. Motoori Norinaga, *Shokanshū*, p. 19. The letter is addressed to Shimizu Yoshitarō (1742–?).

27. Ogyū Sorai, *Bendō*, p. 12.

28. As we saw in Chapter 1, Zhu Xi uses these terms to indicate the distinction between the essential nature of something, as it exists on the level of principle (Ch. *li*, Jp. *ri*), and its activity in the realm of material force (Ch. *qi*, Jp. *ki*).

29. Motoori Norinaga, *Isonokami sasamegoto*, p. 441.

30. This text is a critique of *Kokka hachiron sekihi* (A Rejection of the *Eight Essays on Japanese Poetry*, 1761), by Ōsuga Nakayabu (1712–1776), in which Nakayabu, much like Tayasu Munetake before him, attacks Arimaro's essay from a Song Confucian standpoint. As these commentaries by Norinaga and Nakayabu suggest, Arimaro's essay was a subject of debate for some decades after the initial debate between Arimaro, Munetake, and Mabuchi.

31. Motoori Norinaga, *Kokka hachiron sekihi hyō*, p. 499.

32. My citations of *Naobi no mitama* are from this final 1790 version.

33. Motoori Norinaga, *Naobi no mitama*, p. 57. For English translations of

Naobi no mitama, see Nishimura, "The Way of the Gods," and Wehmeyer, *Motoori: Kojiki-den, Book 1*, pp. 213–47.

34. The specific version of Norinaga's text that Kakumei was responding to was *Michi chō koto no ron*.

35. Ichikawa Kakumei, *Maganohire*, p. 186.

36. The debate between Norinaga and Kakumei is discussed in Mogi, "Kokugaku to jukyō no ronsō," pp. 221–33.

37. Motoori Norinaga, *Naobi no mitama*, p. 56.

38. Ichikawa Kakumei, *Maganohire*, p. 191.

39. Ogyū Sorai, *Benmei*, p. 135. King Jie was the final ruler of the Xia dynasty, and King Zhow was the final ruler of the Shang (Yin) dynasty. Jie and Zhow are famous examples of tyrants, and their tyrannical rule is taken as a sign that they (and their dynasties) had lost the mandate of Heaven, making it acceptable to overthrow them. (I use the Romanization "Zhow" to distinguish this ruler from the Zhou dynasty.)

40. Motoori Norinaga, *Kakaika*, p. 403.

41. Ibid., p. 406. For a discussion of the debate between Norinaga and Akinari, see Burns, *Before the Nation*, pp. 102–30. Burns' analysis is particularly valuable for showing how Akinari, unlike Norinaga, saw community as something contingent, a view tied to how Akinari read texts like the *Kojiki* as products of political conflict, in contrast to Norinaga's reading of this work as the expression of gods that transcend all human negotiations for power.

42. The existence of *Kokuikō* was inconvenient for the Edo school's picture of Mabuchi, but Harumi downplays its centrality to Mabuchi's teachings, explaining that it was simply the product of Mabuchi's frustration with "vulgar Confucians," and should be considered "a slip of the tongue" (Izumi Makuni, *Meidōsho*, p. 159). I discuss the disagreements among Mabuchi's followers over the significance of *Kokuikō* in "Reflections on the Meaning of Our Country," pp. 230–38.

43. Izumi Makuni, *Meidōsho*, p. 158. The *Meidōsho* debate is discussed in McNally, *Proving the Way*, pp. 69–78.

44. Murata Harumi, *Wagaku taigai*, p. 448. Modern scholars sometimes use the term "Wagaku" to indicate a less ideological form of Japanese studies in the Tokugawa period, and contrast this with the nativist ideology of "Kokugaku." This is in line with Harumi's use of "Wagaku" in this text, but it should be kept in mind that the use of "Wagaku" and "Kokugaku" as contrasting terms is not completely consistent, either in modern scholarship or in the Tokugawa period itself (for example, modern scholars typically identify Harumi as a follower of Kokugaku, despite his criticisms of Norinaga).

45. Motoori Norinaga, *Hihon tamakushige*, pp. 329–30.

46. Discussions of Norinaga's political proposals in English-language scholarship can be found in Nosco, *Remembering Paradise*, pp. 225–29, and Matsumoto, *Motoori Norinaga*, pp. 136–56.

47. Motoori Norinaga, *Tamagatsuma*, p. 68.

48. Heidi Buck-Albulet writes about Norinaga's interactions with Akitada, Chōsen, and the Kyoto waka scene more broadly, as well as the relationship of

Ashiwake obune to his early encounters with court poetics, in *Emotion und Ästhetik*, pp. 37–61. See also Jōfuku, *Motoori Norinaga*, pp. 27–52.

49. Motoori Norinaga, *Ashiwake obune*, p. 356.

50. Kanno Kakumyō has argued that Norinaga's breaking down and reconstruction of the notion of authenticity in poetry was a way to maintain the aesthetics of the conservative Nijō school of court poetry, while providing it with a new theoretical basis (Kanno, *Motoori Norinaga*, pp. 67–106). Kanno characterizes Norinaga's criticisms of the Nijō school as criticisms from within, as opposed to how many other Tokugawa figures, such as Mabuchi and Mosui, criticized court poetics from without (pp. 90–92). Watanabe Hiroshi, describing Norinaga's ideal of internalizing poetic elegance from the past, notes that as a result of this process, "In a certain sense, one becomes even more aristocratic than the aristocrats themselves, who at the time, just as they had in the past, maintained authority over the traditional Way of poetry. One perhaps takes on an existence even more courtly (*miyabi*) than the aristocrats who make up the life of the court" (Watanabe, "Michi to miyabi," p. 502).

51. Jōfuku, *Motoori Norinaga*, p. 110.

52. Motoori Norinaga, *Uiyamabumi*, p. 539. For an English translation of *Uiyamabumi*, see Nishimura, "First Steps into the Mountains."

53. Motoori Norinaga, *Ashiwake obune*, p. 267.

54. Motoori Norinaga, *Uiyamabumi*, p. 533.

55. Ibid., p. 534.

56. KKS 1: "toshi no uchi ni / haru wa kinikeri / hitotose o / kozo to ya iwan / kotoshi to ya iwan."

57. KKS 2: "sode hijite / musubishi mizu no / kōreru o / haru tatsu kyō no / kaze ya tokuramu."

58. GSS 1089: "kore ya kono / yuku mo kaeru mo / wakarete wa / shiru mo shiranu mo / Ōsaka no seki."

59. Fujiwara no Teika, *Eiga no taigai*, p. 494.

60. MYS 138: "tamamo nasu / nabiki waga neshi / shikitae no / imo ga tamoto o / tsuyushimo no / okite shi kureba." This is a variant of MYS 131, which contains the similar lines: "tamamo nasu / yorineshi imo o / tsuyushimo no / okite shi kureba" [because I came, leaving her behind like dew and frost, she who slept close to me, clinging like jeweled seaweed].

61. The title of the collection comes from how *tamaboko no* is a *makurakotoba* for *michi* (the Way).

62. From my translation in Shirane, ed., *Early Modern Japanese Literature*, p. 613.

Bibliography

Abbreviations Used in the Bibliography

KMZ   *Kamo no Mabuchi zenshū.* Vols. 1–14, 16–17, 19, 21, 23, 26–27 to date. Edited by Inoue Minoru. Zoku Gunsho Ruiju Kanseikai, 1977–1992.

MNZ   *Motoori Norinaga zenshū.* 23 vols. Edited by Ōno Susumu and Ōkubo Tadashi. Chikuma Shobō, 1968–1993.

NJS   *Nihon jurin sōsho.* 14 vols. Edited by Seki Giichirō. Tōyō Tosho Kankōkai, 1927–1938. Reprint: Ōtori Shuppan, 1971.

NKT   *Nihon kagaku taikei.* 10 vols. Edited by Sasaki Nobutsuna. Kazama Shobō, 1956–1963.

NMSCZ   *Nihon meika shisho chūshaku zensho.* 13 vols. Edited by Seki Giichirō. Tōyō Tosho Kankōkai, 1922–1930. Reprint: Ōtori Shuppan, 1973.

NRI   *Nihon rinri ihen.* 10 vols. Edited by Inoue Tetsujirō and Kanie Yoshimaru. Ikuseikai, 1901–1903.

NSS   *Nihon shiwa sōsho.* 10 vols. Edited by Ikeda Shirōjirō. Bunkaidō Shoten, 1920–1922. Reprint: Ōtori Shuppan, 1972.

OSZ (Kawade)   *Ogyū Sorai zenshū.* Vols. 1–3, 5–6 to date. Edited by Imanaka Kanshi and Naramoto Tatsuya. Kawade Shobō, 1973–1978.

OSZ (Misuzu)   *Ogyū Sorai zenshū.* Vols. 1–4, 13, 17, 18 to date. Misuzu Shobō, 1973–1987.

Primary Texts

Andō Shōeki. *Shizen shin'eidō.* In *Kinsei shisōka bunshū*, Nihon koten bungaku taikei, no. 97, edited by Ienaga Saburō et al., 591–666. Iwanami Shoten, 1966.

Andō Tameakira. *Shika shichiron.* In *Kinsei shintōron • zenki kokugaku*, Nihon shisō taikei, no. 39, edited by Taira Shigemichi and Abe Akio, 422–41. Iwanami Shoten, 1972.

Arai Hakuseki. *Tōga.* In *Arai Hakuseki*, Nihon shisō taikei, no. 35, edited by Matsumura Akira, Bitō Masahide, and Katō Shūichi, 101–44. Iwanami Shoten, 1975.

Chen Chun. *Beixi ziyi*. In *Yingyin wenyuange siku quanshu*, 709:1–61. Taipei: Taiwan Shangwu Yinshuguan, 1983.

Dazai Shundai. *Bendōsho*. In NRI 6:204–30.

———. *Bunron*. In NJS 12.

———. *Dokugo*. In *Nihon zuihitsu taisei* series 1, vol. 17: 261–88. Yoshikawa Kōbunkan, 1976.

———. *Doku Shushi shiden*. In NJS 11.

———. *Keizairoku*. In *Nihon keizai daiten*, edited by Takimoto Seiichi, 9:9–295. Meiji Bunken, 1967.

———. *Keizairoku shūi*. In *Sorai gakuha*, Nihon shisō taikei, no. 37, edited by Rai Tsutomu, 45–56. Iwanami Shoten, 1972.

———. *Rikukei ryakusetsu*. In NRI 6:301–30.

———. *Seigaku mondō*. In *Sorai gakuha*, Nihon shisō taikei, no. 37, edited by Rai Tsutomu, 57–135. Iwanami Shoten, 1972.

———. *Sekihi*. In *Sorai gakuha*, Nihon shisō taikei, no. 37, edited by Rai Tsutomu, 137–92. Iwanami Shoten, 1972.

———. *Shiron*. In NSS 4:285–316.

———. *Shushi shiden kōkō*. In NJS 11.

Fujiwara no Shunzei. *Korai fūteishō*. In *Karonshū*, Nihon koten bungaku zenshū, no. 50, edited by Hashimoto Fumio, Ariyoshi Tamotsu, and Fujihira Haruo, 271–465. Shōgakukan, 1975.

Fujiwara no Teika. *Eiga no taigai*. In *Karonshū*, Nihon koten bungaku zenshū, no. 50, edited by Hashimoto Fumio, Ariyoshi Tamotsu, and Fujihira Haruo, 493–510. Shōgakukan, 1975.

Gion Nankai. *Nankai shiketsu*. In NSS 1:5–32.

———. *Shigaku hōgen*. In *Kinsei bungakuron shū*, Nihon koten bungaku taikei, no. 94, edited by Nakamura Yukihiko, 221–62. Iwanami Shoten, 1966.

Hattori Nankaku. *Nankaku sensei bunshū*. In *Sorai gakuha*, Nihon shisō taikei, no. 37, edited by Rai Tsutomu, 193–231. Iwanami Shoten, 1972.

———. *Nankaku sensei tōka no sho*. In NSS 1:47–66.

———. *Tōshisen kokujikai*. Edited by Hino Tatsuo. 3 vols. Heibonsha, 1982.

Hori Keizan. *Fujingen*. In *Jinsai nissatsu, Tawaregusa, Fujingen, Mukaukyō*, Shin Nihon koten bungaku taikei, no. 99, edited by Uetani Hajime, Mizuta Norihisa, and Hino Tatsuo, 135–246. Iwanami Shoten, 2000.

Ichikawa Kakumei. *Maganohire*. In MNZ 8:183–200.

Ikkai Tomoyoshi and Ikezawa Ichirō, eds. *Jusha*. Edo shijin senshū, vol. 2. Iwanami Shoten, 1996.

Ishikawa Jōzan. *Shihō seigi*. In NSS 10:337–56.

Itō Jinsai. *Chūyō hakki*. In NMSCZ, *Gakuyōbu 1*.

———. *Daigaku teihon*. In NMSCZ, *Gakuyōbu 1*.

———. *Dōjimon*. In *Kinsei shisōka bunshū*, Nihon koten bungaku taikei, no. 97, edited by Ienaga Saburō et al., 49–199. Iwanami Shoten, 1966.

———. *Gomō jigi*. In *Itō Jinsai • Ito Tōgai*, Nihon shisō taikei, no. 33, edited by Yoshikawa Kōjirō and Shimizu Shigeru, 11–113. Iwanami Shoten, 1971.

———. *Mōshi kogi*. In NMSCZ, *Mōshibu 1*.

———. *Rongo kogi*. In NMSCZ, *Rongobu 1*.

Itō Tōgai. *Dokushi yōryō*. In *Nihon shishi, Gozandō shiwa*, Shin Nihon koten bungaku taikei, no. 65, edited by Shimizu Shigeru, Ibi Takashi, and Ōtani Masao, 1–29. Iwanami Shoten, 1991.

Izumi Makuni. *Meidōsho*. In *Kokugaku undō no shisō*, Nihon shisō taikei, no. 51, edited by Haga Noboru and Matsumoto Sannosuke, 125–219. Iwanami Shoten, 1971.

Kada no Arimaro. *Kokka hachiron*. In *Karonshū*, Nihon koten bungaku zenshū, no. 50, edited by Hashimoto Fumio, Ariyoshi Tamotsu, and Fujihira Haruo, 532–66. Shōgakukan, 1975.

———. *Kokka hachiron sairon*. In NKT 7:108–15.

Kaibara Ekiken. *Taigiroku*. In *Kaibara Ekiken • Muro Kyūsō*, Nihon shisō taikei, no. 34, edited by Araki Kengo and Inoue Tadashi, 9–58. Iwanami Shoten, 1970.

Kaihō Seiryō. *Keikodan*. In *Honda Toshiaki • Kaihō Seiryō*, Nihon shisō taikei, no. 44, edited by Tsukatani Akihiro and Kuranami Seiji, 215–346. Iwanami Shoten, 1970.

Kamo no Mabuchi. *Futatabi kingo no kimi ni kotaematsuru fumi*. In NKT 7:147–55.

———. *Goikō*. In *Kinsei shintōron • zenki kokugaku*, Nihon shisō taikei, no. 39, edited by Taira Shigemichi and Abe Akio, 394–420. Iwanami Shoten, 1972.

———. *Ka'ikō*. In *Kinsei shintōron • zenki kokugaku*, Nihon shisō taikei, no. 39, edited by Taira Shigemichi and Abe Akio, 348–56. Iwanami Shoten, 1972.

———. *Kanjikō*. Vol. 8 of KMZ.

———. *Kokka hachiron yogen shūi*. In NKT 7:116–26.

———. *Kokka ron okusetsu*. In NKT 7:127–37.

———. *Kokuikō*. In *Kinsei shintōron • zenki kokugaku*, Nihon shisō taikei, no. 39, edited by Taira Shigemichi and Abe Akio, 374–93. Iwanami Shoten, 1972.

———. *Man'yōkō*. Vols. 1–5 of KMZ.

———. *Niimanabi*. In *Kinsei shintōron • zenki kokugaku*, Nihon shisō taikei, no. 39, edited by Taira Shigemichi and Abe Akio, 357–73. Iwanami Shoten, 1972.

———. *Okabe no nikki*. In *Kinsei kabunshū 2*, Shin Nihon koten bungaku taikei, no. 68, edited by Suzuki Jun and Nakamura Hiroyasu, 127–53. Iwanami Shoten, 1997.

———. *Tabi no nagusa*. In *Kinsei kabunshū 2*, Shin Nihon koten bungaku taikei, no. 68, edited by Suzuki Jun and Nakamura Hiroyasu, 107–26. Iwanami Shoten, 1997.

Kong Yingda. *Maoshi zhengyi*. 6 vols. Beijing: Zhonghua Shuju, 1957.

Kumazawa Banzan. *Daigaku wakumon*. In *Kumazawa Banzan*, Nihon shisō taikei, no. 30, edited by Gotō Yōichi and Tomoeda Ryūtarō, 405–63. Iwanami Shoten, 1971.

Motoori Norinaga. *Ashiwake obune*. In *Kinsei zuisō shū*, Shinpen Nihon koten bungaku zenshū, no. 82, edited by Suzuki Jun and Odaka Michiko, 243–404. Shōgakukan, 2000.

———. *Aware ben*. In MNZ 4:583–88.

———. *Genji monogatari tama no ogushi*. In MNZ 4:169–524.

———. *Hihon tamakushige*. In MNZ 8:327–73.

————. *Isonokami sasamegoto*. In *Motoori Norinaga shū*, Shinchō Nihon koten shūsei, no. 60, edited by Hino Tatsuo, 249–504. Shinchōsha, 1983.

————. *Kakaika*. In MNZ 8:375–413.

————. *Kanji san'on kō*. In MNZ 5:375–433.

————. *Kokinshū tōkagami*. In MNZ 3:1–291.

————. *Kokka hachiron sekihi hyō*. In MNZ 2:491–507.

————. *Kuzubana*. In MNZ 8:121–81.

————. *Naobi no mitama*. In MNZ 9:49–63.

————. *Shibun yōryō*. In *Motoori Norinaga shū*, Shinchō Nihon koten shūsei, no. 60, edited by Hino Tatsuo, 11–247. Shinchōsha, 1983.

————. *Shokanshū*. Vol. 17 of MNZ.

————. *Tamagatsuma*. In *Motoori Norinaga*, Nihon shisō taikei, no. 40, edited by Yoshikawa Kōjirō, Satake Akihiro, and Hino Tatsuo, 7–483. Iwanami Shoten, 1978.

————. *Uiyamabumi*. In *Motoori Norinaga*, Nihon shisō taikei, no. 40, edited by Yoshikawa Kōjirō, Satake Akihiro, and Hino Tatsuo, 511–40. Iwanami Shoten, 1978.

Murata Harumi. *Wagaku taigai*. In *Kinsei shintōron • zenki kokugaku*, Nihon shisō taikei, no. 39, edited by Taira Shigemichi and Abe Akio, 448–51. Iwanami Shoten, 1972.

Ogyū Sorai. *Bendō*. In *Ogyū Sorai*, Nihon shisō taikei, no. 36, edited by Yoshikawa Kōjirō et al., 9–36. Iwanami Shoten, 1973.

————. *Benmei*. In *Ogyū Sorai*, Nihon shisō taikei, no. 36, edited by Yoshikawa Kōjirō et al., 37–185. Iwanami Shoten, 1973.

————. *Chūyō kai*. In OSZ (Kawade) 2:401–59

————. *Daigaku kai*. In OSZ (Kawade) 2:367–99.

————. *Gakuritsu kō*. In *Yamagata Daini isho*. Kōyō Tosho Kankōkai, 1924.

————. *Gakusei hen*. In *Yamagata Daini isho*. Kōyō Tosho Kankōkai, 1924.

————. *Gakusoku*. In *Ogyū Sorai*, Nihon shisō taikei, no. 36, edited by Yoshikawa Kōjirō et al., 187–97. Iwanami Shoten, 1973.

————. *Keishishi yōran*. In OSZ (Misuzu) 1:497–534.

————. *Ken'en zuihitsu*. In OSZ (Kawade) 1:129–212.

————. *Rongo chō*. Edited by Ogawa Tamaki. 2 vols. Heibonsha, 1994.

————. *Seidan*. In *Ogyū Sorai*, Nihon shisō taikei, no. 36, edited by Yoshikawa Kōjirō et al., 259–445. Iwanami Shoten, 1973.

————. *Shigen*. In OSZ (Misuzu) 1:559–61.

————. *Sorai sensei tōmonsho*. In OSZ (Misuzu) 1:421–86.

————. *Soraishū*. In *Ogyū Sorai*, Nihon shisō taikei, no. 36, edited by Yoshikawa Kōjirō et al., 487–546. Iwanami Shoten, 1973.

————. *Taiheisaku*. In *Ogyū Sorai*, Nihon shisō taikei, no. 36, edited by Yoshikawa Kōjirō et al., 447–86. Iwanami Shoten, 1973.

————. *Yakubun sentei*. In OSZ (Misuzu) 2:543–71.

Ōsuga Nakayabu. *Kokka hachiron sekihi*. In NKT 7:167–86.

Takagi Ichinosuke and Hisamatsu Sen'ichi, eds. *Kinsei waka shū*. Nihon koten bungaku taikei, no. 93. Iwanami Shoten, 1966.

Tayasu Munetake. *Karon.* In NKT 7:156–61.

———. *Katei yakugen.* In NKT 7:162–66.

———. *Kokka hachiron yogen.* In NKT 7:99–107.

———. *Okusetsu jōgen.* In NKT 7:138–46.

Yamaga Sokō. *Seikyō yōroku.* In *Yamaga Sokō,* Nihon shisō taikei, no. 32, edited by Tahara Tsuguo and Morimoto Jun'ichirō, 7–28. Iwanami Shoten, 1970.

———. *Yamaga gorui.* In *Yamaga Sokō,* Nihon shisō taikei, no. 32, edited by Tahara Tsuguo and Morimoto Jun'ichirō, 29–315. Iwanami Shoten, 1970.

Yamagata Daini. *Ryūshi shinron.* In *Kinsei seidōron,* Nihon shisō taikei, no. 38, edited by Naramoto Tatsuya, 391–419. Iwanami Shoten, 1976.

Yamamoto Hokuzan. *Sakushi shikō.* In *Kinsei bungakuron shū,* Nihon koten bungaku taikei, no. 94, edited by Nakamura Yukihiko, 263–347. Iwanami Shoten, 1966.

Yamamoto Kazuyoshi and Yokoyama Hiroshi, eds. *Hattori Nankaku, Gion Nankai.* Edo shijin senshū, vol. 3. Iwanami Shoten, 1991.

Yan Yu. *Canglang shihua.* Ichinosawa Torao, ed. *Sōrō shiwa.* Meitoku Shuppansha, 1976.

"Yue ji." In *Raiki,* Shinshaku kanbun taikei, no. 28, edited by Takeuchi Teruo, 556–607. Meiji Shoin, 1977.

Zhu Xi. *Daxue zhangju.* In *Sishu zhangju jizhu,* 1–13. Beijing: Zhonghua Shuju, 1983.

———. *Lunyu jizhu.* In *Sishu zhangju jizhu,* 41–195. Beijing: Zhonghua Shuju, 1983.

———. *Mengzi jizhu.* In *Sishu zhangju jizhu,* 197–337. Beijing: Zhonghua Shuju, 1983.

———. *Shi jizhuan.* Fukino Yasushi and Ishimoto Michiaki, eds. *Shuki Shishūden zenchūshaku.* 9 vols. Meitoku Shuppansha, 1996.

———. *Yue ji dongjing shuo.* In *Shushi bunshū 2,* vol. 5 of *Shushigaku taikei,* edited by Tomoeda Ryūtarō et al., 94–96. Meitoku Shuppansha, 1983.

———. *Zhongyong zhangju.* In *Sishu zhangju jizhu,* 14–40. Beijing: Zhonghua Shuju, 1983.

———. *Zhuzi yulei.* 8 vols. Beijing: Zhonghua Shuju, 1994.

Secondary Works

Abe Yoshio. *Nihon Shushigaku to Chōsen.* Tōkyō Daigaku Shuppankai, 1965.

Amagasaki Akira. *En no bigaku: uta no michi no shigaku II.* Keisō Shobō, 1995.

———. *Kachō no tsukai: uta no michi no shigaku I.* Keisō Shobō, 1983.

Ansart, Olivier. *L'empire du rite: la pensée politique d'Ogyū Sorai, Japon 1666–1728.* Geneva: Librairie Droz, 1998.

Aoki Masaru. *Shina bungaku shisō shi.* Iwanami Shoten, 1943.

Araki Yoshio. *Kamo no Mabuchi no hito to shisō.* Kōseikaku, 1943.

Asayama Yoshirō. "Hattori Nankaku no 'shi' no ishiki—Sorai to Nankaku no Shikyōkan o megutte." *Jōchi daigaku kokubungaku ronshū* 18 (1985): 143–60.

Aston, W. G., trans. *Nihongi.* 1896. Reprint (2 vols. in 1), Rutland, VT: Tuttle, 1972.

Bellah, Robert N. "Baigan and Sorai: Continuities and Discontinuities in Eighteenth-Century Japanese Thought." In *Japanese Thought in the Tokugawa*

Period, 1600–1868: Methods and Metaphors, edited by Tetsuo Najita and Irwin Scheiner, 137–52. Chicago: University of Chicago Press, 1978.

———. *Tokugawa Religion: The Values of Pre-industrial Japan*. Glencoe, IL: Free Press, 1957.

Bitō Masahide. "Dazai Shundai no hito to shisō." In *Sorai gakuha*, Nihon shisō taikei, no. 37, edited by Rai Tsutomu, 487–514. Iwanami Shoten, 1972.

———. "Ogyū Sorai and the Distinguishing Features of Japanese Confucianism." In *Japanese Thought in the Tokugawa Period, 1600–1868: Methods and Metaphors*, edited by Tetsuo Najita and Irwin Scheiner, 153–60. Chicago: University of Chicago Press, 1978.

Black, Alison Harley. *Man and Nature in the Philosophical Thought of Wang Fu-chih*. Seattle: University of Washington Press, 1989.

Bloom, Irene. *Knowledge Painfully Acquired: The K'un-chih chi by Lo Ch'in-shun*. New York: Columbia University Press, 1987.

Bol, Peter K. *"This Culture of Ours": Intellectual Transitions in T'ang and Sung China*. Stanford, CA: Stanford University Press, 1992.

Boot, W. J. "Japanese Poetics and the *Kokka Hachiron*." *Asiatica Venetiana* 4 (1999): 23–43.

Bourdieu, Pierre. *Distinction: A Social Critique of the Judgement of Taste*. Translated by Richard Nice. Cambridge, MA: Harvard University Press, 1984.

Brownlee, John S. "The Jeweled Comb-box: Motoori Norinaga's *Tamakushige*." *Monumenta Nipponica* 43, no. 1 (Spring 1988): 35–61.

Buck-Albulet, Heidi. *Emotion und Ästhetik: Das "Ashiwake obune"—eine Waka-Poetik des jungen Motoori Norinaga im Kontext dichtungstheoretischer Diskurse des frühneuzeitlichen Japan*. Wiesbaden: Harrassowitz Verlag, 2005.

Burns, Susan. *Before the Nation: Kokugaku and the Imagining of Community in Early Modern Japan*. Durham, NC: Duke University Press, 2003.

Butler, Lee. *Emperor and Aristocracy in Japan, 1467–1680*. Cambridge, MA: Harvard University Asia Center, 2002.

Caddeau, Patrick. *Appraising "Genji:" Literary Criticism and Cultural Anxiety in the Age of the Last Samurai*. Albany: State University of New York Press, 2006.

Carter, Steven D. *Householders: The Reizei Family in Japanese History*. Cambridge, MA: Harvard University Asia Center, 2007.

Cassirer, Ernst. *The Logic of the Cultural Sciences*. Translated by S. G. Lofts. New Haven, CT: Yale University Press, 2000.

Chan, Charles Wing-hoi. "On Ogyū Sorai's Critique of Chu Hsi's Program of Learning to Be a Sage." *Monumenta Serica* 46 (1998): 195–232.

Chang Sumei. "Ken'en gakuha to ongaku." *Nihon shisōshi gaku* 37 (2005): 155–72.

Chin, Ann-ping and Mansfield Freeman. *Tai Chen on Mencius: Explorations in Words and Meaning*. New Haven, CT: Yale University Press, 1990.

Chou, Chih-p'ing. *Yüan Hung-tao and the Kung-an School*. Cambridge, UK: Cambridge University Press, 1988.

Chow, Kai-wing. *The Rise of Confucian Ritualism in Late Imperial China: Ethics, Classics, and Lineage Discourse*. Stanford, CA: Stanford University Press, 1994.

Chung, Edward Y. J. *The Korean Neo-Confucianism of Yi T'oegye and Yi Yulgok: A Reappraisal of the "Four-Seven Thesis" and Its Practical Implications for Self-Cultivation*. Albany: State University of New York Press, 1995.

de Bary, Wm. Theodore. "Introduction." In *Principle and Practicality*, edited by Wm. Theodore de Bary and Irene Bloom, 1–36. New York: Columbia University Press, 1979.

———. *Neo-Confucian Orthodoxy and the Learning of the Mind-and-Heart*. New York: Columbia University Press, 1981.

———. "Sagehood as a Secular and Spiritual Ideal in Tokugawa Neo-Confucianism." In *Principle and Practicality*, edited by Wm. Theodore de Bary and Irene Bloom, 127–88. New York: Columbia University Press, 1979.

Derrida, Jacques. *Of Grammatology*. Translated by Gayatri Chakravorty Spivak. Baltimore: Johns Hopkins University Press, 1976.

Dumoulin, Heinrich. *Kamo Mabuchi: Ein Beitrag zur japanischer Religions- und Geistesgeschichte*. Tokyo: Sophia University, 1943.

———. "Kamo Mabuchi: Kokuikō—Gedanken über den 'Sinn des Landes.'" *Monumenta Nipponica* 2, no. 1 (January 1939): 165–92.

———. "Zwei Texte Kamo Mabuchis zur Wortkunde." *Monumenta Nipponica* 11, no. 3 (October 1955): 268–83.

———. "Zwei Texte zum Kadō des Kamo Mabuchi: Uta no kokoro no uchi—Niimanabi." Parts 1 and 2. *Monumenta Nipponica* 4, no. 1 (January 1941): 192–206; no. 2 (July 1941): 566–84.

Eagleton, Terry. *The Ideology of the Aesthetic*. Oxford: Blackwell, 1990.

Elman, Benjamin A. *From Philosophy to Philology: Intellectual and Social Aspects of Change in Late Imperial China*. Cambridge, MA: Harvard University Press, 1984.

Flueckiger, Peter. "Reflections on the Meaning of Our Country: Kamo no Mabuchi's *Kokuikō*." *Monumenta Nipponica* 63, no. 2 (Autumn 2008): 211–63.

———. "The *Shijing* in Tokugawa Ancient Learning." *Monumenta Serica* 55 (2007): 195–225.

Foucault, Michel. *The Order of Things: An Archaeology of the Human Sciences*. New York: Vintage Books, 1994.

Fujihira Haruo. *Karon no kenkyū*. Perikansha, 1988.

Gadamer, Hans-Georg. *Truth and Method*. 2nd revised edition. Translated by Joel Weinsheimer and Donald G. Marshall. New York: Continuum, 1994.

Graham, A. C., trans. *The Book of Lieh-tzu*. London: Murray, 1960.

Haga Noboru. *Edo kabunha no seiritsu to tenkai*. Kyōiku Shuppan Sentaa, 1994.

Haga Yaichi. *Kokugakushi gairon*. Kokugodenshūsho, 1900.

Hall, John Whitney, ed. *The Cambridge History of Japan, Volume 4: Early Modern Japan*. Cambridge, UK: Cambridge University Press, 1991.

Hani Gorō. *Nihon ni okeru kindai shisō no zentei*. Iwanami Shoten, 1949.

Harootunian, H. D. "The Consciousness of Archaic Form in the New Realism of Kokugaku." In *Japanese Thought in the Tokugawa Period, 1600–1868: Methods and Metaphors*, edited by Tetsuo Najita and Irwin Scheiner, 63–104. Chicago: University of Chicago Press, 1978.

————. *Things Seen and Unseen: Discourse and Ideology in Tokugawa Nativism.* Chicago: University of Chicago Press, 1988.

Harper, T. J. "Norinaga on the Translation of Waka: His Preface to *A Kokinshū Telescope.*" In *The Distant Isle: Studies and Translations of Japanese Literature in Honor of Robert H. Brower,* edited by Thomas Hare, Robert Borgen, and Sharalyn Orbaugh, 205–30. Ann Arbor: University of Michigan Center for Japanese Studies, 1996.

Hegel, G. W. F. *The Philosophy of History.* Translated by J. Sibree. 1899. Reprint, New York: Dover, 1956.

Hino Tatsuo. "Bungakushijō no Soraigaku • han Soraigaku." In *Sorai gakuha,* Nihon shisō taikei, no. 37, edited by Rai Tsutomu, 577–89. Iwanami Shoten, 1972.

————. "Engi no bungaku: kobunjiha ni tsuite." *Bungaku* 35, no. 7 (July 1967): 46–59.

————. *Hattori Nankaku denkō.* Perikansha, 1999.

————. "Hattori Nankaku no shōgai to shisō." In *Sorai gakuha,* Nihon shisō taikei, no. 37, edited by Rai Tsutomu, 515–31. Iwanami Shoten, 1972.

————. "Jugaku to bungaku." In *Edo bungaku to Chūgoku,* edited by Suwa Haruo and Hino Tatsuo, 205–25. Mainichi Shinbun Sha, 1977.

————. "'Mono no aware o shiru' no setsu no raireki." In *Motoori Norinaga shū,* Shinchō Nihon koten shūsei, no. 60, edited by Hino Tatsuo, 505–51. Shinchōsha, 1983.

————. *Norinaga to Akinari.* Chikuma Shobō, 1984.

————. "Reigaku e no kie—bungakushijō no Soraigaku • josetsu." Parts 1 and 2. *Bungaku* 36, no. 7 (July 1968): 25–37; no. 8 (August 1968): 86–98.

————. *Sorai gakuha: jugaku kara bungaku e.* Chikuma Shobō, 1975.

————. "Sorai gakuha no yakuwari." In *Nihon no kanshi,* edited by Nakamura Yukihiko, 33–67. Kyūko Shoin, 1986.

Hiraishi Naoaki. *Ogyū Sorai nenpu kō.* Heibonsha, 1984.

————. "Senchū • sengo Sorairon hihan." *Shakai kagaku kenkyū* 39, no. 1 (1987): 63–136.

————. "Soraigaku no saikōsei." *Shisō* 766 (April 1988): 82–101.

Hisamatsu Sen'ichi. *Kinsei waka shi.* Tōkyōdō Shuppan, 1968.

————. *Kokugaku: sono seiritsu to kokubungaku to no kankei.* Shibundō, 1941.

————. *Nihon bungaku hyōronshi: kinsei • saikinsei hen.* Shibundō, 1936.

Hobbes, Thomas. *Leviathan.* New York: Penguin, 1985.

Hume, David. *A Treatise of Human Nature.* 2nd edition. Oxford: Oxford University Press, 1978.

Ibi Takashi. *Edo shiika ron.* Kyūko Shoin, 1998.

Ikegami, Eiko. *Bonds of Civility: Aesthetic Networks and the Political Origins of Japanese Culture.* Cambridge, UK: Cambridge University Press, 2005.

Imanaka Kanshi. *Soraigaku no kisoteki kenkyū.* Yoshikawa Kōbunkan, 1966.

————. *Soraigaku no shiteki kenkyū.* Kyoto: Shibunkaku, 1992.

Inoue Minoru. *Kamo no Mabuchi no gakumon.* Yagi Shoten, 1943.

————. *Kamo no Mabuchi no gyōseki to monryū.* Kazama Shobō, 1966.

Inoue Tetsujirō. *Nihon kogakuha no tetsugaku.* Fūzanbō, 1902.

Ishimoto Michiaki. "Dazai Shundai no shikan ni tsuite—Soraigaku no keishō o megutte." *Nihon bungaku ronkyū* 44 (1985): 79–86.

Itō Masao. *Kinsei no waka to kokugaku.* Kōgakkan Daigaku Shuppanbu, 1979.

Itō Tasaburō. *Kokugaku no shiteki kōsatsu.* Ōokayama Shoten, 1932.

Iwahashi Junsei. *Sorai kenkyū.* Seki Shoin, 1934.

Iwata Takashi. *Motoori Norinaga no shōgai: sono gaku to kiseki.* Ibunsha, 1999.

Jōfuku Isamu. *Motoori Norinaga.* Yoshikawa Kōbunkan, 1980.

Joly, Jacques. *Le naturel selon Andō Shōeki. Un type de discourse sur la nature et la spontanéité par un maître-confuceén de l'époque Tokugawa, Andō Shōeki (1703–1762).* Paris: Editions Maisonneuve & Larose, 1996.

Jullien, François. *La valeur allusive: Des categories originales de l'interprétation poétique dans la tradition Chinoise.* Paris: École Française d'Extrême-Orient, 1985.

Kalton, Michael C. et al. *The Four-Seven Debate: An Annotated Translation of the Most Famous Controversy in Korean Neo-Confucian Thought.* Albany: State University of New York Press, 1994.

Kamiyasu Nagako. *Keiseiron no kinsei.* Aoki Shoten, 2005.

Kanno Kakumyō. *Motoori Norinaga: kotoba to miyabi.* Perikansha, 1991.

Kant, Immanuel. *The Critique of Judgement.* Translated by James Creed Meredith. Oxford: Oxford University Press, 1952.

Katanuma Seiji. *Jugaku to kokugaku—'seitō' to 'itan' to no seiseishiteki kōsatsu.* Ōfūsha, 1984.

Kaufmann, Walter. *Musical References in the Chinese Classics.* Detroit: Information Coordinators, 1976.

Kawashima Kinue. "Ogyū Sorai cho 'Kingaku taiishō' honkoku." *Tōkyō Seitoku Tanki Daigaku Kiyō* 37 (2004): 17–28.

Kazama Seishi. *Kinsei wabun no sekai: Kōkei, Ayatari, Akinari.* Shinwasha, 1998.

Keene, Donald. *World Within Walls: Japanese Literature of the Pre-Modern Era, 1600–1867.* New York: Holt, Rinehart and Winston, 1976.

Kinsei Tōshō Waka Ronshū Kankōkai, ed. *Kinsei tōshō waka ronshū.* Meiji Shoin, 1989.

Kojima Yasunori. "Dazai Shundai to Chōsen tsūshinshi." *Kokubungaku kaishaku to kanshō* 46, no. 7 (June 2001): 40–51.

———. *Soraigaku to han Sorai.* Rev. ed. Perikansha, 1994.

Koschmann, Victor. *The Mito Ideology: Discourse, Reform, and Insurrection in Late Tokugawa Japan, 1790–1864.* Berkeley: University of California Press, 1987.

Koyasu Nobukuni. *Edo shisōshi kōgi.* Iwanami Shoten, 1998.

———. *'Jiken' to shite no Soraigaku.* Seidosha, 1990.

———. *Motoori Norinaga.* Iwanami Shoten, 1992.

———. *'Norinaga mondai' to wa nani ka.* Seidosha, 1995.

———. *Norinagagaku kōgi.* Iwanami Shoten, 2006.

Kubota Keiichi. *Kinsei Reizeiha kadan no kenkyū.* Kanrin Shobō, 2003.

Kurozumi Makoto. *Fukusūsei no Nihon shisō.* Perikansha, 2006.

———. *Kinsei Nihon shakai to jukyō.* Perikansha, 2003.

———. "Nihon shisō ni okeru 'wa' no gainen." *Chiiki bunka kenkyū senkō kiyō Odysseus* 6 (2001): 4–17.

Lau, D. C., trans. *Lao Tzu: Tao Te Ching.* New York: Penguin, 1963.

Legge, James, trans. *The Ch'un Ts'ew with The Tso Chuen.* 1872. Reprint, Taipei: SMC, 1991.

———. *Confucian Analects, The Great Learning, and The Doctrine of the Mean.* 1893. Reprint, New York: Dover, 1971.

———. *The She King.* 1871. Reprint, Taipei: SMC, 1991.

———. *The Shoo King.* 1865. Reprint, Taipei: SMC, 1991.

———. *The Works of Mencius.* 1895. Reprint, New York: Dover, 1970.

Leinss, Gerhard. *Japanische Anthropologie: Die Natur des Menschen in der konfuzianischen Neoklassik am Anfang des 18. Jahrhunderts; Jinsai und Sorai.* Wiesbaden: Harrassowitz Verlag, 1995.

Lidin, Olof G. *The Life of Ogyū Sorai: A Tokugawa Confucian Philosopher.* Lund: Studentlitteratur, 1974.

———. *Ogyū Sorai's "Discourse on Government" ("Seidan"): An Annotated Translation.* Wiesbaden: Harrassowitz Verlag, 1999.

———. *Ogyū Sorai's "Distinguishing the Way": An Annotated English Translation of the "Bendō."* Tokyo: Sophia University, 1970.

———. *Ogyū Sorai's Journey to Kai in 1706, With a Translation of the "Kyōchūkikō."* London: Curzon Press, 1983.

———. "Ogyū Sorai's Place in Edo Intellectual Thought." *Modern Asian Studies* 18, no. 4 (1984): 567–80.

Liu, James J. Y. *Chinese Theories of Literature.* Chicago: University of Chicago Press, 1975.

Lynn, Richard John. "Chu Hsi as Literary Theorist and Critic." In *Chu Hsi and Neo-Confucianism*, edited by Wing-tsit Chan, 337–54. Honolulu: University of Hawai'i Press, 1986.

Maezawa Engetsu. *Dazai Shundai.* Sūzanbō, 1920.

Marceau, Lawrence. "Hori Keizan cho 'Fujingen' josetsu: ren'airon o koete." *Nihon bungaku* 42, no. 11 (November 1993): 47–52.

———. "*Ninjō* and the Affective Value of Literature at the Kogidō Academy." *Sino-Japanese Studies* 9, no. 1 (1996): 47–55.

———. *Takebe Ayatari: A Bunjin Bohemian in Early Modern Japan.* Ann Arbor: University of Michigan Center for Japanese Studies, 2004.

Marra, Michael. "Nativist Hermeneutics: The Interpretive Strategies of Motoori Norinaga and Fujitani Mitsue." *Japan Review* 10 (1998): 17–52.

———. *The Poetics of Motoori Norinaga.* Honolulu: University of Hawai'i Press, 2007.

Maruyama Masao. *Gendai seiji no shisō to kōdō.* Rev. ed. Miraisha, 1964.

———. *Nihon no shisō.* Iwanami Shoten, 1961.

———. *Nihon seiji shisōshi kenkyū.* Tōkyō Daigaku Shuppankai, 1952.

———. *Studies in the Intellectual History of Tokugawa Japan.* Translated by Mikiso Hane. Princeton, NJ: Princeton University Press, 1974.

———. *Thought and Behaviour in Modern Japanese Politics.* Expanded edition. Edited by Ivan Morris. Oxford: Oxford University Press, 1969.

Matsumoto Sannosuke. *Kokugaku seiji shisō no kenkyū*. Miraisha, 1972.

———. *Tennōsei kokka to seiji shisō*. Miraisha, 1969.

Matsumoto, Shigeru. *Motoori Norinaga, 1730–1801*. Cambridge, MA: Harvard University Press, 1970.

Matsushita Tadashi. *Edo jidai no shifū shiron—Min • Shin no shiron to sono sesshu*. Meiji Shoin, 1969.

McCullough, Helen Craig. *Brocade by Night: 'Kokin Wakashū' and the Court Style in Japanese Classical Poetry*. Stanford, CA: Stanford University Press, 1985.

McEwan, J. R. *The Political Writings of Ogyū Sorai*. Cambridge, UK: Cambridge University Press, 1962.

McMullen, James. *Idealism, Protest, and the "Tale of Genji": The Confucianism of Kumazawa Banzan (1619–91)*. Oxford: Oxford University Press, 1999.

———. "Kumazawa Banzan and *Jitsugaku*: Toward Pragmatic Action." In *Principle and Practicality*, edited by Wm. Theodore de Bary and Irene Bloom, 337–73. New York: Columbia University Press, 1979.

———. "The Pathos of Love: Motoori Norinaga and the *Tale of Genji*." In *Kaigai ni okeru "Genji monogatari" no sekai: hon'yaku to kenkyū*, edited by Ii Haruki, 205–27. Kazama Shobō, 2004.

McNally, Mark. *Proving the Way: Conflict and Practice in the History of Japanese Nativism*. Cambridge, MA: Harvard University Asia Center, 2005.

Minamoto Ryōen. *Tokugawa gōri shisō no keifu*. Chūō Kōron Shinsha, 1972.

Minear, Richard. "Ogyū Sorai's *Instructions for Students*: A Translation and Commentary." *Harvard Journal of Asiatic Studies* 36 (1976): 5–81.

Miyake Kiyoshi. *Kada no Azumamaro*. Unebi Shobō, 1942.

Miyake Masahiko. *Kyōto chōshū Itō Jinsai no shisō keisei*. Kyoto: Shibunkaku Shuppan, 1987.

Mogi Makoto. "Kokugaku to jukyō no ronsō." In *Nihon shisō ronsō shi*, edited by Imai Jun and Ozawa Tomio, 206–33. Perikansha, 1979.

Momokawa Takahito. *Uchi naru Norinaga*. Tōkyō Daigaku Shuppankai, 1987.

Murai Osamu. *Moji no yokuatsu: kokugaku ideorogii no seiritsu*. Seikyūsha, 1989.

Muraoka Tsunetsugu. *Motoori Norinaga*. Iwanami Shoten, 1928.

Murayama Yoshihiro. "Dazai Shundai no 'Shushi shiden kōkō': Soraigaku ni okeru 'Shikyō.'" *Shikyō kenkyū* 1 (1974): 13–20.

Nagashima Hiroaki, ed. *Motoori Norinaga no sekai: waka, chūshaku, shisō*. Shinwasha, 2005.

Najita, Tetsuo. "History and Nature in Eighteenth-Century Tokugawa Thought." In *The Cambridge History of Japan, Volume 4: Early Modern Japan*, edited by John Whitney Hall, 596–659. Cambridge, UK: Cambridge University Press, 1991.

———. "Method and Analysis in the Conceptual Portrayal of Tokugawa Intellectual History." In *Japanese Thought in the Tokugawa Period, 1600–1868: Methods and Metaphors*, edited by Tetsuo Najita and Irwin Scheiner, 3–38. Chicago: University of Chicago Press, 1978.

———. "Political Economism in the Thought of Dazai Shundai (1680–1747)." *Journal of Asian Studies* 31, no. 4 (November 1972): 821–39.

―――――. *Visions of Virtue in Tokugawa Japan: The Kaitokudō Merchant Academy of Osaka*. Chicago: University of Chicago Press, 1987.

Najita, Tetsuo, ed. *Tokugawa Political Writings*. Cambridge, UK: Cambridge University Press, 1998.

Nakai, Kate Wildman. "The Naturalization of Confucianism in Tokugawa Japan: The Problem of Sinocentrism." *Harvard Journal of Asiatic Studies* 40, no. 1 (June 1980): 157–99.

―――――. *Shogunal Politics: Arai Hakuseki and the Premises of Tokugawa Rule*. Cambridge, MA: Council on East Asian Studies, Harvard University, 1988.

Nakamura Shunsaku. "'Kishitsu no sei' no yukue—Dazai Shundai ron." *Hiroshima Daigaku kyōiku gakubu kiyō* part 2, 40 (1991): 261–68.

Nakamura Takaya. *Hakuseki to Sorai to Shundai*. Banrikaku, 1942.

Nakamura Yukihiko. *Kinsei bungei shichō kō*. Iwanami Shoten, 1975.

Nakano Mitsutoshi. *Jūhasseiki no Edo bungei: ga to zoku no seijuku*. Iwanami Shoten, 1999.

Nienhauser, William H. Jr., trans. *The Grand Scribe's Records*. Vol. 1 and vol. 7 to date. Bloomington: Indiana University Press, 1994–.

Nishimura, Sey. "First Steps into the Mountains: Motoori Norinaga's *Uiyamabumi*." *Monumenta Nipponica* 42, no. 4 (Winter 1987): 449–93.

―――――. "The Way of the Gods: Motoori Norinaga's *Naobi no mitama*." *Monumenta Nipponica* 46, no. 1 (Spring 1991): 21–41.

Nivison, David. *The Life and Thought of Chang Hsueh-ch'eng (1738–1801)*. Stanford, CA: Stanford University Press, 1966.

Noguchi Takehiko. *Edo bungaku no shi to shinjitsu*. Chūō Kōron Sha, 1971.

―――――. "Itō Jinsai ni okeru bungakuron no seiritsu katei." Parts 1 and 2. *Kokugo to kokubungaku* 44, no. 2 (February 1967): 39–52; no. 3 (March 1967): 31–46.

―――――. "Kobunji gakuha no shi to shisō." *Kikan Nihon shisōshi* 21 (1983): 50–64.

―――――. *Ogyū Sorai: Edo no Don Kihōte*. Chūō Kōron Sha, 1993.

―――――. "Shushigaku ni okeru bungaku no gainen." Parts 1–4. *Bungaku* 35, no. 7 (July 1967): 33–45; no. 8 (August 1967): 56–69; no. 9 (September 1967): 62–73; no. 10 (October 1967): 74–91.

Nomura Hachirō. *Kokugaku zenshi*. 2 vols. Seki Shoin, 1928–29.

Nomura Kanetarō. *Ogyū Sorai*. Sanseidō, 1934.

Norman, E. Herbert. "Andō Shōeki and the Anatomy of Japanese Feudalism." *Transactions of the Asiatic Society of Japan*, 3rd series 2 (1949).

Nosco, Peter. "Nature, Invention, and National Learning: The *Kokka hachiron* Controversy, 1742–46." *Harvard Journal of Asiatic Studies* 41, no. 1 (June 1981): 75–91.

―――――. *Remembering Paradise: Nativism and Nostalgia in Eighteenth-Century Japan*. Cambridge, MA: Council on East Asian Studies, Harvard University, 1990.

Nozaki Morihide. *Michi: kinsei Nihon no shisō*. Tōkyō Daigaku Shuppankai, 1979.

―――――. *Motoori Norinaga no sekai*. Hanawa Shobō, 1972.

Ogasawara Haruo. *Kokuju ronsō no kenkyū*. Perikansha, 1988.

Okada Tahehiko. "Practical Learning in the Chu Hsi School: Yamazaki Ansai and

Kaibara Ekken." In *Principle and Practicality*, edited by Wm. Theodore de Bary and Irene Bloom, 231–305. New York: Columbia University Press, 1979.

Okamura Shigeru. *Mōshi seigi yakuchū*. Fukuoka: Chūgoku Shoten, 1986.

Ōkubo Tadashi. *Edo jidai no kokugaku*. Shibundō, 1963.

Okumura Kōsaku. *Kamo no Mabuchi: den to uta*. Tanka Shinbun Sha, 1996.

Ooms, Herman. *Tokugawa Ideology: Early Constructs, 1570–1680*. Princeton, NJ: Princeton University Press, 1985.

Ōta Seikyū. *Nihon kagaku to Chūgoku shigaku*. Kōbundō, 1958.

Ōtani Masao. "Itō Jinsai no shi to gakumon." *Kokugo kokubun* 48, no. 12 (December 1979): 24–41.

Owen, Stephen. *An Anthology of Chinese Literature: Beginnings to 1911*. New York: W. W. Norton, 1996.

———. *Readings in Chinese Literary Thought*. Cambridge, MA: Council on East Asian Studies, Harvard University, 1992.

Palmer, Richard E. *Hermeneutics*. Evanston, IL: Northwestern University Press, 1969.

Parvulesco, Marguerite-Marie. *Écriture, lecture et poésie: lettrés japonais du 17e au 19e siècle*. Paris: Publications Orientalistes de France, 1991.

Pastreich, Emanuel. "Grappling with Chinese Writing as a Material Language: Ogyū Sorai's *Yakubunsentei*." *Harvard Journal of Asiatic Studies* 61, no. 1 (June 2001): 119–70.

Ricoeur, Paul. *The Rule of Metaphor: Multidisciplinary Studies of the Creation of Meaning in Language*. Translated by Robert Czerny. Toronto: University of Toronto Press, 1977.

Rousseau, Jean-Jacques. *A Discourse on Inequality*. Translated by Maurice Cranston. New York: Penguin, 1984.

Rubinger, Richard. *Private Academies of Tokugawa Japan*. Princeton, NJ: Princeton University Press, 1982.

Sagara Tōru. *Itō Jinsai*. Perikansha, 1998.

———. *Motoori Norinaga*. Tōkyō Daigaku Shuppankai, 1978.

Saigo Nobutsuna. *Kokugaku no hihan: hōhō ni kansuru oboegaki*. Miraisha, 1965.

Saigusa Yasutaka. *Kamo no Mabuchi*. Yoshikawa Kōbunkan, 1962.

———. *Kokugaku no undō*. Kazama Shobō, 1966.

Sakai, Naoki. *Voices of the Past: The Status of Language in Eighteenth-Century Japanese Discourse*. Ithaca, NY: Cornell University Press, 1991.

Sasaki Nobutsuna. *Kamo no Mabuchi to Motoori Norinaga*. Rev. ed. Yugawa Kōbunkan, 1935.

———. *Nihon kagaku shi*. Rev. ed. Hakubunkan, 1942.

Sasazuki Kiyomi. *Motoori Norinaga no kenkyū*. Iwanami Shoten, 1944.

Satō Hitoshi, ed., *Shushigaku no kihon yōgo: Hokkei jigi yakukai*. Kenbun Shuppan, 1996.

Satō Miyuki. *Ayatari to Akinari to: jūhasseiki kokugaku e no hihan*. Nagoya: Nagoya Daigaku Shuppankai, 1993.

Saussy, Haun. *The Problem of a Chinese Aesthetic*. Stanford, CA: Stanford University Press, 1993.

Sawai Keiichi. "Dazai Shundai no 'makoto' kaishaku." *Chūgoku koten kenkyū* 32 (1987): 48–61.

———. "'Giko' no sekai ninshiki: kobunjigaku ni okeru hyōgen yōshiki rikai o megutte." *Nihon bungaku* 39, no. 10 (October 1990): 1–10.

———. *'Kigō' to shite no jugaku.* Kōbōsha, 2000.

Shigematsu Nobuhiro. *Kinsei kokugaku no bungaku kenkyū.* Kazama Shobō, 1974.

Shimada Kenji. *Shushigaku to Yōmeigaku.* Iwanami Shoten, 1967.

Shimizu Masayuki. *Kokugaku no tasha zō.* Perikansha, 2005.

Shiraishi Shinko. "Dazai Shundai 'Bunron' kunshaku." *Kanbungaku kaishaku to kenkyū* 1 (1998): 107–89.

———. "Dazai Shundai no 'dokushi' no yōryō." *Kanbungaku kaishaku to kenkyū* 7 (2004): 133–61.

———. "Dazai Shundai no 'Shiron.'" *Tōhōgaku* 114 (July 2007): 84–100.

———. "Dazai Shundai 'Shisho koden' kō—sono ichi." *Kanbungaku kaishaku to kenkyū* 6 (2003): 75–93.

Shirane, Haruo, ed. *Early Modern Japanese Literature: An Anthology, 1600–1900.* New York: Columbia University Press, 2002.

Smith, Adam. *The Theory of Moral Sentiments.* Oxford: Oxford University Press, 1976. Reprint, Indianapolis: Liberty Classics, 1982.

Spae, Joseph John. *Itō Jinsai: A Philosopher, Educator and Sinologist of the Tokugawa Period.* New York: Paragon, 1967.

Suzuki Eiichi. *Kokugaku shisō no shiteki kenkyū.* Yoshikawa Kōbunkan, 2002.

Suzuki Jun. *Edo wagaku ronkō.* Hitsuji Shobō, 1997.

———. *Tachibana Chikage no kenkyū.* Perikansha, 2006.

Suzuki Jun, Ōnaka Masayuki, and Nakamura Kazumoto, eds. *Motoori Norinaga to Suzunoya shachū.* Kinseisha, 1984.

Suzuki Ken'ichi. *Kinsei tōshō kadan no kenkyū.* Kyūko Shoin, 1996.

Suzuki Torao. *Shina shiron shi.* Kōbundō, 1927.

Tabayashi Yoshinobu. *Kamo no Mabuchi kashū no kenkyū.* Kazama Shobō, 1966.

Tahara Tsuguo. *Motoori Norinaga.* Kōdansha, 1968.

———. *Soraigaku no sekai.* Tōkyō Daigaku Shuppankai, 1991.

———. *Tokugawa shisōshi kenkyū.* Miraisha, 1967.

Tajiri Yūichirō. "Ongaku • kannushi to Soraigaku." *Nihon shisōshi kenkyū* 14 (1982): 16–30.

———. "Soraigaku no reigaku kan." *Nihon shisōshi kenkyū* 11 (1979): 16–27.

Tajiri Yūichirō and Hikita Keiyū. *Dazai Shundai • Hattori Nankaku.* Meitoku Shuppansha, 1995.

Takahashi Hiromi. *Edo no barokku: Soraigaku no shūhen.* Perikansha, 1991.

———. "Soraigaku ni okeru 'shi' ni tsuite." *Nihon shisōshi kenkyū* 5 (1974): 32–41.

Takahashi Toshikazu. *Motoori Norinaga no kagaku.* Osaka: Izumi Shoin, 1996.

Takano Toshio. *Motoori Norinaga.* Kawade Shobō Shinsha, 1988.

Takebe Yoshito. *Dazai Shundai.* Yoshikawa Kōbunkan, 1997.

———. *Dazai Shundai: tenkanki no keizai shisō.* Ochanomizu Shobō, 1991.

Tanaka Kōji. *Motoori Norinaga no shikōhō.* Perikansha, 2005.

————. *Murata Harumi no kenkyū*. Kyūko Shoin, 2000.

Teeuwen, Mark. "Kokugaku vs. Nativism." *Monumenta Nipponica* 61, no. 2 (Summer 2006): 227–42.

————. "Poetry, Sake, and Acrimony: Arakida Hisaoyu and the Kokugaku Movement." *Monumenta Nipponica* 52, no. 3 (Autumn 1997): 295–325.

Thomas, Roger K. "'High' versus 'Low': The *Fude no Saga* Controversy and Bakumatsu Poetics." *Monumenta Nipponica* 49, no. 4 (Winter 1994): 455–69.

————. "Plebeian Travelers on the Way of Shikishima: Waka Theory and Practice during the Late Tokugawa Period." Ph.D. dissertation, Indiana University, 1991.

————. *The Way of Shikishima: Waka Theory and Practice in Early Modern Japan*. Lanham, MD: University Press of America, 2008.

Tillman, Hoyt Cleveland. *Confucian Discourse and Chu Hsi's Ascendancy*. Honolulu: University of Hawai'i Press, 1992.

Tōgō Fukiko. "Dazai Shundai no kobunji hihan to bunshōron ni tsuite." *Kikan Nihon shisōshi* 8 (1978): 44–52.

Toki Zenmaro. *Tayasu Munetake*. 4 vols. Nihon Hyōronsha, 1942–1946.

Tomotsune Tsutomu. *Shigen to hanpuku: Motoori Norinaga ni okeru kotoba to iu mondai*. Sangensha, 2007.

Totman, Conrad. *Early Modern Japan*. Berkeley: University of California Press, 1993.

Tucker, John Allen. *Itō Jinsai's "Gomō jigi" and the Philosophical Definition of Early Modern Japan*. Leiden: Brill, 1998.

————. *Ogyū Sorai's Philosophical Masterworks: The "Bendō" and "Benmei."* Honolulu: University of Hawai'i Press, 2006.

Uchino Gorō. *Edoha kokugaku ronkō*. Sōrinsha, 1979.

————. *Bungeigakushi no hōhō: kokugakushi no saikentō*. Ōfūsha, 1974.

Ueda, Makoto. *Literary and Art Theories in Japan*. Cleveland: Press of Western Reserve University, 1967. Reprint, Ann Arbor: University of Michigan Center for Japanese Studies, 1991.

Usami Kisohachi. *Kinsei karon no kenkyū: kangaku to no kōshō*. Osaka: Izumi Shoin, 1987.

Van Zoeren, Steven. *Poetry and Personality: Reading, Exegesis, and Hermeneutics in Traditional China*. Stanford, CA: Stanford University Press, 1991.

Wakabayashi, Bob Tadashi. *Japanese Loyalism Reconstrued: Yamagata Daini's "Ryūshi shinron" of 1759*. Honolulu: University of Hawai'i Press, 1995.

Wakamizu Suguru. *Sorai to sono monjin no kenkyū*. San'ichi Shobō, 1993.

Waley, Arthur, trans. *The Book of Songs: The Ancient Chinese Classic of Poetry*. New York: Grove Press, 1987.

Wang, C. H. *The Bell and the Drum: "Shih ching" as Formulaic Poetry in an Oral Tradition*. Berkeley: University of California Press, 1974.

Watabe Osamu. *Kinsei waka shisō kenkyū*. Jichōsha, 1991.

Watanabe Hiroshi. *Kinsei Nihon shakai to Sōgaku*. Tōkyō Daigaku Shuppankai, 1985.

————. "'Michi' to 'miyabi'—Norinagaku to 'kagaku'ha kokugaku no seiji shisōshiteki kenkyū." Parts 1–4. *Kokka gakkai zasshi* 87, no. 9–10 (September

1974): 1–85; no. 11–12 (November 1974): 1–75; 88, no. 3–4 (March 1975): 238–68; no. 5–6 (May 1975): 295–366.

Watson, Burton, trans. *Chuang Tzu: Basic Writings*. New York: Columbia University Press, 1964.

———. *Records of the Grand Historian of China*. 2 vols. New York: Columbia University Press, 1961.

Webb, Herschel. *The Japanese Imperial Institution in the Tokugawa Period*. New York: Columbia University Press, 1968.

Wehmeyer, Ann. *Motoori: Kojiki-den, Book 1*. Ithaca, NY: Cornell East Asia Series, 1997.

Weinsheimer, Joel C. *Eighteenth-Century Hermeneutics: Philosophy of Interpretation in England from Locke to Burke*. New Haven, CT: Yale University Press, 1993.

Yamashita Hisao. *Motoori Norinaga to 'shizen.'* Chūsekisha, 1988.

Yamashita, Samuel Hideo. "Compasses and Carpenter's Squares: A Study of Itō Jinsai (1627–1705) and Ogyū Sorai (1666–1728)." Ph.D. dissertation, University of Michigan, 1981.

———. "The Early Life and Thought of Itō Jinsai." *Harvard Journal of Asiatic Studies* 43, no. 2 (December 1983): 453–80.

———. *Master Sorai's Responsals: An Annotated Translation of "Sorai sensei tōmonsho."* Honolulu: University of Hawai'i Press, 1994.

———. "Nature and Artifice in the Writings of Ogyū Sorai (1666–1728)." In *Confucianism and Tokugawa Culture*, edited by Peter Nosco, 138–65. Princeton, NJ: Princeton University Press, 1984.

———. "School Relations in Ogyū Sorai's Miscanthus Patch Academy: The Case of Dazai Shundai (1680–1747)." *Asian Cultural Studies* Special Issue 3 (1992): 273–86.

Yasui Shōtarō. *Nihon jugaku shi*. Fūzanbō, 1939.

Yasunaga Toshinobu. *Ando Shoeki: Social and Ecological Philosopher of Eighteenth-Century Japan*. New York: Weatherhill, 1992.

Yoda, Tomiko. "Fractured Dialogues: *Mono no aware* and Poetic Communication in *The Tale of Genji*." *Harvard Journal of Asiatic Studies* 59, no. 2 (December 1999): 523–57.

Yoshikawa Kōjirō. *Five Hundred Years of Chinese Poetry, 1150–1650*. Translated by John Timothy Wixted. Princeton, NJ: Princeton University Press, 1989.

———. *Jinsai • Sorai • Norinaga*. Iwanami Shoten, 1975.

———. *Jinsai, Sorai, Norinaga: Three Classical Philologists of Mid-Tokugawa Japan*. Tokyo: Tōhō Gakkai, 1983.

———. *Motoori Norinaga*. Chikuma Shobō, 1977.

"Soraigaku an." In *Ogyū Sorai*, Nihon shisō taikei, no. 36, edited by Yoshikawa Kōjirō et al., 629–739. Iwanami Shoten, 1973.

Yu, Pauline. *The Reading of Imagery in the Chinese Poetic Tradition*. Princeton, NJ: Princeton University Press, 1987.

Zhang Longxi. *The Tao and the Logos*. Durham, NC: Duke University Press, 1992.

Index

academies, private, 52, 116–18, 147, 234n4; poetry in, 6, 90, 114, 186; of Sorai, 62–63, 90, 99, 108, 114, 116, 250n3

Agatai no kashū (anthology; Kamo no Mabuchi), 166

Agatai no shūi (anthology; Kamo no Mabuchi), 166

Akinari. *See* Ueda Akinari

alternate attendance (*sankin kōtai*) system, 65, 67, 75

Amaterasu (sun goddess), 194, 198, 207

Amenomori Hōshū, 99

Analects (*Lunyu*), 30–31, 241n39; Jinsai on, 52, 55, 57–59, 86, 105; on the Odes, 48, 55, 57–58, 103, 110; on ritual and music, 85–87, 110; Shundai on, 137; Sorai on, 63–64, 83–87, 103–5, 110–11, 246n80; Zhu Xi on, 48, 86–87, 103, 110

ancient kings. *See* sage kings

Ancient Learning (*kogaku*), 11, 236n18. *See also* Itō Jinsai; Ogyū Sorai; Yamaga Sokō

Ancient Phraseology (*guwenci*; *kobunji*), 11, 21–23, 63, 247n6; and Nankaku, 116–17, 121; and Shundai, 140–42; and Sorai, 11, 63, 91–96, 248nn17,19

Ancient Way (*kodō, inishie no michi*): and Mabuchi, 155–65, 169–71; and Norinaga, 14, 24–25, 28, 175–76, 194–200, 204, 206–7, 211; and poetry, 24–25, 155–62, 169–71, 204, 206–7

Andō Shōeki, 163, 165

Andō Tameakira, 34

Andō Tōya, 62, 116, 118, 122

Ansart, Olivier, 18–19, 250n66

"approving virtue and chastising vice" (*quanshan cheng'e*; *kanzen chōaku*), 34, 47–49, 51, 55; Sorai on, 102–4, 107; Shundai on, 136; in the *Kokka hachiron* debate, 151, 154. *See also* morality

Arai Hakuseki, 66–67, 133, 257n27

Arakida Hisaoyu, 235n5

"Arashi" (The Storm; Kamo no Mabuchi), 167

Arimaro. *See* Kada no Arimaro

artisans, 65, 83, 131

Aruga Chōsen, 203, 261n48

Asayama Yoshirō, 251n7, 252n16

Ashiwake obune (A Small Boat Punting Through the Reeds; Motoori Norinaga), 174–75, 184–86, 191–92, 259n3, 261n48

Atsutane. *See* Hirata Atsutane

authenticity: Arimaro on, 150; of emotion, 1–2, 6, 8, 26–27, 31, 114–15, 122, 142–45, 162, 184, 193; in human nature, 5, 52, 184, 193; Norinaga on, 26–27, 31, 184, 193, 262n50; in poetry, 1–2, 6, 120, 122, 134, 140, 142–43, 145, 150, 162, 172, 262n50; Shundai on, 120, 134, 140, 142–43. *See also* genuineness

authoritarianism, 16, 20, 77, 89

aware. *See* mono no aware

Aware ben (An Explanation of *Aware*; Motoori Norinaga), 177

Azumamaro. *See* Kada no Azumamaro

Beixi ziyi (Chen Chun), 46–47, 242n3

Bendō (On Distinguishing the Way; Ogyū Sorai), 64, 77, 79, 82, 106, 111, 190–91, 247n3, 248n19

Bendōsho (A Treatise on the Way; Dazai Shundai), 118, 157, 256n23, 257n24

Benmei (On Distinguishing Names; Ogyū Sorai), 64, 80, 83, 86–87, 90–91, 104, 107, 242n3

Bian Gong, 247n6

Bitō Masahide, 245n65, 252n30

Bo Juyi, 251n6

Bol, Peter, 36, 43

Book of Changes (*Yi jing*), 106, 239n9

Book of Documents (*Shu jing*), 80, 84, 91, 130, 239nn9,15; and the *Odes*, 106–8

Book of Music (*Yue jing*), 106, 249n44. *See also* "Record of Music"

Book of Odes (*Shi jing*): "Airs of the States" ("Guofeng"), 37–39, 42, 48; Arimaro on, 150; categories of poems in, 37, 241n49; editing of, 48, 51, 114–15, 134, 151; and education, 49, 60, 91; "elegantiae" (*ya*) in, 37–39, 48, 56, 241n49;

Book of Odes (*Shi jing*) (*continued*)
emotion in, 41–42, 48, 55–59, 100–101, 107–8, 112–15, 122, 136, 250n68; *feng* (Airs, moral instruction) in, 37, 56, 239n13, 241n49; "Greater Elegantiae" ("Daya"), 37; "Great Preface" ("Daxu") to, 33, 36–41, 43–44, 56, 150, 182–84, 239nn11,13, 256n19; "Guanju," 37–40, 110, 239n11; "Hymns" ("Song"), 37, 56, 125, 241n49; Jinsai on, 55–60, 101, 242nn51,56; and the *Kokka hachiron* debate, 150–51, 153–54; language of, 101, 113–15, 134; "Lesser Elegantiae" ("Xiaoya"), 37; Mabuchi on, 153–54, 160; Mao tradition of, 32, 34–43, 47–48, 55, 59–60, 101, 107, 109, 112–13, 153, 162, 184, 193, 239n8; morality in, 35–43, 47–49, 55–60, 101, 107, 109–10, 112–13, 136, 151, 153–54, 239n8; and music, 35, 37, 40–43, 106, 108–10, 136, 138, 151–54, 240n17, 256n16; Nankaku on, 122, 125–26, 134, 143, 251n7; Norinaga on, 177; orthodox vs. mutated Odes, in, 37–40, 43, 48; "Shaonan," 37–38, 48, 136; Shundai on, 119, 134, 136, 138, 143; and the Six Classics, 106–14, 143, 242n56; Six Principles of, 56, 241n9; Sorai on, 29, 80, 84, 91, 100–103, 106–15, 248n29, 250n68; and the Way, 60, 113–14; "Zhounan," 37–38, 48, 136; Zhu Xi on, 32, 34–35, 43–52, 55–57, 59–60, 101, 103, 106–7, 110–13, 119, 136–37, 151, 153–54, 189, 256n16
Bourdieu, Pierre, 234n4
brotherly obedience (*ti; tei*), 15, 83–84, 157, 196
Buck-Albulet, Heidi, 261n48
Buddhism, 175, 257n32; Shundai on, 118, 130, 136–37; vs. Confucianism, 9–11, 58, 104, 118, 129–30, 136–37; Zen, 93, 247n8
Bunron (A Discourse on Literary Writing; Dazai Shundai), 119, 141–42

Canglang shihua (Canglang's Talks on Poetry; Yan Yu), 92, 247n9
canon: of Ancient Phraseology, 11, 23, 91–92, 117, 120, 127; Confucian, 31, 33, 43; Japanese literary, 26–27, 186, 209; as model, 2, 114, 205, 208. *See also* Five Classics; Six Classics
Cao Cao, 140
Cao Pi, 100, 140
Cao Zhi, 140
Cen Shen, 98
Changes. See Book of Changes
Chen Chun, 46–47, 189, 240n26, 242n3
Cheng brothers, 128
Chen Liang, 235n7
Chikamatsu Monzaemon, 8–9
China: Japanese trade with, 63; Mabuchi on, 155–61, 169, 171; as model, 1–3, 72; music of, 108, 139; Nankaku on, 121; and nativism, 2, 4–5, 12; Norinaga on, 195–96, 201–2, 207; portrayal in Tokugawa kanshi, 96–98, 100,

123–25; Shundai on, 157. *See also* Chinese language; particular dynasties
Chinese language, 1; and Japanese poetry, 182; Mabuchi on, 159–60; Norinaga on, 175, 182–83; Shundai on, 119; Sorai on, 11, 62–63, 70–71, 90, 92, 94–95, 243n18; vs. Japanese, 62, 70–71, 94, 243n18, 257n27
"Chōan dō" (The Chang'an Road; Hattori Nankaku), 123–24
chōka form, 166–69, 254n1
Chu Guangxi, 124
Chūyō hakki (An Exposition of the *Doctrine of the Mean*; Itō Jinsai), 52
Chūyō kai (Interpretation of the *Doctrine of the Mean*; Ogyū Sorai), 64, 84, 88
class structure. *See* hierarchy, social
commercialization, 3, 65; Norinaga on, 201; Shundai on, 132–33; Sorai on, 10, 75, 88–89
commoners, urban (*chōnin*), 3, 8–9, 26
community, 2, 5, 145, 210; Akinari on, 261n41; Mabuchi on, 259n13; Nankaku on, 122–23, 128, 143, 208; Norinaga on, 26, 28, 259n13, 261n41; Sorai on, 16–18, 99–100, 114, 120
Confucianism: on emotion, 28–32, 162, 188, 190; and government, 15, 199–201; Harumi on, 199; Jinsai on, 58; Korean, 33; and literature, 28–29, 32–34, 211, 238n61; Mabuchi on, 147, 155–58, 162, 165, 171, 201; and modernity, 28–29, 31, 211–12; and nativism, 25, 28–29, 31, 145–46, 211–12, 238n58; Norinaga on, 27, 175, 188–92, 195–96, 200–201, 211–12; Shundai on, 118, 129–30; Sokō on, 10–11; and Sorai, 7–8, 10–11, 13, 16, 29, 86, 143, 211; and the Tokugawa shogunate, 62; vs. Buddhism, 9–11, 58, 104, 118, 129–30, 136–37; vs. Daoism, 9–11, 58; and *wen*, 86, 183. *See also* the Way; particular thinkers
Confucius, 9, 78, 104–5, 111, 128, 133, 140, 191; Daoist portrayal of, 122–23; and the *Odes*, 48, 51, 55–58, 101, 114, 134, 151, 160, 177. *See also Analects*
considerateness (*shu*; *jo*), 54, 105, 241n39
court poetry, 145, 148–49, 203, 255n5, 256n13, 261n48, 262n50
culture: and *bunjin*, 123; Chinese vs. Japanese, 2, 11–12, 145, 151, 171, 196; and emotion, 5–6; and human nature, 4–6, 21, 23–24, 28, 61, 88, 120, 193–94, 208; Japanese, 5, 145, 151, 171, 173, 198–200; of King Wen, 40, 107, 112–13; Mabuchi on, 155–56, 171; Nankaku on, 122, 143, 252n16; and nativism, 5, 11–12; Norinaga on, 27–28, 173, 181, 184, 193–94, 196, 198, 208–9; and Norinaga's critics, 198–200; and objectivity, 67–72; and poetry, 6, 20, 43, 114, 122, 172, 181, 208, 210–12; popular, 67; of sage kings, 60, 74, 94, 106, 157, 163–64; Sorai on, 11, 16–21, 67–72, 77–78, 83–84, 88,

92, 106, 110, 114–15, 120, 122, 237n34; urban commercial, 10; vs. history, 237n33; vs. invention, 19–20; vs. metaphysical norms, 3–5; vs. moral norms, 21; vs. nature, 19–20, 163; and the Way, 3–6, 11, 23, 43, 61, 88, 110. *See also* wen

currency, 66–67, 132, 163, 201

custom (*fūzoku*): Mabuchi on, 153; Norinaga on, 195, 201; and reforms, 72–74, 201; Shundai on, 129, 133, 138; Sorai on, 71–74, 78, 129, 237n34; vs. laws, 73, 78

Daigaku kai (Interpretation of the *Great Learning*; Ogyū Sorai), 64

Daigaku teihon (The Authentic Text of the *Great Learning*; Itō Jinsai), 52

Daigaku wakumon (Kumazawa Banzan), 10

Daitō seigo (Stories of the East; Hattori Nankaku), 117

Dao de jing, 126, 257n25

Daoism, 11; Jinsai on, 9, 52, 58; and Mabuchi, 156, 158, 171; and Nankaku, 122, 126, 128, 251n15; and Norinaga, 194, 196; Shundai on, 131–32, 253n33; Sorai on, 77, 79–80, 88, 246n88, 247n3, 251n15; vs. Confucianism, 9–11, 58; and Zhu Xi, 9, 52, 58

Dazai Shundai, 2, 118–20, 128–42; and Ancient Phraseology, 140–42; on Buddhism, 118, 130, 136–37; critics of, 256n23; and Daini, 164; on Daoism, 131–32, 253n33; on the economy, 131–33; on emotion, 129–30, 134–35, 138, 143, 208; on the gentleman, 129–30, 134, 137, 143; on genuineness, 130, 140–43; on government, 120, 128, 131–37, 142–44, 157; on human nature, 118, 128–31, 142; on institutions, 131–33; and the *Kokka hachiron* debate, 152; and Mabuchi, 157, 162, 256n23, 257n24; on morality, 129–31, 136, 157, 253n50; on music, 118, 130–31, 136, 138–40, 143, 157, 162, 252n30, 254nn50,53; and Nankaku, 13–14, 116, 119–20, 140; on non-action, 132, 253n33; and Norinaga, 178; on poetry, 118–19, 134–37, 140–43, 208; on political economy, 118, 120, 131–33, 135, 137; and politics, 13–14, 119–20, 123, 142; on ritual, 119, 123, 128–31, 144, 157, 252n30; on the sage kings, 128–32, 137–39, 157; and Seiryō, 253n36; on the Six Classics, 118–19, 128, 136, 143; on social hierarchy, 131, 134–35; and Sorai, 13–14, 64, 116, 118–20, 128–36, 138–44, 250n3, 252nn27,30; on the Way, 118–19, 128–33, 136–37, 157; on words vs. tones, 136, 256n16; and Zhu Xi, 118–19, 128, 135–37

de Bary, Wm. Theodore, 16, 19, 234n2

Doctrine of the Mean (*Zhongyong*; *Chūyō*), 46, 240n26; Jinsai on, 52; Sorai on, 64, 77, 79, 84, 88; Zhu Xi on, 47, 79, 241n38. *See also* the Mean

Documents. See Book of Documents

Dōjimon (Questions from Children; Itō Jinsai), 52, 55

Dokugo (Solitary Ramblings; Dazai Shundai), 119, 138–40, 254n53

Dokushi yōryō (Essentials of Reading the Odes; Itō Tōgai), 55

Doku Shushi shiden (Reading Zhu Xi's *Transmissions on the Odes*; Dazai Shundai), 119, 136

Du Fu, 99, 124, 137, 253n47

Du Shenyan, 100

economy: in the Genroku period, 65; market, 133; Norinaga on, 201; and Seiryō, 253n36; Shundai on, 131–33; Sorai on, 73, 75; in the Tokugawa period, 3, 65–67; and trade, 133. *See also* commercialization

Edo school (Edo-ha), 199, 235n5, 261n42

education: and the *Odes*, 49, 60, 91, 106, 110, 134; and poetry, 6–7, 11, 90–93, 114, 127–28, 134; Sorai on, 6–7, 11, 90–93, 106, 110, 114, 127–28, 134

elites, 10, 20; Nankaku on, 120–22, 124, 143–44, 208; Shundai on, 134–35, 137; Sorai on, 2, 7, 22, 83, 91, 97–100, 113–14, 128. *See also* gentleman; rulership; samurai

emotion (*qing*; *jō*): of common people, 134–35, 251n6; communication of, 26–27, 30, 177–79, 184, 189, 192–93, 204, 210–11; and Confucianism, 28–32, 162, 188, 190; and culture, 5–6; elegant, 121; and the Four-Seven Debate, 241n38; and harmony, 46–47; and human nature, 1, 4–6, 9–10, 19, 23, 27, 43–48, 52–54, 105, 130, 176, 184–85, 188, 208; Jinsai on, 9, 52, 55–57, 106; *Kokinshū* preface on, 149–50; liberation of, 6, 12–15, 24–25, 28–29, 32, 142, 210–12; and Mabuchi, 153–55, 171; and the Mao tradition, 35–36, 38–39, 41–42, 112; and morality, 4, 8, 22, 27, 31, 44–48, 54, 109, 154, 189–90, 240n22; and music, 15, 22, 41–42, 44, 108–10, 113, 130, 138, 143, 188; Nankaku on, 120–21, 142, 208; and neoclassical form, 3, 21–23; Norinaga on, 14–15, 23–28, 30–31, 173, 176–80, 183–93, 204, 209, 211, 259n12, 260n25; in the *Odes*, 41–42, 48, 55–59, 100–101, 107–8, 112–15, 122, 136, 250n68; and patterning, 41, 176, 179–80, 183–84, 193, 239n15, 259n12; and poetry, 1–3, 6, 8, 14–15, 32, 43–47, 89–90, 100–106, 109–10, 114–15, 138, 145, 154–55, 160–62, 175, 187, 191–93, 204, 208–9, 249n54, 251n6; regulation of, 4, 6, 15, 21–22, 26, 28–32, 35, 42, 44, 46–48, 68, 108–10, 112–13, 130, 138, 143, 153–55, 160, 185–90, 209–11, 241n38; and rulership, 11, 22–23, 105–6, 113, 134–36, 142–43, 153, 160, 178, 180, 191; Shundai on, 129–30, 134–35, 138, 143, 208; and social norms, 8, 15, 30, 32, 188, 210–12;

emotion (*qing*; *jō*) (*continued*)
Sokō on, 10–11; Sorai on, 8–9, 11–15, 19,
21–23, 28–29, 31, 89–90, 100–102, 103–10,
112–15, 208, 211, 249n54; vs. desires, 189–90,
240n22, 260n25; vs. politics, 13, 31; and the
Way, 5, 12–15, 25, 28, 45–47, 89, 105, 107, 109,
130; Zhu Xi on, 4, 8, 13, 43–48, 53–54, 68, 101,
112–13, 154, 189, 234n3, 240n22, 241n38
empathy: and considerateness, 54, 241n39; and
poetry, 25–27, 30, 52, 55, 59, 101, 104, 106,
122, 134–35, 153, 160, 178, 187–88, 191; and
rulership, 11, 22, 106–8, 113–14, 122, 133–36,
142–43, 153, 160, 178, 191
emperor, Japanese: and Daini, 164–65; Mabuchi
on, 158–59, 172; and Norinaga, 24, 173, 194,
197, 209; restoration of, 164
Europe, 16

faithfulness (*xin*; *shin*), 15, 83–84, 196
feudalism, 3, 163; Shundai on, 131, 133, 135; Sorai
on, 5–6, 12, 76, 105–8, 113, 165; vs. law-based
societies, 5–6, 76, 107–8; vs. markets, 133
fictionality, 186, 190; of poetry, 120, 123–25, 128,
143
filial piety (*xiao*; *kō*), 15, 83–84, 157, 179, 196
Five Classics, 36, 100, 239n9, 249n44. *See also*
Six Classics
five relationships, 163
Four Beginnings (*siduan*; *shitan*), 53–54, 56–57,
68–69, 104–5, 241n38
Four-Seven Debate, 241n38
Four Teachings (*sijiao*; *shikyō*), 106–7, 110. *See
also* Six Classics
Fujiwara no Fuhito, 74
Fujiwara no Shunzei, 186
Fujiwara no Teika, 148
Futatabi kingo no kimi ni kotaematsuru fumi
(Another Reply to Tayasu Munetake; Kamo
no Mabuchi), 153
Fu Xi, Emperor, 127

Gakuritsu kō (Reflections on Musical Pitches;
Ogyū Sorai), 108
Gakusei hen (On Musical Systems; Ogyū Sorai),
108
Gakusoku (Regulations for Learning; Ogyū
Sorai), 64
genbun itchi (unification of spoken and written
languages), 21
gender, 161, 176, 257n31
Genji monogatari (Tale of Genji), 34; and
Banzan, 236n14, 238n59; and Mabuchi, 147,
166; and Norinaga, 27, 174–75, 177, 190, 203
Genji monogatari shinshaku (New Interpretation
of the *Tale of Genji*; Kamo no Mabuchi), 147
Genji monogatari tama no ogushi (The Tale of
Genji, A Small Jeweled Comb; Motoori
Norinaga), 175

Genroku period (Japan), 65–66, 89, 118, 132, 139
gentleman (*junzi*; *kunshi*), 255n9; and Ancient
Phraseology, 93–94; education of, 91, 106,
134; and the mandate of Heaven, 197; and
music, 91, 108; Nankaku on, 121–22, 128, 134,
251n7; and the *Odes*, 91, 121–22, 134, 251n7;
and poetry, 7, 89, 96, 100, 114, 121–22, 137;
Shundai on, 129–30, 134, 137, 143; Sorai on, 7,
83–84, 89–91, 93–94, 96, 100, 106, 108, 114, 143
genuineness (*cheng*; *sei*, *makoto*): Munetake on,
151; Norinaga on, 184–86; Shundai on, 130,
140–43; Sorai on, 87–88, 246n88. *See also*
authenticity
Gion Nankai, 247n9, 251n6
gods, Japanese: and Norinaga, 24, 27, 173–75,
194–200, 202, 209, 261n41
Go'ikō (Reflections on the Meaning of Language;
Kamo no Mabuchi), 147
Gomō jigi (The Meaning of Terms in the
Analects and *Mencius*; Itō Jinsai), 52, 54–56,
242n3
Gongan school, 93, 247n10, 248n11
Gosenshū, 186, 206
government: Banzan on, 10; Daini on, 163–64;
by gentlemen, 91, 96, 114, 143; Harumi on,
199; of King Wen, 248n29; Mabuchi on, 148,
152–53, 158–60; and the Mao tradition, 38–41;
and morality, 15, 106, 195–96, 235n7; and
music, 41, 109, 153; Nankaku on, 117, 122, 128,
143; and nativism, 12, 144; Norinaga on, 24,
178, 190–92, 194–96, 200–202; and the *Odes*,
38–41, 91, 101, 112–13, 242n4; and poetry, 7,
11, 22, 24, 33, 106, 114, 128, 135, 137, 142–44,
149, 152–53, 190–92; Shundai on, 115, 120, 128,
131–37, 142–44, 157; Sorai on, 11, 13, 15, 22, 61,
64–65, 67, 72–76, 78, 81–85, 91, 96, 104–8,
111–14, 144, 165, 209, 237n26, 242n6, 248n29;
and talent, 81–85; and the Way, 61, 64, 72,
107, 111–12, 122, 137. *See also* politics; rulership
Great Learning (*Daxue*; *Daigaku*), 49–52, 64

Han dynasty (China), 11, 44, 74, 92, 97, 108,
123; *Odes* commentaries of, 32, 35–36; poetry
of, 92–93, 140
Hanfeizi, 132
Han shu (History of the Han), 41
Han Yu, 142
harmony (*he*; *wa*): and music, 86, 108–9; Sorai
on, 84–85, 89, 108–9, 112, 197, 246n73; and
talent, 84–85, 89, 109, 112; vs. sameness,
84–85, 197, 246n73; Zhu Xi on, 46–47, 86
Harootunian, H. D., 25–27
Harumi. *See* Murata Harumi
Hattori Nankaku, 2, 116–18, 120–28; and
Ancient Phraseology, 116–17, 121; on China,
121, 124–25; on community, 122–23, 128,
143, 208; on culture, 122, 143, 252n16; on
the gentleman, 121–22, 128, 134, 251n7; and

Mabuchi, 170; and the *Odes*, 122, 125–26, 134, 143, 251n7; on poetry, 117, 120–23, 140, 143, 208; poetry of, 123–28, 234n5; and Shundai, 13–14, 116, 119–20, 140; and Sorai, 14, 116–17, 119–20, 122, 127–28, 142–43

Hayashi Gahō, 62

Hayashi Razan, 62; on the Way, 34, 43

heart (*xin*; *shin*, *kokoro*): of ancient Japanese, 158, 161, 170, 182, 184, 196; and Buddhism, 137, 257n32; Chinese vs. Japanese, 177, 182, 195, 207; consolation of with poetry, 150, 153, 178; cultivation of with poetry, 101, 151, 161, 171–72, 186; of the Four Beginnings, 53, 57, 104–5; of the gods, 194; as the origin of poetry, 40–41, 161, 177, 180, 192, 203; regulation of with music, 87, 109, 151–53; of rulers, 85, 159; subjectivism of, 67, 91, 128, 183; Zhu Xi on, 44–46, 49–50, 53, 91, 128, 189, 257n32. *See also* emotion

Heaven (*tian*; *ten*), 3, 156; and human nature, 19, 43–46, 78–79, 81, 88, 93, 188, 209; Sorai on, 15, 19, 78–79, 197, 209, 236n24; and the Way, 3, 15, 19, 236n24

Heaven-and-Earth: Jinsai on, 9, 58; Mabuchi on, 155–58, 162, 171–72, Norinaga on, 194–95; Shundai on, 132; Sorai on, 7, 79, 103; Zhu Xi on, 44–45

Hegel, G. W. F., 236n23

Heian period (Japan), 166, 174, 238n59, 257n31

He Jingming, 92, 247n6

hierarchy, social, 65–67, 253n36; and humaneness, 105–6; as invention vs. nature, 12; Mabuchi on, 165; and Nankaku, 123; and Norinaga, 26, 201; Shōeki on, 163; Shundai on, 131, 134–35; Sorai on, 17–18, 73, 76, 83, 131. *See also* artisans; commoners, urban; elites; gentleman; merchants; peasants; samurai

Hihon tamakushige (The Secret Jeweled Comb Box; Motoori Norinaga), 200

Hikita Yakara, 242n5

Hino Tatsuo, 21–23, 32, 252n16

Hiraishi Naoaki, 237n26

Hirano Kinka, 116

Hirata Atsutane, 233n1

history, 199–200; Sorai on, 73–74, 102–3; vs. nature, 237n33

"Hito no kyō ni yuku o okuru" #2 (Sending Someone off to the Capital #2; Hattori Nankaku), 125

Hobbes, Thomas, 129, 245n65

Holland, 160

honkadori (allusive variation), 186, 206

Hori Keizan, 174, 248nn12,15,17

humaneness (*ren*; *jin*), 10, 23; Jinsai on, 54, 68, 104; Mabuchi on, 157; Mencius on, 53; Norinaga on, 196; and rulership, 23, 91, 104–6, 111; Shundai on, 132, 157; Sorai on, 18, 64, 69, 91, 104–6, 111–12, 250n66

human nature (*xing*; *sei*): and culture, 4–6, 21, 23–24, 28, 61, 88, 120, 193–94, 208; diversity of, 8, 68, 81–83, 85, 89; and emotion, 1, 4–6, 9–10, 19, 23, 27, 43–48, 52–54, 105, 130, 176, 184–85, 188, 208; and genuineness, 87–88, 185–86, 246n88; goodness of, 48, 53, 83, 87, 129–30, 245n65, 246n88; and Heaven, 19, 43–46, 78–79, 81, 88, 93, 188, 209; and the investigation of things, 50; and Japanese poetry, 148, 185, 193–94, 208; Jinsai on, 52–54, 57, 242n51, 245nn64,65; Mabuchi on, 257n32; Mencius on, 129, 245n65; moral definition of, 4, 8, 13, 44–48, 53, 112–13, 154; and music, 246n88; and Norinaga, 24, 27–28, 176, 184–85, 193–94, 208; original (*benran zhi xing*; *honzen no sei*), 4, 45, 49, 68, 78–79, 154, 171; and poetry, 19, 55, 90, 102, 109, 113–14, 142, 148, 193–94, 208–9; and principle, 3–5, 44–45, 51, 60, 68–69, 79, 171, 255n8; Shundai on, 118, 128–31, 142; Sorai on, 8, 11, 13, 19, 21, 61, 68–69, 76–83, 85, 87–90, 102, 104–5, 108–9, 114, 120, 197, 208–9, 245nn64,65, 246n88; and study, 93; and virtue, 80–81; and the Way, 5, 8, 16, 19–20, 23, 49, 53–54, 68, 76–80, 88–89, 105, 128–29; Xunzi on, 129, 245n65; Zhu Xi on, 3–5, 44–54, 60, 68–69, 78–79, 83, 112–13, 154, 171, 245n64

Hyakunin isshu (Hundred Poems by a Hundred Poets), 146, 174

Ichikawa Kakumei, 196–97

Ikegami, Eiko, 234n4

Ike no Taiga, 123

inborn nature. *See* human nature

India, 160–61, 198

Inoue Tetsujirō, 21, 236n18, 245n65, 252n26

institutions (*seido*): Daini on, 164; Shundai on, 131–33; Sorai on, 72–76, 88–89, 110

investigation of things (*gewu*), 49–51, 59, 102–3, 235n12

Ise monogatari (Tales of Ise), 34, 174, 177

Ise monogatari ko'i (Ancient Meanings of the Tales of Ise; Kamo no Mabuchi), 147

Ishikawa Jōzan, 247n9

Isonokami kō (anthology; Motoori Norinaga), 204

Isonokami sasamegoto (Ancient Whisperings; Motoori Norinaga), 174–80, 187–90

Itō Jinsai, 11, 172, 187; on the *Analects*, 52, 55, 57–59, 86, 105; and Ancient Learning (*kogaku*), 11, 236n18; on Daoism, 9, 52, 58; on emotion, 9, 52, 55–57, 106; on the Four Beginnings, 53–54, 56–57, 68–69, 104–5; on humaneness, 54, 68, 104; on human nature, 52–54, 57, 242n51, 245nn64,65; and the *Kokka hachiron* debate, 256n16; on morality, 52–60; on the *Odes*, 55–60, 101, 242nn51,56; on poetry, 52, 55–60; private academy of, 52, 116;

Itō Jinsai (*continued*)
on ritual and music, 86–87; and Sorai, 9–10, 51, 63, 67–69, 86–87, 104–5, 242n3; and Zhu Xi, 9–10, 51–60, 235n12, 241n38, 242n51
Itō Tōgai, 55, 116, 256n16
Iwahashi Junsei, 245n65
Izumi Makuni, 199

Japanese language: and Mabuchi, 147, 155, 159–60, 162, 169–71; and nativism, 12, 145; and nature, 155, 162; and Norinaga, 173, 175, 181–83, 204; Shundai on, 119; Sorai on, 62, 70–71, 94, 243n18; unification of spoken and written (*genbun itchi*), 21; vs. Chinese, 62, 70–71, 94, 119, 159–60, 182, 243n18, 257n27; and *waka* poetry, 1, 12, 145, 151, 162, 169–71, 181–82, 204; and writing systems, 159–60, 182–83, 257n27
Japanese learning (*wagaku*), 199, 261n44
Jin dynasty (China), 93, 140
Jinmu, Emperor, 164
Jinsai. *See* Itō Jinsai
jokotoba (poetic preface), 180

Kada no Arimaro, 146, 166, 255n8; and *Kokka hachiron*, 147–55, 255n11, 256nn14,16, 260n30
Kada no Azumamaro, 146, 166
Kada no Nobuna, 146
Kaibara Ekiken, 8–9
Kaiho Seiryō, 133, 253n36
Ka'ikō (Reflections on the Meaning of Poetry; Kamo no Mabuchi), 147, 161
"Kajitsu no kankyo" (Idleness on a Summer Day; Hattori Nankaku), 127
Kakinomoto no Hitomaro, 206
Kamakura period (Japan), 74, 139, 164
Kamo no Mabuchi, 2, 11, 145–72, 182; on the Ancient Way, 155–65, 169–71; on China, 155–61, 169, 171; on Confucianism, 147, 155–58, 162, 165, 171, 201; and Confucian views of literature, 153–55, 160, 162; and court poetry, 262n50; and Daoism, 156, 158, 171; disciples of, 199, 235n5, 261n42; on the emperor, 158–59, 172; and Japanese language, 147, 155, 159–60, 162, 169–71; and the *Kojiki*, 170; and the *Kokinshū*, 147, 167; and the *Kokka hachiron* debate, 149, 152–55, 260n30; on the *Man'yōshū*, 147, 161, 166–67, 169–70, 258n56; on nature, 155–56, 162, 165, 171, 208; and Norinaga, 174, 185, 196, 201, 203–4, 207, 259n13; on poetry, 147, 152–55, 160–62, 171–72; poetry of, 165–71, 235n5; on rulership, 153, 158–60, 165; and self-cultivation, 170–72, 257n32; and Shundai, 157, 162, 256n23, 257n24; and Sorai, 155–56, 162, 165, 170–72; on straightforwardness, 157–61, 165, 170, 172; and Zhu Xi, 154, 156, 162, 171

Kamo-ō kashū (anthology; Kamo no Mabuchi), 166
kana syllabary, 182–83
Kang Hai, 247n6
Kanjikō (Reflections on Poetic Epithets; Kamo no Mabuchi), 147
Kanji san'on kō (Reflections on the Three Modes of Pronouncing Chinese Characters; Motoori Norinaga), 175
Kanno Kakumyō, 262n50
Katō Chikage, 146, 166, 199, 235n5
Katō Enao, 146
Katō Umaki, 149, 166, 182
Keichū, 149, 166, 174
Keikodan (Conversations about Learning from the Past; Kaiho Seiryō), 133
Keizairoku (A Record of Political Economy; Dazai Shundai), 118–19, 128, 131–32, 135–37
Keizairoku shūi (Gleanings from *A Record of Political Economy*; Dazai Shundai), 118, 132–33
Ken'en zuihitsu (Jottings from the Miscanthus Garden; Ogyū Sorai), 63–64, 249n54
Kenzō, Emperor, 170
Kingaku taiishō (A General Study of the Koto; Ogyū Sorai), 108–9
kogaku. *See* Ancient Learning
Kogidō (Hall of Ancient Meanings; academy of Itō Jinsai), 52
Kojiki (Records of Ancient Matters): and Mabuchi, 170; and Norinaga, 174–75, 194, 196, 199, 204, 261n41; and Norinaga's critics, 199, 261n41
Kojikiden (Transmission of the *Records of Ancient Matters*; Motoori Norinaga), 174–75, 194
Kojima Yasunori, 26, 236n24, 252n30
Kokinshū, 150, 256n12; and Mabuchi, 147, 167; and Norinaga, 175, 180, 186, 205–6; preface to, 33, 149–50, 255n10
Kokinshū tōkagami (A *Kokinshū* Telescope; Motoori Norinaga), 175
Kokin wakashū sachū ron (A Study of the Marginal Notes in the *Kokinshū*; Kamo no Mabuchi), 147
Kokka hachiron (Eight Essays on Japanese Poetry; Kada no Arimaro), 147–51; debate on, 147–55, 160, 166, 203, 254n4, 255n11, 256nn14,16, 260n30
Kokka hachiron sekihi (A Rejection of the *Eight Essays on Japanese Poetry*; Ōsuga Nakayabu), 260n30
Kokka hachiron sekihi hyō (A Critique of *A Rejection of the "Eight Essays on Japanese Poetry"*; Motoori Norinaga), 192
Kokka hachiron yogen (My Views on the *Eight Essays on Japanese Poetry*; Tayasu Munetake), 151–52
Kokka hachiron yogen shūi (Gleanings from *My*

Views on the "Eight Essays on Japanese Poetry";
Kamo no Mabuchi), 152–53
Kokka hachiron sairon (A Restatement of the
Eight Essays on Japanese Poetry; Kada no
Arimaro), 152
Kokugaku, 233n1, 234n4, 235n5; vs. Wagaku
261n44. *See also* Kamo no Mabuchi; Motoori
Norinaga; nativism
Kokuikō (Reflections on the Meaning of Our
Country; Kamo no Mabuchi), 147, 155–62,
196, 201, 257n24, 261n42
Kong Yingda, 35
Konjaku monogatari, 117
Korai fūteishō (Selections from Poetic Styles
from Ancient Times to the Present; Fujiwara
no Shunzei), 186
Korea, 33, 99, 241n38
Korean language, 99
Kotoba no tama no o (Words on a String of
Jewels; Motoori Norinaga), 175
Koyasu Nobukuni, 27
Kumazawa Banzan, 10, 235n14, 238n59
Kurozumi Makoto, 30, 242n56, 246n73
Kuzubana (Arrowroot; Motoori Norinaga), 196
Kyōchūkikō (Report from a Journey to Kai;
Ogyū Sorai), 252n15
Kyōhō reforms, 66–67
"Kyōkaku" (The Knight-Errant; Ogyū Sorai), 97
"Kyo o kōhoku ni utsusu" (Moving to the
North of the City; Hattori Nankaku), 126–27

language: and Ancient Phraseology, 11, 21–23,
93–96; elegant vs. vulgar, 94, 120–21; and
emotion, 23, 179; of gentlemen, 91, 93–94,
114, 134; and Harumi, 199; and Mabuchi,
160; neoclassical, 1–2, 21–23, 63, 170; and
Norinaga, 27; of the *Odes*, 101, 113–15, 134;
patterning (*wen*) of, 93–94, 176, 179–84,
193; Shundai on, 119, 134; Sorai on, 21–23,
62–63, 70–71, 87, 93–96, 110, 113–15, 243n18;
vernacular, 21, 243n18; vs. music, 41, 87, 110.
See also Chinese language; Japanese language
Laozi, 99; Jinsai on, 9, 52, 58; Mabuchi on, 156;
Norinaga on, 194; Shundai on, 132; Sorai on,
79, 91. *See also* Daoism
laws, 66, 199; Shundai on, 131–32; Sorai on, 73,
76, 78, 109, 129, 250n69; sumptuary, 67, 73;
vs. custom, 73, 78, 129
Legalism, 131–32
Leinss, Gerhard, 245n64
Liang Youyu, 247n6
Li Bo, 96, 124
Lidin, Olof, 242n6
Liezi, 127
Li ji. See Record of Ritual
Li Mengyang, 92, 247n6
Li Panlong, 11, 63, 92–93, 97, 117, 247n6, 248n19
literati (*bunjin*), 6, 123, 143, 251n12

literature, 7, 33–35; and culture, 20; liberation
of, 12–15, 22, 24, 28–32, 104, 112–14, 142–43,
211–12, 250n68; popular, 8; as self-expression,
12, 21–22. *See also monogatari*; poetry
Liu Yuxi, 97
Liuyu yanyi, 64
Lotus Sutra, 137
loyalty (*zhong*; *chū*), 15, 83–84, 105, 196
Lu Xiangshan, 128
Lu Zhaolin, 100

Mabuchi. *See* Kamo no Mabuchi
Maganohire (Dispelling Delusions; Ichikawa
Kakumei), 196–97
makurakotoba (pillow words, poetic epithets),
147, 167, 169, 179–80
Makura no yama (anthology; Motoori
Norinaga), 207
mandate of Heaven (*tianming*; *tenmei*), 195–98,
261n39
Man'yō kai (Explanation of the *Man'yōshū*;
Kamo no Mabuchi), 147
Man'yōkō (Reflections on the *Man'yōshū*; Kamo
no Mabuchi), 147, 258n56
Man'yōshū, 149–50, 152, 254n1; Mabuchi on, 147,
161, 166–67, 169–70, 258n56; and Norinaga,
174, 203–6
Man'yōshū Tōtōmi uta kō (Reflections on the
Tōtōmi Poems in the *Man'yōshū*; Kamo no
Mabuchi), 147
Maoshi jian (Annotations on the *Mao Odes*;
Zheng Xuan), 35, 55
Maoshi zhengyi (Correct Significance of the *Mao
Odes*; Kong Yingda), 35–43, 153, 240n17
Marra, Michael, 259n14
Maruyama Masao, 22, 211, 234n2, 236nn22,23;
on modernity, 12–15, 20; on Norinaga, 14–15,
24–26; on Sorai, 12–19, 28–29, 31–32, 142–43,
236n23,24, 245n65, 252n27
material force (*qi*; *ki*), 4, 8–9, 45, 47, 53, 68, 162,
260n28
Matsudaira Sadanobu, 200
Matsumoto Sannosuke, 25
Matsunaga Teitoku, 203
Matsushita Tadashi, 247n6
McNally, Mark, 233n1, 234n4
the Mean (*zhongyong*; *chūyō*), 15, 67, 83–84. *See
also Doctrine of the Mean*
Meidōsho (A Clarification of the Way), 199
Mencius, 9, 55, 133; on human nature, 129,
245n65; Sorai on, 77–78, 197
Mencius, 240n26; Four Beginnings (*siduan*;
shitan) in, 53, 56–57, 68–69, 104; Jinsai on,
52, 56–57; Sorai on, 68–69, 104; Zhu Xi on,
53–54, 241n38
merchants, 65–67, 83, 253n36; Norinaga and,
173–74, 201; Shundai on, 131; Sorai on, 10, 73;
vs. samurai, 65–66, 76

Michi chō koto no ron (A Treatise on the Matter Called a Way; Motoori Norinaga), 194

Michi chō mono no ron (A Treatise on the Thing Called a Way; Motoori Norinaga), 194

Ming dynasty (China): Confucianism of, 10, 16, 33, 91, 128, 143; poetry of, 11, 63, 91–93, 95, 100, 110, 116–17, 121, 140–41

Mito Learning, 245n65

Mizuno Genrō, 242n5

modernity: and Confucianism, 28–29, 31, 211–12; and literary autonomy, 3, 13–14, 22, 28–29, 31–32, 104, 114, 142–43, 211, 252n16; Maruyama on, 12–15, 20, 142–43; of Norinaga, 24; of Sorai, 12–16, 236n24, 237n28

Momokawa Takahito, 26, 259n13

moneylending, 67, 165, 201

monogatari (tales), 117; and Norinaga, 26, 28, 173, 177, 187, 190, 204. *See also Genji monogatari; Ise monogatari*

mono no aware (the pathos of things), 14, 25–27, 177–80, 191, 204; knowing, 26, 184–90. *See also* emotion

morality: and cultural norms, 21, 43; and emotion, 4, 8, 22, 27, 31, 44–48, 54, 109, 154, 189–90, 240n22; and fiction, 190; and government, 15, 106, 195–96, 235n7; and human nature, 4, 8, 13, 44–48, 53, 112–13, 154; Jinsai on, 52–60; in the *Kokka hachiron* debate, 148–55, 255n11; and literature, 31, 34, 211; and Mabuchi, 154–55, 157, 159, 171; and the Mao tradition, 35–43, 112, 239n8; Maruyama on, 12–15, 22, 236n22; and the Mean, 83–84; and music, 40–42, 109–10, 113, 139–40, 154; in Neo-Confucianism, 16; Norinaga on, 173, 179, 184, 189–90, 196; in the *Odes*, 35–43, 47–49, 55–60, 101, 107, 109–10, 112–13, 136, 151, 153–54, 239n8; and poetry, 8, 29, 33, 52, 59–60, 102–4, 109–10, 112–13, 151, 211; Shundai on, 129–31, 136, 157, 253n50; Sorai on, 7–8, 12–15, 61, 76, 83–84, 101–4, 106, 110, 235n7, 236n22, 237n26, 255n11; vs. politics as content of Confucianism, 2, 7–8, 12–15, 17, 61, 91, 106, 199, 235n7, 237n26; Zhu Xi on, 3–4, 8, 20, 22, 34, 44–49, 51, 53–57, 60, 101–4, 112–13, 154, 234n3, 240n22

Morikawa Akitada, 203, 261n48

Mōshi kogi (Ancient Meanings of the *Mencius*; Itō Jinsai), 52

Motoori Norinaga, 2, 173–209; and Akinari, 182–83, 198–99, 261n41; on community, 26, 28, 259n13, 261n41; and Confucianism, 27, 175, 188–93, 195–96, 200–201, 211–12; and court poetry, 203, 261n48, 262n50; critics of, 196–200; on culture, 27–28, 173, 181, 184, 193–94, 196, 198, 208–9; and Daoism, 194, 196; on emotion, 14–15, 23–28, 30–31, 173, 176–80, 183–93, 204, 209, 211, 259n12, 260n25; and the emperor, 24, 173, 194, 197, 209; and the *Genji*,

27, 174–75, 177, 190, 203; on genuineness, 184–86; and Harumi, 199, 261n44; on human nature, 27–28, 176, 184–85, 193–94, 208; on the Japanese gods, 24, 27, 173–75, 194–200, 202, 209, 261n41; and Japanese language, 173, 175, 181–83, 204; and the *Kojiki*, 174–75, 194, 196, 199, 204, 261n41; and the *Kokinshū*, 175, 180, 186, 205–6; and Mabuchi, 174, 185, 196, 201, 203–4, 207, 259n13; on the *Man'yōshū*, 174, 203–6; on *mono no aware*, 14, 25–27, 177–80, 184, 187–91, 204; on morality, 173, 179, 184, 189–90, 196; on patterning, 176, 179–84, 193, 260n14; on poetry, 24–28, 30, 172–81, 190–94, 203; poetry of, 203–8, 234n5, 235n5; on reforms, 200–202; on rulership, 178, 190–91, 195–96; and Shundai, 178; on Song Confucianism, 23, 183; and Sorai, 11–12, 14, 174, 178, 183–84, 186–87, 190–91, 193–94, 196–97, 201–2, 207–9, 211; and *waka*, 26, 28, 173–75, 177, 179–82, 185–86, 190–91, 203–5, 208, 254n11; and the Way of the Gods, 14, 23–25, 28, 175–76, 194–200, 204, 206–7; and Zhu Xi, 23, 27, 183, 189, 192

Mozi, 132

Munetake. *See* Tayasu Munetake

Murata Harumi, 146, 166, 199–200, 235n5, 261n42

Murata Harumichi, 146

Muromachi period (Japan), 74, 139

music: *Correct Significance of the Mao Odes* on, 40–43, 240n17; court, 108, 139, 253n49; and emotion, 15, 22, 41–42, 44, 108–10, 113, 130, 138, 143, 188; and the gentleman, 91, 108; and government, 41, 109, 153; and human nature, 246n88; in the *Kokka hachiron* debate, 150–54; and the Mao tradition, 35, 37, 40–43; and morality, 40–42, 109–10, 113, 139–40, 154; and the *Odes*, 35, 37, 40–43, 106, 108–10, 136, 138, 151–54, 240n17, 256n16; and poetry, 40–43, 108–10, 113, 136, 138, 150–54, 162, 249n54; popular, 109, 139; and ritual, 20–21, 69, 74, 84–88, 91, 94, 106, 110–11, 131, 151–52, 157, 164, 188, 246nn80,88, 252nn16,30, 257n24; of the sages, 15, 21–22, 99, 108–9, 125, 130–31, 138–39, 151–53, 162, 164, 188, 249n50, 252nn16,30, 253n49; Shundai on, 118, 130–31, 136, 138–40, 143, 157, 162, 252n30, 254nn50,53; and song, 41–42, 109, 138–39, 162, 176; Sorai on, 15, 21–22, 69, 74, 80, 84–88, 90–91, 93, 99, 106, 108–11, 113, 252nn16,30, 256n16; vs. language, 41, 87, 110; and the Way, 86–87, 111, 139; and *wen*, 20, 84, 94, 246n80. *See also* "Record of Music"; song

Nagasaki, 63

Najita, Tetsuo, 17, 237n33, 253n36

Nakamura Yukihiko, 33–34

Nakano Kiken, 118, 146

Nankaku. *See* Hattori Nankaku
Nankaku sensei bunshū (The Collected Writings of Master Nankaku; Hattori Nankaku), 117
Nankaku sensei tōka no sho (Master Nankaku's Jottings under the Lamplight; Hattori Nankaku), 117, 120–22
Naobi no mitama (The Upright Spirit; Motoori Norinaga), 194–96
Nara period (Japan), 159
nativism, 2–3, 7, 234nn3,4; and Confucianism, 25, 28–29, 31, 145–46, 211–12, 238n58; and culture, 5, 11–12; and emotion, 14, 24–25, 29, 144–45, 211–12; and *kokugaku*, 233n1, 261n44; and poetry, 211–12, 234n5; and Shundai, 118; and Sorai, 2–3, 11–12, 14, 144, 245n65. *See also* Kamo no Mabuchi; Motoori Norinaga
nature: and Daini, 164; Mabuchi on, 155–56, 162, 165, 171, 208; as metaphysical principle, 8, 12, 250n66; Norinaga on, 176, 181, 187; Shōeki on, 163; Sorai on, 80; vs. artifice, 19, 80, 141; vs. culture, 19–20, 163, 237n33; vs. history, 237n33; vs. invention, 12, 16, 19–20, 61; vs. Nature, 18. *See also* Heaven-and-Earth; human nature
Neo-Confucianism, 16, 27. *See also* Zhu Xi
Nihon shoki, 162, 170, 199, 204
Niimanabi (An Introduction to Learning; Kamo no Mabuchi), 147, 162
Nijō school, 262n50
ninjōbon (books of human emotions), 8
Noguchi Takehiko, 242n51, 254n50
Nomura Kanetarō, 245n65
Norinaga. *See* Motoori Norinaga
Noritokō (Reflections on *Norito*; Kamo no Mabuchi), 147
Nosco, Peter, 24, 255n11

Odes. See Book of Odes
Ogyū Kinkoku, 116
Ogyū Sorai, 61–115; and Ancient Learning, 236n18; and Ancient Phraseology, 11, 63, 91–96, 248nn17,19; antecedents of, 7–12; authoritarianism of, 16, 77, 89; and Chinese language, 11, 62–63, 70–71, 90, 92, 94–95, 243n18; on commercialization, 10, 75, 88–89; on culture, 11, 16–21, 67–72, 77–78, 83–84, 88, 92, 106, 110, 114–15, 120, 122, 237n34; on custom, 71–74, 78, 129, 237n34; and Daini, 164; on Daoism, 77, 79–80, 88, 246n88, 247n3, 251n15; disciples of, 116; on emotion, 8–9, 11–15, 19, 21–23, 28–29, 31, 89–90, 100–102, 104–10, 112–15, 208, 211, 249n54; on feudalism, 5–6, 12, 76, 105–8, 113, 165; on the gentleman, 7, 83–84, 89–91, 93–94, 96, 100, 106, 108, 114, 143; on genuineness, 87–88, 246n88; on government, 11, 13, 15, 22, 61, 64–65, 67, 72–76, 78, 81–85, 91, 96,

104–8, 111–14, 144, 165, 209, 237n26, 242n6, 248n29; on harmony, 84–85, 89, 108–9, 112, 197, 246n73; on Heaven, 15, 19, 78–79, 197, 209, 236n24; on humaneness, 18, 64, 69, 91, 104–6, 111–12, 250n66; on human nature, 8, 11, 13, 19, 21, 61, 68–69, 76–83, 85, 87–90, 104–5, 108–9, 114, 120, 197, 208–9, 245nn64,65, 246n88; on institutions, 72–76, 88–89, 110; and Jinsai, 9–10, 51, 63, 67–69, 86–87, 104–5, 242n3; and the *Kokka hachiron* debate, 152, 255n11; life of, 61–65; and Mabuchi, 155–56, 162, 165, 170–72; Maruyama on, 12–19, 28–29, 31–32, 142–43, 236nn23,24, 245n65, 252n27; on morality, 7–8, 61, 101–4, 106, 110, 235n7, 236n22, 237n26, 255n11; on music, 15, 21–22, 69, 74, 80, 84–88, 90–91, 93, 99, 106, 108–11, 113, 252nn16,30, 256n16; and Nankaku, 14, 116–17, 119–20, 122, 127–28, 142–43; and neoclassical form, 21–23; and Norinaga, 11–12, 14, 174, 178, 183–84, 186–87, 190–91, 193–94, 196–97, 201–2, 207–9, 211; on the *Odes*, 29, 80, 84, 91, 100–103, 106–15, 248n29, 250n68; on poetry, 2, 6–8, 11, 90–96, 112–14, 208; poetry of, 11, 21–22, 96–100, 123, 234n5; and reform, 64, 72–73, 89, 165; on ritual, 18–21, 64, 69, 74, 80, 84–88, 91, 106, 110–11, 246n88, 249n44, 250n69, 252nn16,30; on rulership, 10–11, 23, 76, 82, 85, 91; on the sage kings, 5–7, 9–10, 15–16, 21–23, 64, 67–68, 72, 74, 78–81, 88–89, 91, 94, 99, 104–9, 111–12, 122, 128, 156, 252nn16,30; and Seiryō, 253n36; and Shundai, 13–14, 64, 116, 118–20, 128–36, 138–44, 250n3, 252nn27,30; on talent, 81–85, 89, 109, 112; on Tokugawa society, 10, 30, 67, 73–76; on translation, 62, 70–71, 243n20; on virtues, 15, 18, 80–88, 90–91, 106, 108, 249n54; on words vs. tones, 110, 256n16; and Zhu Xi, 12–13, 16, 21, 62–63, 67–69, 78, 83, 85, 101–4, 106, 110–13, 171, 234n3, 235n7, 250n68
Okabe no nikki (travel diary; Kamo no Mabuchi), 166
Ono Furumichi, 146–47
Ōoka Tadamitsu, 163
original nature. *See* human nature
Ōsuga Nakayabu, 260n30
Ōtomo no Tabito, 170

Parvulesco, Marguerite-Marie, 7, 234n5
patterning (*wen*; *aya*): and emotion, 41, 176, 179–80, 183–84, 193, 239n15, 259n12; in the "Great Preface," 41, 239n15; Nankaku on, 122; Norinaga on, 176, 179–84, 193, 259n12, 260n14; Sorai on, 93–94. *See also wen*
peasants, 65, 75, 83, 131, 200, 202
plays, domestic-life (*sewamono*), 8
poetic houses (*ie*), 148–49, 203, 255n5

poetry: and the Ancient Way, 24–25, 155–62, 169–71, 204, 206–7; autonomy of, 3, 6, 13–15, 21, 24–25, 28–32, 112–14, 149–55, 190–94; Chinese vs. Japanese, 2, 145, 151–52, 177, 185; and common people, 251n6; and communication, 27, 30, 57–59, 177–79, 184, 192–93; and elegance, 120–21, 251n6; as emotional expression, 1–2, 14, 23, 41, 44, 55, 100–101, 138, 140, 154, 176–77, 185; and empathy, 25–27, 30, 52, 55, 59, 101, 104, 106, 122, 134–35, 153, 160, 178, 187–88, 191; and governing elites, 2, 7, 11, 22, 90–91, 98–99, 109, 113–14, 122, 134–35, 137, 142–43, 153, 160, 178; and human nature, 19, 55, 90, 102, 109, 113–14, 142, 148, 193–94, 208–9; imitative, 1–2, 21–23, 32, 63, 91–93, 100, 120, 127, 140–42, 170, 186, 205, 207–8; Jinsai on, 52, 55–60; as linguistic model, 1, 23, 90, 93, 151, 162, 170–71, 181–82, 204; Mabuchi on, 147, 152–55, 160–62, 171–72; and the Mao tradition, 36; meter in, 170, 180–81; and morality, 8, 29, 33, 52, 59–60, 102–4, 109–10, 112–13, 151, 211; and music, 40–43, 108–10, 113, 136, 138, 150–54, 162, 249n54; Nankaku on, 117, 120–23, 140, 143, 208; Norinaga on, 24–28, 30, 172–81, 190–94, 203; as patterned language, 179–81, 183–84; Shundai on, 118–19, 134–37, 140–43, 208; social context of composition, 6, 90, 99, 108, 114, 117, 146–48, 166, 174, 203–4; Sorai on, 2, 6–8, 11, 90–96, 112–14, 208; study of, 1, 51, 57, 93, 102–4, 135, 149, 161–62, 186, 204. *See also Book of Odes*; *waka* poetry; particular poets
politics: and Confucianism, 12–15, 28–32; and the *Kokka hachiron* debate, 148–55; and literature, 22, 24, 31–32, 112–114; Mabuchi on, 160, 172; and the Mao tradition, 36; and Nankaku, 119, 122, 128; and Norinaga, 24–26, 200–202, 208; and the *Odes*, 29, 112–14; and poetry, 3, 6, 32, 112–14, 128, 149, 208, 212, 255n11; and Shundai, 13–14, 119–20, 123, 142; and Sorai, 2, 14, 29, 31–32, 64–65, 237n26; vs. emotion, 13, 28, 31; vs. morality, 12–15, 17, 237n26; and the Way, 12–15, 19. *See also* government; rulership
post-horse rebellion (*tenma sōdō*; 1764), 164–65
principle (*li*; *ri*): and human nature, 3–5, 44–45, 51, 60, 68–69, 79, 171, 255n8; and individual differences, 18; and the investigation of things, 49–51, 235n12; Jinsai on, 9, 52, 54, 58–59; in the *Kokka hachiron* debate, 149, 153–55, 255n8; and Mabuchi, 155–56, 162, 171; and material force, 4, 8–9, 45, 53, 260n28; Nankaku on, 121; Norinaga on, 23, 183; and the *Odes*, 60, 101, 113; Shundai on, 135–36; and the Six Classics, 106; Sorai on, 8, 69, 79, 91, 102, 111–12; vs. emotion, 10, 121; and the Way, 3, 5, 12, 23, 43–51

printing, 149
public vs. private spheres, 13–15, 18, 21–22, 25, 142, 236n23, 237n26

Qian Qi, 97, 248n22
Qin dynasty (China), 92, 139
Qing dynasty (China), 64

"Record of Music" ("Yue ji"), 44, 52, 99, 188–89, 239n15, 241n38, 249n44, 256n15
Record of Ritual (*Li ji*), 44, 106, 239nn9,15, 241n38, 249n44, 256n15
reforms, 10, 159; Kyōhō, 66–67; Norinaga on, 200–202; Sorai on, 64, 72–73, 89, 165
Reishōin poetry group, 203–4
Reizei Tamemura, 203
rightness (*yi*; *gi*), 4, 45, 53, 196; Jinsai on, 54, 68; and the Mao tradition, 38–39; and the *Odes*, 107; Shundai on, 128–29, 157
Rikukei ryakusetsu (A General Outline of the Six Classics; Dazai Shundai), 118–19, 134–35, 138–39
ritual (*li*; *rei*): *Analects* on, 58, 85–87, 110; and Daini, 164; and human nature, 45, 53, 246n88; internalization of, 18, 246n88; Jinsai on, 54, 68–69, 86–87; and the *Kokka hachiron* debate, 151–52; and the Mao tradition, 38–39; Mencius on, 53; and music, 20–21, 69, 74, 84–88, 91, 94, 106, 110–11, 131, 151–52, 157, 164, 188, 246nn80,88, 252nn16,30, 257n24; Norinaga on, 196; Shundai on, 119, 123, 128–31, 144, 157, 252n30; Shundai vs. Mabuchi on, 157, 257n24; Sorai on, 18–21, 64, 69, 74, 80, 84–88, 91, 106, 110–11, 246n88, 249n44, 250n69, 252nn16,30; and the Way, 86–87, 111, 130; and *wen*, 86, 246n80
Rongo chō (Clarification of the *Analects*; Ogyū Sorai), 64, 84, 86, 105
Rongo kogi (Ancient Meanings of the *Analects*; Itō Jinsai), 52, 55
rulership, 2, 42, 193; and empathy, 11, 22, 106–8, 113–14, 122, 133–36, 142–43, 153, 160, 178, 191; and humaneness, 23, 91, 104–6, 111; Mabuchi on, 153, 158–60, 165; Norinaga on, 178, 190–91, 195–96; Sorai on, 10–11, 23, 76, 82, 85, 91. *See also* government; politics
Ryūshi shinron (Master Ryū's New Thesis; Yamagata Daini), 163

sage kings: as creators vs. moral exemplars, 16, 81; Daini on, 164–65; in the *Kokka hachiron* debate, 151–53; Mabuchi on, 153, 158, 165; the Mao tradition on, 38; music of, 15, 21–22, 99, 108–9, 125, 130–31, 138–39, 151–53, 162, 164, 188, 249n50, 252nn16,30, 253n49; Nankaku on, 125, 128; Norinaga on, 24, 190–91, 195–96; Shōeki on, 163, 165; Shundai on, 128–32, 137–39, 157; Sorai on, 5–7, 9–10, 15–16, 21–23,

64, 67–68, 72, 74, 78–81, 88–89, 91, 94, 99, 104–9, 111–12, 122, 128, 156, 252nn16,30; vs. Japanese gods, 24; Way of, 6, 10, 21–23, 28–29, 38–39, 64, 72, 88–89, 91, 95, 102, 107, 111, 128–31, 137, 165, 171, 190–91
sages: Jinsai on, 11, 52, 58; Seiryō on, 133; Zhu Xi on, 16, 49–51, 81, 128. *See also* sage kings
Saigō Nobutsuna, 25
Sakai, Naoki, 16–19, 243n16, 250n69
samurai: Mabuchi on, 159; Norinaga on, 202; Seiryō on, 253n36; Shundai on, 131–33; Sokō on, 10; Sorai on, 10, 73, 75–76, 85; stipends of, 3, 65–66, 243n6; and trade, 133; vs. merchants, 65–66, 76
Sasaki Nobutsuna, 255n5, 259n3
Sawai Keiichi, 250n68
scholar-officials (*shi*), 65, 114, 119
Seidan (A Discourse on Government; Ogyū Sorai), 64, 72–76, 82, 84–85, 242n4
Seigaku mondō (Dialogue on the Learning of the Sages; Dazai Shundai), 118, 129–30
Sekihi (Pointing out Errors; Dazai Shundai), 119
self-cultivation: and Confucianism, 2, 16, 33, 46, 57–58, 257n32; and the investigation of things, 49, 51, 235n12; Jinsai on, 56, 242n51; and Mabuchi, 170–72, 257n32; and the *Odes*, 106; and poetry, 144, 161; Shundai on, 131, 136–37, 143; Sorai on, 61, 68, 78, 81, 143
Shen Buhai, 132
Shibun yōryō (Essentials of the *Tale of Genji*; Motoori Norinaga), 174–75, 187, 190
Shigen (Origins of Poetry; Ogyū Sorai), 247n9
Shi ji (Historical Records; Sima Qian), 92, 97, 99–100
Shi jing. See Book of Odes
Shi jizhuan (Collected Transmissions on the Odes; Zhu Xi), 55, 153; preface to, 43–44, 48, 51–52, 106–7, 136–37, 189
Shinkokinshū, 150, 152, 186, 206
"Shinsai no gūsaku" (Composed on the New Year; Ogyū Sorai), 98
Shinto, 14–15, 25, 118, 146–47, 173, 199
Shiron (A Discourse on Poetry; Dazai Shundai), 119, 137, 140–41
"Shōnen kō" (Song about a Young Man; Ogyū Sorai), 96, 123–24
Shōtoku Taishi (Prince Shōtoku), 157, 164
Shūishū, 186
Shu jing. See Book of Documents
Shun, King: Mabuchi on, 158; Munetake on, 151; Sorai on, 72
Shundai. *See* Dazai Shundai
Shushi shiden kōkō (The Fatal Errors of Zhu Xi's *Transmissions on the Odes*; Dazai Shundai), 119, 136
Sima Guang, 103
Sima Qian, 92, 97
Sima Xiangru, 96

six arts (*rikugei*), 149, 255n9
Six Classics (*liujing*; *rikukei*), 30; Nankaku on, 120–21; and the *Odes*, 106–14, 242n56; Shundai on, 118–19, 128, 136, 143; Sorai on, 22–23, 106–14, 248n19, 250n68; Zhu Xi on, 106, 136. *See also* Five Classics; Four Teachings
song: in the "Great Preface," 41–42; lyrics vs. tones of, 152, 256nn14,16; and music, 41–42, 109, 138–39, 162, 176; Norinaga on, 176, 179, 181–82, 188, 254n1; and poetry, 150–52, 254n1, 257n28, 259n5; Shundai on, 138–40, 162
Song dynasty (China): Confucianism of, 3, 9–11, 16, 18, 23, 32–34, 43, 45–46, 51–52, 63, 68, 75, 85, 91, 95, 102–3, 121, 128, 136, 143, 153–54, 156, 162, 183, 201; poetry of, 92–93, 121, 140. *See also* Zhu Xi
Sorai. *See* Ogyū Sorai
Sorai school, 7, 28–29, 63–64, 117, 119, 234n3, 253n36; critics of, 199, 247n11; fragmentation of, 14, 116, 142, 234n4; and music, 256n16; and poetry, 13, 32, 97, 141, 234n5; vs. Mabuchi, 155, 162; vs. nativism, 2–3; vs. Norinaga, 196. *See also* Dazai Shundai; Hattori Nankaku; Ogyū Sorai
Sorai sensei tōmonsho (Master Sorai's Responsals; Ogyū Sorai), 64, 85, 95, 102–3
Soraishū (anthology; Ogyū Sorai), 96
Spring and Autumn Annals (*Chunqiu*), 106, 239n9
straightforwardness (*naoshi*), 157–59, 161, 165, 170, 172
subjectivism, 30; Norinaga on, 182–83, 188; Sorai on, 9–10, 67–69, 75, 79, 85, 102–3, 109, 209; of Zhu Xi, 9–10, 57, 78–79, 85, 102–3, 235n12
Sugagasa no nikki (The Sedge Hat Diary; Motoori Norinaga), 234n5
Suga Naoiri, 204
Sugiura Kuniakira, 146, 166
Sugiura Masaki, 146
Sui dynasty (China), 139
sumptuary laws, 66–67, 73
Suzunoya shū (collection; Motoori Norinaga), 204–5, 234n5

Tabi no nagusa (travel diary; Kamo no Mabuchi), 258n49
Taigiroku (Kaibara Ekiken), 8
Taiheisaku (A Proposal for Great Peace; Ogyū Sorai), 64, 71–72, 85, 129, 242n4
Takano Rantei, 116
Takebe Ayatari, 123
Takenouchi Shikibu, 164–65
talent (*cai*; *sai*): Sorai on, 81–85, 89, 109, 112
Tamaboko hyakushu (A Hundred Poems on the Jeweled Sword; Motoori Norinaga), 206–7
Tamagatsuma (The Jeweled Basket; Motoori Norinaga), 203
Tamenaga Shunsui, 8

Tang dynasty (China), 35–36, 43, 74, 108; poetry of, 11, 63, 91–93, 96–97, 100, 117–18, 121, 137, 140–41, 151, 247n9

Tangshi xuan (*Tōshisen*; anthology of Tang poetry), 97–100, 117–18, 124

Tanuma Okitsugu, 200

"Taohuayuan ji" (Record of Peach Blossom Spring; Tao Qian), 126–27

Tao Qian, 126–27

taxes, 67, 75, 200, 202

Tayasu Munetake, 147, 166–67, 203; and the *Kokka hachiron* debate, 148–49, 151–53, 256nn14,16, 260n30

Teeuwen, Mark, 233n1, 235n5

Thomas, Roger, 7

Three Dynasties (China), 74, 76, 91, 140. *See also* Xia dynasty; Yin dynasty; Zhou dynasty

ti yong (*tai yō*; essence and application), 46–47, 191–93

Toda Mosui, 148–49, 166, 262n50

Tōga (Arai Hakuseki), 257n27

Tōgo shi (Poetry after the Tang; Ogyū Sorai), 92

Tokugawa Harusada, 200

Tokugawa Ieharu, 200

Tokugawa Ienari, 200

Tokugawa Ienobu, 66

Tokugawa Ieshige, 163

Tokugawa Ietsugu, 66–67

Tokugawa Ieyasu, 66, 75

Tokugawa shogunate: challenges to, 163–65; and Confucianism, 62; and Norinaga, 25; reforms of, 66–67; and Sorai, 12, 64–65, 73–75, 89. *See also* government

Tokugawa Tsunayoshi, 61–62, 66, 117

Tokugawa Yoshimune, 64, 66–67, 147

Tongjian gangmu (Outline of the *Comprehensive Mirror*; Zhu Xi), 85, 103

Tönnies, Ferdinand, 236n21

Tōshisen kokujikai (An Explanation in Japanese of the *Tangshi xuan*), 118

Tucker, John, 16, 237n28, 242n3

Ueda Akinari, 166, 182–83, 198–99, 261n41

"Uhōshū ni towaruru o shasu" (Expressing Thanks upon the Visit of Amenomori Hōshū; Ogyū Sorai), 99

Uiyamabumi (First Steps in the Mountains; Motoori Norinaga), 175, 204–5

Uji shūi monogatari, 117

"Umazake no uta" (Poem on Delicious Sake; Kamo no Mabuchi), 170

urbanization, 3, 10, 65, 75–76

Usami Kisohachi, 256n16

Usami Shinsui, 133

utopianism, 126–28, 163, 165

Van Zoeren, Steven, 35–36, 240n17

virtue (*de*; *toku*): and emotionality, 4, 45, 53–54, 108, 113, 241n38; and the gentleman, 90–91; Jinsai on, 53–56, 59, 68, 86, 242n51; Mabuchi on, 157–58, 165; and the Mao tradition, 37–40; and music, 85–86, 108, 113, 249n54; Norinaga on, 196; Seiryō on, 253n36; Shundai on, 130, 157; Sorai on, 15, 18, 80–88, 90–91, 106, 108, 249n54; Zhu Xi on, 4, 12, 45, 53–54, 86, 241n38, 250n66. *See also* "approving virtue and chastising vice"; humaneness; morality; rightness

Wadoku yōryō (Guidelines for Reading in Japanese; Dazai Shundai), 119

Wagaku taigai (An Outline of Japanese Learning; Murata Harumi), 199

Wakamizu Suguru, 29, 112, 234n3

waka poetry, 7, 145, 235n5, 238n38, 255n5; and *aware*, 177; and the *Book of Odes*, 100–101; and court nobles, 145, 148–49, 151, 203, 255n5, 256n12, 261n48; and human nature, 148, 185–86, 208; and Japanese language, 1, 12, 145, 151, 162, 169–71, 181–82, 204; and the *Kokka hachiron* debate, 148–55; and Mabuchi, 146, 165–66; and Nankaku, 117; and Norinaga, 26, 28, 173–75, 177, 179–82, 185–86, 190–91, 203–5, 208, 254n1; rhetorical techniques of, 179–81; vs. Confucianism, 191

Wang Jiusi, 247n6

Wang Shizhen, 11, 63, 92–93, 247n6, 248n19

Wang Tingxiang, 247n6

Wang Yangming, 128

Watanabe Hiroshi, 262n50

Watanabe Mōan, 146

the Way (*dao*; *dō*, *michi*): and Ancient Phraseology, 11, 22, 92; and ancient texts, 1–2; as composite name, 110–12; cultural vs. metaphysical, 3–5; and culture, 3–6, 11, 23, 43, 61, 88, 110; in Daoism, 79–80, 88, 122–23, 131–32, 156, 194; and the *Documents*, 107–8; and emotion, 5, 12–15, 25, 28, 45–47, 89, 105, 107, 109, 130; of the Gods, 14, 23–25, 28, 175–76, 194–200, 204, 206–7; and government, 61, 64, 72, 107, 111–12, 122, 137; and Heaven, 3, 15, 19, 236n24; and humaneness, 105, 111; and human nature, 5, 8, 16, 19–20, 23, 49, 53–54, 68, 76–80, 88–89, 105, 128–29; and institutions, 88–89, 110; internalization of, 93, 130–31; as invention vs. nature, 7–8, 12–16, 18–23, 61, 80, 88; of Japan (*Shikishima no michi*), 151; Jinsai on, 52, 54, 58, 105; and literature, 34; and music, 86–87, 111, 139; Nankaku on, 122–23; and the *Odes*, 60, 113–14; and poetry, 2, 19, 29, 32, 45–47, 113, 192; and politics vs. morality, 7–8, 12–15, 61, 237n26; and principle, 3, 5, 12, 23, 43–51; and public vs. private, 12–15, 17–21, 237n26; and ritual, 86–87, 111, 130; of the sage kings, 6, 10, 21–23, 28–29, 38–39, 64, 72, 88–89, 91, 95, 102, 107, 111, 128–31, 137, 165, 171, 190–91;

Shundai on, 118–19, 128–33, 136–37, 157; and the Six Classics, 106, 111, 136–37; Sorai on, 7–8, 10–11, 16, 23, 28, 61, 64, 68–69, 72, 76–89, 91, 94–95, 105–7, 113–14, 122, 139, 171–72, 190–91, 193–94, 197, 236n24; and virtue, 80–85; of the warrior, 159; and *wen*, 34, 43, 86, 94; Zhu Xi on, 3, 5, 9, 12–13, 16, 20, 34, 43–44, 53–54, 68, 79, 111, 128. *See also* Ancient Way
Wei dynasty (China), 92–93, 140
wen (*bun*; culture, literary writing, patterning), 20, 34, 237n34; Sorai on, 83–84, 86, 246n80; and the Way, 34, 43, 86, 94. *See also* patterning
Wen, King, 37–40, 43, 48, 72, 107, 112–13, 248n29
Wen xuan, 98, 100, 127
wisdom (*zhi*; *chi*), 45, 53–54, 69, 81, 85, 157
Wu Guolun, 247n6
Wujing zhengyi (Correct Significance of the Five Classics), 36

Xia dynasty (China), 74, 261n39
Xie Zhen, 247n6
Xijing zaji (Miscellaneous Records of the Western Capital), 96
Xunzi, 15, 102, 129, 245n65
Xu Zhenqing, 247n6
Xu Zhongxing, 247n6

Yakubun sentei (A Guide to Translation; Ogyū Sorai), 62–63, 70–71, 94–95
Yamaga Sokō, 10–11, 236n18
Yamagata Daini, 163–65
Yamagata Shūnan, 116
Yamamoto Hokuzan, 248n11
Yamanoue no Okura, 169
Yamashita, Samuel, 19, 250n3
Yamazaki Ansai, 34, 162, 234n3
Yanagisawa Yoshiyasu, 62–65, 117
Yang Shen, 110
Yan Yu, 92, 247n9
Yao, King: Mabuchi on, 158; Nankaku on, 251n10; Sorai on, 72
Yi jing. See Book of Changes
Yin dynasty (China), 74, 261n39
Yoda, Tomiko, 27
"Yoru, bokusui o kudaru" (Going down the Sumida River at Night; Hattori Nankaku), 124
Yosa Buson, 123
Yoshikawa Kōjirō, 22–23
"Yoshino no hana o mite yomeru" (Composed on Viewing the Blossoms in Yoshino; Kamo no Mabuchi), 167–69
Yuan Hongdao, 93, 247n10
Yuan Kang, 97
Yuan Zhongdao, 247n10

Yuan Zongdao, 247n10
"Yue ji." *See* "Record of Music"
Yue ji dongjing shuo (An Explanation of Rest and Motion in the "Record of Music"; Zhu Xi), 44
Yue jing. See Book of Music
Yue jue shu (Yuan Kang), 97

Zekku kai (Explanation of Quatrains; Ogyū Sorai), 92
Zen Buddhism, 93, 247n8
Zhang Heng, 127
Zheng Xuan, 35, 55
Zhou, Duke of, 72, 158
Zhou dynasty (China), 37, 74, 108, 125
Zhuangzi, 91, 194
Zhuangzi, 70, 122, 251n10; fishtrap metaphor in, 243n20. *See also* Daoism
Zhu Xi: authoritarianism of, 20; criticism of, 4, 8–11, 35, 52, 54, 57, 60, 233n2, 235n7; and Daoism, 9, 52, 58; on emotion, 4, 8, 13, 43–48, 52–54, 68, 101, 112–13, 154, 189, 234n3, 240n22, 241n38; on harmony, 46–47, 86; on human nature, 3–5, 44–54, 60, 68–69, 78–79, 83, 112–13, 154, 171, 245n64; influence of, 33–34; on the investigation of things, 49–51, 59, 102–3, 235n12; and Jinsai, 9–10, 51–60, 235n12, 241n38, 242n51; and the *Kokka hachiron* debate, 151, 153–54, 256n16; and Mabuchi, 154, 156, 162, 171; on *Mencius*, 53–54, 241n38; and metaphysical unity, 3–5; on morality, 3–4, 8, 20, 22, 34, 44–49, 51, 53–57, 60, 101–4, 112–13, 154, 234n3, 240n22; and Norinaga, 27, 189, 192; and the *Odes*, 32, 34–35, 43–52, 55–57, 59–60, 101–3, 106–7, 110, 136–37, 151, 153–54, 189, 256n16; optimism vs. rigorism in, 20; on principle, 3–4, 8, 12, 44–45, 69, 79, 101, 111, 154, 156, 260n28; and public vs. private, 236n23; and ritual and music, 86–87; and Shundai, 118–19, 128, 135–37; on the Six Classics, 106–7, 136; and Sorai, 12–13, 16, 21, 62–63, 67–69, 78, 83, 85, 101–4, 106, 110–13, 171, 234n3, 235n7, 250n68; subjectivism of, 9–10, 57, 78–79, 85, 102–3, 235n12; vs. Ancient Learning, 236n18; vs. the Mao tradition, 34–35, 47–48; vs. nativism, 25; on the Way, 3–5, 9, 12–13, 16, 20, 34, 43–44, 53–54, 68, 79, 111, 128
Zhuzi yulei (Master Zhu's Classified Conversations; Zhu Xi), 50–51
Zigong, 57, 241n39
Zisi, 77, 79–80, 93
Zixia, 58
Zizhi tongjian (Comprehensive Mirror for Aid in Government; Sima Guang), 103
Zong Chen, 247n6
Zuo zhuan, 84–85, 107, 197, 245n71